THE HOUSE & GARDEN
Cookbook

THE HOUSE & GARDEN

Cookbook

COMPILED BY VICKY JONES

CHATTO & WINDUS
LONDON

Acknowledgements

At the end of each recipe, the author's initials are given. Their names are as follows.

CB Christophe Buey, chef at L'Ecole de Cuisine Française, Litlington, East Sussex; NC Nicola Cox; SCP Shona Crawford Poole; SD Silvija Davidson; RD Roz Denny; JD Jim Dodge, pastry chef at the Stanford Court Hotel, San Francisco; HDM Hugo Dunn Meynell; KD Kate Dyson; PF Paola Fletcher; BGM Beryl Gould Marks; JH Jacqui Hurst; MJ Meg Jansch; VJ Vicky Jones; EL Elisabeth Luard; PM Paul Mitchell, chef at The Hunting Lodge restaurant, near Auckland, New Zealand; SM Sallie Morris; AN Ann Norris; MN Mary Norwak; SO Sri Owen; CP Charles Plumex, chef at Le Prieuré restaurant, Thonon-les-Bains, France; JR Jennie Reekie; ER Elisabeth Riely; RS Rena Salaman; MJS Maria José Sevilla; HW Hilary Walden; SJW Sue Jane Warren; SW Stephen Wheeler; AW Anne Williams; AWS Alice Wooledge Salmon.

Photographs: Howard Allman: pages 57, 84, 90, 169. Jan Baldwin: pages 147, 148, 157, 159, 163, 173. Eric Carter: pages 13, 14, 17, 23, 30, 31, 43, 45, 46, 58, 66, 75, 78, 88, 91, 104, 107, 110, 117, 121, 155, 158, 160, 162, 170. Michael Cook: page 109. Alex Dufort: pages 10, 28, 35, 55, 60, 92, 100. Paul Forster: pages 21, 64. Nicky Gibbs: page 176. Tim Hill: pages 27, 63, 77, 87, 124, 143, 181. John Hollingshead: pages 6, 12, 19, 40, 48, 137, 140, 141, 144, 152, 177. Jacqui Hurst: pages 22, 39, 123, 132, 135. Tim Imrie: pages 53, 69, 70, 72, 113, 127, 128. Graham Kirk: front cover, pages 9, 83, 95, 96, 99, 103, 112, 165, 171, 174, 183, 185. Scott Morrison: pages 115, 118, 120. James Mortimer: pages 37, 51. James Murphy: back cover, pages 131, 133, 139, 151, 167, 179, 187. Jasper Partington: pages 54, 106. Fritz von der Schulenberg: pages 18, 32. Chris Thornton: page 149. Simon Wheeler: page 25.

Designed by John Bridges and Jenny Newton

Published in 1992 by
Chatto & Windus Ltd
Vauxhall Bridge Road
London SW1V 2SA

First published by
Chatto & Windus in
hardcover in 1990

© The Conde Nast Publications Ltd

A CIP catalogue record for this book is available
from the British Library

ISBN 0 7011 3702 9

Photoset by Rowland Phototypesetting Ltd
Bury St Edmunds, Suffolk
Printed and bound in Great Britain by
Butler and Tanner Ltd, Frome, Somerset

CONTENTS

INTRODUCTION

The *Wine & Food* section of *House & Garden* magazine has featured literally thousands of imaginative, practical recipes by an impressive group of contributors. This *Cookbook* is a collection of some personal favourites.

Our contributors include professional chefs, cookery writers with a background in home economics, authors who have come to writing about food from other disciplines, and people who are simply accomplished home cooks, providing for family and friends. All have two things in common – a genuine love of good food, and a generosity that is essential to successful entertaining.

Each author has his or her own style of cooking and writing, and no attempt has been made in compiling this book to disguise their individuality. The variety is a vital part of the collection.

Roz Denny, who has contributed a large number of the recipes, has combined her creative flair with her training in home economics to devise a splendid variety of original recipes, as well as to adapt traditional ones to the demands of today's busy cooks. Alice Wooledge Salmon, author of *House & Garden Cooking with Style* (Octopus, 1987), has an inventive and literary style, deriving inspiration from her extensive travels, and drawing from her own eclectic repertoire of culinary ideas. Silvija Davidson's Latvian parentage has given rise to her delight in Baltic cookery, while her self-taught expertise in the techniques of classic French cuisine is applied to all manner of ingredients. Elisabeth Riely's writing has that special freshness and individuality which reflects the best of current American gastronomy, while other cooks draw on the rich fund of European culinary traditions. Elisabeth Luard, for example, lived in Spain for many years, and wrote *European Peasant Cookery* (Bantam Press, 1986); Maria José Sevilla is another Spanish specialist; Rena Salaman is not only an expert in the cookery of her native Greece, but also the creator of many original recipes. Nicola Cox, Anne Williams and Jennie Reekie all live in the English countryside, and tend to write about the customs and recipes of a more British-based cuisine.

Right *Rice with salt cod, garlic and spinach (recipe on page 48); sopa morellana (recipe on page 33); and scrambled eggs with truffles.*

FIRST IMPRESSIONS

Crisp filo pastry parcels; pâtés and mousses; fresh and smoked fish; colourful salads and stuffed vegetables – these tempting first course dishes will stimulate the palate without dulling the appetite

SMOKED SALMON AND PLAICE ROULADE WITH TARRAGON CREAM

Soaking fish in fresh lime or lemon juice is a way of preserving it that has been used for centuries in the Caribbean, South America and the Pacific. Even so, it is obviously essential that if you are going to eat uncooked fish, it must be very fresh to start with. Ideally, buy it from a reputable fishmonger or supermarket wet fish department and tell them that you are planning to eat it raw or, failing that, buy good quality frozen fish fillets which should have been frozen within hours of being caught. Allow them to defrost and then use as soon as they have completely thawed out.

*4 fillets of plaice weighing about 6–8 oz
   (175–250 g) each
Salt and freshly milled black pepper
1½ teaspoons dried tarragon
4 oz (125 g) sliced smoked salmon
Juice of 4 limes
¼ pint (300 ml) double cream*

TO GARNISH
1 ripe avocado

Skin the plaice fillets and remove any bones and dark pieces of flesh from around the stomach. Lay the fillets out and sprinkle each one with a little salt and pepper and a very little tarragon. Put the slices of smoked salmon on top, then roll up the fish fillets, starting at the tail end. Cut each one into 4 rolls and place them in a shallow dish, fairly close together, but not so that they touch. Sprinkle with a little more tarragon (you want to be left with about half a teaspoon) and pour over the lime juice. Leave to marinate for about 8 hours, turning them over several times and liberally basting them with the lime juice.

Remove the rolls of fish from the lime juice and arrange on a serving dish. Add the remaining tarragon to the cream in a basin. Add about half the lime juice, season with salt and pepper, then taste and add a little more of the lime juice if wished. Pour over the fish fillets in the serving dish.

Halve the avocado, peel, remove the stone and cut into slices. Dip these into the remaining lime juice, then use to garnish the edge of the plate. Chill until ready to serve.

Serves 4.   JR

SPICED HERRINGS WITH CUCUMBER SAUCE

Spiced herring fillets (sometimes also slightly inaccurately called matjes herrings) are pickled in a sweet/sour mixture, usually with onions, and can be bought either in packets from supermarkets or

Right *Smoked salmon and plaice roulade with tarragon cream and (below) spiced herrings with cucumber sauce*

loose from fishmongers. They can be served in a variety of ways, but are especially good as a light starter, with sour cream and cucumber sauce.

4 spiced herring fillets, about 8 oz (250 g)
¼ pint (150 ml) soured cream
4 oz (125 g) bulb fennel
½ cucumber
Freshly-milled black pepper

Remove the herring fillets from the preserving liquor and arrange on a serving dish. Strain the liquor and reserve any pieces of onion. Blend with the soured cream. Finely chop the fennel, reserving any pieces of green frond, and cut the cucumber into ¼ inch (5 mm) dice. Add to the soured cream with plenty of freshly-milled black pepper, then pour over the herring fillets. Garnish with the pieces of reserved green frond.

Serves 4.   JR

GLAZED SALMON TARTLETS

Crisp cream cheese pastry tartlets, baked blind and left to cool, are filled with pressed salmon on a lime mayonnaise and yoghurt base and topped with lime aspic. They are perfect for dinner parties, as the glaze allows you to prepare this dish ahead without the tartlets getting tired. Decorative strips of cucumber peel and sprigs of fresh herbs add the finishing touch.

PRESSED SALMON
12 oz (350 g) middle cut of salmon
1 tablespoon sea salt
1 teaspoon white sugar
Grated rind ½ lime
Pepper

FILLING
5 fl oz (150 g) mayonnaise
5 fl oz (150 g) natural thick yoghurt
Lime juice to taste
Salt and pepper

Glazed salmon tartlets

CREAM CHEESE PASTRY
6 oz (175 g) plain flour
4 oz (125 g) soft butter
4 oz (125 g) cream cheese
¼ teaspoon salt

LIME GLAZE
½ pint good aspic, such as Haco
Lime juice to taste

DECORATION
Strips cucumber skin
Sprigs dill, parsley or chervil

PRESSED SALMON
Fillet and skin the salmon. Mix the salt and sugar with a little grated lime rind. Sprinkle some on a plate, lay one piece of salmon on this and sprinkle over some more salt and sugar: lay the second piece of salmon on top and sprinkle with the remaining salt and sugar mixture. Cover and press lightly and leave for 12–48 hours in the fridge. Remove, pat dry and slice very thinly.

CREAM CHEESE PASTRY
Cream the butter until really soft, work in the cream cheese then sift and add the flour and salt; work lightly together and form into 4–6 flattened

discs. Chill, wrapped for 1–2 hours in the fridge. Roll thinly and line 4–6 individual tartlet tins of about 4–5″ (10–13 cm) diameter. Prick the bases, line with tinfoil, fill with baking beans and cook in a hot oven (400°F, 200°C, gas mark 6) for about 8–10 minutes until set.

Remove the beans and tinfoil, turn down the oven to moderately hot (375°F, 110°C, gas mark 5) and continue to cook until light golden brown and completely cooked. Cool on a rack.

LIME GLAZE
Prepare the aspic according to the instructions on the packet and flavour generously with lime juice. Cool until syrupy.

FILLING
Fold the yoghurt into the mayonnaise, adjust seasoning and add lime juice to taste.

DECORATION
Blanch and refresh some strips of cucumber skin. Cut in thin strips.

TO ASSEMBLE
Spread a little mayonnaise filling in the base of the tartlets, arrange thin slices of pressed salmon over this, decorate with cucumber strips and sprigs of herb and cover with a very thin layer of lime glaze. Chill until the glaze sets and the decoration is stuck down then run over another thin layer of glaze and leave to set. Serve on individual plates with a sprig of herb and a slice of lime.

Serves 4–6.   NC

SQUID WITH LITTLE GEM AND SESAME DRESSING

Squid, once a rarity, is now widely available from fishmongers and the wet fish counter of most supermarkets, where it can often be bought ready cleaned. If this is not the case, do not despair as cleaning is a fairly easy process.

Inexpensive and versatile, it can be fried, stuffed, braised, or used in a salad.

1 lb (500 g) squid, cleaned (see below)
2 pints (1.2 litres) boiling water
Juice of ½ lemon
¼ cucumber
4 spring onions
2 teaspoons sesame seeds
2 Little Gem lettuces

DRESSING
2 tablespoons cider vinegar
3 tablespoons sunflower oil
1 tablespoon sesame oil
1 teaspoon Dijon mustard
Salt and pepper to taste

To prepare the squid, cut tentacles from the head just above the eyes, then squeeze to remove the little bone in the centre. Wash and reserve tentacles. Using fingers, pull the quill and innards from the body cavity and discard. Rub away the fine mottled skin from the outside of each squid. Wash and pull off wing pieces and reserve. Turn each squid inside out and wash thoroughly to complete cleaning.

Cut each squid down one side and lay on work-top inside uppermost. Using a sharp knife, lightly mark a fine lattice all over the surface of each squid, taking care not to cut through. Then cut into three strips from tip to base.

Drop the squid into the pan of boiling water to which the lemon juice has been added. Cook gently for about 5 minutes, when the squid will have formed curls and will be quite tender when tested with a skewer. Lift out and drain.

Cut the cucumber into matchsticks. Slice the green tops from two spring onions into 2″ (5 cm) lengths, and slit each end several times with a sharp knife leaving the centre intact: place in ice-cold water and they will form attractive curls. Shred the remainder finely. Dry fry the sesame seeds till just golden and set aside. Place all the dressing ingredients in a screw-top jar and shake well together when required.

Arrange lettuce on serving plates. Pour dressing over squid, add cucumber and shredded spring onion. Spoon onto lettuce, sprinkle over sesame seeds and garnish with spring onion curls.

Serves 4.   SM

EGG AND SPINACH MOUSSES

These mousses, topped with green spinach, make very pretty individual starters.

> *12 oz (350 g) fresh spinach, with a few leaves*
> *of sorrel if available*
> *7 fl oz (200 ml) milk*
> *1 small onion stuck with 4 cloves*
> *1 bay leaf*
> *1 small carrot, halved*
> *1 oz (25 g) butter*
> *1 shallot, chopped*
> *1 oz (25 g) flour*
> *4 size 3 hens' eggs, hard-boiled and chopped*
> *1 dessertspoon dry sherry*
> *1 teaspoon gelatine crystals*
> *3 tablespoons whipping cream, lightly whipped*
> *1 egg white*
> *3 quails' eggs, hard-boiled, peeled and halved, or*
> *2 very small hens' eggs, sliced*
> *Salt and black pepper*

Blanch the spinach and sorrel, if using, then squeeze dry. Divide between the bases of 6 lightly greased ramekin dishes. Cool.

Meanwhile, scald the milk with the onion, bay leaf and carrot and allow to cool for 15 minutes. Strain, reserving the milk only.

Melt the butter in a saucepan and sauté the shallot lightly for 2 minutes. Stir in the flour and cook for about a minute until grainy. Gradually stir in the milk, mixing until smooth. Bring to the boil and simmer for a minute or two until the milk has thickened. Stir in the chopped eggs, sherry and seasoning. Sprinkle the gelatine onto 2 tablespoons of boiling water and stir briskly until dissolved, then mix into the sauce. Cover and cool, stirring occasionally to prevent a skin forming.

Fold in the whipped cream, then whisk the egg white and fold that in. Spoon the mixture on top of the spinach and allow to set.

To serve, run a knife round the edges of the ramekins, turn out onto individual plates and garnish with the quails' or small hens' eggs.

Serves 6.   RD

A PATE OF SARDINES AND LEMON

Simple yet delicious, this pâté is both inexpensive and easy to assemble.

> *8 oz (250 g) can of sardines in olive oil, with oil*
> *drained off and backbones removed*
> *10 oz (300 g) unsalted butter, softened*
> *Juice of 2 lemons*
> *½ teaspoon cayenne pepper*
> *Freshly ground black pepper to taste*
> *Twist of lemon peel and salad leaves to decorate*

Put sardines into a bowl and mash well with a fork. Add butter, and start to blend with a wooden spoon. Add lemon juice and continue blending. (Blending must be slow, or the mixture will overheat and the butter will separate.) Add a little salt, cayenne, and lots of black pepper.

Refrigerate for 24 hours. Take out 1 hour before the meal and serve with crackers, toast or wheat wafers.

Serves 6.   HDM

A pâté of sardines and lemon

CELERIAC REMOULADE WITH SMOKED MEAT

This classic salad can be made up to a week ahead: it strengthens and mellows in character with time. Garnish at the last minute with pickled capers, anchovies, gherkins, or olives. Just be sure the mayonnaise coats the celeriac to keep it from darkening. Try the recipe with various mustards: wholegrain mustard gives this light mayonnaise plenty of texture.

1 egg
3 tablespoons lemon juice
2 tablespoons Dijon or wholegrain mustard
½ pint (300 ml) vegetable oil
½ teaspoon salt
Pepper to taste
1 large celeriac bulb, about 1 lb (500 g) in weight
Red leaf lettuce to line plates
Thinly sliced smoked chicken, ham, or duck, 2 slices for each serving
Cornichons, olives and capers for garnish

First make the mayonnaise. Put the egg in a food processor or blender with the lemon juice and mustard. Turn on the motor briefly to combine them, then in a slow, steady stream add the oil. As the mayonnaise thickens and forms an emulsion, add the remaining oil faster. Sharpen the seasoning with salt, pepper and more mustard or lemon juice if you like. Scrape the mayonnaise into a medium-size bowl and set aside.

Peel the celeriac, cutting off the rough exterior and any spongy interior flesh. Cut the bulb into thin slices, then cut the stacked slices across into matchstick juliennes. As soon as the celeriac is cut, fold it into the mayonnaise, stirring to coat every piece. Cover and chill.

To serve, line 6 serving plates with lettuce. Pile the celeriac on the lettuce, dividing it among the plates. Curl or ruffle the slices of meat and place them attractively around the celeriac. Garnish with cornichons, capers and olives. Serve at once as a first course or salad.

Serves 6–8.   ER

Spiced meat pouches

SPICED MEAT POUCHES

Tasty little canapés that can be prepared and baked in advance. If liked, the same filling can be made into Turkish *borek* by cutting and folding the filo into triangles.

4 sheets filo pastry
2 oz (50 g) butter, melted

FILLING
1 tablespoon olive oil
1 small onion, finely chopped
1 clove garlic, crushed
8 oz (250 g) lean minced beef or lamb
1 teaspoon ground cumin or coriander
1 egg, beaten
2 tablespoons fresh chopped parsley
A little chopped fresh mint or dill, optional
2 oz (50 g) flaked almonds, toasted and lightly crushed
Salt and ground black pepper

First, make the filling. Fry the onion and garlic in the oil for 5 minutes. Add the minced beef or lamb and fry for another 5 minutes. Sprinkle in the spice and season well. Cook for a further minute, then remove and cool slightly.

Beat in the egg, herbs and nuts. Ideally, if you have time, allow to cool completely, as this makes it easier to fill the pouches.

Cut the pastry sheets into 4, brush each quarter well with butter and fold in half. Divide the mixture between the 16 sheets of dough and pull up the edges around the filling like a purse. Press hard to seal, and place on lightly greased baking sheets. Brush the outsides of the pouches with butter.

Bake at 350°F (180°C, gas mark 4) for about 20 minutes until crisp and golden. Allow to cool slightly before removing to a wire tray.

Makes 16.   RD

GINGER AND CORIANDER CHICKEN IN FILO FLOWERS

These make wonderful, quick supper-party dishes because they look so pretty and taste good too. Lay them out on elegant white plates with any accompaniments served separately. The cases can be made beforehand and reheated before serving.

Ginger and coriander chicken in filo flowers

4 sheets filo pastry
1½ oz (40 g) butter, melted, or 4 tablespoons
    olive oil

FILLING
2 tablespoons olive oil
1″ (2.5 cm) cube root ginger, peeled and chopped
2 cloves garlic, crushed
2 shallots or 1 small onion, chopped
1 lb (500 g) boned and skinned chicken breasts,
    sliced thinly in strips
2 teaspoons ground coriander
1 medium courgette, sliced thinly
8 oz (250 g) carton Greek yoghurt thinned with
    3 tablespoons milk
Salt and ground black pepper
Freshly chopped coriander or flat leaf parsley, to
    garnish

Brush the insides of four 4″ (10 cm) flan dishes or Yorkshire pudding bun tins with a little melted butter or oil.

Cut each filo sheet into four and layer into the tins, brushing liberally in between with butter, and arranging the sheets so that the corners alternate, forming a flower shape.

Bake at 375°F (190°C, gas mark 5) for about 7 to 10 minutes until golden and crisp, checking to see that the edges don't burn. Cool in the tins, then remove. If making them in advance, store in a large airtight container.

To make the filling, heat the oil and fry the ginger, garlic and shallot or onion until softened – about 5 minutes. Add the chicken pieces and fry for a further 5 minutes until firm and cooked. Sprinkle in the coriander and stir again.

Add the courgette slices, then cover and cook gently for about 3 minutes until they have just softened. Season well. Stir in the thinned yoghurt and reheat without boiling.

Reheat the filo cases if necessary, then spoon in the filling and scatter over the chopped coriander or parsley. Serve hot.

Serves 4.

NOTE This is also good with a small, sliced green pepper instead of the courgette, but cook pepper at the same time as the onion.   RD

SALMON FILO KOULIBIACS

These little 'turnovers' make particularly good starters or picnic food. Based on the Russian fish and rice pastry called koulibiac, these are not only light and crisp, they are also easier to make.

> 8 oz (250 g) filleted fresh salmon, e.g. from the tail
> 1 large shallot, chopped (save the skin)
> 1 bay leaf
> 4 oz (125 g) basmati rice, rinsed
> 1 tablespoon chopped fresh dill
> 2 tablespoons chopped fresh chives, or 1 spring onion, finely sliced
> 6 tablespoons double or soured cream
> 1 egg, hard-boiled and chopped
> 4 sheets filo pastry
> Salt and ground black pepper
> About 2 oz (50 g) butter, melted, or 3 tablespoons olive oil

Poach the salmon in ½ pint (300 ml) water with the shallot skins, bay leaf and some seasoning, for about 7 minutes, or until firm. Remove the fish, take off the skin and flake. Scoop out the shallot skin and bay leaf.

Return the water to the boil and add the rice and shallot. Bring to the boil, cover and simmer gently for about 12 minutes until cooked and the stock is absorbed. Cool and stir in the herbs, cream, egg and fish.

Cut the sheets of filo in half lengthwise. Brush well with butter or oil and place about an eighth of the mixture at one end of one half-sheet in a mound slightly to one side. Fold over at right-angles to make a triangle, making sure the edges are straight and meet. Then fold over again, on itself, to make another triangle. Continue like this until you have a turnover shape. Remove to a greased baking sheet.

Repeat with the other pastry sheets and filling. Brush the tops well with any remaining butter or oil and bake at 375°F (190°C, gas mark 5) for about 15 minutes or until golden and crisp. Serve warm or cold, with a salad garnish.

Serves 4–6. RD

PARMESAN CHEESE TARTLETS WITH QUAILS' EGGS AND HOLLANDAISE

Although slightly fiddly to make, these tartlets can be prepared in stages beforehand. Eggs, cheese and smoked salmon make an excellent combination.

> PASTRY
> 4 oz (125 g) butter
> 8 oz (250 g) plain flour
> 2 tablespoons freshly grated Parmesan cheese
> Good pinch cayenne pepper
> 2 egg yolks

> SAUCE
> 3 tablespoons wine vinegar
> 1 bay leaf
> A few peppercorns
> 1 blade mace
> 2 egg yolks
> Pinch each salt, ground white pepper and mustard powder
> 4 oz (125 g) unsalted butter, softened

> FILLING
> 16 quails' eggs
> 3–4 oz (75–125 g) smoked salmon
> Sprigs of parsley to garnish

Rub the butter into the flour, cheese and cayenne. Mix to a firm dough with the egg yolks, adding a little cold water if necessary. Wrap in cling film, and refrigerate for half an hour, then roll out and use to line about sixteen 2″ (5 cm) tartlet tins.

Prick the bases and bake blind for 10–15 minutes at 400°F (200°C, gas mark 6). Cool and remove the baking beans.

To make the sauce, reduce the vinegar by boiling down, with the bay leaf, peppercorns and mace, to 1 tablespoon. Strain and reserve.

In a small, heatproof bowl over a pan of gently simmering water, mix the egg yolks with the pinch of salt, pepper and mustard and a knob of butter, until thickened. Gradually mix in the rest of the butter in pieces, taking care not to let the mixture overheat or it will curdle. If it does curdle, splash in

15

some cold water and beat until smooth again. When all the butter is incorporated, remove from heat, and add vinegar.

Poach the quails' eggs for just a minute or two until firm, then remove with a slotted spoon and drain on kitchen paper.

Cut the salmon into 16 strips and form into rolls. Arrange an egg and salmon roll in each tartlet and coat with sauce. Garnish with a sprig of parsley and serve as soon as possible, allowing 2 tarts per serving.

Serves 8. RD

MUSHROOMS WITH PORCINI AND MOZZARELLA

Large flat mushrooms are always popular – even more so when stuffed or, rather, topped. For an extra rich mushroom flavour, add some soaked Italian *porcini* mushrooms and enclose them in a melting blanket of mozzarella.

½ oz (15 g) dried porcini mushrooms
4 large flat mushrooms
A little olive oil
1 small onion, chopped finely
2 cloves garlic, crushed
2 sticks celery, chopped
2 oz (50 g) green bacon, chopped
1 tomato, skinned and chopped
1 oz (25 g) butter
Salt and ground black pepper
2 tablespoons cream
4 oz (125 g) mozzarella cheese

TO SERVE
Sprigs of fresh marjoram
Triangles of toast

Soak the porcini in a little boiling water for 20 minutes. Drain and chop. (The liquid can be used in stocks so don't discard it.)

Brush the mushrooms lightly on both sides with olive oil. Grill for about 5 minutes on each side, depending on the size.

Meanwhile, sauté the onion, garlic, celery, bacon and tomato in the butter until softened. Season well and stir in the cream.

Pile on top of the mushrooms. Slice the mozzarella thinly and arrange on the filling, then return to the grill until just melted and bubbling. Serve immediately, garnished with marjoram and accompanied by toast.

Serves 4. RD

TOMATOES STUFFED WITH CUCUMBER AND FROMAGE FRAIS

A light, pretty starter using a low fat filling flavoured with chopped fresh herbs.

6 large, round, firm tomatoes (not beef ones), skinned
¼ cucumber, peeled and grated
8 oz (250 g) fromage frais
4 oz (125 g) curd or low fat soft cheese
1 tablespoon fresh chopped mint
2 tablespoons fresh chopped chives
2 tablespoons fresh chopped parsley
1–2 teaspoons fresh chopped dill
Salt and ground black pepper

TO SERVE
Mixed cress and endive salad, tossed in vinaigrette dressing

Cut the tomatoes in half and scoop out the seeds. Sprinkle the shells with salt and leave to drain upside down for half an hour.

Sprinkle the cucumber lightly with salt and leave to drain also, in a colander, for the same time. Squeeze dry and mix with the two cheeses, herbs and extra seasoning if needed. Pile into the tomato shells and chill before serving surrounded by the salad. These tomatoes can be prepared a few hours ahead, but some liquid may ooze out, which can simply be poured away.

Serves 6. RD

Mushrooms with porcini and mozzarella, and (in background) tomatoes stuffed with cucumber and fromage frais

SCALLOPS WITH GINGER AND LIME

Ideal for a dinner party, these ingredients can be prepared before the meal and the dish cooked as people sit down. Ask the fishmonger to detach the scallops from their shells, but to return 6 deep shells to you for serving the dish.

18 scallops
12 spring onions
1½" (3.75 cm) piece fresh ginger
1½ limes
2 oz (50 g) butter
Seasoning

Wash the scallops well and slice each in 3 horizontally. Leave to dry on kitchen paper. Trim the spring onions and cut into 1" (2.5 cm) pieces, including some of the green stalks. Peel and finely chop the fresh ginger. Pare the rind from the limes, shred this and put into a sieve, then pour boiling water through it to soften the rind. Squeeze the juice from the limes and reserve.

Sauté the spring onions with the ginger in the butter for a minute, add the scallops and cook very briefly till just opaque. Pour on the lime juice, season and serve in clean, warm scallop shells, sprinkled with the lime rind and surrounded by dressed salad.

Serves 6.   AW

17

Smoked salmon with smoked trout mousse

SMOKED SALMON WITH SMOKED TROUT MOUSSE

Creamy smoked trout mousse enclosed in a wrapping of smoked salmon.

8 oz (250 g) smoked salmon
3 smoked trout
2 tablespoons double cream
1 tablespoon single cream
Worcestershire sauce and lemon juice to taste
Seasoning to taste

Line a pie dish about 9″ (23 cm) in diameter with the smoked salmon, leaving some of the slices hanging over the side of the dish, to cover the mousse later.

Skin and clean the smoked trout, removing any bones, and put in the food processor. Process to a mousse, adding the cream while the machine is running. Add Worcestershire sauce and lemon juice to taste and blend thoroughly.

Pour the trout mousse into the pie dish, making sure that it is well packed, and cover with the overlapping slices of smoked salmon. Cover with plastic film, and refrigerate until ready to use. Turn out on to a serving plate, and decorate if liked.

Serves 6.   PF

ARTICHOKE AND ANCHOVY TARTS

Ideal as a starter or, if served with salads, a light supper course. Make up the cases beforehand, then fill just before serving.

6 oz (175 g) plain flour
3 oz (75 g) each butter and vegetable shortening
2–3 tablespoons fresh grated Parmesan cheese
Ice-cold water

FILLING
2 large globe artichokes
½ Spanish onion, sliced thinly
1 clove garlic, crushed
2 tablespoons olive oil
1 × 14 oz (400 g) can chopped or peeled tomatoes
3 tablespoons dry white wine
1 tablespoon fresh chopped marjoram, or 1 teaspoon dried
1 × 60 g can anchovy fillets, drained and chopped
Ground black pepper

TO GARNISH
Stoned black olives and fresh marjoram sprigs

Rub the flour and fats together until like fine breadcrumbs, then mix in the cheese and just enough water to make a firm dough. Knead gently, then divide into 4 and roll each piece out to fit four 4″ (10 cm) flan cases, or use to make one 8″ (20 cm) flan case if preferred. Prick bases lightly. Chill. Bake blind at 400°F (200°C, gas mark 6) for about 20 minutes until crisp. Cool and store in an airtight container until required.

Pull the leaves off the artichokes, cut out the hairy chokes and peel off any other tough parts. Cut into chunks and boil immediately in salted water with a squeeze or two of lemon juice for about 5 minutes.

Meanwhile, sweat the onion and garlic in the oil until softened. Add the tomatoes, wine, marjoram and pepper. Cook uncovered, on a medium heat, for about 10 to 15 minutes until thick and little liquid remains. Stir in the artichokes and anchovies. Cool.

Spoon into the cases to serve, and garnish with the olives and marjoram. The tarts are best eaten at room temperature.

Serves 4. RD

DUCK BREAST AND ROCKET SALAD WITH ORANGE DRESSING

Roast duck breast fillets, thinly sliced, combine wonderfully well with slices of fresh orange, crunchy water chestnuts and orange dressing.

2 duck breast fillets
2 oranges
8 water chestnuts from a can
Handful rocket or other leaves if preferred

Duck breast and rocket salad with orange dressing

DRESSING
4 tablespoons orange juice
1 tablespoon lemon juice
1 teaspoon Dijon mustard
4–6 tablespoons sunflower oil
Seasoning to taste

Cook the duck breasts according to directions on the packaging. Allow to cool. Finely pare the skin from one orange and cut into shreds. Place these in a small pan with boiling water and simmer for 4 minutes. Drain, rinse and drain again. Reserve shreds of orange peel for garnish.

Peel both oranges, making sure there is no pith, and slice finely. Slice drained water chestnuts. Wash and dry leaves. Prepare dressing by shaking all the ingredients together.

Cut the duck breasts into thin slices. Arrange all the ingredients attractively on serving plates and drizzle over the dressing just before serving. Scatter orange shreds over the top to garnish.

Serves 4–6. SM

COURGETTE AND CHERVIL SOUFFLES WITH SMOKED SALMON

Curd cheese may be used instead of ricotta, but the flavour and texture are a little less delicate. The exact cooking time may vary from 10–15 minutes, depending on the accuracy of the oven thermostat.

6 thin slices of smoked salmon
6 oz (175 g) finely grated small, young
  courgettes
8 oz (250 g) ricotta cheese
Approximately 1½ tablespoons chopped chervil
Salt and freshly ground black pepper
3 egg whites
Crusty wholemeal or granary bread to serve

Line 6 ramekin dishes with the smoked salmon. Pat the courgettes with absorbent kitchen paper to remove excess moisture (there should not be much with young courgettes). Mix with the ricotta and

19

chervil and season with pepper and a little salt. Whisk the egg whites until stiff, but not dry, then lightly fold into the ricotta.

Divide the mixture between the ramekin dishes, place in a baking tin and surround with boiling water. Cook in an oven preheated to 350°F (180°C, gas mark 4) until very lightly set – about 15 minutes. Garnish with chervil and serve.

Serves 6.   HW

SOLE AND RED PEPPER JELLIES WITH RED PEPPER SAUCE

These are rather involved to make, but the results, illustrated on page 99, are stylish and celebratory of the right kind of appreciative guests.

FISH BROTH
3 lb (1.5 kg) bones and heads from lean fish:
   Dover sole (best), lemon sole, plaice
1 large onion, peeled and sliced
2 leeks, cleaned and sliced
8 parsley stalks
4 tablespoons lemon juice
1 large glass dry white wine
½ teaspoon salt

FISH JELLIES
Vegetable oil for moulds and peppers
7–8 leaves gelatine
2½ pints (1.5 litres) fish broth (see above)
Whites and crushed shells of 2 eggs
Dry white wine
Salt and freshly ground black pepper
4 sweet red peppers
8 skinned fillets fresh Dover sole
Handful fresh basil leaves
¾ of a 1¾ oz (50 g) container of red 'caviar'

RED PEPPER SAUCE
Flesh of 2 red peppers (above)
10 oz (300 g) Greek-style yoghurt
Salt and black pepper
Fresh basil

To make fish broth, wash fish bones and heads; remove and discard gills. Chop carcases into convenient sizes and put these into a large, deep pot with onion, leeks, parsley, and lemon juice. Cover with 4½ pints (2.5 litres) cold water, bring this to simmer over a low heat, skim thoroughly, add wine and salt, and simmer, uncovered, for 30 minutes. Strain broth through a colander lined with muslin, cool and refrigerate for several hours.

To begin the jellies, lightly oil 12 oval, metal moulds of 3 fl oz (90 ml) capacity each; put these in the refrigerator to chill. Soak 7 leaves (8 if the weather is hot) of gelatine in a jug of cold water.

Carefully ladle 2½ pints (1.5 litres) chilled fish broth away from its sediment; the liquid should be fairly clear, but it will almost certainly be necessary to clarify it further. To do this, pour all but ½ pint (300 ml) of the broth into a clean pot and place this over a medium heat. Mix egg whites and shells with remaining ½ pint (300 ml). As liquid comes to the boil, whisk in the egg white mixture and continue whisking, slowly and thoroughly, until the broth boils across its surface.

Remove pot from the heat and let it stand, undisturbed, for 10 minutes. Then bring contents just to the boil, twice more, without whisking, leaving 10 minute intervals between each boil. The egg protein forms bonds with fish particles in the broth and draws them out of solution.

Line a large, fine sieve with a triple thickness of muslin and gently ladle in the clarified broth, keeping base of sieve well above surface of the strain liquid. Let contents of sieve drain, undisturbed, for 5 minutes, then discard whites and debris. Lift flavour of the broth with some dry white wine and salt, if necessary, to taste, and ladle 2 pints (1.2 litres) of this into a clean saucepan. Add softened, drained gelatine, and gently heat contents of pan until gelatine has dissolved. Cool.

Meanwhile, lightly oil surface of the 4 peppers and roast them whole under a medium grill, turning as skins blister and blacken all over. Cool under wet kitchen paper to trap steam that loosens their skins, and peel these away. Cut open peppers to remove cores and seeds, wash and dry flesh. Cut the two firmest peppers into small dice and place these in a medium bowl.

Venison liver pâté

VENISON LIVER PATE

The flavour of this dish improves with a day's rest, to allow the flavours to blend.

> 1 lb (500 g) sliced bacon
> 1 lb (500 g) chicken liver
> 2 tablespoons oil or clarified butter
> 1 medium onion, diced
> Grated rind and juice of 1 orange
> 5 sprigs fresh rosemary (2 whole, the leaves from
>   the others chopped)
> 4 fl oz (120 ml) whisky (possibly more)
> 1 lb (500 g) venison liver
> 10 oz (300 g) pork fat
> 1 egg white
> Salt and pepper
> 3½ fl oz (100 ml) cream (or less)

Trim sole fillets, press the flat of a large, heavy knife down the length of each, score the membrane side – several times across – with a sharp knife (these measures reduce distortion in cooking) and gently poach fish in some of the unclarified broth until cooked through. Drain and dry fillets, and when they are cold, cut into small dice and add to the peppers in the bowl.

Chop basil, and put this, plus red 'caviar', among peppers and fish, season with black pepper, mix carefully with hands – the 'caviar' is fragile and breaks easily – and taste; salt will probably not be necessary.

Ladle a thin layer of cooled jelly into each chilled mould and return these to the fridge. When liquid has set, divide sole mixture among the 12 moulds, fill them carefully with jelly and chill till quite firm.

To make the sauce, purée remaining red pepper flesh in food processor; beat purée, to taste, into the Greek yoghurt and season well.

To serve jellies, run a blunt knife round side of each mould, dip briefly into hot water and turn out. Serve 2 per person, garnished with basil, and pass sauce separately.

Serves 6 as a first course.   AWS

Line a large terrine dish generously with slices of bacon, extending them over the sides. Set the dish aside and cover.

Brown the chicken livers in oil or clarified butter. Then remove from the pan and pour off the excess fat, leaving any sediment. Add diced onion, orange rind and juice, chopped rosemary and whisky to the pan. Return to the heat, and flame off whisky, reducing the contents of the pan by half. Remove from the heat.

Mince or process both livers until smooth and then add pork fat in small pieces, again beating or processing until smooth. Add the contents of the pan and beat or process again, then add egg white and beat or process once more. Season to taste, and add more whisky if you want a stronger flavour. Finally, add the cream, beating until it is just incorporated.

Spoon the pâté into the lined dish, smoothing it into the corners, then fold the bacon ends over and place the remaining rosemary sprigs on top. Cover and seal with lightly greased foil, and place in a roasting dish half full of water. Bake in a pre-heated oven at 425°F (220°C, gas mark 7) for 40–45 minutes, or until the pâté is firm in the centre. Leave in the tin until completely cold, then remove the sprigs of rosemary and turn out.

Serves about 10.   PM

Buckwheat blinis with crème fraîche and 'caviar'

BUCKWHEAT BLINIS

Serve with real caviar if you can, but otherwise these little buckwheat pancakes go well with lump-fish roe and crème fraîche. Iced vodka would be the traditional accompaniment.

> 1 oz (25 g) fresh yeast
> ³/₄ pint (450 ml) scalded milk cooled to 85°F
> 8 oz (250 g) sifted buckwheat flour
> 1 tablespoon sugar
> 3 eggs, separated
> 1 tablespoon melted butter
> 1 teaspoon salt

Dissolve the yeast in milk, and stir into 6 oz (175 g) of the flour, and 1 tablespoon sugar. Cover the bowl and set aside in a warm place to rise for about 1½ hours.

Beat egg yolks with melted butter, and stir in remaining flour with salt. Add to yeast sponge, beat well, and leave to rise for another 1½ hours, or until almost doubled in bulk.

Whip the egg whites until stiff but not dry and fold into the batter. Allow to stand for 10 minutes, then cook the pancakes, dropping a small amount at a time onto a hot greased skillet or griddle. Turn to brown lightly on the other side.

Place the blinis on serving plates, with a spoonful of red and black lumpfish roe and crème fraîche. Garnish with chives.

Makes 24 × 2″ (5 cm) blinis.   CW

ASPARAGUS WITH ORANGE, WALNUT AND HONEY DRESSING

A light starter that is more refreshing than asparagus served with the usual rich butter dressings.

> 1 to 1½ lbs (500–750 g) fresh asparagus,
>   trimmed or bases peeled
>
> DRESSING
> Juice 1 orange
> Juice ½ lemon
> 2 teaspoons grated orange rind
> 2 tablespoons extra virgin olive oil
> 1 tablespoon sunflower oil
> 1 teaspoon coarse-grained mustard
> 1 tablespoon clear honey
> 1 teaspoon grated onion (optional)
> Salt and ground black pepper
> 2 oz (50 g) chopped walnuts

Mix all the dressing ingredients together in a screw topped jar and shake well.

Poach or steam the asparagus until the bases are just tender but still of good texture and the heads are not overcooked. If you have a microwave oven, asparagus is excellent cooked in this. Follow your manufacturer's instruction booklet for times, as these can vary.

Drain the asparagus and cool until lukewarm, then arrange on serving plates, coated with honey and orange dressing.

Serves 4.

NOTE This dressing is particularly good tossed into a mixed salad of bitter and astringent leaves, such as sorrel, chicory, Good King Henry, red orach and chives, with the sweetness of the honey and orange juice complementing them nicely.   RD

A PÂTÉ OF BORLOTTI BEANS AND CHEESE

Well-flavoured beans are a suitable substitute to add body to a meatless pâté. This recipe is for a good basic pâté to which you could add your own variations—mould pâtés in baby savarin rings, for example, filling the centres with a salad – raw mushrooms or even more beans.

> 8 oz (250 g) borlotti beans, soaked and cooked,
>   or one 15 oz (425 g) can, drained
> 1 large clove garlic, crushed
> 6 oz (75 g) soft goat's cheese, or ricotta or cream
>   cheese
> 2 oz (50 g) butter, melted
> 2 tablespoons fresh chopped parsley
> 1 tablespoon fresh chopped thyme or dill
> Grated rind of ½ lemon
> Salt and ground black pepper

> TO SERVE
> Diced salad vegetables, or some extra beans or
>   raw button mushrooms

For dried beans, soak overnight, drain, rinse and simmer in water for 50–60 minutes or until they are cooked.

Blend the beans in a food processor or liquidizer, then add the remaining ingredients, blending until quite smooth.

Spoon into four oiled individual moulds or cups and chill until firm. (The pâté will not be as firm as a meat or fish pâté.)

Dip the moulds briefly into hot water to loosen them, and shake out onto serving plates. If the edges look a little rough, simply smooth them with a blunt knife.

Spoon diced salad, or more beans or mushrooms, dressed in a little vinaigrette, into the centre of the moulds and serve attractively garnished with slices of toasted, garlic-flavoured baguette.

Serves 4.

NOTE The pâté can be spooned into a 1 pint (600 ml) dish until firm, then served in spoonfuls on leaves of radicchio, or frisée for example, sprinkled with fresh chopped herbs.   RD

BROAD BEAN TIAN

This is the favourite springtime dish in Provence.

> ¾ lb (350 g) young broad beans, in their pods
> ½ lb (250 g) spinach or Swiss chard leaves
> 6 eggs
> ¼ pint (150 ml) cream or milk
> 3 oz (75 g) freshly grated Parmesan
> 1 teaspoon chopped savory or marjoram
> 2–3 chopped spring onions
> 1 teaspoon salt, freshly-milled pepper
> 1 tablespoon olive oil

Prepare the broad beans; as they are young and tender, string and chop them as for runner beans. Rinse and shred the greens.

Beat the eggs lightly with the cream or milk, grated cheese, herbs, spring onions, salt and pepper. Stir in the beans and the shredded greens.

Oil a shallow heatproof, earthenware dish (diameter about 7–8″, 18–20 cm) and pour in the mixture. Bake the *tian* in a medium oven 350°F (180°C, gas mark 4) for 45 minutes, until the egg is set but still creamy. Serve with bread, black olives, a tomato salad and red wine.

Serves 6–8.   EL

A pâté of borlotti beans and cheese

HOT SOUPS AND COOL SOUPS

From shimmering, savoury jellies, served chilled
as the opener to a summer dinner, to robust
platefuls of steaming winter vegetables, there are
soups for all seasons and every occasion

CHILLED TOMATO ORANGE SOUP

Despite their everyday use, tomatoes and oranges are rarely partnered. Here they make a wonderfully refreshing and fragrant summer soup that is almost exotic for its unusual combination.

> 1½ lb (750 g) ripe tomatoes (or 2½ cups canned
>   Italian plum tomatoes with liquid)
> 2 large oranges
> 1 lemon
> 1 small white onion, chopped
> 2 tablespoons chopped fresh dill or other fresh
>   herb
> Salt and freshly-ground black pepper to taste
> Sour cream or yoghurt for garnish

First, drop tomatoes into a pot of boiling water for 30 seconds or so, depending on their ripeness. Cut in half and squeeze each half over a bowl fitted with a sieve to hold the seeds, catching the juice below. Slip off the skins and discard them with the seeds. Coarsely chop the flesh and combine it with the tomato juice in a food processor or blender.

Grate the zest from the oranges and lemon, and squeeze the juice. For a more refined soup, blanch the zest in boiling water for 2 minutes to remove the bitterness, then drain. Add the citrus zest and juice to the tomatoes with the onion and dill. Combine well, but leave a little texture. Season to taste with salt and pepper. Cover and chill thoroughly in the refrigerator until serving time.

Serve the soup in glass bowls, garnished with a dollop of sour cream or yoghurt.
Serves 4.   ER

KISIEL (STRAWBERRY SOUP)

This Northern European dessert soup can be made with various red fruits, as well as peaches and nectarines, but fresh, ripe strawberries are undoubtedly the favourite.

Served chilled with whipped cream, it makes an excellent finale to a summer meal, and would also be delicious for a late Sunday breakfast.

> 2 tablespoons cornflour
> ½ pint (300 ml) white wine
> 2 oz (50 g) sugar or to taste
> 1 lb 6 oz (675 g) fresh strawberries, hulled
> 2 tablespoons lemon juice
> 2 tablespoons grated lemon zest
> 2 tablespoons Cointreau
> Unsweetened whipped cream and unsalted
>   pistachios chopped fine for garnish

Right (clockwise from top) Chilled tomato orange soup; chlodnik (a summer borsch, page 27); jellied cucumber lime mint soup, page 26; kisiel (strawberry soup); courgette, leek and yoghurt soup, page 26

Using just enough water, make a paste with the cornflour in a pot. Stir in the wine, ½ pint (300 ml) water and the sugar. Bring to the boil and stir: the mixture will thicken. When cool, purée with the strawberries in the food processor or blender. Add the lemon juice, zest and a little more sugar if needed. Chill thoroughly, covered.

Just before serving, stir in the Cointreau. Ladle the strawberry soup into pretty bowls. Float a little whipped cream on top of each and dust with finely chopped pistachios.

Serves 6. ER

JELLIED CUCUMBER LIME MINT SOUP

This is a delicate soup, illustrated on page 25, to precede an elegant main course of salmon or trout, for a light summer dinner – not a robust peasant pottage for lusty appetites. The amount of gelatine is just enough to hold the soup together without making it bounce; to increase yield, double the entire recipe.

> 1 envelope unflavoured gelatine
> 2 fl oz (60 ml) water
> ¾ pint (450 ml) good chicken stock, preferably
>   home-made, with all fat removed
> 1 large cucumber
> 3 spring onions, green tops included, chopped
> 2 fl oz (60 ml) lime juice or more
> 4 tablespoons chopped fresh mint
> 2 tablespoons chopped fresh parsley
> Salt and pepper to taste
> Lime for garnish

Soften the gelatine in the water for a few minutes, then dissolve it in the chicken stock over low heat, stirring. Coarsely chop the cucumber, then combine it in a food processor or blender with the chicken stock, onions and lime juice. Combine the ingredients well, but do not reduce them to a fine purée: a little texture is desirable. Season with herbs and salt and pepper, and taste; sharpen with more lime juice if needed. Pour the mixture into a bowl,

cover and refrigerate for at least 3 hours, until the gelatine is set.

To serve, mix up the jellied soup to redistribute the solids, scoop it into bowls and garnish with thin slices of lime.

Serves 6. ER

COURGETTE, LEEK AND YOGHURT SOUP

This wholesome vegetable soup, illustrated on page 25, is both satisfying and versatile. Make it thick or thin; serve it hot or cold; spice it with cumin, curry or other pronounced seasoning. It is an excellent way to use up giant courgettes, and freezes well if you add the yoghurt later.

> 3 tablespoons vegetable oil
> 8 oz (250 g) leeks, trimmed, quartered
>   lengthwise, and chopped
> 1 lb (500 g) courgettes, chopped
> 2 pints (1.2 litres) chicken stock
> 1 large lemon
> 5 fl oz (150 ml) plain yoghurt
> 1 tablespoon cumin, or to taste
> Salt and freshly-ground pepper to taste
> More yoghurt and fresh coriander leaves for
>   garnish, if desired

In a large pot, heat the oil over medium heat and sweat the leeks, stirring, for about 5 minutes. Add the courgettes and stock. Cut six very thin rounds from the centre of the lemon for garnish, and reserve. From the lemon ends, grate the zest and add, with the juice, to the pot. Bring to the boil and simmer, covered, for about 15 minutes.

Cool the soup, then purée in a food processor or blender with the yoghurt. Season to taste with cumin (start with a small amount and increase), salt and pepper. You may thin it with more stock. Cover and chill thoroughly.

To serve, ladle the soup into individual bowls and swirl in more yoghurt on top. Garnish with the reserved lemon and coriander leaves if you like.

Serves 6. ER

CHLODNIK
(SUMMER BORSCH)

The brilliant deep magenta colour is reason enough to make this summer borsch from Poland, illustrated on page 25. The authentic soup is made with raw beetroot and tops, but this puréed version uses pre-cooked roots that are more readily available. Just be sure to use untreated ones, that is, un-vinegared. By saving the broth to add after cooking, the colour stays beautifully intense.

> 2 lb (1 kg) cooked beetroot (not vinegared)
> 4 tablespoons or more wine vinegar
> 4 oz (125 g) fresh young beet tops (or spinach or Swiss chard)
> 1 large carrot, scrubbed and shredded
> 4 spring onions, green tops included, chopped
> 3 tablespoons chopped fresh dill, or to taste
> For the garnish: chopped cucumber, sliced spring onions, hard-boiled egg and sliced lemon
> Sour cream
> Seasoning

Grate a quarter of the beetroot over a large pot to catch all the juice. Add 2 tablespoons vinegar and 2 pints (1.2 litres) boiling water. Bring slowly to the boil, then cool. Strain, reserving the broth.

In another pot, combine the carrot and onions with 5 fl oz (100 ml) water. Bring to the boil, then add the greens. Cook for 10 minutes, stirring occasionally, until the greens are wilted and tender. Let the vegetables cool.

Meanwhile, grate the remaining beetroot, again keeping all the juice. When the vegetables have cooled, purée them with their liquid in a food processor or blender. Add the grated beetroot and reserved broth – just enough to give a thick but not semi-solid texture. Season to taste with more vinegar and dill. Chill thoroughly, covered.

To serve the chlodnik, ladle it over an ice-cube placed in the bottom of each serving bowl. Garnish with cucumber, spring onion, quartered hard-boiled egg and a slice of lemon. Pass the sour cream on the side.

Serves 10 or 12.   ER

Hampshire watercress and bacon pottage, topped with swirls of cream and crumbled crisp bacon

HAMPSHIRE WATERCRESS
AND BACON POTTAGE

For centuries pottage was the universal food of the peasants. A thick broth containing vegetables, herbs, and usually a grain, such as oats or barley, it could be left to simmer in a large pot over an open fire. Any meat added was almost inevitably bacon, which provided not only a small amount of valuable protein, but also some additional flavour. This is certainly a more refined version than would have been available in the Middle Ages, but it is a recipe with ancient origins.

> 4 rashers streaky bacon
> 1 oz (25 g) butter
> 1 medium onion, peeled and chopped
> 1 large potato, peeled and chopped
> 2 bunches watercress
> 1½ pints (900 ml) chicken or vegetable stock
> ¼ pint (150 ml) single cream
> Salt and freshly milled black pepper

27

Cut the rind off the bacon. Melt the butter in a pan and gently fry the bacon rinds with the onion for 5 minutes. Add the potato to the pan and cook for 3 minutes. Cut about 1 inch (2.5 cm) off the watercress stalks, then roughly chop the remainder. Add to the pan and cook for about 2 minutes. Pour over the stock and bring to the boil. Cover the pan and simmer gently for 20 minutes. Do not overcook or the soup will lose its vivid green colour. Remove the bacon rinds, then sieve the soup or purée it in a blender or food processor. Tip back into the saucepan, reheat gently and adjust the seasoning.

Meanwhile grill the bacon until it is crisp, remove from the pan and roughly crumble. Pour the soup into a tureen, pour the cream round in a swirl and sprinkle with the bacon. Serve immediately, piping hot.

Serves 4. JR

and add to the soup to thicken it. (If using egg yolks, beat them into the soup at this stage.) Heat gently but do not boil. Adjust seasoning, add butter and cream and heat again. Pour into a warm tureen when almost ready to serve.

Cut slices of crust from the sides of the rolls and stick almond slices into the crust so that they look like spiky hedgehogs. Grill briefly to toast the almonds, and float the 'hedgehogs' on the soup. Serve immediately.

Serves 8.

NOTE If you possess a Thermomix, all the soup ingredients except the cream can be placed together in the machine, using half the required quantity. Switch on for 15 minutes, empty the soup into another container and repeat with the remaining half of the ingredients. Add the cream and seasoning and serve as above. KD

HEDGEHOG SOUP

This is one of the oldest of soup recipes, which has its roots in Roman cookery. Often called white soup, and originally thickened with egg yolks, it has a subtle and delicate flavour. If you prefer the idea of egg yolk thickening to cornflour, use 3–4 yolks, beaten into the soup, which must then be heated gently, not boiled.

> *4 oz (125 g) ground almonds*
> *3 pints (1.75 litres) good white stock*
> *1 pint (600 ml) milk*
> *2 tablespoons cornflour or 4 egg yolks*
> *2 oz butter*
> *½ pint (300 ml) single cream*
> *3 bay leaves*
> *Salt, freshly ground pepper*
>
> GARNISH
> *3 small round French rolls*
> *1 packet sliced almonds*

Heat ground almonds with the stock, milk and bay leaves. Simmer gently for about 15 minutes, and liquidize. Slake the cornflour in a little cold water,

Hedgehog soup, with floating almond 'hedgehogs'

POTAGE OF LEEKS, CELERIAC AND POTATOES

This is not a refined soup for an elegant evening but an earthy *potage* with the elusive flavour and celadon colour of celery. Chicken stock is used here rather than water; it slightly masks the celeriac colour and flavour but adds another note. Either way, the soup benefits from the contrasting sharpness of its garnish. Instead of caraway, you might try dried fennel seeds, rye bread croûtons, crumbled bacon, or bits of salty country ham.

> *2 medium leeks*
> *1 large celeriac bulb, about 1 lb (500 g)*
> *2 large potatoes, about 1 lb (500 g) total*
> *2 tablespoons butter*
> *Water or chicken stock to cover, about 2½ pints (1.5 litres)*
> *1 pint (600 ml) rich milk*
> *Salt to taste*
> *White pepper to taste*
> *Caraway seeds for garnish*

Chop off the root end of the leeks and most of the green tops. Slice lengthwise in quarters almost to the root and rinse out any grit under cold running water. Shake off excess water and chop the leeks coarsely. Peel the celeriac and potatoes and cut both into cubes.

Melt the butter in a large pot over medium low heat. Add the leeks and cook, stirring, until wilted. Add the celeriac and potato together with water or stock barely to cover. Put on a tight-fitting lid and simmer slowly for about 40 minutes, until cooked through. Cool somewhat, then purée in a food processor or blender in batches. This much may be done in advance.

Return the soup to the pot, add 1 pint (600 ml) of rich milk, and heat it nearly to boiling point but do not let it actually boil. Season to taste with salt and white pepper, and thin with a little more milk if you prefer. Serve the soup piping hot in bowls, each garnished with half a teaspoon of caraway seeds or your chosen alternative.

Makes about 3 pints (1.75 litres) of warming winter soup. ER

COLD TOMATO AND SWEETCORN SOUP

For the ripest, most flavourful summer tomatoes and the freshest sweetcorn only. Add some Italian, sun-dried tomatoes for their concentration of colour and flavour. (See illustration page 96.)

VEGETABLE BROTH
> *2 carrots, peeled*
> *1 medium onion, peeled*
> *1 leek, washed and trimmed*
> *2 long sticks celery*
> *½ potato, peeled*
> *1 head of garlic, peeled*
> *Bouquet of thyme, bay leaf, parsley*
> *¼ teaspoon salt*
> *4 pints (2.25 litres) cold water*

SOUP
> *2½ lb (1.25 kg) large ripe tomatoes*
> *½ large onion, peeled and sliced*
> *3–4 sun-dried tomatoes, washed*
> *1½ pints (900 ml) broth (above)*
> *Salt*
> *9 oz (275 g) sweetcorn kernels, cut from corn ears with small knife*
> *Freshly ground black pepper*
> *2–3 fl oz (60–90 ml) buttermilk*
> *Plain yoghurt*

To make the broth, quarter the 5 vegetables and place in a deep pot with the garlic, bouquet garni, salt and water. Bring to the boil and simmer, lid ajar, for 1¾ hours. Cool and strain the broth.

To make the soup, peel, seed, and chop the fresh tomatoes, putting flesh and all exuded juices into a medium pot with the onion, the sliced, sun-dried tomatoes, broth, and a little salt. Bring to the boil and simmer for 10–12 minutes, adding 4 oz (125 g) of the sweetcorn for the last 5 minutes.

Purée the soup until very smooth, and season to taste. Reheat with the remaining sweetcorn, simmering for 1 minute. Cool, add buttermilk to sharpen, check seasoning and chill for several hours. Serve each bowlful with a swirl of yoghurt.

Serves 6. AWS

SUCCOTASH CHOWDER

Succotash is a Narragansett Indian word meaning something that is broken into bits. Nowadays, Americans use it to describe a stew of fresh lima beans, corn and other foods.

It can be made with canned or frozen corn and beans if necessary, and is hearty enough for a winter lunch, served with country bread. This version contains no meat (more traditional recipes use bacon grease) and is suitable for vegetarians.

2 cobs of fresh sweetcorn
1½ oz (40 g) butter
2 cloves garlic, crushed
1 medium onion, chopped
2 sticks celery, chopped
1 teaspoon fresh chopped basil
1 teaspoon fresh chopped thyme
2½ pints (1.5 litres) warm milk
2 teaspoons tamari soy sauce
12 oz (350 g) fresh or frozen lima beans or 4 oz (125 g) dried weight, soaked and cooked

Succotash chowder

Salt and ground black pepper
Fresh chopped parsley and chives, or a few small sage leaves

Stand the cobs upright and with a sharp knife strip the kernels off.

Melt the butter in a large saucepan and gently fry the garlic, onion and celery until softened, about 5 minutes. Add the corn and cook for a further five minutes then blend in the basil, thyme, milk, tamari and lima beans. Season well and heat gently until quite hot but not boiling. Serve hot, sprinkled with chopped herbs.

Serves 4–6.   RD

PUCHERO

This recipe from the Philippines is a close relation of Spanish *cocida*. It is best served in wide-brimmed soup plates, either the soup first, followed by the vegetables and meat – as in a French *pot au feu* – or together, as described here.

Chicken, pork and chorizo are combined with chickpeas, sweet potato, plantain and Chinese leaves in this one-pot dish, and a garlicky aubergine sauce is stirred in at the last minute.

8 oz (250 g) chickpeas, soaked overnight in water
3 lb (1.25 kg) chicken, jointed into 8 pieces
12 oz (350 g) lean pork belly, rind removed and cut into chunks
2 medium onions, chopped
4 pints (2.25 litres) water
4 tablespoons groundnut oil
3 cloves garlic, crushed
1 can (14 oz, 400 g) chopped tomatoes
3 tablespoons tomato purée, or to taste
2 chorizos (Spanish sausages)
2 sweet potatoes, or equivalent in pumpkin or potato if liked, peeled and cubed
1–2 plantain (bananas for cooking), peeled and sliced
6–8 Chinese leaves, finely shredded
6 spring onions, shredded to garnish

*(Clockwise from top) puchero; Lancashire hot pot
(recipe on page 81); Genoese minestrone*

AUBERGINE SAUCE
1 large aubergine
1 small onion, chopped
2 cloves garlic, crushed
2 spring onions, trimmed and chopped
Salt and pepper to taste

Place the drained and rinsed chickpeas in a large pan with chicken pieces, pork belly, one chopped onion, and water to cover. Bring to boil, skim if necessary, half cover and cook gently for 45 minutes or until meats are tender.

Set oven to 400°F (200°C, gas mark 6). Score the aubergine with a knife and place in oven for 40–50 minutes till wrinkled on the outside. Strip off skin with a knife, holding the aubergine gently with an oven-glove. Scoop flesh into a food processor with the onion, garlic and spring onions. Beat to a pulp, season and transfer to a serving dish.

Fry remaining onion gently in hot oil, with the garlic, till soft and transparent. Add chopped tomatoes and then the purée, and stir into the meat mixture along with the peeled and sliced chorizos, cubes of sweet potato and plantain. Season to taste, then cook gently for 15–20 minutes.

Just before serving, bring to the boil and add Chinese leaves. Cook for 2 minutes only and scatter with the spring onion before you take the *puchero* and the prepared sauce (which is stirred into helpings of the soup) to the table.

Accompany with fresh bread.

Serves 6–8.   SM

GENOESE MINESTRONE

This is traditionally served with spoonfuls of rich green pesto floating on the surface. Other vegetables in season – carrots, cauliflower, aubergine, potato, for example – can be used, but they will need more cooking than celery and tomatoes.

1 large onion, peeled and chopped
3 cloves garlic, crushed
1 can (1¾ oz, 45 g) anchovy fillets
3–4 tablespoons groundnut oil
2 sticks celery, finely chopped
*4–6 oz (125–175 g) French beans, cut into
    short lengths*
Sprigs marjoram and parsley tied together
2 × 14 oz (400 g) cans chopped tomatoes
2 × 15 oz (425 g) cans borlotti beans
*2–2½ pints (1.2–1.5 litres) chicken stock,
    home-made or from a cube*
*4–6 oz (125–175 g) tiny shell or bow-shaped
    pasta cooked according to packet directions*
Salt and freshly ground black pepper

PESTO
*1 cup fresh basil leaves, or continental parsley,
    plus 2–3 teaspoons dried basil*
2 cloves garlic, crushed
2–3 oz (50–70 g) pine-nuts or walnut pieces
½ pint (300 ml) sunflower or groundnut oil
2–3 tablespoons Parmesan cheese
Seasoning

31

Fry the onion and garlic in the drained oil from the anchovies and the groundnut oil till soft and transparent. Chop the anchovies and add to the pan with celery, French beans, herbs and tomatoes. Cook together for 3–4 minutes.

Add the drained and rinsed beans and the stock, and cook for 10–15 minutes. Add pasta shapes and cook for a further 2–3 minutes. Taste for seasoning and remove herbs if liked.

Meanwhile, make the pesto by placing the herbs, garlic and nuts in a food processor with oil and blending till smooth. Add cheese and season to taste. The pesto should be quite runny, so you may need to add a little boiling water.

Serve the soup in a tureen, drizzle some of the pesto into the centre and serve the remainder separately so that each person spoons a little onto the individual helping. Serve with chunks of warm bread or rolls.

Serves 6–8.   SM

Soup of meat and red beans

CREAM OF SPINACH SOUP

This delicious soup (illustrated on page 87) can be made in minutes with the aid of a liquidizer.

6–7 tablespoons chopped shallot
1½ oz (40 g) butter
1 lb (500 g) fresh, washed spinach leaves
½ teaspoon salt
1½ oz (40 g) flour
2½ pints (1.5 litres) chicken stock
2 egg yolks
5 fl oz (140 ml) double cream
½–1 oz (15–25 g) softened butter

Soften the shallots in the first measure of butter in a covered pan; do not let them brown. Stir in the spinach and salt. When the spinach has wilted, stir in the flour and cook slowly for 4–5 minutes. Add the boiling chicken stock off the heat. Stir to incorporate, then simmer for about 5 minutes.

Blend the egg yolks and cream in a bowl. Beat in ½ pint (300 ml) of hot soup, little by little to prevent curdling. Then gradually add the rest of the

hot soup. Pour back into the saucepan, and stir over a moderate heat for 2 minutes; do not let it boil. Purée the soup in a liquidizer. Bring to simmering point and stir in the softened butter gradually.

Serves 4–6, hot or cold.   BGM

SOUP OF MEAT AND RED BEANS

1¼ lb (625 g) very lean beef (chuck or shin)
1 oz (25 g) butter or margarine
18 oz (500 g) dried red kidney beans, soaked in
    water overnight
2 tins tomato juice, about 18 fl oz (500 ml) each
Salt and pepper

Cut the meat into bite-size cubes. Melt the butter or margarine in a large pan and brown the meat slowly. When lightly browned, add the drained beans and heat through. Pour in the tomato juice, and simmer for 3 hours. Season and serve.

Serves 6.   PF

FRESH TOMATO SOUP WITH BORAGE FLOWERS

This dish looks particularly striking – the vibrant red of the tomato soup with borage blue. Borage (*Borago officinalis*), the bee plant, has a flavour of cucumber and, as such, marries well with salad vegetables. This is a no-cook soup, served cold, which does need overnight marinating.

> *2 lb (1 kg) ripe tomatoes, skinned, seeded and chopped*
> *⅓ cucumber, peeled, seeded and chopped*
> *2 spring onions or 2 tablespoons fresh chopped chives*
> *1 tablespoon chopped red or yellow pepper*
> *½ pint (300 ml) light stock*
> *2 tablespoons cider vinegar*
> *3 leaves of borage*
> *About 24 borage flowers, with hairy sepals removed*
> *Salt and white pepper*
> *Single cream, to serve*

Blend or process everything together except the flowers and cream. Chill overnight and check the seasoning when cold.

Serve, if possible, on a bed of crushed ice and trail whispers of cream into the soup, then scatter over the borage flowers. Naturally, the flowers are best picked just before serving.

Serves 6.   RD

SOPA MORELLANA

The walled medieval town of Morella in Spain has given its name to this clear, strongly-flavoured broth, which is topped with tiny floating choux buns called *buñuelos*.

> FOR THE STOCK
> *1 ham bone (best from Parma ham)*
> *¼ chicken*
> *¼ boiling fowl*
> *Small beef or lamb bone*

> FOR THE CHOUX PUFFS
> *1 oz (25 g) butter*
> *¼ pint (150 ml) milk*
> *2 oz (50 g) flour*
> *2 egg yolks, plus 1 white*
> *Pinch of salt*

Place the stock ingredients in a large pot, cover well with cold water, bring to the boil, and simmer, covered, for 4–5 hours. Skim the surface occasionally and top up with more water if required. Strain and leave the stock in a basin in the fridge overnight. Skim fat off the surface.

To make the choux puffs, place butter, milk and salt in a small saucepan, and bring to the boil. Add flour, blend well and stir over gentle heat until it forms a mass and the inside of the pan is clean. Remove from heat, cool slightly, and beat in egg yolks one at a time, followed by the egg white. Allow to cool completely before piping the mixture (or spooning, if preferred) into small balls onto a baking tray. Bake at 325°F (170°C, gas mark 3) for about 15 minutes, until golden brown.

Reheat broth, check seasoning, and float *buñuelos* on top to serve.

4 pints (2.25 litres) serves 6–8.   MJS

CARROT SOUP WITH CARDAMOM AND JUNIPER

This highly aromatic pair of spices surprises and enhances the decidedly unexotic qualities of the carrot. Prepare the soup a day in advance to allow the flavours to mingle and give its character time to mature.

> *16 green cardamoms*
> *3 large juniper berries*
> *1 oz (25 g) butter*
> *1 large onion*
> *1½ lb (750 g) carrots*
> *3 pints (1.75 litres) chicken broth*
> *Salt*
> *Freshly-ground black pepper*
> *Double cream*

Open and discard the cardamom pods, crush their seeds with the base of a heavy knife handle; crush and chop the juniper berries and drop both spices into a large, heavy pot with the just-melted butter.

Add the peeled and sliced onion and carrots and let all sweat over a low heat, the pot's lid ajar, for about 10 minutes, until vegetables have softened and the spices' fragrance is well-developed. Stir often.

Add broth and a little salt and let simmer until vegetables are cooked. Half-cool the mixture and liquidize, seasoning to taste, until the soup is very smooth and spices are well pulverized. Reheat to serve, swirling a drop of cream round the centre of each bowlful.

Serves 6. AWS

CARROT, CELERY, POTATO AND LOVAGE SOUP

Fresh lovage leaves, with their pungent, slightly maverick flavour of celery, lift a comfortable, everyday soup into one of unusual interest, and (illustrated on page 99) make a small adornment.

1 medium onion, peeled and sliced
10 oz (300 g) carrots (peeled weight), sliced
12 oz (350 g) celery, sliced
1 oz (25 g) butter
6 oz (175 g) potato (peeled weight), cubed
2¾ pints (1.6 litres) home-made chicken broth
Salt and freshly ground black pepper
Leaves of fresh lovage

Using a large, heavy pot, sweat onion, carrots, and celery in butter until softened, stirring occasionally. Add potato, broth, a dash of salt; bring liquid to the boil and allow broth to simmer until vegetables have cooked – a period of some 10 minutes from boiling point.

Remove pot from heat and add 6–7 chopped lovage leaves – these vary in impact and you can always increase their number – cool soup slightly and liquidize, seasoning to taste. Judge whether to add more lovage – it should be quite evident, but not overpowering – and liquidize again until smooth.

Reheat soup to serve, garnishing each bowlful with a frond of lovage.

Serves 6. AWS

PARTAN BREE WITH CRÈME FRAÎCHE

This classic Scottish soup takes on a tangy creaminess if crème fraîche is stirred in just before serving.

3 shallots, finely chopped
1 stick celery, finely chopped
1 oz (25 g) butter
2 tablespoons flour, optional, to thicken soup
½ pint (300 ml) milk
1½ pints (900 ml) fish or chicken stock
8 oz (250 g) crab meat, fresh or frozen
Sprig fresh rosemary
A good pinch cayenne pepper or few drops hot
 pepper or Worcestershire sauce
2 tablespoons brandy
Freshly grated nutmeg
Salt and ground black pepper
4 tablespoons crème fraîche plus a little extra for
 garnish, beaten until smooth
Fresh chopped parsley, to garnish

Gently sauté the shallots and celery in the butter for 10 minutes in a large saucepan until softened. Stir in the flour, if using, and cook for a minute. Then gradually stir in the milk and stock.

Bring to the boil, stirring, add the crab meat, rosemary and seasoning. Cover and turn down to a gentle simmer for 20 minutes. Remove rosemary, and stir in brandy and nutmeg, then blend in the crème fraîche. Reheat just a little but don't boil.

Serve the soup in warm bowls and spoon in some extra cream. Scatter over the parsley.

This can be made in advance and kept chilled or frozen up to the stage of adding the crème fraîche. Finish off before serving.

Serves 6–8. RD

CREAM OF TURNIP SOUP

The distinctive flavour of turnips seems to blend particularly well with game stock. Piquant orange croûtons add a nice finishing touch.

12 oz (350 g) peeled turnip
2 shallots or 1 small onion
1¼–1¾ oz (32–45 g) butter
½ teaspoon caster sugar
1¾ pints (1 litre) game or chicken stock
1 tablespoon potato flour
3–4 fl oz (75–125 g) cream or milk
Little fresh chopped parsley
Salt and pepper

CROUTONS
3–4 slices white or brown stale bread, cut into
*   tiny squares*
1 tablespoon oil
½ oz (15 g) butter
½–1 teaspoon curry paste or powder
Grated rind of ½ orange or clementine

Cream of turnip soup

Finely chop the onion and cut the turnip into thin slices. Sweat in ¾ oz (20 g) of the butter in a heavy pan, sprinkle with sugar and cook gently, without browning, for 20–30 minutes (add a tablespoon or so of stock if the pan gets too dry). Season, add the stock and simmer for 20 minutes, or until completely tender, then purée and return to the rinsed-out pan.

Mix the potato flour with the cream or milk, add to the pan and bring to the boil, stirring. Correct the seasoning and simmer for a minute or two before drawing off the stove. Stir in the remaining butter in little bits to enrich and further thicken the soup, and serve immediately with the croûtons, parsley and some fine shreds of orange or clementine zest.

To make the piquant orange croûtons, heat butter and oil in a frying pan, add the curry paste or powder, orange rind and the squares of bread and fry, tossing, until golden brown. Drain on absorbent kitchen paper and keep warm or reheat before serving.

Serves 4–6.   NC

GERMAN PUMPKIN SOUP

This delicate amber soup has its own fresh innocent flavour; don't be tempted to stir in cream.

1½ lb (750 g) piece pumpkin
¾ pint (450 ml) water
3 cloves
Small piece cinnamon stick
2 tablespoons wine vinegar
2 oz (50 g) butter
Salt, pepper, sugar

Peel the pumpkin, and scoop out the seeds and fibrous middle. Cut the flesh into 1″ (2.5 cm) cubes and put them in a saucepan. Pour in the water – it may appear too little, but pumpkin is very watery.

Stick the cloves and the stick of cinnamon into a piece of the pumpkin flesh so that you can remove them easily. Stew gently with the spices for 20–30 minutes, until the pumpkin is soft. Take out the spices, then purée the pumpkin with its cooking liquid. Stir in the wine vinegar. Heat again and beat in the butter. Season with salt, plenty of freshly milled black pepper, and a little sugar.

Serves 4.   EL

FISH AND SHELLFISH

The most healthful and versatile of foods, fish and shellfish lend themselves to a thousand different treatments, from chowders to kedgeree, terrines to tartares, crêpes to croquettes

MILLE-FEUILLE OF SALMON AND POTATOES

Alternate layers of salmon and potato, with a cream and lemon sauce.

> 4 medium-sized potatoes
> 1 lb (500 g) fresh salmon
> 7 fl oz (200 ml) double cream
> Juice of 1 lemon
> Salt, pepper, small bunch of chives

Peel the potatoes, and slice thinly. Heat a heavy frying-pan, and coat the base thinly with oil. Arrange slices of potato over the base of the pan, overlapping the slices, so that the potatoes adhere during cooking, until the base is covered. Keep any remaining potato for cooking later. Cook the potatoes for 5 minutes on each side, turning in one piece like a pancake, until cooked through and lightly browned. They should form a solid disc when cooked. Using a 3″ (6 cm) circular cutter, make rounds of potatoes and set aside. Repeat until all the potato slices are cooked and cut into rounds. Keep potato discs warm whilst cooking the salmon.

Slice the salmon into escalopes about ½″ (1 cm) thick, season and cook in an oven at 300°F (150°C, gas mark 2) for 4 minutes.

Remove the salmon from the oven, and cut into rounds with the same circular cutter. Arrange alternate layers of salmon and potato rounds on serving plates in the style of a mille-feuille.

Mix together the cream, lemon juice and chopped chives. Season and pour the sauce around the mille-feuilles to serve.

Serves 4.   CP

CABBAGE LEAVES STUFFED WITH PIKE

Pike is difficult to find in England, unless you have an enlightened fishmonger, or angling friends who are prepared to part with their catch.

> 6 cabbage leaves
>
> STUFFING
> 1 lb 4 oz (635 g) fillet of pike, skinned
> 1 lb (500 g) double cream
> 1 egg white
> Salt, pepper
>
> SAUCE
> 1 lb (500 g) peas, shelled
> Knob of butter
> Fresh tarragon
> Salt, pepper, pinch of sugar

Right (Clockwise from top) tartare of trout (see page 38); cabbage leaves stuffed with pike; and mille-feuille of salmon and potatoes

To make the stuffing, first pulverize the fish thoroughly, and pass through a sieve to remove any bones which may remain. Gradually incorporate the cream and egg white bit by bit, blending well, to obtain a smooth, creamy consistency.

Blanch the cabbage leaves, refresh under cold water, and cut away the stalk from each leaf.

Cook the peas with a little boiling water, butter, salt, pepper and sugar, for 10 minutes. Blend in the liquidizer with fresh chopped tarragon, to make a fairly liquid sauce.

Divide the pike mixture between the 6 cabbage leaves, placing a spoonful on each, and wrap the leaves up to form neat parcels. Bake, covered, in the oven for 15 minutes at 325°F (175°C, gas mark 3).

Serve hot, with the pea sauce poured around.
Serves 6.   CP

TARTARE OF TROUT

An elegant starter, using really fresh trout.

TARTARE
1 lb (500 g) fresh trout, filleted and skinned
Juice of 1 lemon
Small bunch of chives
2 dessertspoons olive oil
Salt, freshly ground white pepper

RED PEPPER SAUCE
2 red peppers
½ pint (300 ml) olive oil
Salt, pepper

With a sharp knife, chop the trout finely and season with lemon juice, salt and pepper. Finely chop the chives; add to the trout mixture, together with the two spoonfuls of olive oil. Blend well and refrigerate for a couple of hours.

To make the sauce, place the red peppers in a very hot oven for 15 minutes to loosen the skins. Peel and deseed, then purée the flesh in a blender. Slowly add the olive oil to the red pepper purée, blending all the time, as if making mayonnaise.

Season to taste.

To serve, pour a pool of sauce onto each serving plate. Using two dessertspoons, make egg-shaped *quenelles* of the trout mixture. Place one *quenelle* on each plate, and serve decorated with fresh chives.
Serves 4.   CP

FRESH TUNA WITH GINGER VINAIGRETTE

Fresh tuna is becoming increasingly available from the wet fish counters in good supermarkets, as well as from go-ahead fishmongers. However, if it is not available, the dressing might be served with salmon steaks.

1" (2.5 cm) piece fresh ginger, peeled and finely
*   chopped*
2 large spring onions, white and some of the
*   green parts, thinly sliced*
8 fl oz (225 ml) olive oil
Juice of 2 limes
2 tablespoons soy sauce
2 tablespoons sesame oil
Salt
Freshly ground black pepper
1 bunch fresh coriander or flat-leaved parsley,
*   finely chopped*
6 × 5–6 oz (150–175 g) tuna steaks
Coriander or flat-leaved parsley leaves and slices
*   of lime for garnish*

To make the vinaigrette, stir together the ginger, spring onions, vinegar, olive oil, lime juice and soy sauce, then whisk in the sesame oil and seasonings. Finally, add the coriander or parsley. Grill the tuna under a high heat (or over a barbecue) for 3½–4 minutes on each side, or a little longer for more well-cooked fish.

Spoon some of the dressing onto 6 plates. Add the fish and garnish with coriander or parsley leaves and slices of lime. Serve with crisp salad of mixed lettuce leaves.
Serves 6.   HW

Scallop stir-fry with rice

Heat oil in wok, and sauté carrot, celery, mushrooms and red onion for about 1 minute. Remove from oil, set aside. Add prawns and scallops to wok. Sauté until scallops turn white and firm and prawns turn pink – about 1½ minutes. Add soy sauce, oyster sauce, sugar, sesame oil, pepper, sherry, ginger, garlic and spring onions. Stir in vegetables and sauté for about another 30 seconds. Serve with plain rice.

Serves 2.   CW

SCALLOP STIR-FRY

The ultimate fast food – once the ingredients are prepared, cooking takes less than five minutes.

A Californian interpretation of the Chinese style of cooking, it uses ingredients which are readily available in most supermarkets today, not just the Chinatown emporia of large cities.

> *6 oz (175 g) fresh raw prawns*
> *6 oz (175 g) scallops, sliced in two horizontally*
> *Oil for frying*
> *1 carrot, cut in julienne strips*
> *1 stalk celery, in julienne strips*
> *1 oz (25 g) shitake mushrooms, sliced*
> *1 small red onion, sliced*
> *1 tablespoon soy sauce*
> *2 tablespoons oyster sauce (available from Chinese foodstores)*
> *3–4 teaspoons sugar*
> *½ teaspoon sesame oil*
> *¼ teaspoon black pepper*
> *2 teaspoons dry sherry*
> *1 slice fresh ginger, shredded*
> *½ teaspoon finely chopped garlic*
> *2 spring onions, trimmed and sliced*

STEAMED FRESH SCALLOPS WITH GARLIC

This is a speciality of the Bayee House, an excellent Chinese restaurant in Putney, whose manager, Albert Siu, described the method. Quantities given are *per person* as a first course.

> *3 large fresh scallops, with their coral and rounded half-shells*
> *1 teaspoon minced garlic per scallop*
> *Vegetable oil*
> *Salt*
> *Freshly ground black pepper*

Have your fishmonger clean the scallops and shells; carefully detach coral (the Bayee House does not serve this, but it adds interest and colour) and remove any extraneous tissue from around the side of each white muscle. Put the muscle, with coral, into a rounded half-shell, and top the scallop with a teaspoon (or less, if this is too much) of minced garlic mixed with a little oil and seasoning.

Set each shell in the top of a steamer, or on a rack placed inside a pot large enough to hold the scallops well above the level of simmering water. Cover with a snug-fitting lid and gently steam the fish for 10–15 minutes, or until each scallop is cooked right through and has made its own delectable broth.

Carefully remove each shell from the steamer – so as not to spill the broth – season the contents, and eat without delay.

Serves 1.   AWS

Salt cod with sweet red peppers

SALT COD WITH SWEET RED PEPPERS

Salt cod is a great favourite in Spain, and is used in hundreds of ways. This appetizer, called *pericana*, comes from the region of Valencia.

> *2–3 dried sweet red peppers*
> *About 8 oz (250 g) dried salt cod*
> *6–7 cloves fresh garlic*
> *Olive oil*

Soak the salt cod in cold water for 24 hours, changing the water twice.

Heat a pan of olive oil, remove from heat and 'blanch' the peppers in the hot oil very briefly, taking care not to allow them to burn. Remove and set aside.

Using a heavy frying-pan or griddle, roast peeled garlic cloves until tender and slightly blackened on the outside. Remove and set aside. In the same pan, sweat the salt cod, without oil, until cooked. Flake the fish, discarding skin and bones, and chop the garlic finely. Crumble the fried red peppers, and mix cod, garlic and peppers together in a bowl. Pour over olive oil to taste, check seasoning and serve with crusty bread.

Serves 4.   MJS

SMOKED HADDOCK SOUFFLE CREPES

This is a very popular dinner-party starter.

CREPES
2 eggs
4 oz (125 g) plain flour
½ pint (300 ml) milk
Salt and ground black pepper
Oil, for greasing

FILLING
1 lb (500 g) Finnan haddock
¾ pint (450 ml) milk
1 large bay leaf
2 oz (50 g) butter
1 shallot or small onion, chopped
1 clove garlic, crushed
1 teaspoon curry powder or paste
1½ oz (40 g) flour
5 tablespoons Parmesan cheese
2 egg yolks
3 egg whites
Some flaked almonds, to sprinkle

Blend the crêpe eggs with the flour, milk and seasoning, in a blender or food processor, until the mixture is smooth.

Using a 7″ (18 cm) omelette pan, lightly grease the base and make a batch of lacy thin crêpes, heating the pan well in between each one. Stack the crêpes and keep warm in a clean tea towel.

Meanwhile, poach the haddock in the milk with the bay leaf and black pepper, for about 10 minutes, until it just flakes. Skin, bone and flake with a fork. Discard the bones and skin but strain and reserve the milk.

Melt the butter in a large saucepan and sauté the chopped onion and crushed garlic for about 5 minutes. Stir in the flour and curry powder and cook for another minute.

Gradually blend in the reserved fish milk, stirring until smooth and thickened. Season and add the 2 egg yolks. Stir in the flaked fish and 3 tablespoons of the cheese.

Whisk the egg whites until forming stiff peaks. Beat a spoonful into the mixture, then carefully fold in the rest.

Divide the soufflé mixture into 6, and spoon down the middle of 6 crêpes. Flip over the two edges and place the crêpes down the centre of a large, oval ovenproof dish. Sprinkle over the remaining cheese and almonds, and bake uncovered at 400°F (200°C, gas mark 6) for 20–25 minutes, until risen and slightly crispy. Serve at once – make sure your guests are sitting down first.

Serves 6.

NOTE Despite being a soufflé mixture, the filling is surprisingly adaptable as it can be prepared in advance and baked 25 minutes before you sit down. Any leftover crêpes can be interleaved, wrapped and frozen.   RD

FISH PIE IN FILO PASTRY

This exquisitely delicate pie, which can serve as a starter or main course dish, is at its best when served within half an hour of cooking. However, it is perfect for dinner parties, as it can be assembled a couple of hours in advance and cooked just before it is to be served.

FILLING
8 oz (250 g) mushrooms, rinsed and dried
1 leek (only its white part), trimmed, chopped
*   and rinsed*
2 carrots, scraped and chopped
1 oz (25 g) butter
1 lb 6 oz (675 g) fresh fillet of cod, skinned and
*   boned*
2 spring onions, trimmed and rinsed
2 tablespoons chopped fresh dill
1 tablespoon chopped parsley
3 eggs
2 tablespoons single cream or creamy milk
Salt

PASTRY
1 lb (500 g) packet filo pastry
6 oz (175 g) melted butter

Make a *mirepoix* by putting carrots, leek and mushrooms through the sharp mincing blade of a food processor and processing briefly until the mixture has the consistency of large-sized crumbs. Melt the butter, add the minced vegetables and sauté over medium heat, turning over until all the moisture has evaporated; about 3–4 minutes. Season and keep aside.

Process the remaining filling ingredients until finely chopped and well amalgamated.

Butter a rectangular or square roasting dish, about 15″ × 11″ × 3″ (39 × 28 × 8 cm) or slightly smaller. Unfold the stack of pastry and brush its top layer with melted butter; lift it and line the oven dish as neatly as possible, removing excess length but allowing 2″ (5 cm) overhang on all sides in order to enclose filling. Continue in the same manner until about half of the pastry has been used, which will be about 6–7 sheets. Spread the fish filling evenly into the dish, then top with the *mirepoix*. Fold all four sides of the pastry over the filling, enclosing it and preventing it from spilling. Cover neatly with sheets of pastry that have been brushed with butter as before, until all the pastry has been used. Brush top sheet liberally and trim any excess edges with scissors. Score only the top sheets of pastry carefully and light-handedly – otherwise the filling might spill – into diamond or square serving portions. Sprinkle with a little cold water with your fingertips to prevent the edges of the pastry from curling upwards, and cook in an oven preheated to 375°F (190°C, gas mark 5) for 45 minutes until the top is crisp, puffed up and light golden. Take out and let it stand for 5–10 minutes to solidify and make it easier to serve.

Serves 8 as a starter; 6 as a main course.   RS

NEW ENGLAND CLAM CHOWDER

Fresh clams are difficult, though not impossible to obtain through a fishmonger. Only those that are closed or close when touched should be used.

> *1 quart fresh soft shell clams or 2 × 6½ oz cans*
> *3 oz (75 g) salt pork or green bacon, diced*

> *1 onion, sliced*
> *1 lb (500 g) potatoes*
> *Fresh bay leaf*
> *1 pint (600 ml) milk, scalded*
> *1 oz (25 g) butter*
> *Salt and ground black pepper*

If using fresh clams, steam open, remove from shells, then mince. Reserve any juice. If using canned, reserve juice and mince the flesh.

In a large saucepan, gently fry the diced pork until the fat begins to run. Add the onions and fry until golden brown.

Cut the potatoes into dice and add to the pan together with the clam juices and enough water to cover. Season well and add the bay leaf. Simmer until just tender. Add the clams and simmer for about 10 minutes (less if using canned clams).

Just before serving, add the hot milk and butter. Stir until melted. If possible store for 24 hours in a fridge before re-heating and serving.

Serves 4–6.   RD

SALMON, CUCUMBER AND CORN CHOWDER

A hearty main course soup with a pleasing contrast of sweet and salty flavour.

> *1 tail piece fresh salmon, about 1¼ lb (625 g)*
> *4 oz (125 g) smoked salmon*
> *2 fresh corn cobs*
> *1 cucumber, skinned, seeded and chopped*
> *1 onion, chopped*
> *1 oz (25 g) butter*
> *3 tomatoes, skinned, seeded and chopped*
> *2 medium potatoes, chopped*
> *1″ (2.5 cm) cube fresh ginger, grated*
> *Salt and ground black pepper*
> *A little fresh fennel, to garnish*

Right *(from top) three seafood chowders: snapper and squid chilli, page 44; salmon, cucumber and corn; New England clam chowder*

Fillet and skin the salmon tail, then make a stock with the bones, skin, onion peelings and seasonings in about 3 pints (1.8 litres) of water. Cook for 20 minutes and strain.

Dice the fresh and smoked fish. Stand the corn cobs upright and with a sharp knife strip the kernels off by cutting downwards. Sauté the vegetables in the butter with the ginger for about 5 minutes then add the stock and seasonings. Simmer for about 15 minutes and add the fresh and smoked salmon. Cook for a further five minutes. Serve hot garnished with fennel.

Serves 6.   RD

SNAPPER AND SQUID CHILLI CHOWDER

This is based on a Bahamas recipe, where fresh chillies feature strongly in the native cuisine. Red snapper, a most delicious fish, can be found not only in speciality fish shops but also on fish stalls in city markets supplying West Indian communities.

About 1 lb (500 g) whole red snapper
1 lb (500 g) squid, prepared and skinned
8 oz (250 g) white crab meat
2 limes
2 fresh green or red chillies, seeded and chopped
4 oz (125 g) salt pork or green bacon, diced
1 medium onion, chopped
1 large clove garlic
1 green pepper, diced
1 lb (500 g) potatoes, peeled and diced
Sprig fresh thyme
1 bay leaf
½ teaspoon ground mace
Salt and ground black pepper
Fresh parsley, to serve

Fillet the snapper and skin it (or ask the fishmonger to do this for you).

Put the bones into a large saucepan with onion skins and seasonings. Make a fish stock from this, draining after 15 minutes. Reserve.

Cut the fish and squid into bite-size portions

and marinate with the crab in the lime juice with the chillies for an hour or so. (Take care though when cutting chillies as they can sting, and never, never rub your eyes with chilli-stained fingers!)

Fry the pork gently until the fat runs, then add the chopped onion and garlic. Sauté gently for about 5 minutes.

Add the green pepper and potatoes together with the marinated fish, snapper stock, herbs and mace. Season and simmer for about 5 minutes. Serve garnished with little fresh parsley.

Serves 6.   RD

COTRIADE BRETONNE

This is very popular seafood dish from Brittany which has its origins in the days when the fisherfolk went out to sea with very limited cooking facilities on board their fishing boats.

However, with true French flair and expertise, they were able to produce a dish, some would say a feast, fit for a king.

1½ lb (750 g) fresh fish – cod, haddock or
*   monkfish – skinned and cut into chunks*
3 lb (1.5 kg) fresh mussels
1½ lb (750 g) potato, peeled and diced
2 onions, peeled and chopped
3 leeks, cleaned and sliced
3 oz (75 g) butter
2 cloves garlic, crushed
Seasoning to taste
8 oz (250 g) spinach leaves, finely shredded, or
*   equivalent of frozen spinach*
A little grated nutmeg
½ pint (300 ml) single cream
Chopped parsley

FISH STOCK
A few fish bones from the fishmonger
2½ pints (1.5 litres) water
1 small onion, peeled and quartered
1 stick celery
Salt
Black pepper

Cotriade bretonne

Make the fish stock first. Wash fish bones well, then place in a large pan with water, onion, celery and seasoning. Bring to the boil, skim and simmer gently for 20 minutes. Cool and strain. Reserve 1¾ pints (1 litre) for soup.

Prepare fish and set aside. Clean the mussels by scraping off barnacles with a small knife and pulling away beards. Discard any mussels which are broken or open.

Choose a very large pan with a tight-fitting lid. Fry the potato, onions and leeks in melted butter without browning. Add garlic and cook gently for 3–5 minutes. Pour in fish stock and seasoning, simmer for 8–10 minutes, then add the fish and cook for 4–5 minutes only.

When ready to serve, bring to the boil and add the spinach, nutmeg, cream and mussels. Cover and cook over high heat for 4 minutes till all the shells are open, shaking the pan from time to time.

Serve from the pan into wide soup plates sprinkled with parsley, and eat with French bread.

Serves 8.   SM

HADDOCK AND HAZELNUT CROQUETTES

These are ideal for preparing ahead and, after sealing in hot oil, can be reheated later (next morning, for breakfast, for example) in a moderate oven.

> 1 small onion, chopped
> 1 oz (25 g) butter
> ¼ teaspoon curry powder
> 12 oz (375 g) Finnan haddock, cooked, skinned
>   and flaked
> 1 lb (500 g) floury potatoes, boiled and mashed
> 2 tablespoons fresh chopped parsley
> 2 teaspoons grated lemon rind, optional
> 2 egg yolks
> Salt
> Pepper
> Oil, for deep frying
>
> TO COAT
> Plain flour, for dusting
> 1–2 eggs, beaten
> 3 oz (75 g) natural dried breadcrumbs
> 2 oz (50 g) hazelnuts, chopped

Sauté the onion in the butter for 5 minutes, then add the curry powder and fry for a few seconds.

Mix with the fish, potato, parsley, lemon rind (if using), egg yolks and plenty of seasoning. Chill.

Shape into 8 rolls, using wet hands if the mixture is sticky.

Prepare three bowls with the flour in one, beaten eggs in another and the crumbs and nuts mixed in a third. Coat the rolls in flour, then egg, and finally the crumb mixture. Set aside on a plate.

Pour enough oil to come a third of the way up a deep-fat frying-pan and heat to 375°F (190°C) or until a cube of white bread browns in half a minute. Deep fry the croquettes 2 or 3 at a time until crispy and browned, then drain. Reheat the oil in between batches. If the croquettes show signs of breaking up in the pan, the oil is not hot enough.

Reheat on a baking tray at 375°F (190°C, gas mark 5), for about 15 minutes. Serve with a homemade tartare sauce.

Serves 6–8.   RD

45

Bouillabaisse, the classic fish soup of the Mediterranean

BOUILLABAISSE

This classic Mediterranean dish is really a soup, but sufficiently filling to be served as a main meal. The important thing to remember is to boil rather than simmer the liquor, to mix the oil and water together. Choose from a good mixture of firm, rich seafood and white fish.

*About 4 lb (1.75 kg) fish total weight from the
    following. Choose at least five types: sea
    bass, whiting, monkfish, John Dory, conger
    eel, squid, langoustines, clams, crabs,
    crawfish*

*2 large onions
3 cloves garlic
2 large tomatoes
Pinch saffron filaments
Sprig fresh thyme
3 sprigs fresh fennel
2 bay leaves
2 pieces thinly pared orange rind
Salt
Ground black pepper
¼ pint (150 ml) olive oil
¼ pint (150 ml) dry white wine
Fresh chopped parsley
Slices French bread*

Trim and cut the fishes into good-sized chunks. Skin the squid, pick over the shellfish. Put the firm fish and shellfish on one plate, the white on another. Make a court bouillon, if liked, with the heads, trimmings and any onion peelings. Simmer 15 minutes, then strain. Slice the onion, crush the garlic, skin and chop the tomatoes.

Put the firm fish into a large cast iron casserole, sprinkle over the onions and garlic; tomatoes, saffron, herbs and orange rind. Pour over the oil, wine and cover with court bouillon or water.

Bring to the boil and boil well for 5 minutes. Add the other fish and then boil again for a 5 further minutes.

Serve piping hot, ladled on top of bread slices and sprinkled with parsley.

Serves 6.   RD

MONKFISH CASSOULET

A classic bean dish using monkfish fillets, instead of the traditional ingredients of preserved goose, pork and sausage.

> 6 oz (175 g) dried haricot beans or 15 oz
>   (425 g) can of cannellini beans, drained
> Pinch saffron threads
> 1 lb (500 g) monkfish tail, filleted
> 1 pint (600 ml) water or fish stock
> 1 large bay leaf
> 1 onion, sliced
> 1 small bulb fennel, sliced
> 4 oz (125 g) salt pork or ham, diced
> 2 oz (50 g) smoked bacon, diced
> 1 oz (25 g) butter
> ¼ pint (150 ml) dry cider or white wine
> ½ teaspoon ground mace
> Sprig each of fresh thyme, rosemary and savory
> 4 tomatoes, skinned and quartered
> Salt
> Ground black pepper

> TOPPING
> 6 tablespoons fresh white breadcrumbs
> 3 tablespoons chopped parsley

If using dried beans, soak overnight, and simmer in seasoned water until soft. Reserve. Soak the saffron in a few tablespoons of warm water.

Poach the monkfish in the water with the bay leaf and seasoning until firm; about 10 minutes. Cut into bite-size pieces. Reserve the stock.

Sauté the onion, fennel, pork and bacon in the butter until softened, about 5 minutes.

Add the cider or wine and reserved stock. Stir in the beans, herbs, mace, saffron with its soaking water and the tomatoes. Season.

Bring to the boil, then cover and simmer gently for 20 minutes. Add the fish, and a little extra liquid if you feel it is needed.

Spoon into a shallow gratin dish, sprinkle with the crumbs and herbs then put into an oven at 375°F (190°C, gas mark 5) for about 25 minutes until the topping is crisp. This dish can be made in advance and the oven reheating done when ready to serve. Ideal with warm, crusty baguettes and a salad.

Serves 4.   RD

SPAGHETTI ALLE VONGOLE

Mediterranean clams or vongole – the small whitish, smooth variety – are cheap and make a delicious meal in the Italian manner that will bring you foreign tastes, smells and even sounds, as this is a dish found in every small restaurant of central and southern Italy. Sometimes chopped and skinned ripe tomatoes are added.

Make sure the pasta is neither overcooked, nor dry, but glistens with a good olive oil, and the dish will be mouthwatering.

> 3 lb (1.5 kg) clams
> 7 tablespoons olive oil
> 3 spring onions, trimmed, rinsed and sliced finely
> 2–3 cloves garlic, peeled and crushed
> 3 tablespoons parsley, finely chopped
> 3 tablespoons fresh dill, finely chopped
> Freshly ground black pepper
> 12 oz (350 g) spaghetti
> Salt

Place the clams in a large bowl of cold water and let their grit sink. Lift clams out and repeat the process until the water is perfectly clear. In the meantime, pick out and discard any clams that remain open even after they are tapped.

Heat the oil in a large frying-pan or casserole and sauté the onion gently without browning it; add the garlic and parsley, and sauté briefly until aromatic. Turn heat up, add the clams and stir continuously, coating them in the oil, until they open; about 2–3 minutes.

Remove from heat and let them stand for 1–2 minutes until slightly cooler. Working quickly, pick half the clams out of their shells using your fingers and discard the shells; keep the rest in their shells. In the meantime, discard any that may not have opened. (At this stage, the clams can wait up to 10 minutes, but no longer as they will lose their fresh flavour and become leathery.)

In the meantime, boil the spaghetti in plenty of lightly salted water for about 8 minutes, making sure it is not overcooked, and strain. Heat the clams up, stirring continuously, add pepper and the fresh dill and, after a few seconds, the cooked spaghetti. Mix well, coating the pasta in the oil for a few seconds, and withdraw from heat. Serve immediately on hot plates.

Serves 4 as a starter; 2 as a main course.   RS

RICE WITH SALT COD, GARLIC AND SPINACH

Rice is grown on the plains around the Spanish town of Valencia and forms the basis of dozens of local specialities.

4 oz (125 g) salt cod
14 oz (400 g) shortgrain rice
1 lb (500 g) spinach
4 tablespoons olive oil
10–12 spring onions, trimmed and cut in half
2–3 garlic cloves, unpeeled
1 teaspoon paprika
5–6 strands of saffron
Salt and pepper

Soak the dried salt cod for 24 hours, changing the water twice. Drain, dry the cod, and flake, discarding skin and bones.

To prepare the saffron either roast in a hot pan for a few minutes and crumble, or soak in a little hot water. Heat the oil in a fireproof dish (the Spanish use terracotta, prepared for use on the hob) and brown the cloves of garlic in the oil. Remove and discard. Wash the spinach thoroughly, discard tough stems, and add to the garlicky oil, together with the spring onions. Stir around on gentle heat for 2–3 minutes. Measure the volume of rice in a cup, and set aside double that volume of water.

Add the flaked cod and the rice to the spring onions and spinach, and continue to cook for another 3–4 minutes. Heat the water which was set aside, and add, together with the saffron. Bring to the boil, then place in a medium oven 350°F (180°C, gas mark 4) for about 20 minutes, or until the rice is cooked, taking care not to let it dry out through over-cooking. Check seasoning.

Serves 6 as a first course, or as a light supper or lunch dish.   MJS

Rice with salt cod, garlic and spinach

PAN-FRIED SALMON WITH A QUICK QUARK SAUCE

One of the benefits of pan-frying is that you can make an excellent sauce with the juices in just a few minutes. Quark, a soft cheese with a very low fat content, can be stirred into sauces as a lighter, more tangy alternative to double cream – ideal for fish. Do not, however, allow the sauce to boil after it has been added, or it will curdle. Fromage frais, soured cream or crème fraîche could also be used.

> *1 oz (25 g) butter*
> *1 tablespoon olive oil*
> *4 salmon fillets, about 6 oz (175 g) each, e.g.*
> *   from the tail end*
> *Chopped fresh herbs of your choice such as*
> *   thyme, parsley, dill or basil*
> *2 tablespoons chopped shallots*
> *4 tablespoons dry white wine*
> *½ pint (300 ml) fish stock (use the skin and*
> *   bones from filleting)*
> *Juice ½ small lemon or 1 lime*
> *4 tablespoons quark*
> *A little fresh chopped parsley or more herbs, to*
> *   garnish*
> *Salt*
> *Ground black pepper*

Heat the butter and oil in a wide, heavy-based frying pan and fry salmon fillets for about 4 minutes each side, sprinkling with some herbs if liked. Do not overcook. Season lightly and remove.

Add the shallots to the pan (with a little extra butter if need be) and cook for 2 minutes. Pour in the wine and cook until reduced. Add the stock. (This can be made by boiling the skin and bones from filleting in seasoned water for 20 minutes, if you don't have any to hand!)

Bring to the boil, add the lemon or lime juice and seasoning. Simmer for a few minutes. Mix the quark until smooth then stir into the sauce, reheating but not allowing to boil.

Serve the salmon fillets on warm plates with the sauce and maybe some broccoli florets and a sprinkling of more herbs to garnish.

Serves 4.   RD

BOURGEOIS IN THE F.T.

A good dish for serving to city slickers, this is a high protein, low cholesterol meal wrapped up in the latest financial news. Your guests could even check their share prices whilst negotiating the bones. Bourgeois (or Red Admiral) is a tropical game fish which is imported from the Seychelles and can be ordered from good fishmongers, given a little notice. However, you may have to be prepared to take a whole fish of about 4 to 5 lbs (1.75 to 2.25 kg) in which case, have it all cut into steaks and freeze the remainder for another dinner party. Of course, the recipe can easily be used for salmon, turbot, halibut and even cod steaks. This dish can be prepared in advance.

> *6 cutlets of Bourgeois, about 6–8 oz*
> *   (175–250 g) each*
> *2 carrots, peeled and cut in thin julienne strips*
> *1 small bulb fennel, sliced thinly*
> *2 oz (50 g) pack ready-made herb and garlic*
> *   butter, or 3 tablespoons extra virgin olive oil*
> *2 spring onions, sliced thinly*
> *¼ pint (150 ml) dry white wine*
> *6 tablespoons single cream, optional*
> *Salt and ground black pepper*

First prepare 6 single sheets of newspaper – whichever is appropriate for the occasion. Line them with a sheet of lightly greased greaseproof paper. Check the fish for any large bones and remove, but try to keep the skin intact. Place the fish in the centre of each sheet and season lightly.

Blanch the carrot and fennel in boiling water for 3 minutes, then drain and toss in the butter or oil with the onion shreds. Spoon on top of each fish steak, sprinkle over with the wine and cream if using, and season lightly again. Wrap up well, keeping the joins on top if possible, then place on a baking sheet and bake at 375°F (190°C, gas mark 5) for about 30–35 minutes or until the fish feels firm.

Serve the parcels as they are, for your diners to unwrap, accompanied by sprigs of fresh fennel, if you have any, new potatoes and a green vegetable such as mangetouts.

Serves 6.   RD

SKATE IN LIME AND SAFFRON

The delicate taste of this dish, with the fresh aroma of lime, makes it very special. If you have enough time, the dish is infinitely better when the fish has been marinated for a couple of hours.

4 (or 8 if they are small) pieces of skate wing;
about 2 lb (1 kg)
2 limes
2 tablespoons olive oil
1 oz (25 g) butter
¼ pint (150 ml) dry white wine
2 large pinches saffron, crumbled
Salt and black pepper

Wipe the skate clean and arrange in one layer in a *gratin* dish. Rinse and dry limes. Cut 6–7 strips of zest from a lime, cover with film and keep aside. Squeeze 1½ limes and pour the juice over the skate. Use remaining lime for garnish.

Heat oil and butter gently in a saucepan, add the wine and bring to boil. Add seasoning and the saffron, and bubble for 2–3 minutes until the liquid is brightly coloured. Pour over the fish, cover with foil and let it marinate for 2 hours.

Half an hour before serving baste the fish, replace foil, and cook in an oven preheated to 375°F (190°C, gas mark 5) for 20–25 minutes. Baste the fish once or twice during cooking time.

Pour the juices in a small saucepan, add the reserved lime zest and boil rapidly for 1–2 minutes, until it thickens lightly. Place skate on hot plates and coat with the sauce. Decorate with lime slices.
Serves 4. RS

A CREAMY KEDGEREE

It is intriguing that an Indian peasant dish, *khichiri*, of rice, lentils, eggs and spices, became a British Raj breakfast dish containing smoked haddock. For breakfast, this dish can be made the night before, without the raw egg, reheating and finishing before serving, as spicy hot as you like.

1 lb (500 g) smoked Finnan haddock
Parsley stalks and a bay leaf
1 small onion, chopped
1½ oz (40 g) butter
1 teaspoon turmeric
8 oz (250 g) cooked long grain rice, preferably Basmati
2 large eggs, one hard boiled and one raw and beaten
2 tablespoons fresh chopped parsley or coriander
Salt, pepper and cayenne or hot pepper sauce

Poach the fish in water to cover, with the parsley stalks, bay leaf and pepper, until just cooked: about 10 to 15 minutes. Drain, skin and flake the fish.

Sauté the onion in the butter for 5 minutes, then add the turmeric and fry for a few seconds. Mix in the rice, fish, seasoning, cayenne or pepper sauce to taste, and reheat.

Chop the hard egg white and sieve or very finely chop the yolk. Mix the chopped white into the kedgeree.

Just before serving, mix in the fresh herbs and beaten egg and serve topped with the sieved yolk.
Serves 2–3. RD

SALMON, SAMPHIRE AND DILL SALAD

This is ideal for those who like to serve salmon when entertaining but don't feel up to garnishing a whole fish. Sea bass could also be used, and when samphire is out of season, use blanched asparagus or thin Kenya beans instead, although the flavour is, of course, quite different.

2 lbs (1 kg) fresh salmon, on the bone (a large tail piece would be suitable)
2 tablespoons wine vinegar
Small onion, sliced
Bay leaves, peppercorns and sprigs of dill – for the court bouillon
4 oz (125 g) fresh samphire, rinsed
4 spring onions, sliced
Seasoning

SAUCE
¼ pint (150 ml) soured cream
2 egg yolks
1 teaspoon horseradish relish
Grated rind and juice of a small lemon
2 tablespoons fresh chopped dill
Salt and ground black pepper

Poach the fish for about 15 minutes in 1 pint (600 ml) water, with the vinegar, onion, bay leaves, peppercorns and dill sprigs. Season lightly. Leave to cool in the court bouillon, if possible. Strain the liquor off and boil down to about 4 tablespoons. Cool and reserve.

Skin and flake the fish into bite-size chunks. Mix with the samphire and onion.

Blend all the dressing ingredients together with the reserved fish stock, then mix into the fish. Chill the salad, and serve garnished with a few sprigs of samphire and dill. This is delicious served with hot, buttered new potatoes.

Serves 4.   RD

Terrine of smoked eel and leeks

TERRINE OF SMOKED EEL WITH LEEKS

An excellent combination of flavours and textures, which looks stunning when sliced through.

TERRINE
12 young leeks
1 lb (500 g) smoked eel, skinned and filleted, but in one piece
2 red peppers
7 fl oz (200 ml) aspic jelly

SAUCE
Juice of ½ lemon
3 fl oz (100 ml) olive oil
Salt, pepper

Trim the leeks, washing thoroughly and discarding all the tough greenery and leaving only the tender white part. (The trimmed leeks should approximately equal the length of the terrine in which the dish is to be made.) Cook in plenty of salted, boiling water for about 6 minutes. Remove and refresh in cold water, then drain and set aside.

Make the aspic jelly. Pour a small amount of warmed jelly into the base of a terrine, then cover with a layer of leeks, laid lengthwise. Leave in the refrigerator to set.

Place the red peppers in a very hot oven for 15 minutes to loosen the skins. Peel and cut in half lengthwise, remove the seeds, and wrap the pieces of pepper around the smoked eel.

Place the smoked eel, wrapped in red pepper, on top of the leeks. Pour in more aspic. Fill the terrine with the rest of the leeks, packing them around the eel, and remaining aspic.

Leave the terrine in the fridge, weighted on top, overnight to set.

Make the vinaigrette with olive oil, lemon juice, salt and pepper. It should be sufficiently sharp to offset the richness of the smoked eel.

To serve, turn the terrine out onto a serving plate, and, with a very sharp knife, cut slices about 1″ (2.5 cm) thick. Serve the slices with the vinaigrette sauce poured around.

Serves 6.   CP

POULTRY AND GAME

Quail, duck, goose and even rabbit or chicken all
have the makings of dinner-party fare when
combined with the fresh fruits, herbs and
aromatics which are their natural partners

ROAST QUAIL WITH GRAPES

For this straightforward and subtly-flavoured dish,
the quail are wrapped in vine leaves and pork fat,
and roasted with grapes and a moistening of semi-
sweet Vouvray wine from the Loire.

This preparation (or any other, for that matter) is not worth making with anything other than
the best young quail: freshly-killed, dry-plucked
fowl, raised by small producers who feed their
birds with a mixture rich in grain and protein, and
rear them in clean, non-intensive conditions.

In London, worthwhile fresh quail are available at Harrods, and from restaurant suppliers
Snipe & Grouse who welcome private customers at
their shop in the Chelsea Farmers Market. It is wise
to telephone first (01-376 8514) in order to ensure
that the necessary quail are available.

In certain parts of the country, it is possible to
find poulterers selling birds of quality, and in addition, good small producers.

Unsalted butter
4 best quail, weighing 3–4 oz (75–125 g) each,
    oven-ready and trussed
12 fresh vine leaves (if available), washed and
    dried
4 rectangles of thinly-sliced pork back fat
Small bunch white or 'flame'-coloured grapes
½ pint (300 ml) semi-sweet, non-sparkling
    young Vouvray
Salt and freshly-ground black pepper

Butter breast and thighs of each bird, wrap a stem-
less leaf round each breast, and tie on a piece of back
fat. Place birds, breast up, in an ovenproof dish
with a low side.

Halve and, if necessary, seed grapes, and place
half of these in vessel with the quail. Pour on about
one third of the wine, and centre dish in a 450°F
(230°C, gas mark 8) oven. Put remaining grape
halves into a small, heavy saucepan with the rest of
the wine, and simmer for several minutes until fruit
has just cooked. Retrieve grapes from the saucepan
with a slotted spoon and keep in a warm place.

After quail have roasted for 15 minutes, carefully cut string that secures their barding fat, remove this – together with vine leaves – and return
birds to the oven for 10 minutes, to allow their
breasts to brown attractively.

When quail are ready, reserve them in
warmth, add grapes from the ovenproof dish to the
previously-simmered quantity and set aside. Add
roasting juices to the saucepan containing wine and
grape juice, degrease, and reduce the liquid by one
third. Then, as this simmers briskly, beat in about
1 oz (25 g) butter and season sauce to taste.

Cut trussing string from quail, season birds,
and serve 2 per plate on the optional vine leaves,
flanked by grapes. Pass sauce separately.
Serves 2.   AWS

Right Roast quail with grapes, and (above) matuffi,
a dish of polenta and meat sauce (see page 101)

COLD STUFFED QUAIL

Stuffed quail are better poached than roasted. Poaching in stock keeps them plump and moist. Buy frozen boned quail for this recipe, which is then quite quick and not at all difficult. A lick of aspic improves their appearance.

> *12 boned quail*
> *1 small onion, chopped*
> *1 oz (25 g) butter or 2 tablespoon oil*
> *½ oz (15 g) dried porcini mushrooms (boletus edulis)*
> *6 oz (175 g) fresh mushrooms, finely chopped*
> *1 small chicken breast, diced*
> *Chopped tarragon and parsley*
> *Salt and freshly-ground black pepper*
> *1 pint (600 ml) chicken stock*
> *1 packet aspic*
> *1 tablespoon balsamic or red wine vinegar*
> *4 tablespoons madeira*
> *12 leaves flat parsley*

Cold stuffed quail

Cook the onion in the butter until it is soft, but not brown. While the onion is cooking, put the dried *porcini* in a bowl and pour ½ pint (300 ml) boiling water over them. Leave them to soak.

Add the chopped fresh mushrooms to the onions, and when they have cooked down a little, add the chicken. Turn the mixture on a medium heat until the chicken is cooked and the mushrooms have given off some liquid and reabsorbed it. Drain and add the dried mushrooms, saving their soaking liquid. Season the mixture quite strongly with tarragon, parsley, salt and pepper – remember the taste will fade when the stuffing is cold. Turn the stuffing into a food processor and process it briefly. It should be very finely chopped, not a cream.

Open out the quail. Put about a tablespoon of stuffing into each bird, then reform them, closing them top and tail with wooden cocktail sticks.

Heat the stock and mushroom soaking liquid in a large shallow pan; when it boils, add the quail. Reduce the heat to simmering and cover the pan. Poach the quail for 15 minutes, drain and set aside to cool.

Make up the aspic, substituting the vinegar and madeira for part of the liquid specified on the packet. The aspic is ready when it has cooled to the syrupy stage and is just about to solidify. This can be achieved in moments if a small amount of warm aspic is put in a bowl resting in iced water. Paint the cold quail with aspic. Place one parsley leaf on each bird and give them another coat. Chill to serve.

Pour the remaining aspic into a dish to a depth of about ¼" (0.5 cm). This can be cubed and scattered between the quail on the serving dish.

Serves 6.   SCP

ROAST QUAIL IN BUCKWHEAT NOODLE NESTS WITH PINENUTS

Allow 1–2 birds per person, depending on appetites and menu.

> *4–6 quail (or poussin or young partridge)*
> *2 tablespoons pinenuts*
> *Sprigs of celery or bunch watercress*

MARINADE
1 teaspoon sugar
½ teaspoon salt
1 tablespoon soy sauce
1 tablespoon vermouth or sherry
½ teaspoon grated fresh root ginger
1 teaspoon finely chopped shallot
1 teaspoon oil

BUCKWHEAT NOODLES
2 oz (50 g) buckwheat flour
8 oz (250 g) strong white flour
2 eggs
2 yolks
1 teaspoon pinenut, hazelnut or olive oil
1 teaspoon salt
1–2 tablespoons cold water if necessary

A little pinenut, hazelnut or olive oil

Wipe the birds dry. Mix up the marinade, rub the birds with it and leave to marinate, turning from time to time, for 1–2 hours.

To make the buckwheat noodles, process the flours, eggs and yolks, oil and salt in a food processor until crumbly, then gradually drip in water as the mixture processes until it forms polystyrene-like granules which can be pressed together to form cohesive lumps. Press into 4–5 lumps and keep in a polythene bag.

Roll each piece through the pasta roller, set at its widest, until smooth; then progressively through thinner rollers to the thinnest-but-two setting. Lay on a cloth while you repeat with remaining pieces. Leave to dry for half an hour before cutting if you wish, or cook at once. Then pass through the fine noodle cutter and toss in piles on a tray. Alternatively make up the pasta by hand; knead for 5–10 minutes then roll out very thinly, flour well, roll up and cut into fine noodles. Shake out onto a tray.

Roast the quail for 18–20 minutes until done in a hot oven at 400°F (200°C, gas mark 6), brushing with marinade frequently. If necessary, they can be left in a switched-off or very low oven (under 200°F, 95°C, gas mark ¼, so the birds do not go on cooking or dry out) for up to half an hour.

Roast quail in buckwheat noodle nests

Fry the pinenuts in a little oil until golden.

At the last minute, toss the noodles into plenty of boiling, salted water to which a teaspoon or so of vegetable oil has been added. Boil for 3–5 minutes until 'al dente' then drain. Toss the noodles, seasoning and pinenuts with their oil in the roasting pan juices. Form mounds of noodles into nests on a serving dish and top each nest with a roast bird. Tuck in sprigs of celery leaf or watercress and serve at once.

Serves 4–6.   NC

CHICKEN BREASTS WITH FRESH CORIANDER SAUCE

Simply cooked chicken with a positively-flavoured, low fat sauce.

6 chicken breasts, with skin
Salt and freshly ground black pepper
¾ pint (450 ml) chicken stock
3 fl oz (75 ml) dry vermouth
1 shallot, finely chopped
12 oz (350 g) fromage blanc
Leaves and fine stems from a small bunch (about
    ¼ oz or 7 g) fresh coriander
Salt and freshly ground black pepper

Season the chicken breasts and grill skin-side uppermost for 4 minutes. Turn them over using tongs and grill for a further 4 minutes.

Meanwhile, boil the vermouth with the shallot in a frying pan until only 1 tablespoon remains. Add the stock and boil until the liquid is reduced to 1½ fl oz (45 ml).

At the same time, chop about a third of the coriander and purée with the fromage blanc. Lower the heat beneath the stock and stir in the fromage blanc purée until warmed through, but do not allow it to boil. Season to taste. Cover and remove from the heat.

Skin the chicken and slice or leave whole, as preferred. Spoon some of the sauce onto 6 warmed plates, place the chicken on top and trickle the remaining sauce over the breasts. Garnish with the rest of the coriander leaves, and serve with new potatoes and young broad beans.

Serves 6. HW

VINEGAR CHICKEN

Volaille au vinaigre is one of the classic dishes of France. The trick is in the properly jointed chicken (you could buy these ready-prepared, but not just quarters) and in the professional finish to the sauce. This is a typical reduction sauce from which the cooking butter is skimmed and fresh butter whisked in to 'monte' or thicken the reduced juices. It is a principle that can be applied to any sauté dish, meat or fish, and well worth accomplishing. Serve with fresh tagliatelle.

2 × 2½ lb (1.2 kg) chickens jointed into 8
  pieces
4 cloves garlic – crushed
4 oz (125 g) butter
5 tablespoons wine vinegar
5 tablespoons white wine
1 tablespoon tomato purée
5 tablespoons stock
Salt
Pepper

Season the chicken joints and sauté quickly with the garlic in the butter, turning to brown lightly. Remove from the pan. Deglaze the pan with the wine and wine vinegar. Add tomato purée and stock to the pan and return the chicken joints. Cover and simmer gently for 30 minutes till tender but firm. Remove pieces and skim surplus butter (use a jug so that you can see the butter floating on the top). Reduce remaining liquid by half at the most. Add 2 oz (50 g) butter in small pieces, whisking as for *hollandaise* or *beurre blanc*. Pour the sauce over arranged pieces of chicken and sprinkle with a little chopped parsley.

Serves 8. AN

CHICKEN BREASTS IN WATERCRESS SAUCE

At its best in early spring and summer, the peppery flavour of watercress adds a tangy freshness to this simple dish.

12 oz (350 g) chicken breasts
3 oz (75 g) butter
1 tablespoon oil
2 bunches watercress
6 tablespoons double cream
1 teaspoon lemon juice
Salt
Pepper

Cut across the chicken breasts to give 1″ (2.5 cm) slices. Heat 1 oz (25 g) butter with the oil and cook the chicken pieces over low heat until cooked through and slightly golden. Meanwhile, remove the base of the stems from the watercress, and cook the rest in boiling water for 5 minutes. Drain and dry well and chop finely.

Lift the chicken pieces on to a warm serving dish. Add the watercress to the cooking juices in the pan, with the remaining butter. Simmer for 3 minutes. Stir in the cream, lemon juice, salt and pepper. Pour over the chicken pieces and serve at once with rice or vegetables.

Serves 4. MN

SWEET SOY CHICKEN

This is a simple and delicious way to transform an average chicken into a tasty dish. Ideally, marinate it in the sauce for a couple of hours, or overnight if more convenient.

> *3½ lbs (1.5 kg) fresh chicken, jointed into 4 or 8*
> *Salt and ground black pepper*
>
> MARINADE
> *4 tablespoons light soy sauce*
> *3 tablespoon clear honey*
> *2 tablespoons dry sherry*
> *2 cloves garlic, crushed*
> *1 tablespoon fresh grated root ginger*
> *2 tablespoons sesame oil*
> *1 tablespoon sunflower oil*

Mix all the marinade ingredients together, then pour over the chicken joints. Rub well in, cover and leave to marinate in the fridge.

Place the joints and marinade in a wide shallow ovenproof dish. Season and bake at 375°F (190°C, gas mark 5) for 30 minutes, turning occasionally and basting with the juices, which should gradually reduce down to a dark golden syrup.

Serve the joints hot or chilled with a salad, ideally one containing some unusual salad leaves.

Serves 4.

NOTE This is also an excellent barbecue sauce, but will burn easily if cooked for too long, so par-bake in the oven for half the time and finish over glowing charcoal.   RD

CASSEROLE OF PARTRIDGE WITH RED CABBAGE

Casseroled partridge with cabbage is a dish that appears in many Continental recipe books, from Spain through to Poland. It is particularly suitable for older birds or ones that have been frozen for some months, as the vegetables and liquids help to prevent the birds from becoming too dry. Pheasant can be cooked in the same way.

> *2 large partridges*
> *2 oz (50 g) butter*
> *Salt and ground black pepper*
> *1 small red cabbage*
> *1 onion*
> *1 small cooking apple*
> *About 8 juniper berries, crushed*
> *¼ pint (150 ml) dry red wine*
> *¼ pint (150 ml) game or poultry stock*
> *2 teaspoons sugar*

Truss the birds, then place in a large casserole and smear with the butter, particularly over the breast. Season well. Roast uncovered at 400°F (200°C, gas mark 6) for about 15 minutes until browned.

Shred the cabbage and blanch in boiling water for a minute or two. Drain. Slice the onion, core and slice the apple.

Remove the partridges from the casserole, place the cabbage, onion and apple on the base and scatter over the juniper berries and sugar. Pour over the wine and stock, then season.

Return the birds to sit on top of the vegetables. Baste with any juices and pour over the wine and

Sweet soy chicken with bitter salad leaves

stock. It helps to cover the breasts with butter paper during cooking to stop them from drying out. Cover and return to the oven at 350°F (180°C, gas mark 4) for at least another 30 minutes or until tender. This will depend on the age of the birds.

Cut the birds in half along the breast to serve. Drain the cabbage mixture and thicken the sauce with a little cornflour, if liked, or simply serve the vegetable mixture unthickened. Creamed or boiled potatoes or fresh pasta will accompany this winter dish nicely.

Serves 4. RD

CHICKEN AND HAM BURGOO WITH CORN BREAD

The traditional dish of the American state of Kentucky, burgoo should really be made with squirrel meat, for the sake of authenticity. However, chicken and ham seem more acceptable substitutes for this hearty one-pot meal. It can be cooked outside, in keeping with the American tradition of cook-outs, but is probably easier to cook indoors and reheat over the barbecue in a flameproof pot.

Chicken and ham burgoo with cornbread

1 × 2 lb (1 kg) joint smoked collar bacon
1 × 2½ lb (1.25 kg) chicken
½ teaspoon cayenne pepper
8 oz (250 g) carrots, sliced
8 oz (250 g) potatoes, diced
1 large onion, chopped
3 sticks celery, sliced
14 oz (400 g) can tomatoes
8 oz (250 g) broad beans
4 oz (125 g) cabbage, shredded
8 oz (250 g) sweetcorn kernels
8 oz (250 g) okra, scrubbed and trimmed
1 tablespoon Worcestershire sauce
1 small green pepper, diced
Fresh chopped parsley, to garnish

If the bacon is not lightly cured, you may need to soak it overnight in cold water. Cover the meats with at least 6 pints fresh water, bring to the boil and simmer for about 1 hour. Allow the meats to cool in the liquid, then remove, dice and reserve. Skim any fat from the top.

Return the stock to the pan with the cayenne, carrots, potatoes, onions, celery and tomatoes. (No need for salt as the stock will have salt from the bacon.) Simmer for 15 minutes then add the other vegetables (except the green pepper), the diced meats and Worcestershire sauce. Simmer for a further 10 minutes. Stir in the green pepper, ladle onto plates sprinkled with parsley and serve with slices of buttered cornbread.

Serves 8.

CORNBREAD
7 oz (200 g) yellow cornmeal
3 oz (75 g) plain flour
4 teaspoons baking powder
1 teaspoon salt
3 teaspoons caster sugar
2 size 3 eggs
½ pint (300 ml) milk
2 tablespoons oil

Blend everything to a smooth batter in a processor or blender. If made by hand, beat the liquid ingredients gradually into the dry.

Pour into a well-greased, 8″ (20 cm) sandwich

tin and bake at 400°F (200°C, gas mark 6) for approximately 30–35 minutes. RD

CHICKEN BREASTS BRAISED WITH BACON, CELERIAC, CARROTS AND PEARL ONIONS

In this simple, braised dish, the celeriac mingles with all the other ingredients so that their flavours enhance each other. You can prepare it mostly ahead and do the final braising soon before serving.

> 4 strips streaky bacon, diced
> 2 large chicken breasts, halved and boned
> 8 pearl onions
> 1 large carrot
> ½ celeriac bulb
> ¼ pint (150 ml) chicken stock
> ¼ teaspoon dried thyme
> 2 tablespoons chopped fresh parsley

Cook the bacon in a flameproof casserole or pan, tossing to brown it on all sides. Drain and reserve. In the remaining fat and over medium heat, cook the chicken breasts on both sides until the skin is golden brown.

Meanwhile, peel the onions and cut a shallow cross into the root ends. Peel and cube the carrot and celeriac; each should measure about 6 oz (175 g) in weight. When the chicken is browned, reserve it on a plate. Leaving 2 tablespoons of fat in the pan, lower the heat and brown the onions, stirring to colour them evenly. Put them with the chicken. Cook the root vegetables in the fat (add a little butter if necessary), stirring until lightly browned.

Pour in the stock and stir up to deglaze the dark crusty bits on the bottom. Return the chicken to the pan and surround with the bacon, vegetables and herbs. Cover with a lid or piece of foil and simmer 10 minutes. Uncover and simmer about 10 minutes longer, until the chicken is cooked through but still tender and springy to the touch.

Arrange the chicken on warm serving plates and, with a slotted spoon, put the vegetables and bacon around. Over high heat reduce the braising liquid until concentrated in flavour and thickened in texture. Nap the chicken with this sauce and serve with boiled potatoes or another starch.

Serves 4. ER

SAFFRON-SCENTED WHOLE CHICKEN

Even tiny quantities of saffron have the ability to give striking yellow-orange colour and a warm, flowery sweetness to huge dishes of risotto, paella and bouillabaisse. Here it imparts the same qualities to a whole chicken.

This dish is delicate, delicious and very simple. Saffron adds such a taste of luxury that you need not hesitate to serve it for a special meal.

> 3 lb (1.5 kg) fresh chicken
> ¼ teaspoon saffron threads
> Pinch of salt
> 2 oz (50 g) unsalted butter, softened
> 1 small carrot, quartered
> 1 shallot, halved
> 1 small stick of celery
> Bouquet garni
> Sprigs of chervil for garnish

Gently heat the saffron in a heavy non-stick pan for about 5 minutes. Crush the saffron and beat it into the butter. Place a knob of the saffron-flavoured butter in the cavity of the chicken and rub the remainder over the skin. Place the chicken in a steaming basket and cover with a tight-fitting lid. Steam the chicken over about 440 ml/14 fl oz of gently boiling water – to which the vegetables and bouquet garni have been added – for about an hour. Place the steaming basket, with the chicken still inside, on a large warm plate and keep warm.

Strain the liquid and taste to see if it should be reduced to concentrate the flavours. Check and adjust seasoning.

Slice the chicken and serve accompanied by the juices and garnished with sprigs of chervil.

Serves 4. HW

POULET EN COCOTTE A L'AIL

A true French bourgeois dish with a glorious aroma of garlic. Use the best corn-fed chicken you can find (though this is a marvellous treatment for any chicken) and firm fresh garlic. You can get this all prepared and leave it ready for the oven. Then pop it in and forget it until ready to serve. The garlic is surprisingly delicate treated in this way so don't be afraid of using this quantity.

> *3½ lb chicken*
> *1–2 heads garlic*
> *4–5 tablespoons olive oil*
> *¼ teaspoon Pernod*
> *3–4 slices stale French bread*
> *A good bunch of herbs (3 sprigs fennel, 2 sprigs rosemary, 3 sprigs thyme and a little marjoram)*
> *1 bay leaf*
> *Salt and pepper*
>
> HUFF PASTE
> *8 oz (250 g) plain flour*
> *5 fl oz (150 g) water*
> *½ teaspoon salt*

Whisk together 2 tablespoons oil and the Pernod. Dry the bread in a low oven until crisp. Rub 1–2 cloves of garlic, cut in half, over both sides of the bread, then moisten them with the Pernod-oil, season with salt and pepper and pop inside the chicken. Rub the dry chicken all over with the remaining Pernod-oil.

To make the huff paste, mix the flour, salt and water to a stiff paste, knead until smooth and use to seal the casserole.

In a casserole (preferably earthenware) place 2–3 tablespoons olive oil just to cover the bottom. Make a bed of herbs on this and scatter over the cloves of garlic, separated but unpeeled. Lay the chicken on this, breast up, season with salt and pepper and cover with the lid. Seal the lid in place with huff paste. Set the casserole to cook in a hot oven at 450°F (230°C, gas mark 8) for 1¼ hours. Remove the lid of the casserole at the table so that

Poulet en cocotte à l'ail

you catch the wonderful trapped aroma, and carve the chicken. Serve 2–3 of the cloves of garlic with each serving. Pressed from its paper skin, the purée is mild and delicious.

Serves 4–6.   NC

CHICKEN IN A BOTTLE OF WORCESTERSHIRE SAUCE

Although fairly spicy, this dish is no hotter than a medium-strength curry or Mexican chilli. It is simply chicken breasts marinated in a bottle of Worcestershire sauce, which can be done before you shoot off to work, and then baked in the oven just before the guests turn up.

> *6 chicken breasts, boned and skinned*
> *5 fl oz (142 ml) bottle Worcestershire sauce*
> *About 4 tablespoons sesame seeds*
> *2 oz (50 g) butter, melted*

Put the chicken breasts in a polythene food bag and pour in the sauce. Rub well in, seal the bag and leave to marinate in the fridge for about 6–8 hours.

Drain off the Worcestershire sauce and discard, then coat the breasts on both sides with sesame seeds, pressing them well in. (It doesn't matter much if they are not completely covered.) Lay them in a shallow roasting dish and dribble over the melted butter.

When you are nearly ready to sit down and eat, bake the breasts at 375°F (190°C, gas mark 5) for about 20 minutes, until just cooked.

Cut each breast into slices for an attractive presentation. Baked potatoes, or a bowl of buttered basmati rice, together with an interesting green salad, would be appropriate accompaniments.

Serves 6.   RD

GOOSE LEGS WITH CABBAGE

This hearty winter casserole is an especially popular dish in North Germany.

2 goose legs
1 oz (25 g) fat or goose dripping
2 large onions, chopped
2 lb (1 kg) white cabbage, finely sliced
1 tablespoon wine vinegar
1 dessertspoon brown sugar
4 crushed juniper berries
¼ pint (150 ml) white stock
¼ pint (150 ml) dry white wine
Pepper and salt

Brown the legs in the fat. Add the onions, and continue cooking until they have softened. Add all the other ingredients, season then simmer until the legs are tender. Take out the legs, remove all the bones then dice the meat and put it back in the pot. Reheat and serve with plenty of boiled potatoes.

Serves 4–5.   BGM

GOOSE NECK SAUSAGE

In Eastern and Northern Europe, this is considered one of the best ways to enjoy goose liver. A similar dish exists in the Quercy region of France.

1 goose neck

STUFFING
1 goose liver
8 oz (250 g) streaky bacon
1 small onion
2 tablespoons cooked rice
1 beaten egg
Pepper and salt
3 fl oz (90 ml) sherry or Madeira
Strong stock for cooking

Clean and bone the neck, then sew up one end. Stiffen the liver in a little fat, and mince together with the streaky bacon and onion. Add the rice, mix well together, bind with the egg, and season to taste. Stir in sherry or Madeira. Stuff neck loosely and sew up the open end.

Simmer neck gently in the stock for 50–60 minutes. Remove and allow to cool. Flatten slightly by leaving the sausage between two boards with a weight on top. Slice when cold, having pulled out the sewing threads first.

Serve as a starter, for 6–8.   BGM

PRESERVED GOOSE

Confit d'oie is the basis of cassoulets. It can be used to give a unique flavour to casseroles and stews.

2 lb (1 kg) uncooked, jointed goose legs and
*   wings*
1 oz (25 g) sea salt
1 dessertspoon allspice or mixed spice
Fat, preferably goose fat or pure pork lard

Mix salt and spice together. Rub it well into the meat. Put the meat in a container, cover with foil and leave in a cool place for at least 48 hours.

Brush off surplus salt and spice mixture. Arrange the meat in a terrine, and pour over enough melted fat to cover the joints. Cook with the lid on at 240°F (120°C, gas mark ¼) until the meat is tender – about 2½–3 hours.

Drain joints and arrange in an earthenware

storage jar. Strain the fat over the meat to cover it completely – make certain the fat is at least ¼" (0.5 cm) above the joints to seal them hermetically. Cover the confit and store in the refrigerator.

The goose will keep for several months but, when using only one or two pieces of the confit, make sure that the rest is covered with the fat so it will keep. Duck can be preserved in the same way.

BGM

COUNTRY CASSOULET

A French bean and meat casserole with many local variations, this is best made the day before eating, and then reheated.

> 1–1½ lb (500–750 g) haricot beans
> 4 oz (125 g) smoked ham rind cut in ½" (1 cm) squares
> 2 medium onions, chopped
> 2 cloves of garlic, crushed
> 2 lb (1 kg) diced stewing lamb
> 4 oz (125 g) streaky bacon, chopped
> 1 lb (500 g) Toulouse or other spicy sausages, cut in thick slices
> 8 oz (250 g) preserved goose (confit d'oie)
> Goose fat or lard
> ½–1 pint (300–600 ml) strong meat stock
> Pepper and salt
> 3 tablespoons tomato purée
> Bouquet garni
> Fine white breadcrumbs for topping

Soak the beans overnight in unsalted water. Fry the ham rind until the fat runs, add the beans and the water in which they were soaked, and simmer gently for about 1 hour – the rind should disintegrate during cooking, but adds flavour.

In the meantime, soften the onions and garlic in a heavy, fireproof casserole. Add all the meats and brown lightly. Add the beans, their liquor, and enough meat stock to cover. Stir in the tomato purée and put in the bouquet garni. Season highly. Cover closely, and cook slowly in the oven at 240°F (120°C, gas mark ¼) for at least 2 hours. Check

from time to time and add more stock if necessary.

Remove lid, cover with the breadcrumbs, dot with fat and cook until topping is brown. A hearty red wine accompanies this well.

Serves 6–8. BGM

SWEDISH ROAST GOOSE

This method of cooking goose keeps the flesh moist without retaining too much fat.

> 1 young goose weighing 6–8 lb (3–4 kg)
> Pepper and salt
>
> STUFFING
> 1 lb (500 g) cooking apples, peeled, cored and chopped
> 15–20 prunes, pitted and stewed
> 1 teaspoon powdered cloves
> 1 finely chopped onion, parboiled for 10 minutes in a little water
> Pepper and salt

Remove neck, giblets and wing tips from goose, and set aside for use in other dishes. Cut out surplus fat from inside vent end (to be rendered and used for pastry or as a spread).

Rub the inside of the bird with pepper and salt. Mix stuffing ingredients together and use to stuff goose body. Sew up, or skewer. Prick the breast all over to allow fat to escape. Heat the oven to 400°F (200°C, gas mark 6). Start roasting with the breast down on a grid over a little water in the meat dish. After half an hour, when the fat runs, pour the liquid off, pour in more hot water, and continue roasting with the breast up. Cook until tender, about 2–2½ hours, basting frequently.

When nearly done, pour 4 tablespoons ice-cold water over the breast, and leave oven door slightly open to make the skin crisp. The Swedes

Right (from top) Country cassoulet; Swedish roast goose; ingredients for country cassoulet; goose eggs

carve the breast in strips, reassemble it, reheat, and serve with red cabbage and roast potatoes.

NOTE Alternatively, roast the goose as above but stuff with 5 or 6 large leeks, chopped and seasoned to taste. Serve the leeks with the bird.

Serves 6–8.   BGM

RABBIT IN FILO PASTRY WITH BACON AND RED ONION SAUCE

Crisp parcels of filo pastry enclosing flavoursome rabbit morsels.

1 rabbit
1 medium onion, chopped
1 medium carrot, chopped
1 stick celery, chopped
2 bay leaves
12 fl oz (350 ml) white wine
2 oz (50 g) butter
2 oz (50 g) flour
12 sheets of filo pastry
Clarified butter or oil
3½ oz (100 g) bacon, cut in thin strips
3½ oz (100 g) red onion, thinly sliced
1 oz (25 g) butter
½ pint (300 ml) cream

Place the rabbit in a suitably-sized casserole dish with the chopped onion, carrot, celery and bay leaves. Add the white wine, and top up with water if necessary just to cover. Cover and braise for 2–2½ hours.

Reserve 1 pint (600 ml) of the stock, and leave the rabbit to cool. Remove the flesh from the rabbit, cover and refrigerate. Melt the butter and add the flour to make a roux. Cool slightly, add the reserved stock, bring to the boil and simmer for 10 minutes, then cool and refrigerate. When sauce and rabbit are chilled, combine the two.

Lay 3 sheets of filo pastry on top of each other. Brush the top sheet with melted, clarified butter (oil is a perfectly suitable alternative), then fold the bottom edge of the 3 sheets back over about 2″ (5 cm). Place a quarter of the rabbit mix on the folded section, fold the sides over, brush with clarified butter, and roll up. Brush the top with clarified butter and place on a baking tray.

Repeat with the remaining ingredients, to finish with 4 parcels. Bake for 20–25 minutes at 400°F (200°C, gas mark 6).

For the sauce, sauté the bacon and red onion for one minute with a touch of butter. Then add the cream and reduce. Season to taste.

Serves 4.   PM

Rabbit in filo pastry with bacon and red onion sauce

RABBIT WITH MUSTARD

The British are not very adventurous when it comes to eating rabbit, but the French, especially in the rural areas, enjoy rabbit dishes a great deal. The meat is fresh, lean and succulent, as well as being cheap and readily available.

Rabbit is particularly well complemented with a creamy mustard sauce.

2 tablespoons vegetable oil
6 rabbit portions, thawed if frozen
8 oz (250 g) green streaky bacon
8 oz (250 g) shallots, peeled
1 tablespoon flour
¼ pint (150 ml) light stock or water
2 tablespoons Dijon mustard
Salt and ground black pepper
¼ pint (150 ml) single cream
Sprigs fresh tarragon or parsley

Heat the oil in a large frying-pan, and brown the rabbit portions. Remove to a casserole dish. Add the streaky bacon rashers, cut in half if liked, and the shallots. Brown lightly and add these to the casserole. Sprinkle in the flour, stir up and pour in the wine, stock or water, mustard and seasonings. Bring to the boil, stirring well. Allow to simmer for a minute or two, then pour over the rabbit. Cover and cook at 350°F (180°C, gas mark 4) for about 1 hour.

When tender, remove the rabbit to a serving dish and pour the cream into the sauce. Stir well, reheat gently but do not allow to boil, then serve spooned over the rabbit. Looks pretty garnished with fresh tarragon or parsley.

Serves 4–6.   RD

COLD DUCK WITH ORANGE AND MINT JELLY

The amount of gelatine you will need for this recipe depends on how jellied the stock is. After the gelatine has been added, spoon a small amount of the liquor onto a saucer and place it in the refrigerator to set (the jelly should be very light).

4 tablespoons dry white vermouth
5 fl oz (150 ml) Seville orange juice
Finely grated rind of 1 Seville orange
7 fresh mint leaves, broken
1 pint (600 ml) jellied chicken stock
1 egg white
1 egg shell, crushed
3–4 teaspoons clear honey, to taste

Approximately 2 teaspoons gelatine
1 cooked duck, about 4½ lb (2 kg), jointed or
   boned
Mint leaves for decoration

Boil vermouth until syrupy. Stir in orange juice and rind, mint and stock. Whisk in egg white and shell, and bring slowly to the boil, whisking constantly. Take off heat and leave for 5 minutes. Carefully make a hole in crust on the surface of the liquor, then ladle out the liquor, taking care not to disturb the crust.

Dissolve honey in a little of the heated liquor, then stir into the remaining liquid. Place gelatine in a small bowl, stir in a little liquor, and leave for 5 minutes. Place the bowl over a saucepan of hot water until the gelatine has melted, then, off the heat, stir in the remaining liquor. Add seasoning, and more honey, if necessary, to taste. Leave until just on the point of setting.

If the duck you are using has been jointed, put the pieces on a rack placed over a tray, and spoon a little of the liquor over the meat. Leave aside to set.

Position the mint leaves for the decoration on the portions, and apply 2 or 3 more coats of still just-liquid liquor, allowing each to set before adding the next. Leave any remaining liquor to set, then chop and serve around the duck.

If the duck flesh is off the bone, put the pieces of duck into a bowl, spoon the liquor over and fork through the duck gently. Leave until the liquor is just beginning to set, then carefully transfer the duck to 4 serving plates. Garnish with mint, warm the remaining liquor so it is just liquid and spoon over the duck. Leave to set before serving.

Serves 4.   HW

DUCK BREASTS WITH ORANGE, ONIONS AND TURNIPS

This recipe uses French boned duck breast – *magret* – and, with a vegetable accompaniment, all it needs is a little pasta or crusty rolls to mop up the juices, and perhaps a watercress and chicory salad.

Hannah Glasse's dressed duck (at left); lamb tagine (see page 81); rabbit with mustard (see page 64)

6 boned duck breasts
1 large Spanish onion, peeled and chopped
8 oz (250 g) baby turnips, topped and tailed,
    then diced
1 clove garlic, crushed
1 orange, strips of peel from half the fruit and all
    the juice
3 tablespoons dry sherry
Good pinch dried sage
Good pinch sugar
Salt and ground black pepper

Heat a large, heavy-based frying pan without oil, until it feels really quite hot when you hold your hand above it. Slash the duck breasts a number of times on the skin side, then place skin side down in the pan. This ensures that the fat runs out (there is no need for any extra) and gives a nice dark browned skin. Fry for about 5 minutes, then flip over and cook on the other side, for about 3 minutes if you like your duck pink, or longer if you prefer it more cooked. Season lightly in the pan, then take off the heat and keep warm in a low oven.

Pour off all but about 2 tablespoons of the fat that has run out and sauté the onions, turnips and garlic for 3 minutes, stirring once or twice. Meanwhile, scrape the pith off the orange peel and cut into julienne strips. Add these to the pan along with the juice, sherry, sage, sugar and seasoning.

Bubble up the sauce, cover and cook gently for another five minutes or until the turnips are just cooked. Serve the vegetables spooned alongside the duck breasts.

Serves 6.   RD

HANNAH GLASSE'S DRESSED DUCK

We seem to think of cooking with lettuce as rather French, yet the eighteenth-century English cookery writer, Hannah Glasse, in her *Art of Cookery Made Plain and Easy*, uses lettuce when slow-cooking a duck. She specified a whole duck, but few modern frying-pans are large enough to brown a large duck, so use quarters instead.

> *4 duck quarters or 5 lb (2.25 kg) duck, quartered*
> *Flour, to dust*
> *1 oz (25 g) butter*
> *1 dessertspoon vegetable oil (not in the original recipe, but it does stop the butter from burning)*
> *1 firm round lettuce, shredded*
> *12 oz (350 g) garden peas*
> *½ pint (300 ml) good gravy, or strong giblet stock flavoured with a little dry sherry*
> *A small bunch sweet herbs – marjoram, thyme, parsley and sage*
> *½ teaspoon ground mace or nutmeg*
> *Salt and ground black pepper*
> *1 egg yolk*
> *3 tablespoons double cream*
> *Few sprigs fresh mint, to garnish*

Remove as much loose fat as possible from the duck quarters, then dust with flour. Heat the butter and oil in a large heavy frying-pan and brown the quarters. Remove and drain well.

Sprinkle the base of a large casserole dish with the shredded lettuce and peas and lay the duck on top. Pour over the gravy or stock, snip over the fresh sweet herbs (out of season, use a good pinch of dried marjoram, thyme and sage but fresh pars-

ley), sprinkle over the mace or nutmeg and season well. Cover and cook at 350°F (180°C, gas mark 4) for about ¾ to 1 hour or until tender.

With a slotted spoon, remove the duck and vegetables to a large serving platter. Pour the stock into a small saucepan.

Beat the egg yolk and cream and blend into the stock. Reheat gently, stirring continually until slightly thickened, but do not allow to boil. Pour over the duck. Garnish with chopped mint.

Serves 4.   RD

BARBARY DUCK WITH GREEN OLIVES

A classic dish from Provence.

> *1 Barbary duck weighing 10 lb (4.5 kg)*
> *7 oz (200 g) green olives*
> *3½ oz (100 g) smoked bacon, diced*
> *7 oz (200 g) button mushrooms, sliced*
> *2 large onions, peeled and minced*
> *4 cloves garlic, chopped finely*
> *Olive oil*
> *Bouquet garni; herbes de Provence*
> *1 bottle white Côtes de Provence*

Clean and section the duck. Place 4 tablespoons of olive oil in a fireproof casserole and brown duck on all sides. Remove duck and pour away oil. Lightly cook bacon in the same casserole and remove, discarding the fat produced. In the same casserole toss the minced onion. Cook mushrooms gently in a separate pan with a little oil, allowing their juice to evaporate. Set aside.

When onions are golden, add 1 tablespoon flour, stir and cook for 1 minute, then add the wine, stirring well. Season and add 2 pinches of *herbes de Provence* and a bouquet garni. Return duck, mushrooms and bacon to casserole, stir gently then simmer, uncovered, in a slow oven for 1–1½ hours. Half-way through cooking, add olives and garlic. When cooked, remove duck, skim fat from sauce, reduce if necessary, and serve.

Serves 6–8.   SJW

MAINLY MEAT

Here are aromatic lamb dishes from Morocco
and the Middle East, traditional English ways
of cooking pork, and some inspired ideas
for capturing the richness of wild boar

POTTED RILLONS OF WILD BOAR

Boar is a seasonal meat, its dusky savour well suited to the winter months; a jarful of small morsels, preserved in the age-old manner, effectively extends the season and would make a distinctive Christmas, or Twelfth Night, present. Stay with the suggested cuts – the method ensures tenderness and intensity of flavour.

> 2–3 lb (1–1.5 kg) belly or shoulder of boar
> 4 oz (125 g) additional back-fat
> 1 tablespoon juniper salt
> 3 tablespoons water
> 1 fat, unpeeled clove of garlic
> 1 blade of mace
> 4 allspice berries
> 1 fresh or dried bay-leaf
> 2 sprigs of fresh thyme

Cut the meat into 1½" (3.5 cm) cubes, trimming it carefully of any gristle and membrane. Dice the back-fat quite small. Mix both meats thoroughly with the juniper salt, cover and keep cool for 24 hours. After dry marinating the meat, discard any large pieces of juniper and any liquid which may have formed. Place the meat with the remaining ingredients in a flame-proof pot and bring the water to the boil. Include any bones removed in trimming the meat. Simmer the meat very gently – the liquid should hardly bubble – on top of the stove or in a low oven, 300°F (150°C, gas mark 2)

for 3 to 4 hours, or until the meat offers little resistance to a small skewer.

Once the meat is tender, drain the contents of the pan, reserving the fat but discarding the bones, mace, allspice and herbs. Transfer the meat to a heavy-based frying pan and toss quickly over a fairly high heat to caramelize the surface appetizingly (the flavour can take the addition of very little light, raw sugar at this stage, for a more pronounced caramel note). Either serve immediately – with sautéed potato or root vegetable purées and a sharpish sauce, or a hunk of good country bread and a little salad – or pot up for future use in the traditional manner.

Pack the browned meat into stoneware pots or glass jars and cover lightly until ready to coat with rendered fat. Strain reserved fat and juices through a fine sieve and cool, until the fat can be separated off and poured over the potted meat. Aim to cover the meat with a ½" (1 cm) layer of fat. Cover and keep chilled until ready to use, when the fat should be melted down and the chunks of meat reheated in a little of the fat. Serve as above.

Serves 8 as a snack.   SD

Right A feast of wild boar (clockwise from bottom right): Boar liver cooked in red wine and herbs; boar chops sauced with morello cherries and liquorice (centre) page 71; wild boar sausage with pickled walnuts and mushrooms; gilded apples, page 72; terrine of forest boar, page 70; leg of roast boar

TERRINE OF FOREST BOAR

Use an inexpensive, fat-rich cut for the forcemeat layer, lean fillet for the strips of marbling. It would be as well to order caul fat a week in advance.

2 lb (1 kg) boar loin, or other lean meat
1 lb (500 g) boar belly or shoulder
12 oz (350 g) flare fat ⎫ from
8 oz (250 g) smoked, streaky ⎬ range-reared
    bacon ⎭ pork
8 oz (250 g) caul fat
2 tablespoons juniper salt

WINE MARINADE
½ pint full-bodied red wine
1 tablespoon red wine vinegar
1 tablespoon virgin olive oil
2–3 diced, aromatic vegetables – white of leek,
    celery, carrot, parsnip as available
2 shallots, peeled and sliced

1 large garlic clove, peeled
6 juniper berries
2 allspice berries
2 black peppercorns
1 blade of mace
1 cinnamon stick
12 oz peeled, cooked chestnuts, soaked in
    3–4 tablespoons brandy
2 oz (50 g) dried forest mushrooms, soaked,
    rinsed, drained and chopped
1 small truffle, peeled and diced (optional)
2–3 peeled cloves of oven-baked garlic
12 juniper berries, crushed
½ teaspoon ground mace
½ teaspoon ground allspice
Grinding of milled black pepper
1 teaspoon sea salt

GLAZE
2 tablespoons Madeira
A little concentrated game stock
1 sheet leaf gelatine

Potted rillons of wild boar; recipe on page 68

Dice lean meat finely and cube fat meat roughly. Coat each type of meat with the juniper salt and store separately, cool and covered, for 12–24 hours.

Meanwhile, place wine marinade ingredients into a non-reactive saucepan, bring to the boil, and simmer gently for 15 minutes (the diced vegetables may be caramelized lightly in the oil before adding to the marinade, if time allows). Keep cool until needed.

Brush or rinse excess juniper salt off the meats, and strain the marinade over each type of meat, still keeping the two meats separate. Marinate meats for 12–36 hours as convenient.

Dice 8 oz (250 g) of the flare very finely and set aside. Soak the caul in vinegared warm water for 15 minutes to soften and deodorize, drain and pat dry, stretch it out gently and drape into a 2 pint (1.2 litre) terrine dish. Drain the marinaded meats thoroughly, discarding all but a spoonful of the wine marinade.

Mix together the diced lean meat, diced flare, and truffle, if using, and set aside.

Mince together finely the cubed fat meat,

remaining flare, smoked bacon, and about 4 oz (125 g) of the crumblier chestnuts, drained. Blend in (a food processor may be used for this stage as for the mincing) the garlic, spices and seasoning, reserved marinade and chestnut-soaking brandy, then gently stir in remaining chestnuts – whole if possible – and mushrooms. Layer the two types of meats in the terrine, beginning and ending with the minced meat, and mounding up in the centre. Bring the caul over and around the meat, tucking edges down the sides of the terrine.

Bake in a water-bath in a medium-hot oven, at 350°F (180°C, gas mark 4) for about an hour, or until juices run clear when a skewer is inserted, and the meat has pulled away from the sides of the dish.

Cool, then pour off and retain juices. Chill the terrine and juices separately. The terrine may be weighted if wished; this will make it easier to cut and serve, but the compacted meat will be a little less juicy. Strain off any juices and reserve.

To make the glaze, degrease reserved juices (which will probably have set). Heat and melt these gently and make up to ¼ pint (150 ml) with the Madeira and additional stock. Soak the leaf gelatine in a little warm water, and dissolve the softened gelatine thoroughly in the hot (but not boiling) juices. Chill until almost setting, then spoon over the terrine. Chill until one hour before serving.

Serves 12. SD

CHOPS OR CUTLETS OF WILD BOAR SAUCED WITH MORELLO CHERRIES AND LIQUORICE ROOT

A simple treatment for any small, tender cuts and one which ensures the meat keeps well both before and after cooking, if need be. Dried morello cherries from America are now widely available at wholefood stores and good grocers.

4 chops or cutlets of boar, about 8 oz (250 g) without bone, 10–12 oz (300–350 g) with bone
1 tablespoon juniper salt (optional)

WINE MARINADE
½ pint (300 ml) full-bodied red wine
1 tablespoon balsamic vinegar
1 tablespoon muscovado sugar
1 stick liquorice root
1 fat clove of garlic, peeled
1 shallot, peeled and sliced
1 fresh bay leaf
6 juniper berries
2 allspice berries

MORELLO SAUCE
1 tablespoon dried morello cherries, soaked in 5 tablespoons red wine with ½ stick cinnamon
½ pint (300 ml) game stock, or good chicken stock
1" (2.5 cm) piece unsweetened liquorice stick (or 2 small pieces sweetened liquorice)
1–2 tablespoons wild fruit jelly
Salt and pepper
4 oz (125 g) stoned fresh morello cherries, lightly cooked (optional)

Trim meat of any excess fat and coat with juniper salt if wished. Meanwhile, make up the marinade by bringing all the ingredients to the boil, then simmering gently for about 15 minutes in a non-reactive saucepan. Wipe any salt off the meat and cover with cooled marinade. Keep covered and cold for 1–3 days.

Heat a little light oil in a heavy-based, deep frying pan. Drain and dry the meat, discarding the marinade. Sear and caramelize the chops or cutlets quickly over a fairly high heat, then fry gently for about 10 minutes on each side until nicely browned. Cover the pan and continue to cook the meat in its own juices over the lowest possible heat until tender – another 30 to 40 minutes, depending on thickness. Meanwhile simmer the soaked cherries and cinnamon gently in the wine for about 5 minutes and strain, separately reserving cherries and wine.

Transfer cooked meat to a warm plate and rest, covered, in a low oven. Deglaze the frying pan with the wine, scraping any sediment into the liquid. Add the stock and liquorice and reduce, stirring, until liquorice is dissolved, and the sauce a

Gilded apples

8 Cox Pippin apples, or sound Golden
  Delicious when necessary
8 oz (250 g) boar sausage-meat
2 oz (50 g) seedless raisins, soaked in
  2 tablespoons sweet Madeira
1½ oz (40 g) pinenuts, lightly toasted
1 teaspoon balsamic vinegar
Good pinch of powdered cinnamon
Good grating of nutmeg
1 rounded teaspoon muscovado sugar
A little boar-lard or butter
1 dessertspoon maple syrup or honey
Additional Madeira
1 yolk of egg, beaten with ½ teaspoon water
1 generous pinch powdered saffron

Core the whole apples, but do not peel. Score the skin of each once round the circumference and twice vertically from the top to the circumference line. Beat together the sausage-meat (remove skins from sausages and break down the filling), drained raisins, nuts, vinegar, spices and sugar and divide this filling between the apples, packing down until all the mixture is used up. Place the apples in a greased fireproof dish and pour in a spoonful of water. Dot the top of each apple with a little boar-lard or butter and dribble on maple syrup or honey and Madeira. Bake in a medium-hot oven for 35–55 minutes, until soft but not collapsed. Remove the dish from the oven and carefully strip the top half of peel off each apple. Beat together the egg yolk and saffron and brush this over the (peeled) top half of each apple. Replace in the oven for 5 minutes to 'gild'. Serve hot with roasts and hams, or on their own, with any rich juices collected in the dish.

Serves 8.   SD

little syrupy. Strain through a fine sieve into a fresh saucepan, add the reserved cherries and a little fruit jelly, and season to taste (unsweetened liquorice will demand more fruit jelly to balance flavours than will sweetened). Add any fresh, cooked cherries to the sauce, heat through, and transfer chops and sauce to a hot serving dish.

The chops will become more succulent for 15–20 minutes' resting. If making the dish in advance, cool cooked chops and sauce quickly and store in the refrigerator, reheating gently to serve.

Serves 4.   SD

GILDED APPLES

This recipe is in keeping with a centuries-old British predilection for blending the sweet and the savoury; use boar sausages for the filling, and make sure to 'dore with the yolks of eyroun', or brush with egg yolk for the effect of gilding.

MARTINMAS STEAKS

The feast of Martinmas, the patron saint of horsemen and all domestic animals, was celebrated in great style in Scotland until comparatively recently. November was the farmworkers' annual holiday, and the Saint's Day on the 11th heralded its beginning. The more benevolent farmers and landowners would kill a steer and distribute it among their employees and tenants and, for many of the poorer families, this was the only time they ate beef all year. A traditional dish for the richer elements of society was steaks made from minced venison and pork, dipped in egg and breadcrumbs, fried and served with redcurrant jelly or Cumberland sauce.

> 8 oz (250 g) venison
> 8 oz (250 g) pork belly
> 1 small onion
> 1 teaspoon dried thyme or 1 tablespoon fresh thyme
> 4 crushed juniper berries
> 1 tablespoon malt whisky
> Salt and freshly milled black pepper
> 2 tablespoons seasoned flour
> 1 egg, beaten with 1 tablespoon water
> 3 oz (75 g) fresh white breadcrumbs
> Oil or fat for frying

Finely mince the venison and pork or process thoroughly in a food processor. Grate the onion and add to the meat with the thyme, juniper berries, whisky and seasoning. Mix well and form into 4 flat cakes, about ½″ (1 cm) thick.

Dip each steak in the seasoned flour, then the egg and finally the crumbs, so that they are evenly coated. Fry in shallow oil or fat over a medium heat for 12-15 minutes until golden brown. Drain well and serve piping hot with redcurrant jelly or Cumberland Sauce.

Serves 4. JR

OSSO BUCO

This classic Italian casserole of shin of veal with wine and tomatoes is nothing without cremolata. Although cremolata is no more than a finely chopped mixture of parsley and garlic with grated lemon zest which is sprinkled onto the slowly cooked veal when it is served, the effect is astonishingly vibrant.

The freshness of the lemon is essential to the taste of the dish.

> 1 oz (25 g) clarified butter
> 3 lbs (1.5 kg) shin of veal cut in slices at least 1″ (2.5 cm) thick
> 1 large tin (about 2 lbs/1 kg) Italian plum tomatoes
> ½ bottle dry, white Italian wine
> Salt and freshly-ground black pepper
> 1 small clove garlic, very finely chopped
> 6 tablespoons finely chopped parsley
> Finely grated zest of 1 lemon

Heat the butter in a large, heavy casserole and brown the veal pieces on both sides in two or three batches. Pack them into the casserole in one layer – so that the bone marrow which is one of the high spots of the dish does not slip out when the veal is cooked – and add the wine. Boil briskly until the wine is reduced by approximately half, then add the tomatoes and their juice. Leave the tomatoes whole and just pinch out the cores with your fingers. Add salt and pepper and cook, covered and very slowly on top of the stove or in a cool oven, at 275°F (140°C, gas mark 1) until the meat is melting off the bones.

Combine the garlic, parsley and lemon zest to make the cremolata.

Traditionally, osso buco is served with a saffron-flavoured risotto made with arborio rice. If you decide to serve it this way, you may wish to reduce the liquid in the casserole by fast boiling. However, it is excellent with creamed potatoes and with the sauce left pretty liquid. Either way, sprinkle each serving of meat with a generous spoonful of the cremolata.

Serves 6. SCP

COLD VEAL WITH A LIGHT APRICOT SAUCE

Veal is excellent cold, especially served slightly pink, with a tangy fruit sauce. Use a rolled shoulder or fillet joint for this, not breast which tends to be rather fatty.

This dish is perfect for buffets, or after-theatre suppers, as it can be prepared ahead.

2–3 lb (1–1.5 kg) rolled joint of veal
12 dried apricots
½ pint (300 ml) light stock
½ pint (300 ml) dry white wine
1 teaspoon dried thyme
About 6–8 thin rashers streaky bacon, derinded
1 onion, sliced thinly
1 tablespoon mango or other fruit chutney
2–3 tablespoons fromage frais or natural yoghurt
Salt and ground black pepper
A few halved unsalted pistachios, to garnish

Soak the apricots overnight in the stock and wine, then drain, reserving the liquid, and chop.

Season the joint, sprinkle over with half the thyme and press half the chopped apricots on top. Cover tightly with the bacon rashers.

Put the remaining apricots, onions and thyme in the base of a roasting pan and place the veal on top. Pour in the reserved liquid. Cover with foil. Roast at 375°F (190°C, gas mark 5) for 30 minutes per lb if you like your veal pink, plus 30 minutes for well done. Uncover the veal to brown for the last 20 minutes or so. Remove the veal and cool. Strain the pan liquid into a jug, cool and skim off any fat. Reserve the apricots and onion.

Purée the liquid with the pan apricots, onions and chutney, then adjust the seasoning. Stir in the fromage frais or yoghurt. Serve the veal sliced, with sauce, and scatter over the pistachios.

Serves 4–6.   RD

QUICK SAUTE OF VEAL KIDNEYS

Kidneys are very much part of the traditional English breakfast, and delicious for lunch or supper.

1 veal kidney, about 8 oz (250 g)
1½ oz (40 g) butter
Juice 1 small orange
1 teaspoon coarse grain mustard

2 tablespoons medium dry sherry
2 tablespoons single cream
Salt and pepper

TO SERVE
4–6 rashers lean streaky bacon, rinded
1 large tomato, halved
Olive oil, preferably garlic flavoured
Fresh chopped parsley

Peel the thin membrane from the kidney, cut into ½" (1 cm) slices and snip out core with scissors.

Roll the bacon rashers neatly and skewer together. Halve the tomato, brush with oil and season. Grill both, turning the bacon once, then keep them warm.

Heat the butter in a sauté pan until foaming, then fry the slices of kidney for 2 to 3 minutes, turning occasionally until just done. Take care not to overcook.

Add the juice, mustard, sherry and seasoning. Simmer for two minutes until reduced by a third, then stir in the cream.

Serve immediately.

Serves 1–2.   RD

SHROPSHIRE COLLARED PORK

There are a number of different ways of 'collaring' meat. Often the joint is simply sprinkled with a few herbs or spices, rolled up, tied with a piece of tape or string (like a collar) and boiled. Sometimes the meat is brined prior to cooking, or else, as in this recipe, it is brined for 24 hours after cooking.

FOR THE STUFFING
6 oz (175 g) fresh white breadcrumbs
Grated rind of 1 lemon
2 tablespoons chopped parsley
2 teaspoons chopped fresh marjoram
6 anchovy fillets, finely chopped
1 teaspoon grated nutmeg
1 egg, beaten
Salt and freshly milled black pepper

Quick sauté of veal kidneys

FOR THE MEAT
3 lb (1.5 kg) boned lean pork belly
1 pig's trotter
1 carrot, sliced
1 leek, sliced
1 stick celery, roughly chopped
About 12 peppercorns

FOR THE BRINE
1½ pints (900 ml) water
½ (300 ml) malt vinegar
1 oz (25 g) salt
1 oz (25 g) soft brown sugar
6 cloves

First make the stuffing. Put all the ingredients into a basin, bind with the egg, and season to taste.

Lay the meat out flat, spread evenly with the stuffing to within 1″ (2.5 cm) of the edge, then roll up and tie with string. Put into a pan with other meat ingredients, cover with water and bring to the boil. Skim off any scum, then cover and simmer gently for 2½ hours. Remove from the heat and allow to cool in the cooking liquor.

Heat brine ingredients gently until sugar has dissolved. Remove from heat. Place pork in a deep bowl, pour over cold brine and leave for 24 hours. Drain thoroughly and serve pork cold with salad.
Serves 8–10. JR

PORK CHOPS IN MINT

Mint is normally associated with lamb, but it goes equally well with pork, as this old recipe of Eliza Acton's proves. Chopped fresh mint is mixed with flour to form a thick crust round the chops, which keeps them very moist during grilling, as well as giving a superb flavour.

¼ pint (150 ml) milk
2 oz (50 g) chopped fresh mint
2 oz (50 g) flour
Salt and freshly milled black pepper
4 pork chops

Pour the milk into a shallow plate. Mix together the mint, flour and seasoning. Dip each chop in the milk and then thickly coat with the flour and mint mixture. Put under a moderate grill and cook for 15 minutes, turning once.

Serves 4. JR

SUFFOLK SOPS

Sops, or Spread Toasts as they are also known, are a direct descendant of medieval trenchers. Before platters were in general use in manor houses, large pieces of bread known as trenchers, about 5″ (13 cm) × 8″ (20 cm) and 1″ (2.5 cm) thick were used instead. The meat etc. was placed on them and the juices, gravies and sauces would soak or 'sop' into them.

The trenchers were not, however, generally eaten by those lucky enough to dine in such a grand manner, but were kept and handed on to the poor. Indeed, it was considered very bad manners to bite into your trencher and thus spoil the dinner of the less fortunate.

Ideally you should use sweet-cured Suffolk ham for this recipe, but failing that (and it is not easy to obtain) use a good quality cooked ham or even gammon off the bone.

Should you then have access to free-range eggs as well, you will have a feast of great simplicity fit for a king.

6 oz (175 g) cooked ham (see above)
4 tablespoons double cream
4 thick slices of bread
2 oz (50 g) butter
10 eggs
Salt and freshly milled black pepper

Finely chop the ham and put into a small saucepan with the cream. Heat gently. Toast the bread on both sides, then spread with the ham mixture and put into a warm oven while preparing the eggs. Melt the butter. Beat the eggs and season with a little salt and pepper. Add to the pan and scramble lightly, then quickly spoon the eggs over the ham mixture and serve at once.

Serves 4. JR

GEORGIAN MARBLED TONGUE AND HAM

Potting meat, i.e. pressing it into a pot and then sealing it with clarified butter, lard or suet, was one of the earliest methods of food preservation. The addition of Worcestershire sauce is a modern adaptation, but it does improve the flavour.

8 oz (250 g) cooked tongue
8 oz (250 g) cooked ham or gammon
6 oz (175 g) softened butter
¼ teaspoon grated nutmeg
2 teaspoons Worcestershire sauce
Salt, if necessary, and black pepper

Finely mince the tongue and ham, or process separately in a food processor. Divide the butter in half, put into separate bowls and beat lightly. Add the tongue to one and the ham to the other and mix well. Season the tongue with the nutmeg and pepper. Add the Worcestershire sauce to the ham and

Right *(clockwise from right) Martinmas steaks, page 72; pork chops in mint; Suffolk sops (in foreground); pommes dorées, page 78; Georgian marbled tongue and ham; Cornish chicken and gammon pie, page 80*

beat again. Season both with salt if necessary.

Lightly butter a small dish. Spread a third of the tongue over the base, then cover with half the ham in small lumps, about the size of a walnut. Spread over another third of the tongue, then the last of the ham in lumps, and finally spread with the remaining tongue. Cover with a sheet of greaseproof paper or clingwrap, place a weight on top and leave for at least 4 hours in a cool place.

Serves 8 as a starter with hot toast or 6 as a main course with salad. JR

POMMES DOREES

A medieval dish which, despite meaning golden apples in French, has nothing whatever to do with fruit. The origin is Norman, the *pommes* being little spicy balls of cooked pork and *dorées* referring to the practice of making food golden.

Pommes dorées were made golden by being dipped in crisp batter. It was usual for half the balls to be dipped in plain batter and the other half either to have parsley added to the batter or to be dipped in parsley after frying so that they were a brilliant green against plain gold.

> *1 lb (500 g) cooked pork*
> *2 oz (50 g) currants*
> *½ teaspoon ground ginger*
> *¾ teaspoon ground mace*
> *1 teaspoon soft brown sugar*
> *Salt and freshly milled black pepper*
> *2 eggs, beaten*
>
> FOR THE BATTER
> *3 oz (75 g) plain flour*
> *1 oz (25 g) self-raising flour*
> *1 egg*
> *¼ pint (150 ml) milk*
> *3 tablespoons very finely chopped parsley*
> *½ teaspoonful salt*

Finely mince the pork, add the currants, ginger, mace and soft brown sugar. Season well and bind

with the eggs. Lightly flour your hands and form the mixture into balls about 1½″ (4 cm) in diameter. Sift the flours with the salt. Make a well in the centre, add the egg and half the milk and beat to a smooth batter, then beat in the remaining milk. Divide the batter in half and stir the parsley into one half. Dip the pork balls into the batter then fry in deep fat until golden brown and crisp.

Serves 4. JR

AMERICAN SUGAR-GLAZED HAM

A delicious treatment for a special home-cooked ham is to baste it during the final period of roasting with a sweet spicy glaze. The flavours are wonderfully complementary.

Quantities given are sufficient for a 10–12 lb (4.50–5.50 kg) ham joint; adjust proportionally for larger or smaller joints.

American sugar-glazed ham; ham and spinach roll; ham rolls à la basquaise

6 oz (175 g) muscovado or dark soft brown
    sugar
3 tablespoons maple syrup or clear honey
2 tablespoons cider vinegar
1 tablespoons mustard powder
Juice of 2 small oranges
Whole cloves, to stud

Mix all the glaze ingredients together well.

Cook the ham as usual. About three-quarters of an hour from the end of cooking, cut off the rind, score the fat with a sharp knife in a criss-cross pattern and stud with cloves.

Spoon over the glaze and return to the oven, basting about three times.

Cool the joint out of the pan. The glaze and juices can be used again if covered with a thin layer of melted fat and stored in the fridge for up to three weeks.   RD

HAM AND SPINACH ROLL

Served cold, this delicious pie is ideal for picnics or summer buffets.

1 × 13 oz (375 g) pack frozen puff pastry,
    thawed
8 oz (250 g) fresh spinach leaves, washed
8 oz (250 g) raw pork, minced
8 oz (250 g) lean raw ham, minced
1 medium onion, finely chopped
2 tablespoons fresh chopped parsley
½ teaspoon dried thyme
½ teaspoon dry sherry
3 tablespoons dry sherry
Grated rind ½ lemon
Salt and ground black pepper
3 hard-boiled eggs, peeled
Beaten egg, for glazing

Roll the pastry out thinly to a rectangle roughly 14 × 12″ (36 × 30 cm). Place on a baking sheet.

Cook the spinach briefly, then drain very well, squeezing dry between two dinner plates, and chop finely. Cool.

Mix all the ingredients together except for the pastry, eggs and glaze.

Spoon half down the centre of the pastry. Place the whole hard-boiled eggs on top in a line, cover with the rest of the filling and mould around the eggs.

Slash the pastry edges at intervals, slanting diagonally, and brush the tips with glaze.

Now, pull the strips over the meat alternately in a criss-cross fashion and press well to seal each strip, and the two ends. Brush all over with glaze.

Bake in a preheated oven at 400°F (200°C, gas mark 6) for about 25 minutes until golden brown, then reduce the heat to 350°F (180°C, gas mark 4) for a further 35 minutes to cook the meat.

Remove, cool on the tray and slide off onto a wire tray to get quite cold.

Serves 6.   RD

HAM ROLLS A LA BASQUAISE

A Mediterranean dish for slices of ham. Grilling the peppers imparts a delicious flavour and is well worth the effort.

1 large red pepper
1 large green pepper
2 tablespoons olive oil
1 onion, sliced
4 fresh tomatoes, skinned and chopped
1 tablespoon tomato paste
Salt and ground black pepper
1 sprig fresh thyme
2 sage leaves, chopped
2 tablespoons fresh chopped parsley
6 green olives, stoned and sliced
6 black olives, stoned and sliced
12 thin slices ham

Grill the peppers under a high heat until the skins burn and split, turning frequently. Peel the skins off, core, de-seed and slice.

Heat the oil and gently fry the onion and pepper strips, then add the tomatoes, paste, seasoning and herbs. Simmer for 10 minutes.

Add the olives, then divide the mixture between the 12 ham slices and roll up. Spread any leftover mixture on the base of a baking dish and put the rolls on top.

Bake at 375°F (190°C, gas mark 5) for about 15 minutes until well heated through. Serve hot with crisp bread and a green salad.

Serves 4.   RD

CORNISH CHICKEN AND GAMMON PIE

There are numerous Cornish recipes for pies which are filled with cream after baking. Likky pie, which was similar to this one, but used only bacon and leeks, was served on high days and holidays. Chicken breast fillets would not, of course, have been used originally.

12 oz (350 g) shortcrust pastry
3 boneless chicken breast fillets, weighing in total
    about 12 oz (350 g)
2 thick gammon steaks, weighing in total about
    12 oz (350 g)
2 oz (50 g) chopped parsley
1 small onion, very finely chopped
¼ teaspoon ground mace
Salt and freshly milled black pepper
¼ pint (150 ml) chicken stock
Milk for glazing
¼ pint (150 ml) double cream

Roll out just over half the pastry to line an 8 ″ (20 cm) diameter deep-pie plate. Cut each chicken fillet into three and lay in the base of the pastry-lined plate. Season well with salt and pepper. Cover with the parsley, then scatter over the onion. Cut the gammon into about 6 pieces and lay them on top. Sprinkle with mace and more pepper. Pour over the chicken stock. Damp the pastry edges.

Roll out the remaining pastry for the lid and place in position. Seal the pastry edges, then trim and flute them. Roll out any pastry trimmings and make into leaves to decorate the pie. Make a hole in

the top of the pie for the steam to escape, then brush all over with milk. Bake in a moderately hot oven, 375°F (190°C, gas mark 5) for 1¼ hours, then remove from the oven.

Bring the cream to just below boiling point in a small saucepan, then pour into the pie before serving, using a funnel if necessary. Serve hot, as soon as possible once the cream has been added.

Serves 4–6.   JR

BOEUF A LA MODE

A potentially tough piece of beef is larded with pork fat and then cooked slowly in delicious, tenderising liquids.

About 3–4 lb (1.5–1.75 kg) piece rolled beef –
    e.g. brisket, or top rump or aitchbone or
    unsalted silverside
4–6 oz (125–175 g) pork or bacon fat, cut into
    thin strips
1 onion and 3 carrots, sliced
2 bay leaves, sprig each fresh thyme and
    rosemary
1 calf's foot, sawn into three
½ pint (300 ml) red wine
½ pint (300 ml) good beef stock
3 fl oz (100 ml) brandy
Salt and ground black pepper

With a larding needle, thread the pork fat strips through the meat. Secure the meat neatly.

Place the onions and carrots in the base of a large casserole and stand the meat on top. Sprinkle over the herbs and squeeze the calf's foot pieces around the sides. Pour over the wine, brandy and stock, season well, cover and bake at 325°F (170°C, gas mark 3) for about 3 hours or until quite tender.

Remove the meat and slice it up. Scoop any marrow jelly from the calf's foot into the sauce then discard the bones. Strain the stock and thicken if liked with a little cornflour, or liquidize with the vegetables and herbs. Pour a little over the meat and hand the rest separately in a sauce boat.

Serves 6.   RD

LANCASHIRE HOT POT

There are many variations on the theme of the hot pot. Traditionally, it was often cooked in the residual heat of the local baker's oven after the day's bread had been baked. Lancashire hot pot, illustrated on page 31, is usually made in a deep earthenware casserole, glazed brown, with a domed lid, which can be removed toward the end of cooking to allow the potatoes to brown.

> 3 lb (1.5 kg) best end neck lamb chops (there
>   should be about 12)
> 3 lamb's kidneys, halved and skinned
> 1 oz (25 g) seasoned flour
> 3 lb (1.5 kg) potatoes, peeled
> 2 onions, peeled and sliced
> 3–4 carrots, peeled and sliced
> 2 sticks celery, sliced
> 2–3 bay leaves
> ¾ pint (450 ml) lamb or chicken stock
> 1 oz (25 g) butter, melted
> Parsley to garnish

Trim any excess fat from the lamb, then toss in seasoned flour. Snip core from each kidney with scissors and toss in remaining flour.

Prepare vegetables. Slice the potatoes neatly and place in a pan of cold water. Bring to the boil and cook for 2 minutes. Drain well, then place a layer of potato slices (about half) on the base of a large ovenproof casserole, followed by onion, carrots, celery and bay leaves. Season to taste. Place kidneys and lamb chops on top, fitting in the pieces like a jigsaw. Finally, cover with neat slices of overlapping potato. Pour the prepared stock down the side of the dish. Brush potato slices with melted butter, and lay a piece of buttered greaseproof paper on top. Cover with a well-fitting lid and set in moderate oven 375°F (190°C, gas mark 5) for about 1¾ hours.

Remove lid and paper, then brush with remaining butter and return to a slightly hotter oven for 30–45 minutes to brown and crisp the potatoes. Scatter with parsley before serving if liked, and serve straight from the casserole.

Serves 6.   SM

LAMB TAGINE WITH ARTICHOKES AND FENNEL

In Morocco and Algeria, rich aromatic stews are cooked in conical earthenware pots called *tagines* (see page 66). The shape of the lid is supposed to encourage steam to drop back into the stew to help moisturize it. However, any casserole with a slightly domed lid should achieve excellent results.

> 2 tablespoons oil
> 1 medium onion, grated
> ½ lemon
> 1½ (750 g) lean stewing lamb (e.g. boned
>   shoulder)
> 1" (2.5 cm) cube fresh ginger, grated, or
>   1 teaspoon ground
> Salt and ground black pepper
> 3 young globe artichokes
> 4 tomatoes, skinned and chopped
> 2 medium heads fennel
> 3 tablespoons fresh chopped coriander leaves
> ¼ pint (150 ml) water
> Some black olives, to serve

Heat the oil in a large cast-iron casserole and gently fry the grated onion. Cut the lemon into thin slices and add to the pan. (This gives a pithy bitterness which Western palates may not like, so thinly pare the rind first, remove the pith, cut the flesh into slices and add rind and flesh only.)

Cut the lamb into bite-size chunks and add to the pan with the grated ginger and seasoning. Cook until browned, about 15 minutes.

Strip the leaves from artichokes, trim the bases of any woody bits, and scoop out the spiky choke with a spoon. Cut the bases into quarters and drop into cold water with a squeeze of lemon juice to prevent them from darkening. Dip the tomatoes briefly in boiling water, skin and chop; slice the fennel. Add the vegetables to the pan with the coriander and water. Cover and simmer gently for about another 20 to 30 minutes or until the meat is tender. Add the olives five minutes before the end of the cooking time. Serve with rice, couscous or simply chunks of sesame bread.

Serves 4–6.   RD

81

LAMB BIRIYANI WITH PUMPKIN CHUTNEY AND CUCUMBER

This is an adaptation of a southern Indian dish of spiced meat layered with rice – a kind of elaborate and subtly-flavoured pilaff. The original recipe came from a book called *Indian Regional Cookery* (now out of print) by Meera Taneja. This version, sharpened by chutney and cooled with cucumber, although no longer authentic, is, however, intriguing and delicious, and appropriate for a small crowd. For the chutney, advance planning is necessary; it should mature for at least a month.

LAMB BIRIYANI

2 lamb shoulders, boned by butcher
4 oz (125 g) ghee
3 large onions
18 oz (550 g) natural yoghurt
6 fresh green chillies, tops off
8 large cloves garlic, peeled
A 2" (5 cm) piece root ginger, peeled
Salt
2 teaspoons black cumin seeds
10 green cardamoms
9 cloves
A good handful each of fresh mint and coriander
*   leaves*
Strained juice of 6 lemons
1 lb (500 g) basmati rice

Trim lamb of excess skin, fat, and connective tissue. Cut into small cubes, and weigh out 4 lb (1.75 kg) of these; submerge them in cold water for an hour. Use any remaining lamb for another purpose.

Meanwhile, melt 3 oz (75 g) ghee in a wide sauté pan, mince onions and fry these slowly until golden-brown. Drain with a slotted spoon and mix with yoghurt, discarding used ghee.

Cut up chillies, garlic and ginger, and purée these to a paste – with the aid of a little salt – in the food processor. Drain lamb and press out water; smear meat with paste and leave for 1 hour.

Bruise cumin seeds with the base of a heavy knife-handle; add to yoghurt with whole cardamoms, cloves, chopped mint and coriander, lemon juice. In due course, add lamb and its paste and mix well. Cover and marinate meat for 5 hours, stirring occasionally.

Transfer all to a large, deep pot – such as a heavy stock pot, 10" (25 cm) across by 6" (15 cm) deep, with a close-fitting lid – salt mixture and simmer it slowly, atop the stove, for 30–40 minutes or until lamb is tender; keep pot half-covered and stir contents occasionally. There should be quite a lot of sauce. Rinse rice in 3 changes of cold water and blanch for 3 minutes in 1½ pints (900 ml) salted, boiling water; drain rice well and reserve.

When lamb is ready, taste for salt, remove meat and sauce from the pot and clean this; smear remaining ghee over bottom and half way up side. Line bottom of pot with ⅓ of rice, cover with half of meat and sauce. Strew with half of remaining rice, spread with the rest of meat and sauce, cover with rice. Top with a very snug lid and bake biriyani in a 375°F (190°C, gas mark 5) oven to finish cooking the grain. A gas oven will require some 30–40 minutes; a traditional electric one may take up to twice as long.

To serve, bring pot to the – well-insulated! – table, remove lid (beware of steam), fork up rice, and dig deep into layers.

Serves 10, with pumpkin chutney and cucumber as follows.

PUMPKIN CHUTNEY

The quantities given here fill two 2 lb (1 kg) jars, and one of 1 lb (500 g) capacity.

4¼ lb (1.85 kg) firm pumpkin (gross weight),
*   seeded, peeled, cut into ¾" (2 cm) chunks*
1½ large onions, peeled and chopped
3 large cloves garlic, peeled and chopped
3 oz (75 g) sultanas
2 teaspoons black peppercorns and 1 teaspoon
*   black mustard seeds, crushed together in a*
*   mortar*
A 1" (2.5 cm) piece root ginger, peeled and
*   grated*
1 stick cinnamon

Lamb biryani with pumpkin chutney and cucumber with mint; with Milleens cheese and salad to follow

2 teaspoons salt
1 lb (500 g) soft light brown sugar
1¼ pints (750 ml) white wine vinegar

Put everything into a deep, heavy pot, bring vinegar to the boil, and simmer contents – uncovered and skimming when necessary – until chutney thickens to a jam-like consistency; the process will take about an hour and 40 minutes. Stir constantly at the end or chutney will stick nastily. Leave it somewhat liquid and ladle immediately into hot, dry sterilized jars; cover with sterilized lids. Let the chutney ripen for at least 4–8 weeks before opening the containers.

CUCUMBER WITH MINT

Two 18 oz (550 g) cucumbers
Salt
1 small onion
A handful of fresh mint leaves

Peel, trim, and seed cucumbers. Cut flesh into ⅜″ (1 cm) cubes, salt these lightly and allow them to drain for an hour or so in a colander. Rinse well and drain again.

Peel and mince the onion finely. Toss cucumber with minced onion and mint.

Serves 10 as a condiment. AWS

83

Persian-style rice and lamb mould

PERSIAN-STYLE RICE AND LAMB MOULD

Rice moulds with their crisp 'skins' are a classic of Persian cuisine. They are made by pressing cooked rice round the base and sides of a mould, then baking with a filling. Although not strictly traditional, this is easier to turn out if the rice is first mixed with eggs and yoghurt.

> 12 oz (375 g) basmati rice, unrinsed
> 2 egg yolks
> 5 oz (150 g) tub thick natural yoghurt
> 2 oz (50 g) butter or ghee, melted and cooled
> 1 lb (500 g) minced lean lamb or beef
> 1 tablespoon oil
> 1 onion, chopped
> 2 cloves garlic, crushed
> 1 teaspoon ground coriander (optional)
> ¾ pint (450 ml) stock
> 2 tablespoons tomato purée
> 6 dried apricots, chopped
> 2 oz (50 g) raisins
> 2 oz (50 g) walnuts, chopped
> Salt and ground black pepper

It is important not to rinse the rice so that it is slightly sticky. Cook the rice in plenty of boiling water on a medium boil for 10 minutes. Drain but don't rinse. Cool.

Beat together the yolks, yoghurt and half the cool but still runny butter, then mix in half the rice. Mix the remaining half of rice with the rest of the runny butter and check the seasoning.

Brown the mince in the oil for 3 minutes in a large frying-pan, then add the onion, garlic and coriander, and fry, stirring for 3 minutes.

Stir in the stock, tomato purée, dried fruits and seasonings. Bring to the boil, then simmer, uncovered, for 15–20 minutes until the liquid has nearly gone. Mix in the nuts.

Grease a loose-bottomed 9″ (23 cm) round deep cake tin with a little butter, and line base with a circle of buttered foil or greaseproof paper.

Spoon in all the egg rice and, with the back of a spoon, work it up the sides of the tin, leaving sufficient on the base to cover. Pat well to firm.

Spoon in half the meat, then half the buttered rice. Repeat the layers finishing with rice, and cover with buttered foil. Stand the tin on a baking sheet and bake at 350°F (180°C, gas mark 4) for 1 hour. Allow it to stand for 15 minutes afterwards, dip the tin briefly in cold water, then invert onto a plate and shake out.

Top with onion rings fried gently in butter until golden, and some parsley or coriander leaves.
Serves 4.   RD

SPICED CURRIED LAMB

Despite the fact that they will eat steak tartare with no qualms at all, many people are slightly dubious about eating other meat raw and, while pork and all poultry should always be thoroughly cooked, lamb is delicious eaten raw. This particular recipe is for a very lightly spiced, curried lamb; however if you would like a slightly hotter mixture you could also add a very finely chopped green chilli as well. Although it can be served with any number of salads, it goes particularly well with cucumber mixed with yoghurt and a little fresh mint.

1 lb (500 g) lean lamb, preferably from the leg
4 rounded tablespoons mayonnaise
1" (2.5 cm) piece root ginger, minced
1 tablespoon garam masala
3 tablespoons chopped fresh coriander
Salt and freshly milled black pepper

TO GARNISH
Coriander sprigs (optional)
Lemon slices

Cut off any excess fat or sinew from the lamb and grind or mince finely. Turn into a bowl and add the mayonnaise, ginger, garam masala and two-thirds of the coriander. Mix well together and season to taste with salt and pepper. Make into 4 cakes and place on a serving dish. Sprinkle with the remaining chopped coriander and garnish with the coriander and lemon.

Serves 4.   JR

LAMB WITH SALTED LEMON

Whole lemons preserved with salt are fundamental to the Moroccan kitchen and are used here in a stew of lean lamb and new potatoes which is flavoured additionally with saffron.

This is a boon recipe when time for preparation is tight because, unusually, the meat is not browned before the liquid is added, and, once the ingredients have been prepared, is left to simmer.

6 tablespoons olive oil
1 clove garlic, crushed
1 small piece (size of garlic clove) fresh ginger, crushed
¼ teaspoon powdered saffron
2 lbs (1 kg) boneless lamb, leg or neck fillet, cubed
2 Spanish onions, finely chopped
1 salted lemon
2 lbs (1 kg) scraped new potatoes
Salt
Freshly-ground black pepper

Put the oil, crushed garlic, ginger and saffron into a big, wide pan. Add the lamb and turn to coat it with the oil. Add the onions.

Divide the lemon into quarters, remove and discard the flesh and pith, and add the skin to the pan with enough water to cover the lamb. Bring to the boil, lower the heat and simmer until the lamb is almost tender. This may take up to two hours.

Add the potatoes and continue cooking until the potatoes are tender. If there is still too much liquid, take out the meat and vegetables and keep them warm, while reducing the sauce by fast boiling. Season with salt, if needed, and freshly-ground black pepper.

Lamb with salted lemon can be cooked in advance and reheated. It can also be frozen.

Hot French bread and a mixed green salad complete this easy meal.

Serves 4–6.

NOTE Free-range chickens, which have more flavour than battery birds, are also excellent cooked this way. Cut one bird into about 10 pieces and halve the cooking time.   SCP

SALTED LEMONS

7 fresh, firm, thin-skinned lemons
7 tablespoons sea salt

Wait until you can find thin-skinned lemons before making this preserve, since coarse, pithy lemons are not nearly as good.

Scrub the lemons with warm water and a soft brush, and scald a Kilner or Parfait jar which is large enough to hold all the fruit.

Using a stainless-steel knife, cut six of the lemons lengthwise as if into quarters, but not right through. Pack a tablespoonful of salt into each one and pack them tightly into the jar. Add the remaining salt and strained juice of the seventh lemon. Top up with boiling water to cover the fruit. Close the jar tightly and leave it for two or three weeks in a cool, dark place.

Once matured, salted lemons keep well for many months.   SCP

MAINLY VEGETABLES

Whether served as accompaniments to meat or
fish, or as main-course dishes in their own right,
these imaginative vegetable recipes are suitable, or
easily adapted, for vegetarians

PROVENCAL TIAN D'EPINARDS

A dessert made with spinach, this dates from the
seventeenth century. It is cooked in a *tian* – a
shallow red earthenware dish – and is still eaten in
Vaucluse at the end of a meal, but can also accompany savoury dishes. This traditional open tart
combines spinach with spinach beet, but it can be
made with spinach alone.

> *1 lb (500 g) spinach*
> *½ lb (250 g) spinach beet*
> *Pinch salt*
> *Boiling water*
> *2 oz (50 g) melted butter*
> *1 oz (25 g) white breadcrumbs*
> *2 oz (50 g) currants*
> *1 oz (25 g) ground almonds*
> *½ pint (300 ml) single cream*
> *2 tablespoons sugar*
> *Nutmeg*
> *2 whole eggs*
> *2 egg yolks*
> *4 oz (125 g) puff pastry*

Blanch spinach and spinach beet in a little lightly
salted boiling water for 1 minute. Drain and chop.
Mix in the melted butter. Stir breadcrumbs, currants and ground almonds into the cream. Then
mix in the spinach, sugar and nutmeg. Add the
beaten whole eggs and egg yolks. Line a 9" (23 cm)
tian – if you have one – or a flan plate with the
pastry. Pour in the spinach mixture. Bake at 425°F
(220°C, gas mark 7) for 10 minutes, then lower heat
to 350°F (180°C, gas mark 4) and cook for a further
30 minutes. Serve hot.

For 6 people. BGM

SPINACH SOUFFLE

Delicately flecked with green, this classic soufflé is
seasoned with Parmesan and anchovy essence,
combined to give a pleasant saltiness.

> *1 tablespoon chopped shallot*
> *½ oz (15 g) butter for frying*
> *6 oz (175 g) blanched, chopped spinach*
>
> PANADA
> *1½ oz (40 g) butter*
> *2 oz (50 g) flour*
> *½ pint (300 ml) boiling milk*
> *2 teaspoons anchovy essence*
> *4 egg yolks, and 5 egg whites*
> *Salt and pepper to taste*
> *1½–2 oz (40–50 g) grated Parmesan cheese*

Right *(from top right) Spinach soup (recipe on page
32); Provençal tian d'epinards; spinach soufflé; raw
spinach and hot bacon salad (recipe on page 111);
Bavarian ham and spinach torte, page 88*

Soften the shallot in melted butter, add spinach and stir and cook until moisture evaporates.

To make the panada, melt the butter and stir in the flour, then cook for 1–2 minutes; do not let it brown. Still stirring, add the milk off the heat, stir vigorously until smooth, then add spinach, anchovy essence and pepper. Stir and cook for about 1 minute. Remove from heat and beat in the egg yolks one by one. Check seasoning. Beat the egg whites and salt until stiff and dry. Add about a quarter to the panada, and stir in all except 1 tablespoonful of the cheese. Very gently fold in the rest of the egg whites.

Butter the bottom and sides of a 2½ pint (1.5 litre) soufflé mould. Pre-heat oven the 400°F (200°C, gas mark 6). Put the mixture into the prepared mould, and sprinkle the top with the remaining tablespoon of cheese. Place in the middle of the oven, and immediately turn heat down to 375°F (190°C, gas mark 5). Cook for 25–35 minutes, by which time soufflé should have risen and be a delicate brown.

Take out of the oven, and leave aside for 4–5 minutes to become firm, before serving.

Serves 4. BGM

BAVARIAN HAM AND SPINACH TORTE

A light lunch or supper dish illustrated on page 87, which, by omitting the ham, could be adapted for vegetarians.

> *7 oz (200 g) puff pastry, can be frozen*
> *8 oz (250 g) cooked ham, coarsely chopped*
> *1½ lb (750 g) minced cooked spinach mixed with butter*
> *3 hard-boiled eggs, chopped*
> *5 fl oz (140 ml) light creamy béchamel sauce*
> *Pepper, salt*
> *Egg for glazing*

Line a shallow, 9″ (23 cm) circular mould with half the pastry. Divide ham and spinach in half, season and arrange in alternate layers on top of the pastry. Put the eggs on top, then cover smoothly with the béchamel. Cover with the rest of the pastry, decorate with any trimmings, and make a hole in the centre. Glaze with beaten egg. Bake at 350°F (180°C, gas mark 4) for 40–45 minutes.

Serves 4. BGM

Filo roll with feta and spinach

FILO ROLL WITH FETA AND SPINACH

This classic Greek pie suits many occasions, from stand-up buffets to a first course for formal dinners. Make it up in advance, ready for baking, then cook it when required. However, it is equally good served cold.

> *5–6 sheets filo pastry, thawed*
> *1½ oz (40 g) butter, melted*
> *1 lb (500 g) fresh leaf spinach, blanched, or ½ lb (250 g) frozen*
> *3 spring onions, chopped*
> *7 oz (200 g) feta cheese, crumbled or grated*
> *1 egg, beaten*
> *1 tablespoon fresh chopped dill*
> *Sesame seeds, to sprinkle*
> *Salt and ground black pepper*

Lay a sheet of pastry on a lightly greased baking sheet. Brush lightly all over with butter. Top with another two sheets of pastry, brushing in between with more butter.

Squeeze the spinach quite dry, then chop. Mix with the onions, cheese, egg, dill and seasoning. (Watch the salt, as feta cheese can be quite salty.) Spread the filling on the pastry, then top with the remaining pastry sheets, brushing in between with more butter.

Roll up like a Swiss roll and brush all over with the last of the butter. Scatter over sesame seeds. If you wish to bake this later, then keep it chilled until required. Bake at 375°F (190°C, gas mark 5) for about 25 to 30 minutes until golden and crispy. Allow to stand for a few moments before cutting into slices.

Serves 4.   RD

SPINACH AND RICOTTA

Rather like a flan without pastry, this vegetable dish can be served hot or cold, sliced like a cake.

> 1 oz (25 g) butter or margarine
> 18 oz (500 g) spinach
> 9 oz (275 g) ricotta
> 1 medium onion
> 1 oz (25 g) dried mushrooms (porcini)
> 3 eggs
> 1 oz (25 g) Parmesan
> Chopped parsley
> Breadcrumbs, and butter to grease tin

Put the mushrooms in a little hot water. Cook the spinach, well washed, in as little water as possible. Drain very well and chop. Slice the onion thinly and cook in butter in a heavy-based frying-pan until transparent, then add the drained mushrooms, finely sliced. Add a good pinch of chopped parsley, cover with a lid and cook slowly until the mushrooms are cooked. Remove pan from heat. Add the spinach, together with salt and pepper to taste and Parmesan cheese.

Put the ricotta in a bowl and break it up evenly with a fork, then add to spinach mixture. Beat the eggs in a basin and add to spinach.

Butter a pie dish about 9″ (23 cm) in diameter, and sprinkle with breadcrumbs. Pour in the spinach mixture and spread it evenly. Sprinkle the top with breadcrumbs, dot with butter and bake in the oven (350°F, 180°C, gas mark 4) for 30–40 minutes. When cooked, turn it out and allow to cool on a cake rack. Serve hot or cold.

Serves 6.   PF

LENTIL AND SPINACH CREPE TIMBALE WITH TOMATO COULIS

A spectacular layered centre-piece that can be prepared ahead and re-heated when required.

CRÊPES
> 2 oz (50 g) each wholewheat and white plain
>   flour
> Salt
> 2 eggs
> ½ pint (300 ml) milk
> A little oil

FILLINGS
> 12 oz (350 g) fresh spinach leaves, chopped
> 2 shallots, chopped
> 1 clove garlic, crushed
> 1 oz (25 g) butter
> A little fresh grated nutmeg
> 8 oz (250 g) ricotta cheese
> 1 oz (25 g) fresh Parmesan cheese
> 6 oz (175 g) red lentils
> 1 small onion, chopped
> 2 medium tomatoes, peeled and chopped
> ¼ pint (450 ml) water or vegetable stock
> Pinch dried basil
> Salt and ground black pepper

Make the batter by mixing the crêpe ingredients in a processor or blender. Using a small pancake pan, make 12–14 thin crêpes about 8″ (20 cm) in diameter. Cool and cover.

89

Sweat the spinach, chopped shallots and garlic in the butter for about 5 minutes in a covered saucepan. The spinach should be wilted and soft. Stir in the nutmeg, ricotta and Parmesan cheeses. Season well.

Cook the lentils with the rest of the ingredients for about 25 minutes until quite soft. Season well. Set aside.

Grease a charlotte russe tin or 2-pint (1.2 litre) basin. Line the base and sides with crêpes, cutting to fit where necessary. Halving the crêpes helps.

Now make layers of the two fillings and crêpes, finishing with a crêpe. Fold over any crêpes from the sides, cover with greased foil, pressing the edges well to the sides.

Steam or boil the mould for about 1 hour. Unmould to serve, allow to stand for a few minutes before cutting into wedges. Hand the tomato coulis separately.

TO MAKE THE COULIS

Sweat 1 large chopped onion and 2 cloves of crushed garlic in 1 oz (25 g) butter and 1 tablespoon olive oil. Add 2 lbs (1 kg) of skinned and chopped fresh tomatoes, 1 teaspoon sugar, 2 teaspoons fresh chopped basil and plenty of seasoning. Simmer for 20 minutes, then strain and serve.

Serves 6–8.   RD

Carrot and ginger pilau in a spinach crown

CARROT AND GINGER PILAU IN A SPINACH CROWN

This could form the basis of a vegetarian main meal, or a more elaborate accompaniment to a simple grill or roast.

> 1 large onion, half sliced thinly, half chopped
> 3 tablespoons groundnut oil or ghee
> 2 cloves garlic, crushed
> 1" (2.5 cm) cube fresh root ginger, finely grated
> 1 fresh green chilli, seeded and chopped
>   (optional)
> 2 carrots, peeled and coarsely grated
> 8 oz (250 g) basmati rice, rinsed
> Good pinch saffron strands
> ¾ pint (350 ml) light stock or water
> 1 cinnamon stick
> 1 teaspoon ground coriander
> 1 lb (500 g) fresh leaf spinach, well washed and
>   slightly chopped
> 1 teaspoon garam masala powder
> Salt and ground black pepper

TO SERVE
> Either some fresh pistachio nuts, chopped, or
>   toasted almond flakes

Lightly fry the chopped onion in half the oil or ghee with one clove of garlic, the ginger and chilli, if using, for 3 minutes. Add the carrots and rice, stir well and cook for 2 minutes. Add saffron (crushing between fingers), the stock, spices and seasoning.

Bring to the boil, cover and turn down to a gentle simmer for about 12 minutes. Meanwhile, in a large saucepan sauté the sliced onion in the remaining oil or ghee, with the other clove of garlic, for 3 minutes. Add the spinach – it should not need any extra water as enough should be clinging to the leaves. Sprinkle over the garam masala and stir well to mix in. Cover and simmer on a low heat for about 5 minutes. Season.

Spoon the spinach around the edge of a serving platter and pile the rice in the middle. Scatter over the nuts and serve hot.

Serves 4–6.   RD

SPINACH PUFFS

Serves as a starter, as a hot canapé with drinks, or as a main course accompaniment.

> *2 lb (1 kg) spinach*
> *2 level tablespoons flour*
> *5 fl oz (140 ml) béchamel sauce*
> *Pepper, salt*
> *Pinch nutmeg*
> *2 eggs, separated*
> *Oil for deep frying*

Cook, drain and purée the spinach. Put it in a pan over a low heat, and stir until all the liquid evaporates. Remove from heat, let it cool slightly, stir in the flour, then add the béchamel. Add egg yolks and seasoning. Beat egg whites until stiff and dry. Fold them in gently. Drop dessertspoons of the mixture into the hot oil and fry until the puffs are crisp. Serve immediately.

Serves 4.   BGM

Potato and parsnip amandine (above; recipe on page 98); cucumber shells with creamed spinach

CUCUMBER SHELLS WITH CREAMED SPINACH

Cucumber makes an excellent hot vegetable, and when halved and seeded, a surprisingly good container for a filling.

> *2 cucumbers*
> *1 lb (500 g) fresh leaf spinach*
> *1 oz (25 g) butter*
> *1 oz (25 g) flour*
> *½ pint (300 ml) hot milk*
> *Freshly grated nutmeg*
> *Salt and ground black pepper*

> TOPPING
> *2 tablespoons dried breadcrumbs*
> *2 tablespoons chopped nuts*
> *2 tablespoons freshly-grated Parmesan*

Cut each cucumber into three then peel, halve and scoop out the seeds. Steam or blanch the shells until just tender but still holding their shape. Drain well and stand in a shallow ovenproof dish.

Trim and wash the spinach then cook, with no extra water, in a covered saucepan for about 5 minutes. Drain well and squeeze dry. This can be done by pressing the spinach between two dinner plates held over a sink. Chop roughly.

Make a roux with the butter and flour and cook for 2 minutes, then gradually add the milk, stirring until smooth and thickened. Season well and add the nutmeg to taste. Simmer for 2 minutes then stir in the spinach. Spoon the spinach into the cucumber shells. Mix the crumbs, nuts and cheese and sprinkle over. The vegetables can be prepared to this stage for reheating later.

Before serving, bake at 375°F (190°C, gas mark 5) for about 20 minutes until bubbling and lightly browned.

Serves 6.   RD

91

Gratin of crunchy vegetables

GRATIN OF CRUNCHY VEGETABLES

This dish can keep warm or be reheated (microwave is best) if the vegetables are kept underdone.

*A mixture of: carrots, courgettes, celery, florence
  fennel, cauliflower and thick ends of Chinese
  leaf; about 1½ lb (750 g) altogether*

SAUCE
*½ teaspoon finely chopped ginger
1 teaspoon finely chopped shallot
2 tablespoons oil
8 fl oz (250 g) chicken or vegetable stock
2 tablespoons cornflour
2 tablespoons sherry or white wine
2 tablespoons cream
1 tablespoon light soy sauce
½ teaspoon sugar
¼ teaspoon salt
1 teaspoon chicken fat (optional)*

Keeping the vegetables separate, cut up the carrots, courgettes and celery into thumbnail-sized bits and the florence fennel into small segments; break the cauliflower into florets and cut the Chinese leaves into thick slices. Steam the vegetables until nearly cooked but still nice and crisp; fennel, celery and cauliflower take longest, followed by carrot and courgette, while Chinese leaf takes the least time. Remove each vegetable as it's done. Mix together the stock and cornflour, the sherry, cream, soy, sugar, salt and chicken fat. Heat a wok or large pan and add the oil, ginger and shallot. Toss for about 30 seconds then add the vegetables; stir-fry until glistening then stir and add the sauce. Bring to the boil, stirring, and boil until the sauce thickens before turning into a shallow gratin dish.

Serves 4.   NC

AUBERGINE DHAL

Yellow split peas, or dhals, make the basis for wonderful, quickly cooked main meals with whatever seasonal vegetables, eggs, nuts and spices you have to hand. Serve with rice or bread – preferably Indian naan or chapatis.

*8 oz (250 g) split peas
1 pint (600 ml) stock or water
2 onions, chopped
1 large bay leaf
2 teaspoons black mustard seeds
2 tablespoons oil or butter
1 clove garlic, crushed
1" (2.5 cm) cube fresh root ginger, peeled and
  grated
1 small green pepper, sliced
1 teaspoon turmeric
1 teaspoon mild curry powder or garam masala
1 medium aubergine, diced in chunks
2 large tomatoes, skinned and chopped
Salt and pepper*

TO SERVE
*2–3 hard boiled eggs, quartered
Fresh chopped coriander or parsley*

Cook the peas in the stock with one of the onions, the bay leaf and some seasoning for 25 minutes until soft.

In a separate pan, fry the mustard seeds in the

oil for about 30 seconds until they start popping, then add the remaining onion, garlic, grated ginger and pepper. Sauté gently for about 5 minutes until softened.

Sprinkle in the spices, stir up and fry for another minute, then add the remaining ingredients with a little extra water just to moisten. Season well, then simmer gently for about 10 minutes. Spoon in the split peas, reheat, then serve hot garnished with the egg quarters and coriander or parsley.

Serves 4–6.   RD

PUFFED PUMPKIN

Simple to prepare, the earthy flavour of this purée is quite delicious with plain-roasted game birds, or a joint of roast pork.

>   *2 lb (1 kg) piece pumpkin*
>   *2 oz (50 g) butter*
>   *Salt and pepper*
>   *1 level teaspoon nutmeg*
>   *2 eggs*

Peel and chunk the pumpkin. Cook it gently in a lidded pan with very little water – it has plenty of its own.

When the pumpkin is soft (it takes about the same time to cook as does potato), drain off any excess water and purée the pulp. Return it to the pan and dry it off further. Beat in the butter. Season the pumpkin purée with salt, pepper and nutmeg, and set it aside to cool for a moment.

Separate the eggs and stir the yolks into the purée. Whisk the whites and fold them in thoroughly. Butter a soufflé dish. Pour in the mixture to within two fingers' width of the top.

Bake at 350°F (180°C, gas mark 4) for 20 minutes, until the purée is puffed and golden. It will keep quite happily in a warm oven until you are ready to serve.

Serves 4–6.   EL

MARINATED VEGETABLE KEBABS

Best in summertime, cooked over charcoal on a barbecue, these could at a pinch go under the grill.

>   *1 lb (500 g) small, new potatoes*
>   *1 lb (500 g) aubergines*
>   *Salt*
>   *1 large onion*
>   *1 large red pepper*
>   *1 large yellow pepper*
>   *8 oz (250 g) firm button mushrooms*
>   *Freshly ground black pepper*
>   *2 cloves garlic, finely chopped*
>   *6 tablespoons finely chopped fresh herbs*
>   *4 fl oz (125 ml) olive oil*

Boil or steam the new potatoes in their skins until they are just cooked. Drain them and transfer to a large mixing bowl.

Cut the unpeeled aubergines into 1″ (2.5 cm) cubes. Put the cubes in a colander, salt generously, and leave to drain for half an hour. Rinse, dry and add the cubes to the potatoes.

Peel and quarter the onion and separate outside layers. If onion is very large, cut each piece in two.

Cut the red and yellow peppers into pieces about the same size as the onion segments, discarding the stalks and seeds. Add the onion and peppers to the bowl, together with the mushrooms, their stalks trimmed level with the caps.

Add salt, plenty of coarse black pepper, the garlic and herbs. Pour over all the oil and use your hands to mix thoroughly so that each vegetable piece is filmed with oil. Leave to marinate for at least two hours, but not much more than half a day.

Immediately before cooking the vegetables, thread each variety onto one or more flat-bladed skewers – mixing the onion and pepper segments if you like, as these do cook evenly together. Cook the kebabs on a charcoal grill, basting them once or twice with the marinade.

Sliding the vegetables off their skewers in straight lines onto a serving dish makes an attractive presentation.

Serves 4–6.   SCP

MUSHROOM SUPPER DISH WITH A LIGHT CREAMY CRUST

It is possible to bake fromage frais, quark or crème fraîche as a light, tangy topping but the mixture should be stabilized first with butter and beaten eggs to keep it from separating. This topping is ideal for a moussaka, or with this all-vegetable casserole.

> 1 lb (500 g) mushrooms, sliced – a mixture of cultivated and wild would be nice
> 2 clove garlic, crushed
> 2 tablespoons walnut oil or extra virgin olive oil
> 1 oz (25 g) butter
> 3 courgettes, sliced thickly
> 2 medium leeks, sliced thickly
> ½ pint (300 ml) vegetable stock
> 1–2 tablespoons flour, optional
> 1 tablespoon fresh chopped thyme or 1 teaspoon dried
> 2 tablespoons fromage frais or quark or crème fraîche
>
> TOPPING
> 1 lb (500 g) fromage frais
> 1 oz (25 g) butter, melted
> 3 eggs, beaten
> Freshly grated nutmeg
> 2 tablespoons freshly grated Parmesan
> Salt and ground black pepper

Put the mushrooms, garlic, oil and butter into a heavy-based saucepan, cover and cook for about 10 minutes, shaking the pan occasionally, until mushrooms are just cooked.

Blanch the courgettes and leeks in the vegetable or chicken stock until only just cooked – about 3–5 minutes. Strain off liquor and reserve.

Sprinkle the flour into the mushrooms (if you want a slightly thickened sauce), stir, then gradually add the reserved stock. Bring to the boil, stirring, then add the courgettes and leeks. Season and add the thyme. Cook for 2 minutes, mix in the fromage frais, quark or crème fraîche and spoon the mixture into a heatproof casserole.

Beat the topping ingredients together, except for the Parmesan, and pour over the vegetables. Sprinkle over the Parmesan, then bake at 375°F (190°C, gas mark 5) for about 30 minutes until light-golden and cooked on top.

Serves 4.   RD

YELLOW PEPPER LASAGNE

This vegetable version of a classic pasta dish is unusual and good.

Alternate layers of wholewheat and green lasagne are filled with a sweet yellow pepper sauce and topped with three cheeses.

> 1 lb (500 g) fromage blanc
> 1 egg and 1 yolk
> Salt and black pepper
> Cayenne pepper
> 4 oz (125 g) wholewheat lasagne
> 2 oz (50 g) green lasagne
> Butter
> 2 large sweet yellow peppers
> 2 large onions, peeled
> 3 large cloves garlic, peeled
> 2 large carrots, peeled
> 7 oz (200 g) mozzarella cheese
> Grated Parmesan cheese

Set fromage blanc to drain of its whey in a plastic sieve lined with muslin. After 2–3 hours, whisk the drained cheese with the egg and extra yolk and season to taste with salt, pepper, and cayenne.

Boil the wholewheat lasagne for 15 minutes in plenty of salted water; boil the green lasagne for 10 minutes. Drain pieces of pasta side by side on kitchen paper.

Butter a 9 × 2″ (23 × 5 cm) circular Pyrex dish.

Slice seeded peppers into thin strips, very thinly slice the onions, chop the garlic, and grate the carrots. Sweat all of these vegetables in butter, in a wide sauté pan, until the peppers and onions have softened; they will greatly reduce in volume. Season well.

Grate the mozzarella cheese.

Yellow pepper lasagne (right), with an inspired salad

Line the bottom and side of the Pyrex dish with a layer of wholewheat lasagne. Spread on ⅓ of the vegetables, and top with ⅓ of the fromage blanc mixture (spread this with a wet spoon). Strew with ⅓ of the mozzarella and some grated Parmesan. Cover with the green lasagne, then half each of the remaining vegetables, fromage blanc, mozzarella, and some more Parmesan. Top with wholewheat lasagne and the rest of the vegetables, fromage blanc and two cheeses.

Trim the edges with a knife and bake at 375°F (190°C, gas mark 5) for about 40 minutes, until the top bubbles and browns attractively.

Serves 4–6.   AWS

STEAMED SEA-KALE

Sea-kale, a delicate and delicious vegetable, is best steamed, since boiling dissolves the valuable salts, and lessens the flavour. In the past, sea-kale was widely cultivated for its blanched shoots, which were considered a delicacy. It has now become a rare vegetable, and in order to have a supply, the best solution is to grow it.

Allowing 4 oz (125 g) sea-kale per person, trim and wash the vegetable, then steam for about 40–45 minutes. Test occasionally with a sharp knife. When tender, serve with melted butter or hollandaise sauce.   BGM

95

VEGETABLE PAELLA

La Mazorca – The Corncob – is a 'natural foods' restaurant in Alicante whose chef, Pepa Ruiz, improvises paellas from the wide range of excellent local vegetables. This is an adaptation of Pepa's recipe, using less oil than she would.

1 small sweet red pepper
2 slim, dried mild chilli peppers; in Alicante, cooks use round dried peppers called ñoras, unavailable here – buy an alternative at Lina Stores in London W1, or use mild chillis you've dried yourself
½ large head garlic, peeled
Olive oil
Salt
4 oz (125 g) carrots, peeled weight
4 oz (125 g) courgettes
½ large onion, peeled
5 oz (150 g) tomatoes, peeled and seeded weight
4 oz (125 g) mushrooms
3 oz (75 g) slim green beans
3 oz (75 g) young, tender peas
10 oz (300 g) Spanish paella rice or Italian risotto rice
Pinch of saffron threads
Fresh rosemary and thyme
Vegetable broth and water

De-seed the sweet pepper and slice into thin strips, cut up the chillis and garlic, and sauté all with oil, using a paella pan or a large, deep frying pan, until the pepper is soft. Set the strips aside and purée the garlic, chilli, oil and some salt in a food processor. Reserve.

Roughly chop the carrots, courgettes, onion, tomatoes and mushrooms. In a little oil, sauté first the carrots, then the courgettes, until each is three-quarters cooked; set aside. Sauté the onion in oil until half done, add the tomatoes and mushrooms, and simmer until most of their liquid has gone. Reserve.

Slice the beans into short lengths, then boil these, followed by the peas, in boiling, salted water until nearly done. Reserve.

Clean the frying pan, pour in ¼″ (5 mm) depth

Clockwise from right: Steamed fresh scallops with garlic (recipe on page 39); cold tomato and sweetcorn soup (recipe on page 29); vegetable paella

of oil, add the rice and stir over a low heat for 4–5 minutes until the grains become opaque. Stir in the saffron and herbs; add everything but the beans, peas, and pepper strips, and cover with about double the ingredients' volume of broth (adding water if needed to make this up). Add salt. Bring liquid to simmer, cover and cook – without stirring – for 20 minutes (introducing beans and peas for the last 10), or until the rice has absorbed the broth and is tender, the grains still separate. Remove the lid for the last 5 minutes. Correct seasoning and serve the paella, adorned with red pepper strips.

Enough for 4. AWS

SWISS CHARD EN PAPILLOTE WITH TAHINI CREAM

Chard leaves are ideal for enclosing fillings as they have neither the strong flavour of spinach nor the chewy texture of cabbage. Basmati rice is used for the filling because of its lovely aroma, but patna is also suitable.

12 large Swiss chard leaves

FILLING
1 onion, chopped
1 clove garlic, crushed
1" (2 cm) cube fresh root ginger, grated
1 oz (25 g) butter
2 tablespoons olive oil
4 oz (125 g) basmati rice, uncooked
1 teaspoon each ground turmeric, cumin,
  fenugreek and coriander
¾ pint (450 ml) water or vegetable stock
Salt and ground black pepper
2 oz (50 g) shelled unsalted pistachio nuts
3–5 tablespoons natural yoghurt, preferably
  ewes' milk

SAUCE
6 tablespoons tahini (sesame paste)
1 clove garlic, crushed
Juice of ½ lemon
Water, to mix

Trim and chop the chard stems. Blanch the leaves until just limp and bright green. Drain and cool.

Sweat the onion, garlic, ginger and chard stems in the butter and oil for about 5 minutes. Add the rice and stir-fry until opaque, then add the spices. Fry for a further minute.

Pour in the water or stock, season well, bring to the boil, then cover and simmer gently for 15 minutes. Stir in the nuts and yoghurt.

Spread the chard leaves out and spoon the filling into the centre of each. Fold up like parcels and arrange, join sides down, on a platter. Cover and keep warm.

Blend the tahini with the garlic, lemon juice, salt and enough water to make a consistency of pouring cream. Serve the sauce separately.

Serves 6.   RD

WATERCRESS FLAN

Bacon, while adding a pleasant saltiness to the filling, could be left out when catering for vegetarians. Add an extra ounce (25 g) of walnuts and additional Parmesan to the filling instead.

8 oz (250 g) shortcrust pastry
1 oz (25 g) grated Cheddar cheese
8 oz (250 g) back bacon rashers
1 oz (25 g) butter
2 bunches watercress
4 oz (125 g) button mushrooms
6 oz (175 g) cottage cheese
2 eggs
1 oz (25 g) chopped walnuts
Salt and pepper
1 oz (25 g) grated Parmesan cheese

Work the Cheddar cheese into the pastry and line an 8" (20 cm) flan ring. Prick lightly with a fork and line with foil, and bake at 400°F (200°C, gas mark 6) for 15 minutes. Remove foil and continue baking pastry for 5 minutes. Meanwhile, chop the bacon and cook in the butter until just cooked but not coloured. Poach the watercress in a little water for 5 minutes, drain and chop. Mix the bacon and watercress and place on the base of the pastry case. Chop the mushrooms and mix with the cheese, eggs, walnuts, salt and pepper. Pour into the flan case and sprinkle with Parmesan cheese. Bake at 350°F (180°C, gas mark 4) for 35 minutes. Serve freshly baked and warm.

Serves 4–6.   MN

SPICED PARSNIP AND COCONUT FALAFELS

Little patties, traditionally made with chick peas in the Middle East.

1 lb (500 g) parsnips, peeled
1 tablespoon toasted desiccated coconut
1 tablespoon cream or yoghurt
1 oz (25 g) butter
1 egg, beaten
4 oz (125 g) fresh breadcrumbs, white or brown
1½ teaspoons mild curry powder
Salt
Ground black pepper
Sesame seeds, for coating, optional
Vegetable oil, for frying

Boil the parsnips until just tender. Cut out any tough fibres and mash the flesh. Mix with all of the remaining ingredients except seeds and oil. Taste to ensure the mixture is well seasoned. Chill until firm.

With wet hands, shape the mixture into small patties and coat in the sesame seeds.

Heat enough oil to come ½" (1 cm) up the sides of a frying pan, and fry the patties until golden brown, about 2–3 minutes on each side. Serve hot or cold.

Makes about 12.   RD

COURGETTE AND GOATS' CHEESE SOUFFLES

The creamy sweetness of courgettes combined with tangy goats' cheese is a successful liaison.

4 medium courgettes
1 shallot, finely chopped
1 clove garlic, crushed
1 oz (25 g) butter
1½ oz (40 g) flour
2 oz (50 g) creamy goats' cheese, without rind
4 tablespoons cream
2 eggs, separated
2 tablespoons fresh grated Parmesan
Salt and ground black pepper
Flaked almonds, to sprinkle

Cut the top quarter lengthwise off each courgette. They are not needed for this recipe but can be used elsewhere. Preheat the oven to 375°F (190°C, gas mark 5).

With a melon baller or teaspoon, scoop out the flesh, leaving the shells intact. Chop the flesh very finely and mix with the shallot and garlic. Season the shells.

Steam the shells for 3 minutes, or simmer in the minimum of water. Drain well, upside down.

Meanwhile, sweat the courgette mixture in the butter for 5 minutes until quite pulpy. Stir in the flour, cook for a further minute. Cut the cheese up and stir in until melted then add the cream, egg yolks, Parmesan and plenty of seasoning.

Whisk the egg whites until stiff and carefully fold in, then pile into the courgette shells.

Sprinkle with the almonds and bake for 25 minutes until risen and golden. Serve immediately.

Serves 4.   RD

POTATO AND PARSNIP AMANDINE

The flesh of baked potatoes is mixed with parsnip purée and topped with almonds (see page 91).

4 baking potatoes, about 6 oz (175 g) each
A little oil, for brushing
8 oz (250 g) parsnips, peeled and diced
1 oz (25 g) butter
2–3 tablespoons milk or cream
1 teaspoon mild curry powder
1 small onion, chopped finely
3 oz (75 g) mature Cheddar or Gruyère, grated
Salt and ground black pepper
2 egg yolks
About 1 oz (25 g) slivered almonds

Score around the middle of the potatoes with a sharp knife, then rub with a little oil. This helps keep the skins tender. Place on a baking sheet and bake at 400°F (200°C, gas mark 6) for about 1 hour, when the flesh inside should be fluffy and cooked.

Meanwhile, boil the parsnips in lightly salted water until tender. Drain and mash or purée in a food processor.

Cut the potatoes in half and carefully scoop out the flesh. Mash it well, making sure there are no lumps. (This is best done by hand, as machines can make the potato rather sticky.) Add the butter and milk or cream, then the parsnip and rest of the ingredients except the almonds. Season well.

Spoon back into the potato shells, and press on the almonds. The potatoes can be chilled at this stage (but not frozen) to be reheated later.

Return to the oven for a further 15 to 20 minutes until golden brown and piping hot.

Serves 4–8.   RD

VEGETABLE GRATIN

This gratin is a seasonal favourite, begun as a way of employing leftovers, but now made, each summer and autumn, as a succulent end in itself.

Potatoes, pumpkin and courgettes are first cooked separately, to retain individual character. The secret ingredient here is watercress, with its peppery flavour.

> 7 oz (200 g) farmhouse Cheddar
> 3 oz (75 g) stale bread of good character,
>   crusts on
> 2 medium potatoes, peeled
> 6 oz (175 g) pumpkin flesh
> Salt
> 1 lb 2 oz (550 g) courgettes
> Olive oil
> 1½ bunches watercress
> 4 large cloves garlic, peeled
> 1 egg
> Freshly ground black pepper

Cut cheese and bread into cubes – the former about ¼″ (5 mm) across, the latter somewhat larger – and put them into a roomy bowl.

Cube potatoes and pumpkin to a size roughly between those of the cubes above, and boil each, in turn, in salted water, until just cooked. Drain, cool, and add to the bowl.

Top and tail courgettes and slice them across into thin rounds; salt these, and use a wide, low-sided pan dribbled with olive oil to sauté courgettes, over high heat, until cooked and starting to colour. Cool, and add to the bowl.

Oil a 10″ (25 cm) porcelain gratin dish with a 1¼″ (3 cm) upright side.

Chop watercress leaves and mince the garlic; mix well, with the egg and plenty of seasoning, into the bowlful of ingredients.

Pile the vegetable mixture across the gratin dish, mounding it in the centre; dribble on a little olive oil, and bake the gratin at 400°F (200°C, gas mark 6) for 30 minutes until cheese has melted and the bread is deeply-coloured.

Serves 4, with a green salad (for 6–8 people, make 2 gratins). AWS

Vegetable gratin (in foreground); carrot, celery, potato and lovage soup (recipe on page 34); sole and red pepper jellies with red pepper sauce (see page 20); avocado and tongue salad (see page 105)

BEETROOT ROULADE WITH HORSERADISH

Root vegetables make particularly good roulades as there is no need for a white sauce base, which makes for greater simplicity and better flavour.

> 8 oz (250 g) raw unpeeled beetroot
> ½ teaspoon ground cumin
> 1 oz (25 g) butter
> 2 teaspoons grated onion
> Salt and ground black pepper
> 4 eggs, separated

> FILLING
> ¼ pint (150 ml) double cream, lightly whipped
> 2 teaspoons white wine vinegar
> ½ teaspoon English mustard
> 1 teaspoon sugar
> 3 tablespoons fresh chopped parsley
> 3 tablespoons horseradish relish

99

Cook the beetroot by steaming or boiling until just tender. Peel, then purée in a food processor or blender. Beat in the cumin, butter, onion and plenty of seasoning.

Line and grease a Swiss roll tin. Preheat the oven to 375°F (190°C, gas mark 5).

Beat the yolks into the beet mixture, then whisk the egg whites until stiff and carefully fold in. Spoon into the tin.

Bake for about 15 minutes until firm and springy to the touch. Turn out onto a sheet of greaseproof paper on top of a cooling rack. Carefully peel off the paper in strips and then cover with a clean tea towel until cold.

Combine all the filling ingredients and spread on the base of the roulade. Roll on the roulade up from the narrow end. (Don't fret if it cracks slightly – that shows it's nice and light.) Chill until required. It looks pretty served in slices garnished with finely-chopped beetroot, celery and flat parsley leaves.

Serves 6.   RD

BROCCOLI WITH ORANGE CREAM SAUCE

Bright green, lightly-cooked broccoli, served with a trickle of orange cream sauce.

1½–2 lb (750 g–1 kg) broccoli spears

ORANGE CREAM SAUCE
1½ oz (40 g) butter
3 fl oz (75 g) double cream
A little grated orange rind
2 tablespoons orange juice
Squeeze lemon juice
Salt and pepper

Prepare the broccoli, stripping the stems if necessary. Plunge into plenty of boiling, salted water (or steam) until cooked but still crisp. Drain and refresh with about a teacup of cold water to set the colour and arrest the cooking but not to cool too much. Drain and set in a serving dish.

Broccoli with orange cream sauce

ORANGE CREAM SAUCE
Chop up the butter and heat gently to melt. Add the cream, orange rind and juice, the lemon and seasoning and heat through, shaking the pan, until it boils and thickens (can be prepared and reheated briefly). Pour over the broccoli and serve.

Serves 4–6.   NC

BROAD BEANS A LA RONDENA

Cheap and delicious, this Spanish dish, whose name comes from the Andalusian town of Ronda, makes a perfect summer lunch.

Coarse country bread of good character is essential to mop up the juices.

2 lb (1 kg) young broad beans in their pods (or
*   1½ lbs (750 g) mature beans, podded)*
3–4 oz (75–125 g) salt-dried ham (prosciutto)
*   or bacon*
3 cloves garlic
1 large onion
6 tablespoons olive oil
Large glass of water
Small glass dry sherry or white wine
Salt and pepper

TO FINISH
1 tablespoon fresh breadcrumbs
1 tablespoon chopped parsley
2 hard-boiled eggs, shelled and sliced

Top and tail the beans, and chop them into short lengths – following the swell of each bean. Do not do this in advance, as the beans go an odd navy blue colour at the edges. Cube the ham or bacon finely. Peel and chop the onion and garlic.

Warm the oil in a casserole. Put in the onion and garlic and fry for a moment without allowing it to take colour. Add the chopped ham or bacon. Fry for a moment longer. Add the beans, sherry or wine, the water, salt and freshly-milled pepper, and bring all to the boil. Cover and stew gently for 1½ hours – this can be done in a gentle oven at 325°F (170°C, gas mark 3). Check intermittently and add water if necessary. When the beans are tender, bubble up the stew uncovered for a moment to evaporate any excess liquid.

Stir in the breadcrumbs and the parsley. Reheat, taste and add more salt and pepper if necessary. Decorate with slices of hard-boiled egg.

Serve the bean stew in soup-plates, with plenty of bread to mop up the rich juices.

Serves 4.   EL

MATUFFI

The attraction of this *polenta*, illustrated on page 53, is in the layering of the cooked maize meal – finished to a softer consistency than is usual – with the wine-laced meat sauce; when sufficiently well-seasoned, *matuffi* is a dream of a country dish.

1½ oz (40 g) dried ceps (in Italian, porcini)
1 large onion, 1 medium carrot, peeled
1 stick celery
2 large cloves garlic, peeled
3 tablespoons olive oil
1 oz (25 g) butter
10 oz (300 g) minced lean beef
8 oz (250 g) minced lean pork

Large glass of good Chianti, plus more at the end
½ pint (300 ml) home-made beef stock
1½ lb (750 g) tinned Italian plum tomatoes, weighed without their juice
Bouquet of sage, basil, bay leaf
Salt and freshly-ground black pepper
10 oz (300 g) coarse or medium-ground yellow maize meal
2½ pints (1.5 litres) cold water, plus additional boiling water
Grated Parmesan cheese

To make the sauce, rehydrate mushrooms by soaking them in hot water for 20 minutes; drain well and chop.

Chop onion, carrot, celery, and garlic; using a wide, heavy casserole, sweat these in oil and butter till vegetables have softened and onion is turning golden. Add meats and stir until the flesh has coloured. Mix in mushrooms, Chianti, stock, tomatoes (breaking these up with a wooden spoon), herbs and some salt. Bring liquid to the boil and briskly simmer the sauce, over low heat and without a lid, for 40 minutes. Taste for seasoning, adding salt and pepper and a very modest amount of Chianti. Cool the sauce and refrigerate for several days to allow its flavours to mature.

When preparing to serve the matuffi, bring salted cold water to the boil and very slowly pour in the maize meal, beating with a wooden spoon to prevent the formation of lumps. Let polenta cook over low heat for 25 minutes, stirring constantly, and periodically adding enough boiling water to keep the mixture smooth and loose but cohesive. Meanwhile, heat the meat sauce separately.

When polenta is ready, season it well and line up 4 low soup dishes. Using a very large implement, spoon into each a layer of polenta, followed by spoonfuls of sauce, followed by more porridge and another layer of sauce, until all the polenta is used. Strew well with Parmesan and eat immediately, followed by a green salad.

Serves 4.   AWS

SALADS FOR ALL SEASONS

From a simple composition of fresh leaves –
lettuce, endive, chicory, corn salad and rocket – to
substantial combinations of crisp winter
vegetables, these salads are for year-round eating

A SALAD FROM THE GOLDEN STATE

In Berkeley, across the Bay from San Francisco, Bill Fujimoto's Monterey Market is a neon-lit mad-house of superb produce – much of it organically grown – sold at rock-bottom prices.

The ebullient and knowledgeable Bill (California-born, of Japanese descent) is one of the great characters of a city not noted for the inarticulate. His discourse on the Market's three kinds of 'organic salad mix' – of which they sell 40–50 cartons a day – deftly encompasses the foggy northern coastal climate suited to growing lettuce, the criteria for a good 'mix' (based on a *mesclun* assortment of curly endive, rocket, and various small, *whole* leaves) and the characteristic local addition of Oriental or Central American greenery like *mizuna*, *shiso* or amaranthus, introduced to the state by immigrant farmers.

To make a salad, here, which is redolent of California's diversity, proceed as follows: infuse some cold-pressed, extra-virgin olive oil with chunks of peeled and bruised fresh ginger, refrigerating for two days. When ready to use, bring oil to room temperature and drain.

For each person, use some *un*-infused oil to sauté separately, till just cooked, a few peeled baby carrots; a quarter of red onion, peeled and sliced; a quarter of seeded sweet yellow pepper, unpeeled and sliced. When cooled, turn each vegetable in snipped fennel leaves and a little of the ginger oil.

Coat a mixture of small leaves – oak leaf, red chicory, curly endive, *mâche* – plus rocket and purple basil, in the gingery oil. Arrange these across plates with a tangle of vegetables, a pansy or two – and some tiny chillies just for looks; grind on black pepper and serve. AWS

FIRE-DRIED WALNUTS AND PECANS

Barbara Tropp is a native of New Jersey, author of an exhaustive volume called *The Modern Art of Chinese Cooking* (published by William Morrow), and chef-proprietor of a San Francisco restaurant named the China Moon Café, where sparkling things happen with Chinese home cooking. Unexpected ingredients like sun-dried tomatoes or baby squash meet pot-browned noodles, and these unusual crisp nuts are one of Barbara Tropp's array of Hunanese 'little dishes' that begin a meal. The recipe is adapted from Miss Tropp's book.

8 oz (250 g) plump, perfect walnut and pecan halves
2 teaspoons corn or peanut oil
¼–½ teaspoon Maldon sea salt
1½–2 tablespoons caster sugar

Right *A salad from the Golden State, with (at left) fire-dried walnuts and pecans*

Mesclun salad with warm bacon, roquefort and raspberry dressing

Cover nuts with boiling water; soak for 30 minutes. Drain, pat dry, and spread evenly on a large, heavy baking sheet lined with a triple thickness of kitchen paper.

Dry for 30 minutes in centre of a 300°F (150°C, gas mark 2) oven. Turn sheet, reduce heat to 250°F (130°C, gas mark ½), and check at 10-minute intervals. Remove nuts from oven when almost dry, with a little moisture left at the core.

Warm a wok or heavy sauté pan over moderate heat till hot. Swirl in oil, add nuts, stir with a wooden spoon till glossed with oil and warm to the touch; do not scorch.

Mix in ¼ teaspoon salt, and slowly add sugar, ½ tablespoon at a time, until you reach an agreeable sweetness. The taste should be lively and sweet, with a hint of salt; add more of this if necessary. Stir constantly while seasoning; the process takes 3–4 minutes. Salt and sugar will melt and adhere to nuts, creating a shiny crunch.

Serve hot or cold as an hors d'œuvre for 10–15 people.   AWS

MESCLUN SALAD WITH WARM BACON, ROQUEFORT AND RASPBERRY DRESSING

Bacon fat imparts the most delicious flavour to salad dressing – even better if it is accompanied by small crisp strips of lean streaky bacon and a sweet fruit vinegar like raspberry.

A mesclun is a mixed leaf salad of whatever delicious leaves are available. Gardeners can grow great quantities of rocket, purslane, spinach, sorrel and nasturtium with the greatest of ease and add these leaves to a prepared mixture of sliced endive, radicchio, crisp lettuce or whatever else happens to be in season. The sheer variety of leaves is a great talking point when entertaining – even better if you scatter the top with a selection of nasturtium, violet or hyssop flowers.

About 2 lbs (1 kg) total weight mixed prepared salad leaves
4 oz (125 g) Roquefort or other crumbly blue-veined cheese
8 oz (250 g) crustless white bread, diced
Vegetable oil, for frying
4 tablespoons walnut or virgin olive oil
8 oz (250 g) lean rinded streaky bacon, diced
2 tablespoons raspberry, cider or other fruit vinegar
1 tablespoon brandy
Ground black pepper

Mix the leaves well together. Crumble the cheese and mix this in too.

Fry the diced bread in about ¼″ (6 mm) of hot vegetable oil until crisp and golden. Drain and cool. Discard the oil and wipe the pan clean.

Heat the walnut or olive oil in the pan, then fry the diced bacon over a moderate heat until crisp but not burnt.

Stir in the vinegar and brandy, season with pepper to taste then bubble up for half a minute, scraping the pan well. Keep the dressing warm until ready to use, then pour it over the leaves and toss well with the croûtons. Eat immediately.

Serves 8.   RD

SEA-KALE AND CHICKEN SALAD

Raw sea-kale makes an excellent salad with cooked chicken and mayonnaise.

> *1 breakfast-cup diced cooked chicken breast*
> *½ cup chopped raw sea-kale*
> *½ cup mayonnaise*
> *White pepper and salt*
> *Sprigs of watercress to garnish*

Mix together the chicken, sea-kale and mayonnaise. Season to taste, and garnish with watercress.
Serves 4 as a starter. BGM

CREOLE COLESLAW

This is a lighter and spicier version of a traditional American (and British) favourite.

> *¼ each red and white cabbage, finely shredded*
> *¼ Spanish onion, sliced thinly*
> *4 tablespoons good olive oil*
> *½ bouillon cube dissolved in 3 tablespoons*
> *   boiling water*
> *3 tablespoons wine vinegar*
> *2 tablespoons fresh chopped parsley*
> *1 tablespoon fresh chopped basil*
> *1 teaspoon fresh chopped thyme*
> *Few drops hot pepper sauce (optional)*
> *Salt*
> *Freshly ground black pepper*
> *1 medium carrot, grated*
> *1 tablespoon caraway seeds, to sprinkle*

Toss the cabbage and onion in the oil and leave for an hour.

Mix the strong stock with the vinegar, herbs, pepper sauce (if using) and seasoning. Mix into the cabbage and let stand for another hour or two, to allow the flavours to blend.

Spoon into a serving bowl and sprinkle over the grated carrot and the caraway seeds.
Serves 4–6. RD

AVOCADO AND TONGUE SALAD

The blandness of avocado is an excellent foil for pickled ox tongue.

> *1¼ lb (625 g) meat from a boiled, pickled ox*
> *   tongue, well-chilled – preferably one prepared*
> *   at home according to a standard recipe*
> *6 oz (175 g) chopped walnuts*
> *9 oz (275 g) raw, tender spinach*
> *6 oz (175 g) batavia, oak-leaf or other*
> *   interesting lettuce leaves*
> *3 ripe avocados weighing 10 oz (300 g) each*
> *Juice of one lemon*
> *2 tablespoons red wine vinegar*
> *4 fl oz (125 ml) olive oil*
> *Salt*
> *Black pepper*
> *3 spring onions*
> *3 hard-boiled eggs*

Cut tongue into lardon-like pieces and place these in a large salad bowl.

Lightly toast walnuts for 10–15 minutes in a 300°F (150°C, gas mark 2) oven, cool nuts and add them to the bowl.

Stem spinach, wash with the lettuce and dry well. Use a large, sharp knife to shred both sorts of leaf across into thin strips. Add these to the bowl and toss the contents with your hands.

Halve avocados, discard stones and skins and slice flesh lengthwise into slim sections; to prevent discoloration, set aside in a bowl of water acidulated with lemon juice.

Make a vinaigrette with vinegar, olive oil, and seasoning; mince the white part of the spring onions and add to the dressing. Chop eggs and stir in two-thirds of these.

When ready to serve the salad, drain the avocado and add to the bowl. Pour on vinaigrette and carefully but thoroughly toss the contents, using your hands for best results. Strew the remaining chopped egg across the top, and present, with salad servers.

Enough for 6 as a light main course, eaten with good bread. AWS

WINTER SALADS

Good winter salads are really no more difficult than summer ones. There are not many herbs about, it is true, so for potato salad, substitute spring onion to decorate and flavour the dish. This has the advantage that onion-haters can easily pick them out. To make spring onion curls, cut the onions into short lengths, slit each one several times, leaving ½″ (1 cm) or so whole at the bottom, and put them in iced water for an hour or two, or overnight.

Beetroot salad is flavoured with toasted coriander, only a hint of vinegar and good olive oil. Buy freshly-boiled beetroot that have not been ruined with acetic acid, or boil your own. Then ball, dice or grate the beets and toss them in a dressing of eight parts mild olive oil, to one part balsamic or wine vinegar, seasoned with ground toasted coriander seeds (heat them in a small pan then grind them in a pepper grinder), salt and freshly-ground black pepper.

For a green salad with radicchio the dressing is another vinaigrette which is light on vinegar. This time the formula is eight or more parts of sunflower oil to two of walnut oil and one of wine vinegar, seasoned to taste with salt, pepper and some light French mustard. **SCP**

HOME-SPROUTED BEANS

Sprouting your own beans and seeds is very satisfying and provides a constant fresh supply of tasty and highly nutritious food, which is an excellent sandwich filling or salad ingredient.

Old beans will not sprout easily, so buy in a new supply if those you have are more than a year old. Generally speaking, beans take about 2–5 days to sprout. If yours haven't sprouted within 48 hours, they are probably too old, so discard them and start again.

Suitable beans are green or brown lentils, chick peas, mung beans, aduki beans, soya beans, haricot beans and flageolet beans. It is a good idea to sprout two or three types of beans at the same time for variety.

METHOD

First, rinse 2–3 tablespoons of beans and place in a large jar with water to cover. Cover this with cheesecloth, muslin or a clean J-Cloth, secured with an elastic band.

Leave overnight, then drain through the cloth top, refill with water through the cloth, shake gently and drain immediately. Lay the jar on its side in a shaded, fairly warm place.

Rinse and drain twice a day until the beans have sprouts at least twice their length (don't let them get too long). If you can't use them at once, then bag in polythene and store in the fridge, but use within a few days.

Use fresh sprouts for all sorts of dishes, or simply sprinkle over hot meals in the same way as grated cheese. They are excellent in salads, over pilaffs or casseroles, in stuffings and croquettes. They also make a pretty garnish. **RD**

A winter salad

TOFU AND LENTIL SPROUT SALAD

Here is a healthy salad using home-sprouted lentils tossed in a delicious honey soy dressing. It makes an excellent starter.

Tofu is made from coagulated soya milk, in a process similar to the making of cottage cheese. It is extremely nutritious, but rather bland in flavour. Smoked tofu has more character, and is now widely available from health food shops and delicatessens. Here, it is grilled before being cubed and mixed with the dressing.

8 oz (250 g) smoked tofu bean curd
Leaves of frisée or other frilly lettuce
4 oz (125 g) oyster mushrooms, sliced if large
1 carrot, sliced thinly lengthwise with a
*   vegetable peeler*
2 spring onions, chopped
4 oz (125 g) whole green beans, topped, halved
*   and blanched*
About 2–3 handfuls of freshly sprouted lentils,
*   mung or aduki beans*

DRESSING
2 tablespoons vegetable oil
1 tablespoon sesame oil
1 clove garlic, crushed
1 tablespoon fresh chopped ginger
2 oz (50 g) walnut pieces
2 tablespoons light soy sauce
1 tablespoon dry sherry (optional)
1 teaspoon clear honey
1 tablespoon wine vinegar
Salt and ground black pepper

Grill the smoked tofu until browned, then cut into bite-size cubes.

Line four salad plates with the frilly lettuce, mixing different coloured leaves if available.

Shake all the dressing ingredients together in a screw-topped jar.

Mix the salad foods together, then toss in the dressing. Pile portions onto the lettuce leaves, and serve at once.

Serves 4.   RD

Tofu and lentil sprout salad

SUMMER COLESLAW

Light summer coleslaw includes fine shreds of Chinese leaves, or any other salad greens, grated mooli (the long white radish), bean sprouts, mange-tout, watercress and grated carrot. The addition of chickpea sprouts lends an interesting texture and taste to this salad.

4 oz (125 g) small head Chinese leaves,
*   shredded*
8 oz (250 g) mooli, grated
4 oz (125 g) carrot, grated
4 oz (125 g) bean sprouts
4 oz (125 g) mangetout peas, cooked 3 minutes
*   and drained*
2 oz (50 g) chickpea sprouts
4 spring onions, finely shredded
1 bunch watercress

DRESSING
2 tablespoons herb vinegar
½ teaspoon salt
Freshly ground black pepper
2 cloves garlic, peeled and crushed
½ carton (225 g) Greek yoghurt
6 tablespoons sunflower oil

Toss all the salad ingredients together in a large bowl, reserving some of the watercress. Cover with clingfilm and chill for up to 2 hours.

Just before serving, blend vinegar, seasoning, crushed garlic and yoghurt together. Whisk in oil and pour over the salad ingredients. Toss well and spoon onto plates garnished with reserved sprigs of watercress.

Serves 4–6. SM

CALIFORNIA SHREDDED CHICKEN SALAD

The peanut butter gives the dressing a delicious Oriental flavour.

6 boneless chicken breasts, skinned
½ cucumber
2 sticks celery
3 spring onions
4 oz (125 g) mangetout, blanched
2 oz (50 g) fresh thin ribbon pasta
Sunflower oil, for frying

DRESSING
1 clove garlic, crushed
2 teaspoons grated fresh ginger
1 tablespoon smooth peanut butter
2 tablespoons fresh chopped coriander
Pinch each sugar and dry mustard powder
4 tablespoons light soy sauce
4 tablespoons rice wine vinegar
2 tablespoons sunflower oil
2 tablespoons sesame oil
Few drops Chinese hot chilli oil

Poach the chicken in light stock for 15 minutes or until cooked. Cool in the stock for an hour or two, then refrigerate. When needed, tear the chicken into chunky bite-size strips.

Slice the cucumber, not too thinly, then cut the slices into shreds. Slice the celery and onions diagonally and halve the mangetout.

Put all the dressing ingredients into a screw-top jar and shake to blend. Mix everything together in a large bowl and chill for 2 hours.

Just before serving, snip the pasta into manageable lengths and fry in hot oil until golden and crispy. Drain well and cool. Serve the salad accompanied by the crispy noodles.

Serves 6. RD

BROWN BASMATI, OLIVE AND GREEK CHEESE SALAD

Although not quite as fragrant as the refined white variety, wholegrain basmati rice still seems to have an elegance, and is delightful for a light summer salad. The fresh lemon and olive oil dressing should be added while the rice is still hot so that the flavour has time to develop.

8 oz (250 g) basmati rice, rinsed
2 tablespoons extra virgin olive oil
Juice 1 small lemon
A quarter of cucumber, halved
1 stick celery
4–6 oz (125–175 g) good black olives
6 oz (175 g) firm white Greek cheese, e.g. feta,
*   haloumi or kefalotiri*
2 tablespoons fresh chopped parsley or mint
*   (optional)*
Chicory and watercress or rocket leaves
Salt
Ground black pepper

Cook the basmati rice according to instructions on the packet. Drain and toss in the oil and lemon juice. Season lightly, especially with the salt to allow for the strong flavour of the olives and the salty Greek cheese.

Cut the cucumber and celery into slanting slices. Stone the olives and cube the cheese. Toss them into the rice when it has cooled. Mix in the herbs. Chill.

Serve on a large platter for a buffet dish, or individual plates for a starter, garnished with the chicory and cress.

Serves 4–6. RD

A salad of mixed leaves

CARROT AND TURNIP SALAD WITH CORIANDER DRESSING

Lightly blanched tender root vegetables, left to cool in a flavoursome coriander dressing, make a delicious salad accompaniment for cold meats.

12 oz (350 g) carrots, peeled and thinly sliced
8 oz (250 g) young turnips, unpeeled and thinly sliced
8 spring onions, sliced

DRESSING
3 tablespoons walnut, hazelnut or olive oil
2 tablespoons sunflower oil
2 tablespoons wine vinegar
Pinch mustard powder

2 teaspoons clear honey
3 tablespoons fresh chopped coriander
Salt and ground black pepper

Blanch or steam the vegetables for just 2 to 3 minutes, until still quite crisp. Drain and mix with the spring onions. Mix up the dressing in a screw top jar and toss into the vegetables while they are cooling. Chill lightly until ready to serve.

Serves 4.   RD

BYESSAR (MOROCCAN BROAD BEAN SALAD)

A salad-purée much like the Middle Eastern hummus, a dish of *byessar* brings tears of home-sickness to the eyes of emigrant Moroccans.

1 lb (500 g) shelled broad beans
2 cloves garlic, peeled and roughly chopped
1 teaspoon chopped marjoram
1 teaspoon powdered cumin
Salt and freshly milled pepper
¼ pint (150 ml) good olive oil

TO FINISH
2–3 spring onions
1 teaspoon paprika
½ teaspoon chilli powder
½ teaspoon powdered cumin
1 tablespoon olive oil

Put beans in a saucepan with enough salted water to cover, and simmer for 15 minutes, until tender. Place in the blender with ½ cup of their cooking liquid, garlic, marjoram, cumin, pepper and a level teaspoon of salt. Pour in enough cold water to cover beans. Add olive oil and process the mixture to a purée. Taste and adjust the seasoning.

Trim and finely chop the spring onions and stir them in. Transfer the purée to a bowl.

Mix the paprika and cumin with the olive oil, and dribble a scarlet swirl over the pale green purée.

Serve warm, with pitta bread for scooping.

Serves 4–6 as a first course.   EL

SALMON AND ASPARAGUS PINWHEEL SALAD

Although similar to a roulade, this takes a fraction of the time and looks equally attractive. Each omelette is topped with thin slices of smoked salmon and asparagus spears before it is rolled up. Cool before slicing.

> *16 spears asparagus*
> *2 beaten eggs*
> *2 tablespoons cold water*
> *Salt*
> *Fresh-milled black pepper*
> *4 thin slices smoked salmon*

> GRAVLAX DRESSING
> *2 tablespoons Dijon mustard*
> *½ teaspoon English mustard*
> *2 teaspoons caster sugar*
> *1–2 tablespoons herb vinegar*
> *6–8 tablespoons sunflower oil*
> *Salt*
> *Freshly-milled black pepper*
> *8 stems fresh dill; keep a few sprigs for garnish*
> *   and chop remainder*

Trim the ends from the asparagus spears and cook in boiling water for 4–5 minutes or until just tender. Drain well and reserve.

For the omelettes, add water and seasoning to eggs. Cook half the mixture in a lightly oiled 8″ (20 cm) frying pan on one side only, until set and golden. Cool slightly in the pan, top with salmon and four asparagus spears placed in pairs along the length of the omelette. Roll up and lift out of pan. Make second omelette in the same way.

Make the dressing by blending mustard, sugar and vinegar together, then whisking in the oil to make a creamy sauce. Add the seasoning and some chopped dill.

Allow half an omelette per person. Slice, and garnish with remaining asparagus spears, dill sprigs and sauce.

Serves 4.   SM

Beet and apple salad with two cheeses and walnuts

BEET AND APPLE SALAD WITH TWO CHEESES AND WALNUTS

There are a number of delicious beetroot salads – this one, with fresh horseradish and apple, is ideal for a light lunch.

> *About 1 lb (500 g) raw, unpeeled beetroot*
> *3 tablespoons fresh grated horseradish*
> *½ red apple, preferably Washington Red, grated*

> DRESSING
> *2 tablespoons fresh chopped chives*
> *4 tablespoons mayonnaise*
> *1 tablespoon wine vinegar*
> *1 dessertspoon whole-grain mustard*
> *Good pinch sugar*
> *Salt*
> *Fresh ground black pepper*

> TO SERVE
> *4 oz (125 g) mould-ripened goats' cheese*
> *4 oz (125 g) blue cheese, e.g. Roquefort, Stilton*
> *   or, for colour, Blue Cheshire*
> *12–16 large fresh walnuts*
> *4 fresh celery sticks*

Scrub the beetroot: do not peel or cut the skin. Boil whole in salted water until tender – about 20 minutes depending on the size. Cool in the water, then peel and grate. Stir in the horseradish and apple.

Mix the dressing ingredients together and stir into the salad. Check the seasoning. Chill.

Serve in small mounds on plates accompanied by thin slices of cheese, the walnuts and celery.

Serves 4–6.   RD

CAJUN COLD RICE

Cajun cooking is supposed to be hotter and more rustic Louisiana cooking than Creole, the food of the town folk. But the following dish is not really a simple rice salad, suggesting that the distinctions have become blurred.

8 oz (250 g) American long grain rice
1 pint (600 ml) chicken stock
3 tablespoons good olive oil
1 tablespoon wine vinegar
1 teaspoon dry mustard powder
1 clove garlic, crushed
Yolk of 1 hard-boiled egg, mashed
Pinch cayenne
¼ pint (150 ml) mayonnaise
4 tablespoons chopped green olives
2 sticks celery, sliced thinly
2 tablespoons diced dill pickle cucumber
1 small red pepper, chopped
Salt and freshly ground black pepper

TO SERVE
4–6 whole Webbs lettuce leaves
1 hard-boiled egg plus white from dressing yolk
Small tomato wedges
Fresh chopped parsley

Simmer the rice in the chicken stock in a covered saucepan for about 15 minutes, until all the stock has been absorbed.

Mix together the oil, vinegar, mustard, garlic, mashed egg yolk and cayenne, with a little seasoning, then toss into the rice as it cools. Chill in the refrigerator until needed.

Mix in the mayonnaise, chopped olives, celery, pickles and red pepper. Check the seasoning.

Serve spooned into the lettuce leaves and garnish with the chopped egg, tomato and parsley.

Serves 4–6.   RD

HOT BACON AND RAW SPINACH SALAD

Raw spinach leaves, tossed in hot dressing, with crisp bacon and croûtons, illustrated on page 87.

1 lb (500 g) washed and trimmed tender spinach
6 oz (175 g) diced streaky bacon
1 clove garlic, crushed
White wine vinegar
Pepper, salt if needed
Croûtons of fried bread

Tear spinach leaves into small pieces. Fry bacon and garlic gently until fat runs and bacon is crisp. Remove bacon, add a little vinegar to the pan, and mix with the fat. Toss the spinach in the pan, mix in with the bacon, and allow to heat but not cook. Serve with crisp croûtons.

Serves 4.   BGM

SALAD OF PUMPKIN AND MARIGOLD

The cubed, just-cooked flesh of the pumpkin or another of the firm, orange-fleshed winter squashes like Hubbard or Queensland blue, is very agreeable linked to the crunch of lettuce, Mediterranean rocket, and freshly-fried breadcrumbs. The slightly bitter petals of pot marigold complement the spice and zest of rocket, and their colour, with the squash, is wonderful.

For each person, cover a dinner plate with lettuce leaves – batavia and oak-leaf, for instance – and a moderate amount of Mediterranean rocket (its impact is strong) tossed in seasoned hazelnut or

111

walnut oil. Then plunge 5 oz (150 g) per person of pumpkin or the flesh of one other of the winter squashes – cut in ½″ (1 cm) cubes – into boiling, salted water; the squash will cook within 30–60 seconds.

Drain cubes thoroughly, place in a sauté pan coated with a heated film of the same oil as used for the lettuce, and toss pumpkin in this, on a high flame, for some 30 seconds. Add salt and a small handful of dried, home-made crumbs of wholemeal bread; toss for 30 seconds longer, and distribute squash with crumbs over lettuce. Strew pumpkin and leaves with the petals of pot marigold, grind on pepper, and serve.   AWS

PERIGORD SALAD

In the same way that the products of Normandy, like apples, cider and cream, team up so well together, so do those of the Périgord, like goats' cheese, walnuts and walnut oil. There is no doubt that walnut oil is a luxury, but the flavour it adds to certain salads, especially when it is a main course like this one, certainly justifies the expense. Once the bottle or tin has been opened, store it in the fridge, or it may go off.

Périgord salad

FOR THE SALAD
8 oz (250 g) curly endive
8 oz (250 g) radicchio
1 small head of celery
8 oz (250 g) cauliflower florets
5 oz (150 g) good quality French salami, sliced
6 oz (175 g) goats' cheese
4 oz (125 g) walnuts, roughly chopped

FOR THE DRESSING
6 tablespoons walnut oil
3 tablespoons wine vinegar
3 teaspoons Meaux mustard
A pinch of brown sugar
Salt and freshly milled black pepper

Wash and thoroughly dry the endive and radicchio. Tear roughly into pieces and place in the base of a large salad bowl. Chop the celery and break the cauliflower florets into small pieces and scatter over the endive and radicchio. Cut the salami into quarters and arrange on the top, then crumble over the goats' cheese and sprinkle with the walnuts. Cover with clingwrap and place in the fridge until the salad is required.

Blend all the ingredients for the dressing together in a screw-topped jar and shake well until thoroughly blended.

Pour over the salad just before serving and toss lightly together.

Serves 6.   JR

AMERICAN SALAD DRESSINGS

For simple green salads, American variations on a basic vinaigrette might include fresh citrus juices, chilli sauce, crushed pineapple, melted bacon fat, ground pecan nuts, often with extra quality virgin olive oil and balsamic vinegar, or Japanese rice wine vinegar.

Thicker dressings, such as those included here are based on homemade mayonnaise, with the addition of anchovies and fresh herbs, or sweet red pepper and chilli sauce.

GREEN GODDESS

A dressing inspired in the mid-1920s by William Archer's play, *The Green Goddess*, and created at San Francisco's Palace Hotel. It should be made with fresh herbs only, which rather restricts the season to the summertime.

> *½ pint (300 ml) good homemade mayonnaise*
> *4 anchovy fillets, finely chopped*
> *1 large spring onion, chopped*
> *2 tablespoons tarragon vinegar*
> *2 tablespoons fresh chopped parsley*
> *2 tablespoons fresh chopped tarragon*
> *3 tablespoons fresh chopped chives*
> *Freshly ground black pepper*

Blend everything together and serve on the day of making.

ROASTED PIMIENTO

An adaptation of Thousand Island Dressing which is in turn based on Russian Dressing.

> *1 medium red pepper*
> *½ pint (300 ml) homemade mayonnaise*
> *3–4 tablespoons sweet chilli sauce*
> *3–4 tablespoons chopped dill pickles*
> *1 chopped green pepper*
> *2 chopped hard-boiled eggs*
> *A little thin cream (optional)*

Grill the red pepper under a high heat, turning it frequently, until it blisters and chars. Peel, rinse and de-seed, then chop finely or pulverize.

Mix the pepper with the other ingredients, adding cream if it seems a little thick. Serve on the same day as making. RD

SALADE GRIBICHE

The strong flavours and contrasting textures of this salad make it interesting enough to serve as a starter. Accompany with good bread.

Salade gribiche

> *¼ cucumber, diced*
> *½ lettuce, shredded coarsely*
> *4 oz (125 g) mangetout*
> *1 stick celery, diced*
> *8 cherry tomatoes*
> *1 hard-boiled egg*
> *2 oz (50 g) Emmenthal cheese, cubed*
> *A stick of broccoli*

> SAUCE GRIBICHE
> *1 teaspoon mustard*
> *2 fl oz (50 g) wine vinegar*
> *5 fl oz (150 g) olive oil*
> *1 shallot, chopped*
> *1 teaspoon each capers and chopped gherkin*
> *Salt and pepper*

Blanch broccoli for one minute in boiling salted water. Blanch mangetout in the same way.

Pound the yolk of the hard-boiled egg to a paste, and mix with mustard and a drop of vinegar. Slowly add oil, whisking well so it emulsifies, then add vinegar and seasoning to taste. Add shallot, capers and gherkins. Pour sauce onto serving plates and arrange salad and cheese on top. Decorate with chopped egg white.

Serves 4. CB

PICKLES AND PRESERVES

A store-cupboard stocked with home-made
chutneys, syrups, jams and jellies preserves the
summer fruits and flowers and adds a distinctive
flavour to year-round cooking

SPICED VINEGAR

This recipe is suitable for pickling most vegetables,
such as onions, red cabbage, beetroot and so on.
You may add more spices, like chillies, if you like
your pickles fiery hot, but the recipe here is for
average British palates.

It is much cheaper to buy your own individual
spices loose, than to use the supermarket jars of
ready-mixed spices.

Wine vinegars make a milder pickle, and are
ideal for using with the delicate flavours of mushrooms or red peppers. Experiment with the flavoured kinds, like tarragon, garlic or cider, or add a
dash of raspberry vinegar for special flavour.

Malt vinegar, which, strictly speaking, is not
vinegar at all, as it is not made from wine, is better
for more robust and traditionally British pickles
like onions and red cabbage – the clear distilled sort
has the same strength as the dark brown malt
variety, but shows off the dark hues of colourful
vegetables like beetroot.

For every 4 pints (2.25 litres) of vinegar you
need ½ oz (15 g) black peppercorns; ¼ oz (7 g)
coriander seeds; a few crushed bay leaves; 2 whole
chillies (dried or fresh); 1″ (2.5 cm) fresh ginger,
chopped; 3 cloves garlic, halved; ½ oz (15 g) cloves;
½ oz (15 g) celery seed; ½ oz (15 g) mace flakes; ½
oz (15 g) mustard seed.

Simmer the spices with the vinegar for 15
minutes (open the window as the acrid fumes will
make your eyes water), then strain, cool and use
as directed.   AW

RASPBERRY VINEGAR

Fill a jar with fresh ripe raspberries, mash them
lightly and cover with white wine vinegar and seal.
After one month, strain off the liquid and put it into
a clean bottle with a few fresh berries. It is delicious
added to salad dressings and can also be used to
make a refreshing summer cordial – dilute one part
vinegar to five parts cold water, add a teaspoon of
sugar per glass and serve with ice cubes.   JH

HERB AND SPICE VINEGAR

1¾ pints (1 litre) red or white wine vinegar
Large handful each tarragon, basil, parsley,
*   summer savory*
4 red chilli peppers
4 cloves
20 black or white peppercorns

Mix all the ingredients together, cover and leave to
stand for four weeks. Strain, label and bottle. Another highly fragrant and spicy vinegar, which may
be varied according to the fresh herbs which are
available; the above selection gives a good balance
of flavouring.   MN

Right *Three spicy vinegars (background), with jars
of pickled eggs, piccalilli and green tomato chutney*

CITRON VINEGAR

This is a particularly delicious vinegar for mayonnaise or an oil-and-vinegar dressing.

1¾ pints (1 litre) white wine vinegar
2 lemons
2 limes
½ orange
Pinch salt
Pinch paprika

Put the vinegar into a pan. Thinly slice one of the lemons, with its peel on, and add to the pan. Grate the rinds of the other lemon, limes and orange into the pan. Add the juice from one lime, with the salt and paprika. Bring to the boil and cool completely. Put into a screw-top jar or bottle, and leave in a warm, sunny place for two weeks, before straining, bottling and labelling. **MN**

SUMMER GARDEN VINEGAR

This is a highly aromatic vinegar, easily made by the keen gardener.

5 pints (2.75 litres) red or white wine vinegar
Large handful each tarragon, scented rose petals,
  fennel, nasturtium flowers
2 garlic cloves, peeled
10 button or pickling onions, peeled
1 oz (25 g) dried elderflowers
1 large sprig thyme
3 bay leaves
3 cloves
1 oz (25 g) salt

Put all the ingredients into a large bowl. Cover with a cloth and leave to stand for four weeks. Strain, bottle and label. **MN**

FLOWER VINEGAR

1¾ pints (1 litre) white wine vinegar
2 oz (50 g) edible flowers

A selection of flowers may be used, including old-fashioned scented roses, elderflowers, thyme and marjoram flowers, violets, pinks, and the flowers of basil and garlic. Spread these on a piece of clean paper, and dry in a sunny place for two days. Put into a bottle with the vinegar and seal tightly. Leave in a warm sunny place for two weeks before straining, bottling and labelling. This vinegar has a delicate flavour which is best used with a lightly flavoured oil for salads. **MN**

STRONG GARLIC VINEGAR

1¾ pints (1 litre) red or white wine vinegar
4 large garlic cloves
2 small onions
2 bay leaves
2 sprigs tarragon
4 cloves
Large pinch each ground nutmeg and salt

Put the vinegar into a jar and add the crushed garlic and chopped onions. Add the other ingredients and seal tightly. Leave in a warm sunny place for three weeks before straining, bottling and labelling.

For 'country vinegar', omit the bay leaves, but include two elderflower heads and two large sprigs of mint. **MN**

STERILISING AND POTTING

To prevent chutneys going mouldy, it is important to sterilize the jars. Wash them thoroughly, then stand them without lids on a baking sheet in a low oven for about ½ hour.

Spoon hot mixture into them, allowing about ½" (1 cm) of headspace. Top with a waxed paper disc then seal with clear plastic covers. If you have vacuum seal jars (but not traditional screw tops), then omit the plastic film and cover with the original lids just after potting.

Chutneys and pickles with vinegar are best sealed with plastic if they are to be stored for some time as the acid eats into metal tops.   RD

Aubergine, okra and fresh coriander relish; and creole chow chow

AUBERGINE, OKRA AND FRESH CORIANDER RELISH

The perfect accompaniment to an Indian meal, and good with bread and cheese.

>   *1 lb (500 g) aubergines, cut in thick chunks*
>   *4 teaspoons salt*
>   *8 oz (250 g) okra, sliced*
>   *4 celery sticks, chopped*
>   *1 large onion, chopped*
>   *2 cloves garlic, crushed*
>   *2 pints (1.2 litres) white malt vinegar*
>   *1–2 tablespoons curry powder*
>   *1 dessertspoon ground allspice*
>   *2 tablespoons tomato purée*
>   *4 oz (125 g) soft brown sugar*
>   *2 tablespoons chopped fresh coriander leaves or 2*
>   *teaspoons ground coriander*
>   *1 teaspoon ground ginger*

Sprinkle the aubergines with salt and leave to drain in a colander overnight. Do not rinse, but pat dry with kitchen paper. Cook in a preserving pan with everything else, simmering for about 30 minutes. Pot in clean sterilized jars.

Makes about 2½ lb (1.25 kg).   RD

TOMATO AND SWEET PEPPER RELISH

Sweet red peppers are ideal for relishes, marrying well with the combinations of sweet, sour and spicy. This relish makes a delicious change to the usual drab-coloured autumn chutneys.

>   *3 lb (1.5 kg) red firm tomatoes, quartered*
>   *1 lb (500 g) onions, chopped*
>   *3 large red peppers, seeded and chopped*
>   *2 celery stalks, chopped*
>   *½ lb (250 g) raisins*
>   *1 lb (500 g) cooking apples, cored and chopped*
>   *1 lb (500 g) granulated sugar*
>   *2 oz (50 g) fresh root ginger, peeled and finely*
>   *grated*
>   *1½ pints (900 ml) cider or white malt vinegar*
>   *2 tablespoons ground cumin*
>   *1 tablespoon mustard seeds, 6 cloves, 6 allspice*
>   *berries (tied together in a small muslin bag)*

Put everything into a large preserving pan and bring to the boil. Simmer for about 1 hour until slightly pulpy and reduced, stirring occasionally.

Remove and discard bag of spices, pot in clean sterilized jars and seal.

Makes about 6 lb (2.75 kg).   RD

117

GREEN TOMATO CHUTNEY

This recipe is a perfect way to clear your windowsills of the rows of green tomatoes that have failed to ripen at the end of the season. It makes a soft, dark brown chutney, which will keep for a year or more.

> 4 lb (1.75 kg) green tomatoes
> 1 lb (500 g) onions
> 2 cooking apples
> 1 tablespoon ground allspice or 1 teaspoon each ground cinnamon, cayenne, paprika and ginger
> 2 teaspoons salt
> 2 teaspoons mustard powder
> ½ pint (300 ml) malt vinegar

Chop the onions and soften them by simmering in a few tablespoons of the vinegar while you slice the tomatoes (saving any juice), and peel, core and roughly chop the apples. When the onions are nearly soft, add all the other ingredients except the remaining vinegar. Simmer until the mixture is soft, stirring occasionally. Add the rest of the vinegar, and boil until the chutney reaches a jam-like consistency. Pour into jars and seal in the usual way before storing in a cool dry place.   AW

GOOSEBERRY CHUTNEY

Delicious with English cheese or cold meats.

> 4 lb (1.75 kg) gooseberries
> 1 lb (500 g) dark soft brown sugar
> 2 pints (1.2 litres) vinegar
> 1 lb (500 g) onions
> 1½ lb (750 g) seedless raisins
> 4 oz (125 g) mustard seeds
> 2 oz (50 g) ground allspice
> 2 teaspoons salt

Wash the berries and cut off tops and tails. Put the sugar and half the vinegar into a pan, then boil together until a thin syrup forms. Peel and chop the onions finely and add to the pan with the raisins, bruised mustard seeds, allspice and salt. Simmer for 10 minutes.

Put the remaining vinegar into a pan with the gooseberries and boil until tender. Put the two mixtures together and simmer for 1 hour until golden brown and thick, stirring occasionally. Put into hot jars and cover with vinegar-proof lids. Keep for a month before using.   MN

BREAD AND BUTTER PICKLE

A pretty pickle and simple to make. Serve with cheese, ham or sliced cold beef and, of course, bread and butter.

> 2 cucumbers, washed and sliced thinly
> 12 oz (350 g) small or button onions
> 1 large green, red or yellow pepper, seeded and sliced
> 3–4 tablespoons coarse salt

Piccalilli with bread and cheese

SPICED VINEGAR
1 pint (600 ml) cider vinegar
½ lb (250 g) granulated sugar
1 tablespoon mustard seeds, 1 teaspoon dill seeds,
    6 cloves (tied together in a muslin bag)

Place the vegetables in a colander, sprinkle with the salt and toss to incorporate. Leave to drain overnight then pat dry.

Meanwhile, boil the vinegar solution ingredients for 5 minutes. Arrange the vegetables in clean sterilized jars and pour over the vinegar. Press the vegetables down well, topping up with extra vinegar to cover by about ¼″ (6 mm). Seal and store for up to 2 weeks before using.

Makes about 3 lb (1.5 kg).   RD

PICCALILLI

If you want to serve this as a crisp pickle on the side of the plate, stick to the ingredients below. If you prefer a softer chutney to spread on sandwiches, add extra vinegar and cook the vegetables for longer. The piccalilli will keep for up to a year.

2–3 cauliflowers
1 lb (500 g) French beans
1 lb (500 g) pickling onions
Salt
5 chillies
1 oz (25 g) fresh ginger
2 pints (1.2 litres) white wine vinegar or more
2 tablespoons flour
1 tablespoon turmeric
4 tablespoons celery seeds
4–5 tablespoons mustard powder
4 oz (125 g) light muscovado sugar (optional)

Chop the cauliflowers into small pieces, trim and slice the beans, peel and halve the pickling onions. Put all these vegetables into a large china or glass bowl and leave for 24 hours, sprinkled with salt.

The next day, rinse the vegetables, drain them well and transfer to a large pan. Split the chillies, remove the seeds and chop the flesh. Peel and finely

chop the ginger. Put the chilli and ginger in the pan, add the vinegar and bring to the boil. Simmer for 5–10 minutes. Strain the vegetables, reserving the vinegar. Mix the spices with the flour in a saucepan, adding the sugar if you are using it, and gradually whisk in the hot vinegar. Simmer for 10–15 minutes until it has thickened, while you pack the vegetables into warm jars. Pour in the thickened vinegar until the vegetables are completely covered, then seal.   AW

CREOLE CHOW CHOW

Chinese migrant railroad workers in mid-nineteenth-century America are thought to be responsible for introducing their hot pickled vegetables, or chow, into American cuisine. This is a recipe from an old Creole book which has been adapted, scaled down and generally made more manageable. It's not unlike our own Indian-inspired piccalilli.

1 small cauliflower, broken in small florets
½ lb (250 g) white cabbage, shredded
1 lb (500 g) cucumber, diced
½ lb (250 g) button onions, peeled
1 green pepper, seeded and diced
2 red peppers, seeded and diced
1 lb (500 g) whole French beans
1½ lb (750 g) green tomatoes, chopped
5 tablespoons coarse salt

PICKLE
2 oz (50 g) fresh horseradish, grated
8 cloves garlic, crushed
4 oz (125 g) French mustard
¼ pint (150 ml) salad oil
4 pints (2.25 litres) cider vinegar
2 tablespoons mustard seed
6 oz (175 g) light soft brown sugar
½ oz (15 g) turmeric

Put all the vegetables into a large colander, sprinkle over the salt, stir well to mix then leave to drain for 12 hours. Stir occasionally to make sure the salt is evenly distributed.

Put all the pickle ingredients into a large pre-serving pan. Bring to the boil then simmer for 5 minutes. Add the drained vegetables (there is no need to rinse them). Stir well and bring to the boil. Simmer for 15 to 20 minutes. The vegetables should be still a little crisp.

Pot straight away in sterilized jars and seal. Store for about 2 weeks before opening.

Makes about 8 lb (4 kg).   RD

MUSHROOM KETCHUP

Before the days of commercially-bottled sauces, and powdered stocks and flavourings, this was a common concoction kept to add zest to soups and stews. If you come across a batch of dark-gilled field mushrooms, perhaps slightly battered and being offered for sale cheaply at some market stall, this is a simple way to make use of them.

> 2 lb (1 kg) dark field mushrooms
> 2½ oz (65 g) salt
> Up to ¼ pint (150 ml) wine vinegar
> 1–2½ tablespoons brandy
> 1" (2.5 cm) piece fresh ginger
> A few blades of mace
> A few black peppercorns

Wipe the mushrooms clean and put them in a glass or china dish, sprinkling them with salt. Cover and leave in a cool place for 3 days, turning occasionally and pressing the mushrooms against the side of the dish with a spoon to extract the juice. After 3 days a fair amount of liquid will have been drawn out of the mushrooms.

Place the dish in the oven at 325°F (170°C, gas mark 3) for 60 minutes, then strain the contents through a sieve, pressing hard with a spoon to extract all the juices. Throw away the mushrooms. Measure the liquid and add ¼ pint (150 ml) of vinegar and 2 tablespoons of brandy to every pint (600 ml). Pour into jars or bottles made of tough glass, and seal while still hot. Stand the jars or bottles in a pan of water and bring to a slow

Picked onions

simmer, removing them after 15 minutes. This process will stop the ketchup from fermenting.

Use sparingly in soups, casseroles, or pâtés, but remember that the ketchup contains quite a bit of salt, so don't overseason your dish.   AW

PICKLED ONIONS

These taste completely different from commercial pickled onions, being much less sharp and slightly softer. Peeling the onions is time-consuming, so try to enlist some help!

If your eyes water horribly, it may help to hold a piece of bread between your teeth.

Peel the onions, using a stainless-steel knife, trying not to nick the flesh as this will discolour later. Trim off the roots and put the whole onions into a china or glass bowl. Cover with a wet brine of 2 oz (50 g) of kitchen salt to 1 pint (600 ml) water. Leave in the brine for 36–48 hours, then drain, rinse very well and pack into jars.

Cover with the cold spiced vinegar, seal and leave for 2–4 weeks. The onions lose their texture after about 9 months.   AW

PICKLED EGGS

Once a common sight on pub counters, these traditional British pickles have now largely been superseded by packets of crisps. However, home-made pickled eggs go extremely well with cold meats or with the customary glass of bitter, and are the perfect accompaniment to winter picnics.

Take a dozen eggs and hard-boil them for 10 minutes. For easy peeling, transfer them to the sink and remove the shells under water. Meanwhile, boil up 1½–2 pints (750 ml–1.2 litres) of malt vinegar together with 1″ (2.5 cm) piece of root ginger, ¼ oz (7 g) coriander seeds and ½ oz (15 g) white peppercorns. Pack the eggs into a wide-mouthed jar, cover with the hot vinegar and add two whole chillies, then seal. The eggs are best left a couple of weeks before eating so the white is tinted brown by the vinegar. AW

MAKING JELLIES

Jellies are similar to jams, but they are made with the juice of the simmered fruit only, and the fruit itself is discarded. The juice is left to drip through a jelly bag to ensure clarity.

Choose firm, just-ripened fruit. Cut out any blemishes. Cook with the measured water in a preserving pan until soft and pulpy. Stir occasionally. Spoon into a flannel jelly bag and allow to drip through naturally until no more drips form. Do not push through as this will result in a cloudy finish. Measure the juice and allow 1 lb (500 g) of granulated sugar to each pint (600 ml) of juice.

Wash out the preserving pan and dissolve the sugar in the juice stirring occasionally until it dissolves. Bring to the boil then simmer until setting point is reached. To test for this, spoon a little onto chilled saucers. Wait for a few minutes then run your fingers over the top. If a skin forms and wrinkles, the jelly is ready.

Allow the jelly to stand for a few moments, then skim off any scum with a slotted spoon.

Pour into small hot sterilized jars, seal and label. RD

HERB JELLIES

Take advantage of an autumn glut of fresh garden herbs and surplus cooking apples, storing flavour-ful jellies to accompany winter roasts. Windfall apples can be used but cut out any bruises.

BASIC JELLY
5 lb (2.25 kg) cooking apples or crab apples
4 pints (2.25 litres) water
About 2¼ (1.35 kg) sugar
Suggested herbs – fresh basil, rosemary, thyme,
  rose geranium, lemon verbena and spearmint

Wash the apples, but do not peel or core, and cut into chunks if large. Stew gently with the water in a large preserving pan until soft and pulpy.

Strain through a jelly bag for at least 4 hours until it completely stops dripping. Complete as for 'Making Jellies' above.

ADDING THE HERBS
For clear jellies either tie up in a muslin bag and boil with the sugar, or chop and stir in after skimming.

Allow 6 to 8 tablespoons of mint or basil, or thyme and verbena – about 4 to 6 of rosemary.

Clear rosemary or thyme jellies look attractive potted with sprigs in the jars but leafy mint or basil go limp. RD

Herb jelly

121

SPICED ROWANBERRY JELLY

Berries from the Rowan tree (or Mountain Ash) make a delicious sweet-tart jelly with a delicate, palate-clearing back-bite – perfect with rich game such as venison, hare or mallard. It has a stunningly pretty colour.

2 lb (1 kg) rowanberries, stripped from the stalks
1 lb (500 g) cooking apples
1 pint (600 ml) water
About 1½ lb (750 g) granulated sugar
Strips of peel from 1 lemon
1 teaspoon cloves

Simmer the berries and apples in the water until pulpy, about 15–20 minutes. Then proceed as for 'Making Jellies' on previous page, tying the lemon strips and cloves in a muslin bag. Remove the muslin bag before potting.
Makes about 3 lb (1.5 kg). RD

GOOSEBERRY AND ELDERFLOWER JELLY

Elderflowers have a wonderful muscatel fragrance and a particular affinity with gooseberries. Happily, they are in season at the same time – around the end of May or early June.

Like gooseberry jam, this turns a delicate pink when cooked.

5 lb (2.25 kg) gooseberries, topped and tailed
2 pints (1.2 litres) water
About 2¼ lb (1.10 kg) granulated sugar
4–5 large heads elderflowers

Stew the gooseberries gently in the water until they are quite soft and pulpy, for about 15 minutes, stirring occasionally.

Complete as for 'Making Jellies' on previous page, tying the elderflowers in a muslin bag. Remove the bag then pot in small jars and seal.
Makes about 4 lb (1.75 kg). RD

ELDERBERRY JELLY

Delicious with duck as well as a sweet jam.

2½ lb (1.25 kg) elderberries
2 lb (1 kg) cooking or windfall apples, quartered
1½ pint (900 ml) water
About 2 lb (1 kg) sugar
Peel strips from 1 orange
1 stick cinnamon

Strip the elderberries from the stalks with a fork, then simmer with the apples in the water for about 20 minutes until pulpy. Proceed as for 'Making Jellies' on page 121, tying orange peel and cinnamon in a muslin bag. Remove bag before potting.
Makes about 3 lb (1.5 kg). RD

RASPBERRY JAM

This does not take long to make, it sets easily and has a lovely fresh flavour. Using 1 lb (500 g) sugar to every 1 lb (500 g) raspberries, gently mash fruit and heat until juice flows. Add warmed sugar, dissolve and bring to boil. After three minutes, test mixture; it should have reached setting point. Remove from heat, and jar immediately. Cover the jars when cold. JH

WHOLE STRAWBERRY JAM

An unusual French recipe. By spreading the cooking process over three days, the boiling time is kept to a minimum.

4 lb (1.75 kg) small just-ripe strawberries
4 lb (1.75 kg) sugar, preferably sugar with
  pectin
Juice of 1 lemon

Right *Raspberry jam with Scotch pancakes*

Left to right: Raspberry vinegar; confiture de vieux garçons; strawberry and raspberry syrup

Hull and wash the strawberries. Drain well and put them in a large bowl with layers of sugar between. Leave overnight.

The next day, put strawberries, lemon juice and sugar in a heavy pan, bring to the boil slowly and boil gently for 3 minutes. Remove from the heat and leave overnight.

The next day, boil for 6 minutes; leave overnight again. The third day boil for 7 minutes, stirring lightly to distribute the fruit. Remove scum if necessary. Pot and cover.

This method for making jam keeps the full flavour, and the strawberries remain whole.

Makes 6–7 lb (3.3–3.50 kg). BGM

LA CONFITURE DE VIEUX GARCONS (BACHELORS' JAM)

Not all bachelors are master chefs, so this delightful conserve is made without any cooking, though not without expense. It consists of just-ripe soft fruits – strawberries, raspberries or other fruits – preserved in alcohol as they ripen to perfection.

The result, after being left to mature for a month or so, is a liqueur and intoxicated fruit which may be served with ice-cream, added to fruit salads, used to flavour many luscious desserts or eaten in a small glass after a meal.

Strawberries, raspberries, other fruit in season
Alcohol, this can be eau-de-vie, brandy, rum,
even whisky
1 lb (500 g) granulated sugar to each 1 lb
(500 g) fruit

Choose just-ripe strawberries. Hull and clean them and place whole in a crock or wide-mouthed glass jar. Add the same amount of sugar. Cover with alcohol. When raspberries come into season, add them with more sugar, ensuring that they are always covered with alcohol. Add any other fruit as it comes into season; stoned cherries, apricots, or peaches. Always use the same kind of alcohol and seal very firmly between additions. Leave to mature for at least 1 month.   BGM

REDCURRANT BAR-LE-DUC

This French jam is quite delicious. Patience is needed, however, in the pricking of each currant to allow the sugar to penetrate the fruit. This prevents shrivelling and keeps the currants plump.

2 lb (1 kg) redcurrants
3 lb (1.5 kg) sugar

Remove stalks from the currants, wash and drain. Prick each one gently and put them in a preserving pan with the sugar. Leave overnight, The next day, stir and bring slowly to the boil. Boil for 3 minutes. Leave standing until a skin begins to form, stir gently to distribute the fruit, then pot in tiny jars and cover.

Fills 8–10 small jars.   BGM

ELDERBERRY SYRUP

The Swedes produce a range of fruit syrups throughout the year from a wide range of flavourful wild berries such as *lingon* or *hjortron*; elderberry syrup is equally popular, as is elderflower

champagne. The syrups are mixed with *brännvin* (vodka), with sparkling wine, or with mineral water according to taste.

2–2½ lb (1 kg) elderberry clusters
1 pint (600 ml) water
12 oz (375 g) sugar per pint (600 ml) strained
juice

Wash berries quickly and strip from the stalks with a fork. Tip into a large saucepan or preserving pan with the water, bring to the boil and simmer for about 10 minutes. Strain through a double thickness of dampened muslin draped over a bowl or through a steel sieve for about 30 minutes, pressing down a little on the pulp to help extract juices. Discard the pulp and return the strained juice to a clean saucepan. Add the sugar and heat the syrup gently until the sugar has dissolved completely. If using immediately, bring to the boil and cool before use. Otherwise, ladle the syrup into clean, warm bottles, leaving 1″ (2.5 cm) headspace before sealing by tying down corks with string, or closing clamp tops.

Place bottles in a hot water bath and process for 20 minutes at 190°F (88°C). Remove and cool. Corks may be coated with melted wax to seal and preserve syrup.

Makes about 1¾ pints (1 litre).

NOTE This method applies to all fruit/berry syrups, though quantities of sugar may vary.   SD

STRAWBERRY AND RASPBERRY SYRUP

Equal quantities of strawberries or raspberries
and caster sugar

Hull and pick over the berries. Put them in a basin, cover with sugar and leave overnight. The next day, mash the berries, rub them through a nylon sieve or liquidize and strain. Simmer juice for 10–15 minutes over a very low heat. Cool. Add the syrup to fruit salads and fruit cups, or pour over ice-cream.   BGM

BAKING BREADS AND CAKES

Here are variations on the theme of bread, with appetising additions of cheese, olives, herbs and nuts to the basic dough, as well as breakfast muffins and teatime cakes

PUMPKIN BREAD

Pumpkin has a delicate flavour that works just as well with savoury foods as with sweet ones. Used in this recipe, it makes a loaf that stays moist and does not stale too quickly.

> *1 lb (500 g) pumpkin, cooked and puréed*
> *1 lb (500 g) strong wholemeal flour*
> *2 teaspoons instant dried yeast*
> *½ teaspoon salt*
> *½ pint (300 ml) milk*
> *Beaten egg, to glaze*
> *2 tablespoons dried pumpkin seeds, roughly*
> *   chopped*

Stir the flour, yeast and salt together, then mix in the pumpkin purée and milk. Beat in the mixer or processor to make a firm dough which comes cleanly away from the sides of the bowl. If making by hand, knead well until smooth, firm and elastic. Cover with oiled clingfilm and leave to rise until doubled in volume.

Turn the dough onto a lightly floured surface, knead briefly, and break into 6 even pieces. Form each piece into a smooth ball, and place in a row in a buttered 2 lb (1 kg) loaf tin. Cover and leave until risen. Brush the top of the loaf with beaten egg and sprinkle with pumpkin seeds. Bake in a preheated oven at 400°F (200°C, gas mark 6) for about 50 minutes until the loaf sounds hollow when tapped underneath (cover the top if necessary). Turn out and leave to cool in a wire rack.   HW

PARSLEY BAPS

These have a soft crust, and being light and delicate in flavour, are particularly versatile.

> *14 oz (400 g) strong plain flour*
> *2 oz (50 g) oat bran*
> *½ teaspoon salt*
> *2 teaspoons instant dried yeast*
> *4 tablespoons chopped parsley*
> *2 oz (50 g) unsalted butter, melted*
> *½ pint (300 ml) milk*

Stir the flour, bran, salt, yeast and parsley together, then add the butter and sufficient milk to make a soft dough. Beat in a food mixer until the dough comes cleanly away from the sides of the bowl, or knead by hand to make a smooth, firm dough. Cover with oiled clingfilm and leave to rise until doubled in volume. Turn out onto a lightly floured surface, knead briefly and roll out to ¾″ (2 cm) thick. Stamp out 8 circles using a plain 3″ (7.5 cm) cutter. Place the circles on a floured baking sheet, cover with oiled clingfilm and leave to rise. Bake in a preheated oven at 400°F (200°C, gas mark 6) for about 15 minutes until well risen and golden. Dust lightly with flour mixed with oat bran.

Makes 8 baps.   HW

Right *(clockwise, from top right) parsley baps; pumpkin bread; herb spiral, page 129; potato and chive bread, page 128; neo-Georgian cheese bread, page 128*

(Clockwise, from top right) pumpkin bread, page 126;
neo-Georgian cheese bread; potato and chive bread;
parsley baps, page 126; herb spiral

NEO-GEORGIAN CHEESE BREAD

This recipe is based on a traditional Russian
Georgian bread, which was made in individual
portions resembling cheese flans and sold by street
hawkers. The quality of the cheese is important –
use a genuine Greek ewe's milk feta and a mature
Lancashire. (If the Lancashire is still young when
bought, leave in a cool place for a while to
improve.) The bread is irresistible when still warm
from the oven, but it is also delicious when cold
and ideal for casual meals and picnics, especially
accompanied by a crisp salad.

12 oz (350 g) granary flour
1½ teaspoons instant dried yeast
5–6 fl oz (150–175 ml) milk
1½ oz (40 g) unsalted butter, softened
8 oz (250 g) feta cheese, crumbled
1 lb (500 g) Lancashire cheese, crumbled
2 eggs, 1 beaten for glazing
Freshly-ground black pepper
2 tablespoons chopped parsley

Stir the flour and yeast together. Add the milk and
butter, and beat together in food mixer to form a
soft, pliable dough that comes cleanly away from
the sides of the bowl. If making by hand, bring
ingredients together and knead until soft, pliable
and elastic. Cover with oiled clingfilm and leave to
rise until doubled in volume. Mix the two cheeses
together with a fork, then work in the egg and
black pepper, followed by the parsley. Turn the
dough onto a lightly floured surface, knead briefly
and roll out to a circle 21–22″ (53–55 cm) in
diameter. Fold the dough back over the rolling-
pin, lift it carefully and place centrally over a buttered 8″ (20 cm) cake tin lined with foil, allowing
the excess dough to drape over the sides. Add the
cheese mixture, making sure it fills the tin completely. Lift the excess dough over the filling,
allowing it to fall into pleats, and twist the edges
together in the centre to form a knob. Cover
loosely with oiled clingfilm and leave to rise. Brush
with beaten egg and bake in a preheated oven at
400°F (200°C, gas mark 6) for about 40 minutes
until risen and golden. Remove loaf from tin and
cool on a wire rack. HW

POTATO AND CHIVE BREAD

This recipe produces a moist loaf: steam rather than
boil the potatoes to prevent the purée, and therefore the dough, from being too wet.

1 lb (500 g) strong plain flour
1 teaspoon instant dried yeast
½ pint (300 ml) milk
½ teaspoon salt
6 oz (175 g) potatoes, peeled and cut into small
  pieces
2 oz (50 g) soft cheese or unsalted butter
3 tablespoons chopped chives
Melted unsalted butter for glazing

Steam the potatoes over boiling salted water until
tender. Drain well, mash until smooth and beat in
cheese or butter. Mix the flour, salt and yeast

together, then add to potato mixture with sufficient milk to make a firm dough. Add the chives towards the end of mixing. Beat in a food mixer until the dough comes cleanly away from the sides of the bowl, or knead by hand to make a firm, smooth dough. Cover with oiled clingfilm and leave to rise until doubled in volume. Knead briefly, then shape to fit a buttered 2 lb (1 kg) loaf tin. Brush the top with melted unsalted butter, cover with oiled clingfilm and leave until the dough fills the tin. Bake in a preheated oven at 425°F (220°C, gas mark 7) for 40–45 minutes until golden brown. Turn out to cool on a wire rack.   HW

then roll out to a rectangle, about 8½″ × 6″ (21.5 × 15 cm). Brush the dough with melted butter, leaving a ½″ (1.25 cm) border clear on one of the long sides. Spread spinach over, keeping the border clear. Sprinkle with herbs and black pepper. Dampen the clear border, roll up like a Swiss roll and seal dough well. Brush all over with melted butter, cover with oiled clingfilm and leave until well risen. Brush the top with egg and milk glaze, sprinkle with a little Parmesan cheese, then bake in a preheated oven at 425°F (220°C, gas mark 7) for about 35–40 minutes until risen and brown. Transfer to a wire rack to cool.   HW

HERB SPIRAL

With its appetising green spiral of fresh herbs and spinach, encased in garlic-flavoured dough, this loaf is attractive when sliced and extremely moreish when eaten.

11 oz (325 g) strong plain flour
½ teaspoon salt
1½ teaspoons instant dried yeast
1 oz (25 g) unsalted butter, melted
2 garlic cloves, peeled and finely crushed
4–5 fl oz (125–150 ml) milk

FILLING
1½–2 oz (40–50 g) unsalted butter, melted
6 oz (175 g) spinach purée, cooked and well
  drained
2 tablespoons each finely chopped parsley,
  tarragon, basil, thyme, rosemary
Freshly-ground black pepper
1 egg beaten with a little milk, for glazing
Freshly-grated Parmesan cheese

Stir the flour, salt and yeast together, then add the butter, garlic and sufficient milk to form a soft, pliable dough. Beat in a food mixer until dough comes cleanly away from the sides of the bowl or knead by hand until elastic. Cover with oiled clingfilm and leave to rise until doubled in volume. Turn onto a lightly floured surface, knead briefly,

OLIVE BREAD

Most recipes for olive bread seem to be Greek and call for chopped, pitted olives. But this has strong-tasting, whole black olives, using stones and all. This bread is better cooked under a grill than baked in the oven. It goes particularly well with thinly sliced salami, or tomato salad.

4 fl oz (125 ml) milk
1 teaspoon sugar
1½ teaspoons dried yeast
1 egg, beaten
2 tablespoons olive oil
4 fl oz (125 ml) natural yoghurt
1 lb (500 g) unbleached plain white flour
½ teaspoon salt
4 oz (125 g) small black olives

Heat the milk to lukewarm, about 110°F (43°C), and mix with the sugar and yeast. Whisk the mixture and set it aside in a warm place for about 10 minutes, or until the yeast has dissolved and frothed up. Stir in the egg, oil and yoghurt.

Sift the flour and salt into a bowl, make a well in the middle and pour in the yeast mixture. Stir, gradually drawing in the flour around the well, to make a soft dough.

Turn the dough onto a floured surface and knead for about 10 minutes or until it is smooth and elastic. Form the dough into a ball and roll it in a lightly oiled bowl. Cover the bowl with a damp cloth and leave in a warm place until the dough has doubled in size.

Turn the dough onto a floured surface, punch it down and lightly knead in the olives. Divide the dough into 6 pieces and shape each into a flat circle, stretching it to a diameter of about 6″ (15 cm).

Arrange the shaped dough on lightly oiled baking sheets, cover with damp cloths and leave to rise for about 20 minutes. Just before cooking, brush the tops with milk. Place the sheets, one at a time, under a very hot preheated grill. The bread should be about 3″ (7.5 cm) from the heat. Grill the olive bread for 2 to 3 minutes on each side, or until cooked through and lightly browned. Serve either hot or warm.

Makes 6.   SCP

CORNMEAL HERB BREAD

Flecked with herbs, and flavoured with Parmesan, this bread is guaranteed to disappear as soon as it comes out of the oven.

> 3 tablespoons dried yeast
> Warm water
> 3 fl oz (90 ml) extra virgin olive oil
> 1½ lb (750 g) strong flour
> ½ lb (250 g) cornmeal
> ½ oz (15 oz) salt
> 2 oz (50 g) freshly grated Parmesan cheese
> 2 tablespoons fresh rosemary
> 2 tablespoons fresh sage

Dissolve yeast in 1¾ pints (1 litre) warm water, in the mixing bowl of an electric mixer or food processor with bread-making attachment. Leave for 10 minutes, so that the yeast can dissolve properly, then add olive oil, flour, cornmeal and salt. Mix on medium to low speed, until the dough wipes clean the sides of the bowl. Add cheese and chopped herbs and mix again until they are thoroughly incorporated.

Set aside and cover with a cloth or plastic film. Leave in a warm place until about doubled in size.

Take out of bowl and shape into 2 round loaves, then place them on a greased and cornmeal-dusted baking sheet. Brush with olive oil, score surface with a sharp knife and leave to rise again until doubled in size. Bake in a preheated oven at 375°F (190°C, gas mark 5) for 45–50 minutes.

Makes 2 loaves.   JD

PROSCIUTTO AND HAZELNUT BREAD

Parma ham, or *prosciutto*, packs a great deal of flavour into very little bulk; a little goes a long way. Here, used together with hazelnuts, prosciutto flavours an interesting bread to serve with plain first courses like artichokes and asparagus, or with cream cheeses.

> 8 oz (250 g) wholewheat flour
> 8 oz (250 g) strong white flour
> 2 teaspoons sea salt
> 2 oz (50 g) prosciutto, very finely chopped
> 2 oz (50 g) shelled hazelnuts, coarsely chopped
> ½ oz (15 g) fresh yeast or 1 teaspoon dried
> About ½ pint (300 ml) warm water
> 2 tablespoons hazelnut or olive oil

Put the flours into a large bowl. Add the salt, prosciutto and nuts and mix them lightly together.

Combine the yeast with a little of the warm water and stir. Set aside in a warm place for about 10 minutes until the yeast has dissolved and begins to froth. Combine the remaining warm water with the oil.

Add the liquids to the flour all at once and stir to form a soft dough. Turn the dough onto a floured surface and knead it lightly.

Rinse, dry and oil the bowl. Form the dough into a ball, turn it in the oiled bowl and cover with a damp cloth or plastic bag. Leave it to rise in a warm place until the dough has doubled its original bulk.

Knock the air out of the dough and knead it again lightly. Set it in a well-oiled loaf tin measuring about 10″ × 3½″ × 3″ (25 cm × 9 cm × 7.5 cm). Cover and leave to rise again until the dough has doubled in volume.

Bake in a hot oven preheated to 450°F (230°C, gas mark 8) for 15 minutes, then reduce the heat to 400°F (200°C, gas mark 6) for 15 minutes. Turn the loaf out of its tin and return it to the oven until it sounds hollow when tapped. Cool the loaf on a wire rack.

Makes 1 loaf.   SCP

COURGETTE AND ONION BREAD

This is an Italian-style savoury bread which is excellent on a picnic with cheese or salami. The leftovers are also good toasted the next day and spread with a soft cheese such a Bel Paese, Pipo Crem or even Philadelphia cream cheese.

> *12 oz (350 g) courgettes, grated*
> *Salt, to sprinkle*
> *1¼ lb (625 g) strong (bread) flour*
> *1 teaspoon salt*
> *1 sachet easy yeast*
> *3 oz (75 g) onion, finely chopped*
> *2 oz (50 g) stoned black olives, chopped*
> *½–¾ pint (300–450 ml) tepid water*
> *Olive oil, to glaze*

Layer the grated courgettes in a colander, sprinkling fairly lightly in between with salt. Leave to drain for half an hour, then rinse and pat dry with kitchen towel.

Mix the flour, teaspoon of salt and yeast in a large bowl then add the courgettes, onion and olives. Mix to a firm but still pliable dough with the water added gradually. You may not need it all.

Knead well on a floured surface for about 10 minutes. This mixture is best made by hand or kneaded by a mixer, rather than processor, otherwise the vegetable texture will be lost.

Divide the dough into 2 and either shape into ovals on a lightly greased baking sheet or place in two 1 lb (500 g) loaf tins. Glaze the tops with olive oil and leave to prove until doubled in size.

Bake at 425°F (220°C, gas mark 7) for about

Poppy seed knots

35–40 minutes, checking the tops don't burn before the bases are cooked. The bases should sound hollow when turned out and tapped. If not, return them to cook further. Turn out to cool on a wire rack to avoid the bases turning soggy.

Makes two 1 lb (500 g) loaves.   RD

POPPY SEED KNOTS

To demonstrate just how simple breadmaking can be using the new easy blend yeasts, a recipe for homemade dinner rolls that can be quickly mixed and served, freshly baked, just before a meal, whether a simple supper or special dinner.

> *1 oz (25 g) butter*
> *1½ lb (750 g) strong (bread) plain flour or a*
> *   mixture of half wholemeal and half strong*
> *   white flour*
> *1 teaspoon salt*
> *1 sachet easy yeast*
> *¾ pint (450 ml) tepid milk*
> *Beaten egg, to glaze*
> *Black poppy seeds or sesame seeds, to sprinkle*
> *   over the rolls*

131

Rub the butter into the flour and salt. Mix in the yeast. Beat in the milk and knead well for at least 10 minutes by hand or 5 minutes in a food processor or electric mixer.

Divide into 12 pieces and roll each out to a long sausage, pulling if necessary, on a lightly floured board. Tie into a knot.

Place on a lightly greased baking sheet, glaze well with egg and sprinkle with seeds. Cover loosely with lightly oiled cling film or foil and leave in a warm place until about doubled in size.

Bake at 400°F (200°C, gas mark 6) for about 15 minutes. Allow rolls to cool slightly before serving freshly baked.

Makes 12.   RD

Sourdough bread

SOURDOUGH BREAD

The technique of using sourdough dates back in America to the days of the Gold Rush, when yeast was not readily available. This recipe cheats slightly, by using yeast as a failsafe, but the flavour and texture are the same.

SOURDOUGH STARTER
1 lb (500 g) grapes, off the stem
Warm water
12 oz (350 g) plain white flour

BREAD
5 tablespoons warm water
2 sachets active dry yeast
½ pint (300 ml) starter (see above)
10 tablespoons warm water
1 lb 1 oz (525 g) strong white flour, unbleached
1 tablespoon salt
1 egg white

To make the starter, mash the grapes thoroughly to release the juice. Place in a covered container at room temperature for 48 hours.

Strain the fermented juice from the pulp. Add enough warm water to make 1 pint (600 ml), stir in flour and replace cover. Leave at room temperature overnight. The starter is then ready to use, or it can

be kept for longer if required. Add 1 pint (600 ml) warm water and then 12 oz (350 g) flour daily if starter is to be kept at room temperature. If it is to be refrigerated, add the water and flour twice weekly.

When starter is ready, make the bread. Pour 5 tablespoons warm water into a bowl. Sprinkle the dried yeast onto the water and set aside.

Pour ½ pint (300 ml) sourdough starter into a mixing bowl, then add 10 tablespoons warm water. Add 6 oz (175 g) of bread flour and mix, either in a food processor with a bread-making attachment, or by hand, until the dough foams (about 2 minutes), then add the yeast mixture. Mix thoroughly until blended, add remaining flour and salt and mix again.

Take the dough out of the bowl and knead on a lightly floured work surface until dough becomes smooth and elastic. This takes about 10 minutes. Place dough in a lightly greased bowl and cover with a damp cloth. Put bowl in a warm place, and leave until doubled in size.

Place dough back on the lightly floured surface and form into a round loaf. Place loaf on a baking sheet greased and dusted with maize meal. Allow to rise in a warm place covered with a damp cloth until doubled in size.

Heat the oven to 450°F (230°C, gas mark 8).

Bring about 2 pints (1.2 litres) water to the boil. Brush risen loaf with beaten egg white and score it across the top with a sharp knife. Place loaf in hot oven, with a baking tin of boiling water placed on the shelf below for 10 minutes or until the loaf begins to take colour. Then remove the water, turn the oven down to 375°F (190°C, gas mark 5) and bake loaf for another 35–45 minutes, or until it is well browned.

Makes 1 loaf.   JD

GREEK EASTER BREADS

These traditional Easter sweet dough breads are ideal for breakfast or mid-morning breaks. By preparing the rolls the night before, and leaving them to prove for the second time overnight in the refrigerator, they can be ready to bake first thing in the morning.

They look pretty (and very Greek) with coloured or hand-painted eggs nestling in the centre, and are best eaten the same day they are baked.

1 lb (500 g) strong (bread) flour
1 teaspoon ground cinnamon
2 oz (50 g) caster sugar
1 sachet easy yeast
2 oz (50 g) butter, melted
2 tablespoons clear honey
2 teaspoons almond essence
4 fl oz (125 m) tepid milk
2 eggs, beaten
Extra beaten egg, to glaze
2 oz (50 g) flaked or nibbed almonds, to sprinkle
Extra warmed honey, to glaze

Sift the flour and cinnamon into a bowl or food processor. Mix in the sugar and yeast.

Mix together the butter, honey, essence, milk and eggs, then beat into the dry ingredients. Knead for about 10 minutes by hand or 5 minutes by machine until you have a smooth, pliable but firm dough. Cover with lightly greased cling film and leave to rise until doubled in size. This may take longer than usual with the extra fat and sugar.

Knock back and divide into about 12 portions. Make two long rolls with each portion, pulling and rolling as necessary on a lightly floured board.

Twist the two rolls together then curl into a circle, sealing the ends with some beaten egg. Stand on a lightly greased baking sheet. Glaze all over with beaten egg and sprinkle over the nuts. Repeat with the remaining dough until you have 12 circlets. Cover the dough lightly with greased cling film and leave to prove and rise again.

Bake at 400°F (200°C, gas mark 6) for about 15 minutes, until cooked. Remove and cool. While the breads are cooling, brush or trickle over some extra honey.

Makes about 12.   RD

Greek Easter breads

133

BRIOCHE LOAVES

Home-made brioche baked in long narrow loaves is an excellent freezer standby if you like brioche toasted – for breakfast, or with potted shrimps, or with *foie gras*. The recipe makes two loaves.

> 2 tablespoons water
> 2 teaspoons sugar
> ½ oz (15 g) fresh yeast or 1 scant teaspoon
>   granulated dried yeast
> 1 lb (500 g) strong white bread flour
> 1 teaspoon salt
> 6 large eggs, lightly beaten
> 8 oz (250 g) lightly salted butter, softened
> 1 egg yolk beaten with 2 tablespoons water to
>   glaze

Heat the water to lukewarm (about 43°C, 110°F) and add a pinch of sugar and the yeast. Whisk and set aside in a warm place for about five minutes, or until the yeast has dissolved and frothed up.

Sift the flour, salt and remaining sugar into a warm bowl. Make a well in the centre and add the beaten eggs and the yeast mixture. Using your hand or a wooden spoon, incorporate the flour into the liquid to make a well-blended dough. Add the butter and work it in thoroughly with your hands. At this stage the dough is so soft it appears completely unworkable but it will calm down a bit during its two rising periods.

Cover the bowl with a damp cloth or plastic wrap and leave it to rise for at least two hours, probably longer, until it is light and airy.

Knock the air out of the dough and transfer it to a clean bowl. Cover it again and chill overnight. The dough will rise again very slowly and it is this slow rising which gives the brioche its distinctive fine texture.

Brush two loaf-tins generously with melted butter and set them on a baking sheet. Turn the dough on to a lightly-floured surface and knead it briefly with well-floured hands. Don't worry if it is still too soft to knead properly. Divide the dough into two pieces and shape them to fit the tins. Drop the dough into the tins, cover them and leave the loaves to rise until they have at least doubled in volume – by the time the brioche is baked it will probably have tripled its size, so pick tins which are on the big side.

Brush the tops of the loaves with egg glaze and bake them in a preheated moderately hot oven (400°F, 200°C, gas mark 6) for 30 to 35 minutes. Rest the loaves in their tins for five minutes before turning on to a wire rack to cool.   SCP

OLIVE OIL BREADSTICKS

Delicious to nibble with drinks, or as an accompaniment for soups, these are best served as soon as they have cooled.

> 1 oz (25 g) dried yeast
> Warm water
> 3 fl oz (90 ml) extra virgin olive oil
> 1½ lb (750 g) strong bread flour
> ¾ oz (20 g) salt
> Sesame or poppy seeds

Dissolve yeast in 14 fl oz (400 ml) warm water in the mixing bowl of the food processor. Leave to stand for 10 minutes. Add oil, flour and salt, and mix on medium speed with bread-making attachment until dough has elasticity and leaves the sides of the mixing bowl cleanly.

Leave the dough to rest in a warm place for 20 minutes. Divide the dough in half, and shape into oblong loaves 12″ (30 cm) long. Oil the underside of 2 baking sheets and place the loaves on these. Brush with olive oil and cover with plastic film. Leave to prove for about 1 hour. Remove the plastic wrap and brush with more olive oil. Cover the loaves generously with sesame or poppy seeds.

Starting at the end of each loaf, cut slices of dough approximately 1″ (2.5 cm) wide and gently stretch them to double their length. This is most easily done on a greased baking sheet. Place sticks about 1″ (2.5 cm) apart on a greased baking sheet. Do not prove again, but bake immediately in a moderately hot oven (400°F, 200°C, gas mark 6) for approximately 10–12 minutes or until brown.

Makes about 40 sticks.   JD

BLUEBERRY MUFFINS

The classic American breakfast muffin.

> 5 oz (150 g) unsalted butter
> 4 oz (125 g) sugar
> 2 fl oz (60 ml) milk
> 12 oz (350 g) plain flour
> 1 tablespoon baking powder
> 1 teaspoon salt
> 4 large eggs
> 1 lb (500 g) blueberries (blackcurrant can be substituted)

Pre-heat oven to 400°F (200°C, gas mark 6). Line a bun tin with paper baking-cups.

Combine the butter and sugar in the food processor and blend until light and creamy. Add the milk slowly to the creamed butter, mixing at medium-low speed.

Sift together the flour, baking powder and salt. With mixer at low speed, stir in one egg, then a quarter of the flour mixture. Stop the mixer and scrape down the sides of the bowl. Repeat three or more times until all the eggs and flour have been incorporated into the batter. Mix at medium-low speed until the mixture is completely smooth.

Pour 2 tablespoons of batter in each paper cup and top with 1 tablespoon of blueberries, or blackcurrants if using. Turn the oven down to 375°F (190°C, gas mark 5) and bake muffins until the tops are golden brown and the centres spring back when lightly touched.

NOTE Frozen blueberries or blackcurrants can be used if fresh ones are unobtainable. Do not defrost them before use.

Makes 24 muffins. JD

Blueberry muffins

PUMPKIN AND PECAN MUFFINS

Ingredients can be prepared at night, the dry and the wet ready for mixing in the morning.

> 8 oz (250 g) plain flour
> ½ teaspoon salt
> 2 teaspoons baking powder
> 2 teaspoons mixed spice
> Grated rind 1 small orange
> 2 oz (50 g) light soft brown sugar
> 3 oz (75 g) pecan nuts, chopped
> 2 eggs
> 1–2 oz (25–50 g) butter, melted
> 4 fl oz (125 ml) milk
> 6 oz (175 g) fresh or canned pumpkin purée

Sift the dry ingredients into a large bowl. Lightly grease a 12-section deep muffin or bun tin. Mix the eggs, butter, milk and pumpkin together.

Lightly and quickly blend the two lots of ingredients together with a fork. It doesn't matter if a few small lumps of flour remain. Don't overmix or the muffins will be tough.

Spoon immediately into the tins, filling to about two thirds. Bake at 400°F (200°C, gas mark 6), for about 25 minutes. Allow to stand for a minute or two before turning out.

Makes 10–12. RD

BANANA CAKE

This rich American cake serves as a sumptuous dessert, with ice-cream on the side.

4 oz (125 g) butter
12 oz (350 g) sugar
2 eggs, beaten
10 oz (300 g) plain flour
½ teaspoon baking powder
1 teaspoon bicarbonate of soda
½ teaspoon salt
5 tablespoons buttermilk
1 teaspoon vanilla essence
3 large ripe bananas, puréed
4 oz (125 g) chopped pecan nuts

BUTTERCREAM ICING
8 oz (250 g) salted butter
12 oz (350 g) icing sugar
1 tablespoon vanilla essence
1 egg white

Cream butter and sugar together thoroughly, then add beaten eggs. Sift dry ingredients, and add alternately with buttermilk, vanilla and banana purée to the butter, sugar and eggs, beating vigorously for 3 minutes after all ingredients have been incorporated, until mixture is light and fluffy. Stir in the pecans, and pour into a 10″ (25 cm) cake tin, which has been greased and floured. Bake for 30–40 minutes at 350°F (180°C, gas mark 4).

To make icing, cream butter and sugar together, add vanilla and egg white, and beat until fluffy. When cake is cool, cover with icing.

Makes one 10″ (25 cm) cake.   RD

PORTUGUESE CHRISTMAS CAKE

Bôlo rei, meaning king's cake, is a traditional Christmas recipe from Portugal combining a plain, nutty bread with a sweet, rich topping of glazed dried and glacé fruits.

1 oz (25 g) fresh yeast
3 oz (75 g) caster sugar
2 fl oz (60 ml) milk
12 oz (350 g) plain flour
2 oz (50 g) chopped hazelnuts
1 oz (25 g) sultanas
Grated zest of 1 orange
3 egg whites
2 egg yolks
2 fl oz (60 ml) port
1 tablespoon melted butter

TOPPING
Icing sugar
6 tablespoons warm apricot jam
A selection of dried and glacé fruits, e.g. cherries, angelica, dried peaches, apricots, pears
1 oz (25 g) whole hazelnuts

Prepare a leaven by mixing the yeast, one teaspoon of caster sugar and three tablespoons of the milk together in a bowl. Set it aside in a warm place to become frothy. This will take about half an hour.

Mix together the flour, caster sugar, chopped hazelnuts, sultanas and orange zest in a large bowl. Make a well in the centre of this dry mixture and set it aside.

When the leaven has risen, whisk together the egg whites and yolks till they are light and fluffy. Add the port, the remainder of the milk and the melted butter to the eggs. Pour the egg mixture into the well in the flour mixture and add the raised leaven. Mix well with the hands to form a firm dough. Knead and then place the dough evenly in a greased and floured 9″ (23 cm) ring mould. Set this aside to rise in a warm place for about 1½ hours.

When the dough has risen, dust the top with icing sugar and bake at 400°F (200°C, gas mark 6) for about 35 minutes. The cake is cooked when a skewer inserted into the middle comes out clean.

Cool the cake thoroughly on a wire rack and then brush the whole surface of the cake with 2 tablespoons of warm apricot jam. Decorate the top heavily with the dried and glacé fruits and the whole hazelnuts and then glaze the fruit with the remainder of the apricot jam. Store in an airtight container as it dries out rather quickly.   MJ

Clockwise, from top: kerstkrans, page 138; Portuguese Christmas cake; love cake

LOVE CAKE

An interesting recipe from Sri Lanka, spiced cashew nut cake or love cake probably dates back to the Dutch colonisation of the island in the seventeenth century. Readily available ingredients such as cashew nuts and spices are used to create an adaptation of a traditional European cake. Today love cake is still made in Sri Lanka by the descendants of those early Dutch settlers, but the origins of its name remain a mystery.

7 eggs, separated
1 lb (500 g) caster sugar

14 oz (400 g) raw cashew nuts, finely chopped
8 oz (250 g) semolina
½ teaspoon ground cinnamon
½ teaspoon ground nutmeg
½ teaspoon ground cardamom
¼ teaspoon ground cloves
2 tablespoons clear honey
1 tablespoon sweet sherry
Grated zest of 1 lemon

DECORATION
Toasted cashew nuts
Glacé cherries
Clear honey

Line an 11″ (28 cm) round cake tin with a double thickness of greaseproof paper. Brush the inside with melted butter.

Whisk egg yolks and caster sugar together until light and fluffy. Fold in the cashew nuts, semolina, spices, honey, rose water, sherry and lemon zest.

Whisk the egg whites until they form stiff peaks and fold these into the mixture. Pour into the baking tin and bake at 350°F (180°C, gas mark 4) for approximately 1 hour and 10 minutes. When cooked, the cake should be nicely browned and a skewer inserted into the middle should come out slightly moist.

Cool the cake thoroughly in the tin, then turn out and remove greaseproof paper. Decorate the top of the cake with toasted cashew nuts and glacé cherries. Dribble some honey over the nuts to create a glaze. MJ

KERSTKRANS

As a complete departure from fruit cake, try this Dutch Christmas pastry, *kerstkrans* (or Christmas crown, illustrated on page 137), which is a delicious and easily prepared combination of almond paste, ground hazelnuts and glacé cherries.

4 oz (125 g) hazelnuts
8 oz (250 g) glacé cherries
12 oz (350 g) almond paste
2 eggs
1 teaspoon lemon juice
1 lb (500 g) puff pastry
1 teaspoon milk

DECORATION
Glacé icing made with 6 oz (175 g) icing sugar,
  one tablespoon cold water and ¼ teaspoon
  lemon juice
Flaked, browned almonds
Halved glacé cherries
Angelica leaves

Prepare the almond filling by placing the hazelnuts and glacé cherries in a food processor and blending till the mixture is fairly fine. Add the almond paste cut into small pieces and process again until the ingredients are thoroughly mixed. Lastly, add one egg and the lemon juice and process again till a thick paste is achieved. Set aside.

Roll out the puff pastry on a floured surface to form a 34″ (86 cm) × 7″ (18 cm) strip. Trim to neaten the edges.

Place the almond filling in a narrow strip along the length of the pastry, leaving about 2″ (5 cm) at either end. Dampen the edges of the pastry with cold water, fold the two ends in on top of the almond filling, and then carefully seal the long edges over each other to form a long, narrow roll.

Place the pastry roll, seam side down, on a baking sheet lined with greaseproof paper. Dampen the two ends and bring them together to form a neat ring. Brush the pastry ring with one beaten egg and the milk. Bake in a hot oven, 425°F (220°C, gas mark 7), for 15 minutes and then reduce heat to 400°F (200°C, gas mark 6) for a further 20 minutes. At the end of this time, the pastry should be nicely brown and slightly risen.

Cool the ring on a wire rack and then decorate the top with glacé icing, cherries, angelica and browned almonds. MJ

SIMPLE SAVARIN

Using easy blend yeast, a savarin ring is not difficult to make, and makes a splendid dessert, filled with soft fruits and served with cream.

6 oz (175 g) strong (bread) flour
1 teaspoon salt
3 oz (75 g) softened butter (plus extra for
  greasing)
1 tablespoon caster sugar
Grated rind of 1 small lemon
1 sachet easy yeast
3 eggs (size 3), beaten
3–4 tablespoons tepid milk

SYRUP
2 oz (50 g) caster sugar
2 tablespoons clear honey
3 fl oz (100 ml) water
2 tablespoons kirsch or white rum

FILLING
3 tablespoons warmed apricot jam
1 lb (500 g) mixed soft fruits, e.g. strawberries,
raspberries, cherries, grapes and kiwi
Extra kirsch or rum, optional

Simple savarin and rum baba

Rub a 9" (23 cm) savarin ring mould thoroughly with butter, then dust lightly with flour. It is essential that the tin is well prepared if the savarin is to turn out successfully. If you are using a new tin, make sure it is thoroughly seasoned.

Rub the butter into the flour and salt, then stir in the sugar, lemon rind and yeast. Beat the eggs with the milk and mix well into the flour, beating until it is very smooth – about 10 minutes by hand or 5 by machine. Cover and leave until doubled in size. This may take time as the mixture is rich.

Knock the dough back and knead again, then place into the ring mould, levelling with the back of a spoon. The mould may look a little uneven, but it will level out on cooking. Leave to prove again until about three quarters of the way up the sides.

Bake at 400°F (200°C, gas mark 6) for 15–20 minutes until browned on top and cooked underneath. Cool slightly, then loosen the edges and turn out. Cool completely but return the savarin to the tin for the soaking.

Simmer the sugar, honey and water together for 5 minutes. Add the kirsch or rum, then slowly pour around and into the savarin. Allow it to soak well in before turning the ring out again, onto a large plate.

Brush all over with the warm jam and fill with the fruit, which may be tossed in some more kirsch or rum beforehand. Serve chilled with whipped or pouring cream.

Makes one savarin to serve 6.

NOTE The same mixture, with 2 oz (50 g) of currants added, can be used to fill about 6 rum baba moulds. Bake for just 10–15 minutes, soak in the same syrup, and fill with cream.   RD

DUCK'S EGG SPONGE WITH APPLE AND MARMALADE FILLING

Ducks' eggs make marvellous whisked sponges, as one gets the richness without the high animal fat. Because egg sizes vary, it's best not to specify exact measurements but balance up the sugar and flour to suit the egg weight. Apples and oranges are combined with cream cheese for the filling.

3 ducks' eggs
Their weight in plain flour, sifted, and the same
weight in caster sugar
Grated rind of one large orange

FILLING
2 cooking apples, peeled
Juice of 1 orange
2 oz (50 g) caster sugar
4 oz (125 g) cream or curd cheese
2–3 tablespoons orange jelly marmalade

TO DECORATE
Icing sugar
A few jonquil flowers
Some strips of blanched orange rind

Grease an 8–9″ (20–22 cm) ring spring tin and line the base with greaseproof paper. Preheat the oven to 325°F (170°C, gas mark 3).

Whisk the eggs in a large, clean bowl either by an electric hand machine on a high setting (but not in a food processor), or by hand over a pan of gently simmering water, until the foam holds its shape leaving a trail when drawn back on itself.

Now, gradually sprinkle in the flour and grated orange rind, and fold in gently until incorporated. Spoon into the prepared tin and bake for 50–60 minutes, until the sponge is firm and springy to touch.

Leave to cool partially in the tin, then turn out onto plate and allow to cool completely. Peel off the paper.

Meanwhile, cook the apples with the orange juice until pulpy. Sweeten to taste, cool and mix with the cheese. Split the cake in two, spread each side with marmalade and fill with the apple cream. Sandwich together, dust with icing sugar, and decorate with the flowers and orange rind strips.

Serves 6–8.   RD

Walnut cake

Sieve the flour. Separate the egg yolks from the whites. Mix together flour, sugar, egg yolks, baking powder, melted butter and Grand Marnier. Beat egg whites until stiff, and gently fold in to the mixture. Add ground nuts. Butter a 2 lb (1 kg) loaf tin, and pour in the mixture.

Bake for about 45 minutes at 375°F (190°C, gas mark 5), until the cake is a pale golden colour and cooked through.

Makes one loaf.   MJS

WALNUT CAKE

One of the gastronomic legacies left by the Moorish occupation of Spain is the Spanish predilection for nuts. Almonds are much favoured, especially in Andalusia, and are used in both savoury and sweet dishes. This recipe for walnut cake, *bizcocho de nueces*, comes from the region of Valencia.

7 oz (200 g) walnuts, crushed lightly
7 oz (200 g) sugar
3½ oz (100 g) butter
3½ oz (100 g) plain flour
1 teaspoon baking powder
4 eggs
2 tablespoons Grand Marnier

CHOCOLATE FONDANT CAKE

For those who dislike fruit cakes, this is a wickedly rich chocolate cake, mousse-like in consistency and an ideal alternative to either Christmas cake or Christmas pudding.

It is an easy recipe, bound to please any lover of chocolate, but, once cooked, it needs to be left for three days to set in the refrigerator so must be made in advance.

8 oz (250 g) plain chocolate
8 oz (250 g) caster sugar
4 tablespoons strong black coffee

8 oz (250 g) unsalted butter, cut into small
  pieces
4 eggs, lightly beaten
1 tablespoon plain flour

CHOCOLATE MARZIPAN
3 oz (75 g) plain chocolate, melted
4 oz (125 g) marzipan

CHOCOLATE GLAZE
4 oz (125 g) plain chocolate
2 oz (50 g) unsalted butter
3 tablespoons water

DECORATION
Chocolate flakes
Chocolate leaves
Icing sugar

Melt the chocolate, sugar and coffee in a bowl over a pan of hot water. When melted, remove the mixture from the heat and allow to cool slightly. Add the small pieces of butter, stirring well to dissolve after each addition. Add the eggs and mix thoroughly. Lastly, beat in the flour. Line an 8″ (20 cm) *moule à manqué* tin with aluminium foil, allowing it to come up higher than the sides of the tin. Brush the foil with melted butter and pour in the cake mixture.

Cook in a *bain-marie* on top of the cooker for 45 minutes. Do not allow the water to boil; just simmer very gently.

Remove the cake from the *bain-marie* and finish baking it in a very cool oven, 275°F (135°C, gas mark 1), for half an hour. Cool the cake in the tin and then refrigerate the cake, still in its tin, for three days (it appears uncooked even after baking, but sets when chilled).

After three days have elapsed, the cake may be finished. Melt the plain chocolate in a bowl set over a pan of simmering water. Prepare the chocolate marzipan by mixing the marzipan with the melted chocolate in a food processor until well combined. Roll into a ball and chill in the refrigerator for about 15 minutes.

Meanwhile, carefully turn the cake out onto a serving dish and remove the aluminium foil. Roll out the chocolate marzipan on a surface lightly dusted with icing sugar, and form it into a circle the size of the top of the cake. Lay the marzipan circle on top of the cake.

Make the chocolate glaze by stirring all the ingredients in a bowl over a pan of hot water till dissolved. Cool slightly, then pour over the cake so that it is completely and evenly covered.

Just before the chocolate glaze is completely set, decorate the top of the cake with flaked chocolate (which can be made by running the blade of a sharp knife over a block of chocolate) and some chocolate leaves.

The latter can be made by dipping the underside of rose leaves in melted chocolate and then peeling them off carefully when the chocolate has set (chocolate leaves are also available, ready-made, from good supermarkets). Dust the top of the cake lightly with icing sugar.

To serve, cut the cake with a sharp knife which has been first run under hot water and then wiped dry. Store cake in the refrigerator.   MJ

Chocolate fondant cake

SNACKS AND SAVOURIES

Celeriac crisps, savoury peanut brittle and
Yarmouth straws are irresistible with pre-dinner
drinks, while after-dinner savouries include
devils-on-horseback and anchovy tartlets

ANCHOVY TARTLETS

A hot and salty snack for late night nibbling.

½ recipe for cheese sablé dough (see page 150)
¼ pint (150 ml) double cream
1 teaspoon anchovy essence
Cayenne pepper
6 anchovy fillets

Roll out the cheese sablé dough, cut into rounds
and line 12–18 small tartlet tins. Prick the bases
lightly with a fork and bake at 375°F (190°C, gas
mark 5) for 7 minutes. Whip the cream to stiff
peaks and flavour with anchovy essence and cayenne pepper. Cut the anchovy fillets into thin
strips. Spoon the cream into the pastry cases and
top with a lattice of anchovy pieces. Return to the
oven for 3–4 minutes. Serve very hot.

Serves 6. MN

YARMOUTH STRAWS

An after-dinner savoury which could be served at
any time, these are really cheese straws with a
filling of kipper fillet as an added dimension.

8 oz (250 g) shortcrust pastry
8 oz (250 g) kipper fillets
1 oz (25 g) grated Parmesan cheese
1 egg

Roll out the pastry thinly into two 3″ (7.5 cm) wide
strips. Grill the kipper fillets, remove the skin and
any bones, and mash the flesh. Spread the kipper on
one piece of pastry and sprinkle with half the
cheese. Brush a little beaten egg round the edge of
the pastry and top with the second piece, pressing
the edges together lightly. Brush with the remaining beaten egg and sprinkle with cheese. Cut into
¾″ (1.75 cm) strips. Place on a lightly greased
baking sheet and bake at 350°F (180°C, gas mark 4)
for 12 minutes. Serve hot.

Serves 6. MN

BLUE CHEESE CRISPS

These little cheese and walnut biscuits are delicious
with pre-dinner drinks.

4 oz (125 g) self-raising flour
4 oz (125 g) butter
2 oz (50 g) blue cheese
2 oz (50 g) mature Cheddar cheese
Salt and pepper
2 oz (50 g) finely chopped walnuts

Right *(clockwise from top) cooked marrow bones;
Camembert cheese (deep-fried, in centre); devils on
horseback, page 144; Yarmouth straws; anchovy
tartlets; blue cheese crisps; various cheeses*

Sieve the flour into a bowl and rub in the butter until the mixture resembles fine breadcrumbs. Crumble in the blue cheese. Grate the Cheddar cheese finely, and add to the flour with plenty of salt and pepper. Mix well to form a dough. Chill for 30 minutes.

Roll the dough into about 30 balls, and roll each ball in the chopped walnuts. Place on lightly greased baking trays, and press out lightly with a fork dipped in cold water. Bake at 400°F (200°C, gas mark 6) for 10 minutes. Leave on the baking sheets for about 5 minutes and lift carefully onto a wire rack to cool. Store in an airtight tin.

Makes about 30.   MN

MILLE-FEUILLE OF BRIE

This dish is equally good as a starter, or as an after-dinner savoury, served with grapes.

7 oz (200 g) puff pastry
5 oz (150 g) Brie cheese
2 oz (50 g) butter
2 oz (50 g) Greek yoghurt
1 oz (25 g) hazelnuts

Roll out the puff pastry into a rectangle about 12 × 6" (30 × 15 cm) and bake in a hot oven at 450°F (230°C, gas mark 8) for 25 minutes until brown. Remove and leave to cool.

Place the Brie and butter in the food processor and blend to a thick paste. Add the yoghurt and process again just enough to mix. Season well.

Roast the hazelnuts. Keep some whole for decoration, and chop the rest.

Add half of the chopped nuts to the cheese mixture, and keep the rest for decoration.

When the pastry is cool, cut it into three rectangles about 4" (10 cm) wide. Separate each piece horizontally into two layers, and use the cheese mixture to sandwich between the layers, keeping some to cover the top. Smooth the top well, and trim the edges of the mille-feuilles. Cut into portions and decorate with the rest of the nuts.

Serves 6.   CB

Eggs stuffed with prawns and crabmeat

DEVILS ON HORSEBACK

The classic after-dinner savoury, illustrated on page 143, which can double as a hot canapé.

12 large plump prunes
12 blanched almonds
6 rashers streaky bacon
3 medium slices white bread
Oil for frying

Soak the prunes until they swell (about 2 hours), then drain. Carefully remove the stones and replace with an almond. Derind the bacon rashers, cut each one in half, and smooth out thinly with a broad-bladed knife. Wrap a piece round each prune, securing with a cocktail stick. Put under a hot grill, turning once, until the bacon is crisp.

While the 'devils' are cooking, cut 4 circles of bread from each slice, using a pastry cutter. Fry the circles until crisp and golden. Put a prune on each piece of bread and serve 2 to each person as a savoury.

Serves 6.   MN

EGGS STUFFED WITH PRAWNS AND CRABMEAT

The recipe for these tiny stuffed eggs comes from Thailand, where they are known as *khai kwan*, or 'precious eggs'.

2 dozen quails' eggs, boiled for 3 minutes

STUFFING
8 oz (250 g) large uncooked prawns, shelled
4 oz (125 g) cooked crabmeat (white meat only)
1 tablespoon chopped coriander leaf
2 cloves garlic, chopped
Freshly ground black pepper
1/2 teaspoon salt
1 tablespoon Thai fish sauce (nam pla)
4–5 tablespoons thick coconut milk or single cream

BATTER
3 oz (75 g) plain flour
6 fl oz (175 ml) warm water
1 tablespoon vegetable oil
1/4 teaspoon salt

Peel and halve the eggs. Scrape out the yolks, set aside the halves, and put the yolks in a bowl.

Chop or mince the prawns, and mix them with all the other stuffing ingredients, except the coconut milk or cream. Add this mixture to the yolks in the bowl, and mix well with a fork. Add the coconut milk or cream, incorporating a spoonful at a time, until the mixture is well blended and moist. You may find you need less than 5 tablespoons of the cream.

Divide the filling into 48 equal portions and put one portion into each half egg white, piling up the filling and shaping it so that you end up with the shape of a whole quail's egg.

To make the batter, put the flour, water, oil and salt in a bowl, and beat until smooth. Dip each of the stuffed eggs in the batter and deep-fry in hot oil (350°F, 180°C) for about 3 minutes or until golden brown, keeping the filling downwards while frying. Take them out with a slotted spoon and drain on absorbent paper.

Serve hot or cold as a starter on a bed of lettuce dressed lightly with *nam chim* (Thai sweet-and-sour chilli sauce), or use *nam chim* as a dip if the *khai kwan* are handed around as an appetizer with drinks.
Makes 48.   SO

TINY TEA EGGS

This is a novelty appetizer which you can serve at a drinks party or as the start of a home-cooked Chinese meal. Hand them round on a salver with a small dish of ground Szechuan red peppercorns mixed with sea salt for dipping into.

12 quails' eggs, hard-boiled and unpeeled
1 pint (600 ml) black tea (try smoky lapsang souchong or the stronger keemun)
1 tablespoon soy or oyster sauce
1 star anise
Good pinch salt

With a teaspoon, tap the shells all over to craze them. Put in a saucepan with the rest of the ingredients and bring to the boil. Simmer gently for 15 minutes, checking that the liquid doesn't boil dry. Remove with a slotted spoon and when cool enough to handle, peel.

Serve warm, if possible.   SO

EGGS PRINCESS

If quails' eggs are fresh – i.e. not near their sell-by date, so they don't spread out when cooked – and fried in very hot fat or oil, they make pretty, round frilly shapes.

Then they can be popped onto any flat contrasting morsel – toasted croûtes, rounds of buttered bread, baked open-cup mushrooms, small lettuce leaves and so on. The following is just one idea. Another would be to spread toasted rounds of French bread with *tapénade*, and top each with a fried quail's egg.

12 small size leaves of crisp round lettuce
12 thin slices small good salami, e.g. Italian or
*   Hungarian*
12 quails' eggs, broken into egg-cups (this can be
*   done in batches)*
1 oz (25 g) butter
1 tablespoon sunflower or olive oil
Ground black pepper

First, spread out the lettuce leaves on a platter and top each with a slice of skinned salami.

When ready to serve, heat the butter and oil until quite hot in a large frying pan and fry the eggs quickly. The fat should be hot enough to make the whites go frilly round the edge.

Scoop out onto the salami, grind over some pepper and hand round as soon as possible. Your guests can fold up the lettuce leaves slightly to eat all at one go. Don't bite into the yolk or it might dribble onto your chin.

Makes 12 bite-size servings.   RD

QUAILS' EGG AND VINEGAR BACON TARTLETS

The perfect party snack, these can be prepared ahead and assembled quickly at the last minute.

6 oz (175 g) plain flour
Good pinch cayenne pepper
3 oz (90 g) butter or margarine
1 oz (25 g) freshly grated Parmesan cheese

FILLING
1 lb (500 g) sweetcure streaky bacon, de-rinded
*   and chopped*
1 teaspoon French mustard
1 tablespoon raspberry vinegar
3 tablespoons fromage frais
1 spring onion, chopped
12 quails' eggs

Make the pastry first by rubbing the flour, cayenne and fat together then mixing in the Parmesan cheese and combining with enough cold water to make a firm dough.

Roll out thinly and use to line 12 tartlet cases, re-rolling if necessary. Prick the bases lightly, and chill for 20 minutes while you preheat the oven to 400°F (200°C, gas mark 6).

Bake the cases for 12–15 minutes until crisp, then cool and remove. These can be stored in an airtight tin for a few days until needed.

To make the filling, preheat a heavy-based frying pan until quite hot. Add the chopped bacon and stir well, then turn down to a medium heat, stirring occasionally until the fat runs and the bacon crisps up.

Pour off as much fat as possible. Mix the mustard and vinegar and pour into the pan, stirring. Cook until nearly evaporated. Off the heat, blend in the fromage frais until creamy, add the spring onion then spoon into the tartlet cases. If liked, the filling can be cooked ahead to this stage and then reheated gently when required in a warm oven just before serving.

Wipe out the pan, add 3 tablespoons sunflower oil or a good ounce of butter and break the quails' eggs into egg-cups in batches. Fry for about a minute and scoop out on top of the bacon.

Alternatively, hard-boil the eggs, peel and halve then place 2 halves on each bacon-filled tart. Eat them as soon as possible.

Makes 12 tartlets.   RD

PROSTINNANS SILL

This delicious Swedish herring snack is known as the Vicar's wife's favourite.

2 double fillets of Majtes or salt herring (soak
*   salt herring in cold water for 2 hours)*
1 small knob of butter
3 or 4 young, tender leeks, washed and trimmed
1 tablespoon or so of unsalted butter
3 freshly hard-boiled eggs, still warm (or boil
*   and shell in advance, then warm in hot water*
*   just before incorporating)*
¼ pint (150 ml) thick cream, stiffly whipped

Prostinnans sill, served with sour cream

Chop herring fillets (well drained, if appropriate) into neat, bite-sized pieces and warm gently in the knob of butter. Shred the leeks very finely and melt (do not brown) in the tablespoon of butter in a separate pan – this may take about 10 minutes. Dice the shelled eggs finely, and combine quickly with the hot herring and leek – a warm mixing bowl is desirable. Finally, fold in the whipped cream deftly, and pile the warm mixture immediately onto rounds of buttered, dark, soft rye bread, small crispbreads, or the larger-size 'Rahms' ready-made croustade shells, which may be heated and crisped in the oven.

Makes 18–24.   SD

CELERIAC CRISPS

Served hot, these make the perfect partner for roasted poultry, pork or winter game. Left to cool they are good with drinks.

1 large celeriac bulb
Vegetable oil to a depth of several inches for
   deep-frying

Peel the celeriac bulb and slice it into rounds, as thin as possible. Drop the slices into a bowl of cold water acidulated with a tablespoon or two of lemon juice or vinegar.

147

Heat the oil in a deep pan. Drain the celeriac and dry thoroughly on both sides with paper towels. When the oil is hot, drop some slices into the fat and cook for about 5 minutes, until they turn brown and crisp. Watch carefully: when they begin to colour they brown rapidly. Do not crowd them in the pot but deep-fry them in batches.

Remove the cooked slices with a slotted spoon, allowing excess oil to drip back into the pan. Drain them in one layer on paper towels and salt lightly. Serve the celeriac crisps while still hot with roasted poultry, pork or winter game.

Serves 4.   ER

BACON-FILLED PIRAGI

Rich or time-consuming yeast-raised doughs invariably have a festive air – and aroma – about them. No Latvian festivity, winter or summer, would be complete without trays full of *piragi* – savoury, bread-dough and smoked bacon rolls. Occasionally they would accompany bowls of light soup in the manner of Russian *pirozhki*, but they are most often encountered as the ideal party snack, whether served hot or cold.

Bacon-filled piragi

Other fillings exist, based on savoury fish, cabbage or soft cheese mixtures, but this is undoubtedly the most popular.

> *½ lb (250 g) smoked pork in the form of speck,
> pancetta or poitrine fumée (this could well be
> a piece of meat already used to flavour a
> casserole or sauerkraut)*
> *½ lb (250 g) streaky bacon – could be green if
> pork is well smoked*
> *1 medium onion, peeled and finely chopped*
> *½ teaspoon freshly-grated nutmeg*
> *Freshly-ground black pepper*
> *Additional pinch of salt if required*

> YEAST DOUGH
> *1 tablespoon dried yeast, or 1 oz (25 g) fresh
> yeast*
> *2 tablespoons warm water*
> *1 teaspoon sugar, if using dried yeast*
> *8 fl oz (250 ml) milk*
> *2½ oz (65 g) unsalted butter*
> *1 lb (500 g) strong, plain unbleached flour*
> *1 teaspoon salt*
> *2 tablespoons thick, soured cream*
> *1 egg, beaten*
> *Additional egg, beaten with 2 tablespoons water
> to form egg-wash*

Finely dice the pork and bacon. Fry gently in an ungreased pan until the fat runs (if pork has seen casserole-use, fry bacon first). Remove the meat from the pan with a slotted spoon and gently soften the onion in the bacon-fat. Remove when soft, and add, with 1 tablespoon of the rendered fat, to the drained meat. Add nutmeg, pepper to taste, and a little salt if the meat was not very salty. Set the mixture aside to cool while preparing the dough – chilling in the refrigerator will make for easier mounding of the filling.

Cream the yeast with the water (and sugar, if using dried yeast) and set aside for 10 minutes until activated. Scald the milk and butter in a saucepan, then cool to blood temperature. Sift the flour and salt into a warm mixing bowl, and form a well in the centre. Pour milk-and-butter, soured cream and egg into the well and gradually incorporate liquids into flour with a wooden spoon, or the dough hook of a food-mixer. Once amalgamated, leave the dough to rest 10 minutes, then turn out onto a floured surface and knead vigorously for 10 minutes (or continue with the mixer dough-hook) until the dough feels elastic.

Place in a greased bowl, cover, and set aside in a warm place to prove and rise until double the original volume (about 1½ hours).

Knock back the dough, knead briefly, then roll and stretch the dough on a floured surface to form a large rectangle (about 15″ × 22″/40 × 55 cm). Facing the shorter side of the rectangle, make 8 rows of 4 or 5 small mounds of filling, starting 1″ (2.5 cm) from the edge. Fold the dough-edge nearest you over the first row and filling, and using a 2″ (5 cm) round pastry cutter or rim of a glass, cut out a semi-circle round each dough-covered mound. Ensure edges are well sealed before transferring to a greased baking sheet. Neaten the pastry rectangle edge roughly, retaining trimmings, and repeat the procedure until you have formed 40 or 48 piragi. If you have sufficient dough trimmings and fillings, re-knead and roll out the dough and make some more pastries.

Piragi may be bent round in a crescent shape before baking, if wished. Arrange piragi on greased baking trays, ensuring they are not touching, and brush lightly with egg-wash. Leave to rise a further 10 minutes while the oven is heating. Bake at a fairly hot temperature (400°F, 200°C, gas mark 6) for 10–12 minutes, until golden-brown. Serve hot, warm or cold.

Makes 40–48.

NOTE The same dough may be used to make another traditional savoury yeast pastry from Latvia – ķimeņmaizītes, or caraway rolls. Small portions of the risen dough are formed into balls the size of a large marble, and placed on greased baking sheets. Make a deep indentation into each by pushing a thumb firmly into the centre of each ball of dough. Brush with egg-wash as before, then press a small piece of unsalted butter (about ¼ teaspoon) into the indentations, and sprinkle generously with caraway seeds.

Bake for 8–10 minutes in a hot oven, and serve either hot or cold.   SD

Turkish cheese boreks

TURKISH CHEESE BOREKS

Best served while still warm, these crisp, cigar-shaped filo pastry rolls are excellent with pre-dinner drinks, as part of a *mezze*.

> *1 lb (500 g) feta cheese, crumbled*
> *1 egg yolk*
> *Freshly-chopped mint*
> *1 egg white, lightly beaten*
> *1 packet of filo pastry*

Mix the cheese with parsley to taste, and add yolk of egg to mixture.

Cut a double layer of filo pastry into rectangles about 9 × 5″ (23 × 13 cm) working quickly and keeping extra pastry under a damp teacloth to prevent it drying out. Put a sausage-shaped layer of cheese filling diagonally across the corner of each rectangle, and starting from that corner, roll the pastry up diagonally, folding the sides as you go, to make a neat parcel shaped like a cigar, and using the egg white to stick the pastry together.

Deep fry in hot oil until crisp and brown, drain on kitchen paper, and serve.

Makes about 30 boreks.   VJ

CHEESE SABLES WITH MUSTARD CREAM

These rich cheese shortbreads make good appetizers, and may be served as plain biscuits or with this mustard cream filling.

6 oz (175 g) plain flour
¼ teaspoon salt
Pinch mustard powder
6 oz (175 g) butter
6 oz (175 g) mature Cheddar cheese
¼ pint (150 ml) double cream
3 teaspoons wholegrain mustard

Sieve the flour, salt and mustard powder into a bowl. Rub in the butter until the mixture resembles fine breadcrumbs. Grate the cheese finely into the bowl, then mix and press together to make a soft dough. Wrap in foil and chill for 1 hour.

Roll out thinly on a floured board (the dough is rather fragile) and cut into 2″ (5 cm) rounds. Place on ungreased baking sheets and bake at 375°F (190°C, gas mark 5) for 12 minutes, until golden. Leave on the baking sheets for 5 minutes and lift carefully onto a wire rack to cool. Store in an airtight tin.

To serve, whip the cream to soft peaks and fold in the mustard until evenly coloured. Sandwich pairs of biscuits with this filling.

Makes about 24.   MN

CURRIED HOT NUTS

Very quick to make, with no cooking skill required, these mixed nuts just need to be reheated for a few minutes in the oven before nibbling.

2 tablespoons sunflower oil
1 teaspoon curry paste
1 lb (500 g) mixed, unsalted nuts (blanched almonds, shelled hazelnuts, pecans, Brazils and unsalted cashews)
½ teaspoon garlic salt
Fine sea salt or crushed rock salt, to sprinkle

Heat the oil in a saucepan and cook out the curry paste for a few seconds. Stir in the mixed nuts and garlic salt.

Fry gently until the nuts are lightly cooked but not too browned. Sprinkle over the salt and serve warm. They can be reheated.

Serves 4–6 as a savoury.   RD

POTTED CHEESE WITH WALNUTS

These make unusual gifts, covered with large cellophane jam pot covers, and secured with elastic bands which can then be disguised with pretty, thin ribbon.

6 oz (175 g) mature red Leicester, Cheshire or Cheddar cheese, grated
2 oz (50 g) freshly grated Parmesan cheese
2 oz (50 g) butter, softened
1 tablespoon chopped chives, or spring onion tops
½ teaspoon ground mace
2–3 oz (50–75 g) roughly chopped walnuts
Capers and small sprigs of rosemary or thyme, to garnish
Ground black pepper

Blend the cheeses and butter until smooth, then stir in the chives or onion, mace, nuts and pepper.

Divide between four ramekins, swirl the tops attractively, and garnish with the capers and herbs.

Chill until ready to give away, or serve with toast.

Makes 4.   RD

SAVOURY PEANUT BRITTLE

These Indonesian snacks, *rempeyek kacang*, are delicious any time, but go particularly well with drinks: pre-dinner or cocktail party.

To achieve the right crispy brittle texture, they are fried first in the frying-pan, then in the wok.

Potted cheese with walnuts (left) and curried hot nuts

4 oz (125 g) fine rice powder
8 fl oz (240 ml) cold water
2 kemiri (candlenuts)
1 garlic clove, peeled
1 teaspoon salt
2 teaspoons ground coriander seed
5 oz (150 g) shelled peanuts (halved if large)
Vegetable oil for frying

Sift the rice powder into a deep bowl. Liquidize the candlenuts and garlic using half of the water and pour this into the rice powder. Add the salt and ground coriander and the remaining water. Mix well, and add the halved peanuts.

Heat 8 fl oz (240 ml) of oil in a non-stick frying-pan. Take up a tablespoon of the batter with some nuts in it, and pour it quickly into the frying-pan. You can do 5–6 spoonfuls at a time; fry these for about 2 minutes. Then remove them from the pan with a slotted spoon and put them to drain on a plate lined with paper towels. Repeat this until all the batter is used up.

Pour the remaining oil from the frying-pan into a wok, adding about 2 more cupfuls, and heat this oil to 350°F/180°C. Fry the half-cooked rempeyek, perhaps 8 or 10 at a time, in the hot oil for 2 minutes until golden brown, turning them several times. Drain and leave to cool.   SO

DEVILLED MUSHROOMS

Quickly made from everyday ingredients, these are a welcome treat at any time of day.

1 lb (500 g) medium-sized flat mushrooms
4 oz (125 g) butter
½ pint (300 ml) double cream
2 teaspoons Worcestershire sauce
1 teaspoon wholegrain mustard
Fingers of dry toast

Wipe the mushrooms but do not wash them. Leave them whole and fry in butter until just tender. Drain off surplus liquid and place the mushrooms in a shallow ovenware dish. Season the cream with sauce and mustard, and pour over the mushrooms. Put under a medium grill until very hot and bubbling. Serve the mushrooms at once with fingers of hot dry toast.

Serves 4–6.   MN

DEVILLED SARDINES

A storecupboard savoury for after dinner.

12 sardines canned in oil
3 medium slices white bread
½ oz (15 g) butter
½ oz (15 g) plain flour
2 teaspoons anchovy essence
1 teaspoon Worcestershire sauce
¼ pint (150 ml) chicken stock
½ teaspoon lemon juice
2 tablespoons single cream
Watercress or parsley sprigs

Bone the sardines and re-form the fish. Toast the bread, remove crusts and cut each slice into four strips. Place in a single layer in a shallow ovenware dish. Place a sardine on each one and sprinkle with a little of the oil from the can. Heat in the oven at 350°F (180°C, gas mark 4) for 5 minutes.

Meanwhile, melt the butter in a small pan. Work in the flour and cook for 30 seconds, stirring

well. Add the anchovy essence, sauce and stock, and stir over a low heat until thick and creamy. Stir in the lemon juice and the cream. Pour over the sardines and heat in the oven for 2 minutes. Serve at once garnished with watercress and parsley.

Serves 6.   MN

GOURMANDISES GRUYEROISES

This is based on a Valais peasant dish described in *Cooking with Pomiane* (Bruno Cassirer, 1962).

2 small tomatoes, or 1 medium
2 oz (50 g) grated Gruyère
2 rashers unsmoked streaky bacon, cut in half, rind and bone removed
2 thickish slices wholemeal bread – such as Poilane's sourdough
Dijon mustard

Gourmandises gruyeroises

Remove skin and pips from tomatoes and lightly chop the flesh. Toast one side of each slice of bread.

Spread untoasted sides generously with mustard. Pile mixture of cheese and tomato firmly on to the mustardy side of the slices, pressing gently and taking care that it comes right to the crust all of the way round.

Grill until cheese goes golden. Lay two half rashers on each slice and grill until starting to brown. Dust lightly with freshly ground pepper, and serve.

Serves 1 or 2. HDM

DARK AND WHITE CHOCOLATE COLETTES

For those who enjoy fresh Belgian chocolates, these little chocolate cases filled with a ganache of white chocolate are an attractive alternative. They do take a little time to make, but are not difficult. You could offer them as presents, nestling on small china plates, when flowers or wine seem inappropriate. They are always well received.

5 oz (150 g) bar dark chocolate (such as Sainsbury's Deluxe Chocolate for Cooking)
A little grated dark chocolate, optional

FILLING
24 large seedless raisins
3 tablespoons white rum
7 oz (200 g) white chocolate
7–8 tablespoons double cream
3 oz (75 g) unsalted butter
2 egg yolks

Break up the dark chocolate and put into a heatproof bowl. Melt slowly over a pan of gently simmering water. Do not allow to overheat or the chocolate will 'seize' and go lumpy. If you have a microwave oven, heat for 2–2½ minutes on full, depending on the wattage, then stir until smooth.

Using a teaspoon, line about 24 petit four paper cases with the chocolate, about half a spoon at a time and spreading it around with the tip of the spoon. Leave to reset on a cooling tray, then very carefully peel the cases off, if you like, although they can be left on.

Put the raisins into a small saucepan with 2 tablespoons of the rum. Heat gently then leave to cool.

Meanwhile, melt the white chocolate with the cream and butter in the same way, over a gentle heat or in the microwave oven. Stir in the remaining spoon of rum and the egg yolks. Allow to cool until thickened, then beat until smooth and the consistency of thick mayonnaise. Spoon into a nylon piping bag fitted with a ½″ (12 mm) star nozzle.

Put a rum-soaked raisin into each case, then pipe a whorl of the white chocolate ganache on top. Sprinkle with a little grated chocolate if liked. Leave in the fridge until ready to give away.

Makes about 24. RD

HAZELNUT AND COFFEE CLOUDS

Although not strictly speaking sweets or savouries, these little, crisp meringues nevertheless are greatly enjoyed at the end of a meal with coffee.

They can be made in advance and stored in an airtight container.

2 egg whites
4 oz (125 g) caster sugar
1½ oz (40 g) ground roasted hazelnuts
2 teaspoons coffee essence

Whisk the egg whites until forming stiff peaks, then gradually whisk in the caster sugar until you have a stiff and glossy mixture. Fold in the ground nuts and essence.

Pipe in small stars or spoon in small mounds onto a baking sheet lined with greased greaseproof, Bakewell or rice paper.

Bake at 300°F (150°C, gas mark 2) for about 25 minutes, or until crisp. Remove with a palette knife onto a cooling tray.

Makes about 24. RD

153

MOVEABLE FEASTS

Chilled soups and salads, a cold galantine, salmon
in a pastry case and home-made brioche have all
the makings of a perfect picnic. With cake and
fruit to follow, here is a sensational outdoor feast

GALANTINETTE

A boned, stuffed bird is certainly good cause for
compliments at a picnic, but the average home
cook requires much time struggling to bone the
bird neatly in the first place.

However, this simpler version should draw
equally admiring gasps of delight.

  18 back rashers of bacon, derinded
  1½ lb (750 g) turkey breast fillets, sliced
  3 tablespoons dry sherry
  1 lb (500 g) stewing pork, minced
  ½ lb (250 g) chicken livers, finely chopped
  1 onion, chopped
  2 cloves garlic, crushed
  3 oz (75 g) butter, melted
  3 tablespoons brandy
  1 teaspoon thyme
  2 oz (50 g) pistachios or 20 stuffed olives
  3 oz (75 g) fresh white breadcrumbs
  3 tablespoons fresh chopped parsley

Place a large sheet of foil on baking sheet and
lightly grease. Lay the bacon rashers in two lines
with the 'oyster' ends meeting in the middle. Overlap the slices very slightly.

Toss the fillets in the sherry and lay them on
top in a long line down the centre. Season well.

Mix everything else together, season well and
spoon on top of the fillets.

Draw the outer edges of the rashers up and
over the filling and press well down. Wrap over the
foil, sealing the ends well.

Bake at 350°F (180°C, gas mark 4) for about
1¼ hours. Allow to cool and chill in the foil.
Unwrap, remove any jelly or meat residue (use
these in the courgette soup, page 158, if liked) and
cut into slices. Overwrap in cling film to stop the
galantinette turning brown in the air.

Serves 8–10.   RD

SPICED CARROT SALAD

This is a good portable vegetable salad as it can be
dressed in advance without turning limp.

Serve it with small wedges of Little Gem
lettuces, as they hold their shape and can be easily
eaten with fingers.

  1 lb (500 g) carrots, grated
  2–3 oz (50–75 g) raisins
  2 oz (50 g) flaked or slivered almonds, toasted
  ¼ pint (150 ml) well-flavoured vinaigrette
  1 teaspoon ground cumin
  Salt and pepper

Simply toss everything together and store in a well-
sealed picnic container until required. Can be made
the night before, but not frozen.

Serves 6.   RD

Right Galantinette, with spiced carrot salad

RARE LAMB SALAD WITH HAZELNUT DRESSING

This is a particularly good mixture of flavours, colours and textures, and needs only simple accompaniments such as the courgette and tomato salad and new potatoes, or crusty bread and fingers of crisp Little Gem lettuces.

> 2 lb (1 kg) lean rolled leg or shoulder of lamb
> 3 tablespoons hazelnut oil
> 4 oz (125 g) shelled hazelnuts, lightly toasted
> 1 medium onion, ideally red, sliced thinly
> 4 oz (125 g) thin green beans, tailed, halved and
>   lightly cooked
> Salt and ground black pepper

Season the lamb lightly, then roast at 375°F (190°C, gas mark 5) for about 45–50 minutes. Cool, then cut into thin slices and then shreds. Mix in a bowl with the oil and nuts, and check the seasoning.

Meanwhile, soak the onion slices in cold water for about 2 hours. Mix with the lamb and nuts, and the cooked beans. Cover and chill for a further two hours then cover ready for transporting.

Serves 6–8.   RD

COURGETTE AND TOMATO SHREDDED SALAD

This simple salad makes a light, refreshing accompaniment to the rare lamb salad with hazelnut dressing described above.

> 1 lb (500 g) courgettes
> 8 oz (250 g) firm tomatoes
> Juice of 1 small lemon
> Salt and ground black pepper

Trim the courgettes (don't peel them), then grate coarsely into a large bowl. Dip the tomatoes briefly into a bowl of boiling water, then peel and skin. Cut into quarters, remove the seeds then slice the flesh. Mix this into the courgettes with the lemon

juice and seasoning to taste. Chill the salad thoroughly before packing into a rigid picnic container for easy transportation.

Serves 6.   RD

FRESH BITTER LEMON CRUSH

A light and refreshing drink.

Chop 3 lemons and a small orange into chunks, then blend in a food processor or liquidizer until pulpy. Add icing sugar to taste and either some sprigs of lemon balm or mint, or a few shakes of Angostura Bitters. Strain through a sieve, rubbing well with a ladle. When you've squeezed as much juice as possible from the pulp, discard it. Transport the juice concentrated, ready to dilute with sparkling mineral water.   RD

SALMON NELSON

This is the fish equivalent of Beef Wellington. Ask your fishmonger to fillet and skin a large tail piece of salmon. Serve with home-made *rémoulade* sauce.

> 2 lb (1 kg) tail piece salmon, skinned and filleted
> 2 tablespoons fresh chopped chives
> Few sprigs fresh sorrel or parsley or dill, chopped
> Juice 1 small lemon
> 2 × 12 oz (375 g) packs frozen puff pastry,
>   thawed
> 2 tablespoons semolina
> 1 egg, beaten
> Salt and ground black pepper
>
> SAUCE
> 2 egg yolks
> ¼ pint (150 ml) extra virgin olive oil
> ¼ pint (150 ml) sunflower oil
> 2 tablespoons white wine vinegar
> 1 teaspoon Dijon mustard
> 2 tablespoons capers, chopped
> 1 tablespoon gherkins, chopped

Courgette and tomato shredded salad, with salmon Nelson, and rare lamb salad with hazelnut dressing

Season the salmon fillets and flavour with the herbs and lemon juice. Lay them on top of each other.

Roll out one pastry piece to a shape about 1½" (4 cm) larger all round than the fish. Prick it well and place on a baking sheet. Bake at 400°F (200°C, gas mark 6) for 15 minutes until golden brown. If it has risen, then press down. Sprinkle over the semolina, and brush the edges with beaten egg. Lay the fish on top. Roll out the remaining pastry so that it is large enough to overlap completely. Fit over the top and press well to seal. Trim the edges and crimp.

Re-roll any trimmings and cut out long thin strips if you want to decorate the pie. Brush all over with more egg, then make a lattice pattern on top with the strips. Press firmly onto the pastry top and glaze again. Return to the oven and bake for 15 minutes then reduce the heat to 350°F (180°C, gas mark 4) for a further 40 minutes, checking to see the pastry doesn't burn.

Cool, then loosen the base with a thin palette knife and transfer the pie onto a thin board.

Make the sauce as you would a mayonnaise, in a food processor or by hand, beating the oil gradually into the seasoned egg yolks. When thick and creamy add the remaining ingredients. Slice pie thinly, and hand sauce separately.

Serves 6–8.   RD

157

Courgette and fresh tomato soup, and potted trout

COURGETTE AND FRESH TOMATO SOUP

This soup tastes equally good hot or cold so it can be adapted right at the last minute to our unpredictable climate.

> 1 lb (500 g) courgettes, chopped
> 1 onion, chopped
> 1 oz (25 g) butter
> 2 tablespoons olive oil
> 1 lb (500 g) tomatoes, peeled and chopped
> 1½ pints (900 ml) light stock
> ½ pint (300 ml) dry white wine or cider
> 5 large leaves fresh basil, chopped
> 1 orange, grated rind and juice

Sweat the courgettes and onion in the butter and oil for about 10 minutes in a large covered saucepan.

Add the rest of the ingredients, bring to the boil, then simmer for 20 minutes.

Blend until smooth and serve hot from a Thermos or cold. Garnish with some thin slices of tomato and fresh sprigs of basil.

Serves 6.   RD

POTTED TROUT

Very quickly made and ideal for your guests to nibble while you unpack the rest of the hamper.

> 8 oz (250 g) filleted smoked trout, skinned
> 2 oz (50 g) curd or cream cheese, softened, or
>   2 fl oz (65 ml) cream
> 2 oz (50 g) butter, softened
> 1 tablespoon fresh chopped chives or spring
>   onions
> ¼ teaspoon ground ginger
> Ground black pepper
> Cayenne and chopped parsley, to garnish

Mash the trout with a fork then blend with the cheese or cream, butter, chives or onions, ginger and pepper. Do not put through a blender. The mixture should have some texture.

Spoon into small ramekins, garnish and cover with cling film until required. Serve with bread sticks, or brioche rolls.

Serves 3–4.   RD

PARSNIP AND APRICOT SOUP

An adaptable first course, which can be served hot or cold. The combination of root vegetables, root ginger and the fruity sharpness of apricots is particularly pleasing.

> 1 small onion, chopped
> 1" (2.5 cm) cube fresh root ginger, peeled and
>   grated
> 2 tablespoons sunflower oil
> 12 oz (375 g) parsnips, peeled and diced

12 oz (375 g) carrots, peeled and diced
3 pints (1½ litres) light stock
4 oz (125 g) dried apricots, chopped
Salt and ground black pepper
Small tub fromage frais, if serving hot
½ pint (300 ml) buttermilk, if serving chilled
Some chopped chives or flaked almonds, to serve
  (optional)

Gently fry the onion and ginger with the oil in a large saucepan for 5 minutes. Add the parsnips and carrots, stir, cover and sweat on a low heat for 10 minutes. Add the stock, apricots and seasoning. Bring to the boil, then cover and simmer for 30 minutes until softened. Blend in a liquidizer or food processor until smooth.

If serving hot, add swirls of fromage frais; to serve cold, chill then mix in the buttermilk. Check the seasoning if served chilled as it may need more. Garnish with chives or almonds if liked.

Serves 4–6.   RD

Parsnip and apricot soup

CURRIED APPLE SOUP

Here's an unusual soup that is an excellent way of using cooking apples.

It takes minutes to prepare and can be served hot or, if you have time, chilled, when it is equally good, if not better.

2 lb (1 kg) cooking apples
1 medium onion
½ oz (15 g) butter
1 level tablespoon mild curry powder
1¾ pints (1 litre) chicken stock
Bay leaf
1 level tablespoon sugar
Seasoning
½ small carton single cream

Peel, quarter, core and slice the apples. Slice the onion and sauté it in the butter in a saucepan for about 5 minutes, then stir in the curry powder and cook for a further minute or two. Add the apples, bay leaf and stock, and bring to the boil. Season, lower the heat and simmer, covered, for 10 minutes until the apples are really soft.

Remove the bay leaf and liquidize the soup. Taste it and add the sugar (it should need very little) and a little more curry powder if you like – remember that this takes about 10 minutes to develop its full flavour, so don't go overboard! Adjust the seasoning, stir in the cream and either heat through and serve with Melba toast, or chill well.

Serves 6.   AW

RIFREDDO SUSANNA

Layers of veal, mortadella and prosciutto baked with beaten egg and Parmesan, to form a succulent terrine-like loaf, which is perfect for picnics or cold buffets.

1 lb 2 oz (550 g) thin slices of veal
5 oz (150 g) thinly sliced mortadella
5 oz (150 g) thinly sliced prosciutto
4 oz (125 g) grated Parmesan
4 eggs

Sausage in brioche, and rolls of brioche dough

Beat eggs with a fork and add the Parmesan.

Butter a deep cake tin or something similar in shape, and put in first a layer of mortadella, then a slice of veal dipped in beaten egg, then a slice of prosciutto. Continue this procedure until all of the ingredients are used up. Dot the top with butter and cover the dish with foil. Cook in a bain-marie in the oven for 2 hours, at 350°F (180°C, gas mark 4). When it is cooked, tip the terrine out of the tin and weigh it down while it cools.

Serve cold, thinly sliced, preferably the day after it is made. (This dish does not require salt, as the ingredients are quite salty.)

Serves 6. PF

PICNIC BRIOCHE

Instead of bread or rolls, why not make a fuss of picnic guests with home-made brioches. The use of easy-blend sachets of yeast (not to be confused with the dried granular type) takes much of the guess-work out of yeast cookery.

The baby brioches below are delicious hol-lowed out and filled with cold salmon or chicken mixed with a good home-made mayonnaise.

2 oz (50 g) butter
9 oz (275 g) strong plain flour
¼ teaspoon salt

160

1 sachet easy blend yeast
2 eggs
3 tablespoons warm milk
Extra beaten egg, to glaze

Rub the butter into the flour and salt until it resembles fine breadcrumbs. Stir in the yeast. (Note – easy-blend types of yeast must not be mixed with liquid first.)

Beat the eggs and milk and then mix into the flour and knead until smooth. Cover with lightly greased cling film and leave in a warm place until doubled in size. In summer this shouldn't take more than about an hour.

Knock back the dough, divide into six pieces and knead lightly. Tear off about a quarter of each piece and shape both into round balls.

Drop the larger of each ball into six well-greased 4" (10 cm) brioche tins, press a slight hollow on the top, glaze with some beaten egg and top with the smaller balls. If you haven't any brioche tins, then divide the dough into eight and use deep patty tins.

Glaze the tops well, cover with greased cling film and leave to rise again to about double the size. Bake at 425°F (220°C, gas mark 7) for about 15 minutes until golden brown. Turn out and cool.

To serve – use like rolls or remove the tops, hollow out and fill with creamy fish or meat salad.
Makes 6. RD

SAUSAGE IN BRIOCHE DOUGH

Use the same brioche dough recipe as above.

Mix some chopped fresh sage, parsley and marjoram into one pound of best quality sausage meat. Then roll to a neat shape about 8" (20 cm) long. Roast on a greased baking tray at 350°F (180°C, gas mark 4) for about 40 minutes. Cool and roll in flour to cover the surface.

Make up the brioche dough to the first proving. Knock back and roll out on a lightly-floured board to a rectangle large enough to wrap up the whole sausage.

Enclose the sausage completely in the dough, sealing with beaten egg. Glaze well, cover with greased cling film and leave to prove until doubled in size.

Bake at 425°F (220°C, gas mark 7) for about 20 to 25 minutes until golden brown. Cool on a wire tray, slice when quite cold.

Serves 4–6.
NOTE: like all home-made yeast dishes, brioches are best eaten fresh but can be made about 24 hours in advance. If you want to freeze them, do so as soon as they have cooled. RD

A TERRINE OF PIGEON AND PORK

This is a rather neat little meat roll which is easy to carve. The quails' eggs are optional.

12 oz (375 g) smoked streaky bacon, derinded
4 wood pigeon breasts, skinned and diced
1 lb (500g) lean pork, diced
1 onion, chopped
1 clove garlic, crushed
1 tablespoon oil
3 tablespoons fresh chopped parsley
1 teaspoon dried thyme or 2 sprigs fresh, chopped
3 tablespoons dry sherry
8 quails' eggs, hard-boiled and peeled (optional)
Salt and ground black pepper

Chop about a quarter of the bacon and lay the rest out in overlapping slices on a large sheet of lightly oiled foil on a flat baking sheet. Mix chopped bacon with the meats, onion, garlic, oil, herbs, sherry and seasoning. Arrange mixture down the middle of the bacon slices in a thick line. If using quails' eggs, press these into the mixture, also in a line.

Draw the bacon slices up over the meat enclosing it in a roll, and then overwrap firmly but not too tightly in the foil. Bake at 350°F (180°C, gas mark 4) for about 1½ hours. Cool, pour away any fat, then chill without unwrapping. Unwrap when quite cold and firm. Serve cut in fairly thick slices.
Serves 6–8. RD

American picnic cake

AMERICAN PICNIC CAKE

An excellent cut-and-come-again cake with a delicious creamy icing.

8 oz (250 g) self-raising flour
1 teaspoon baking powder
Pinch of salt
½ teaspoon cinnamon
4 oz (125 g) dark soft brown sugar
2 fl oz (65 ml) sunflower oil
2 eggs
Rind and juice of 1 orange
6 oz (175 g) carrot, grated
4 oz (125 g) walnuts, chopped
3 oz (75 g) raisins

ICING
2 oz (50 g) unsalted butter, softened
4 oz (125 g) cream or curd cheese, softened
4 oz (125 g) icing sugar, sifted
½ teaspoon vanilla essence

Sift the flour, baking powder, salt and cinnamon into a large bowl. Add the sugar.

Beat the oil, eggs, rind and orange juice together, then beat into the flour and sugar, mixing well. Stir in the carrots, walnuts and raisins, spoon into a greased and lined 2-lb (1 kg) loaf tin. Bake at 325°F (170°C, gas mark 3) for 1 to 1¼ hours. Cool in the tin upside down, then demould and split in half.

For the icing, simply cream everything together. Sandwich the two cake halves together and swirl the rest on top. Decorate with some broken walnuts and thin strips of fresh orange rind.   RD

VINEGAR CAKE WITH SOFT FRUITS

In this old-fashioned fruitcake, the wine derivative *vin aigre* is used, in combination with bicarbonate of soda, as the principal leavening agent (acid + alkali = carbon dioxide bubbles), reinforced by the belt-and-braces measure of a little baking powder. Be reassured – the cake does not taste vinegary.

Serve this with fresh raspberries and blueberries, sprinkled with demerara sugar and anointed at the last minute with a few drops of raspberry vinegar.

Butter for cake tin
14 oz (400 g) plain flour
½ teaspoon baking powder
6 oz (175 g) cold, unsalted butter
6 oz (175 g) soft, light brown sugar
5 oz (150 g) dried currants
4 oz (125 g) raisins
1 beaten egg
4 fl oz (125 ml) milk, plus more for the end of
    the process
Scant 3 tablespoons white wine vinegar
1 teaspoon bicarbonate of soda
Fresh blueberries and raspberries
Petit Suisse cheese
Demerara sugar
Raspberry vinegar

Butter the base and side of an 8½″ (21 cm) circular cake tin with a 3″ (7.5 cm) side.

Sift flour and baking powder into a large bowl, dice butter and rub this in to the dry ingredients; stir in sugar, dried fruits and beaten egg.

Pour all but a few tablespoons of the milk into the jug and mix in the vinegar. Heat remaining milk slightly and dissolve in this the bicarbonate of soda. Add milk and soda to milk and vinegar; the blend will froth wildly and should be quickly poured over the bowl's contents and rapidly incorporated. Add further milk, if necessary, in order to bring the batter to a dropping consistency, and spoon all into the buttered tin. Smooth the mixture and make a slight dip in the centre, where the cake will otherwise rise too high.

Bake cake at 375°F (190°C, gas mark 5) for 30 minutes; lower the heat to 350°F (180°C, gas mark 4) for 45 minutes more, then to 325°F (170°C, gas mark 3) for 30–40 minutes further, until a skewer inserted in the centre emerges clean and hot.

Cool cake completely, remove from tin, and serve cut into thin slices, with the fresh fruits and some mashed Petits Suisses strewn with demerara sugar and a little raspberry vinegar.

Makes one 8½″ (21 cm) circular cake which keeps well. AWS

Fruit tartlets with lemon cream

FRUIT TARTLETS WITH LEMON CREAM

It seems pointless to take elaborate puddings to a picnic. The journey itself would necessitate a somewhat solid and indestructible texture. Small wonder that fresh fruits and a pot of cream are normally popular. So, on a similar theme, serve a pile of light crisp tartlets flavoured with orange flower water, a bowl of prepared fruits and some tangy lemon curd cream for guests to put together on site.

PASTRY
4 oz (125 g) plain flour
2 oz (50 g) cornflour
2 tablespoons icing sugar
5 oz (150 g) unsalted butter, softened
2 egg yolks
1 tablespoon orange flower water or 1 teaspoon
*   vanilla essence*

TOPPING
5 oz (150 g) soured cream or curd cheese,
*   softened*
3 tablespoons lemon curd, preferably home-made
1 lb (500 g) fresh berry fruits – e.g.
*   strawberries, raspberries, pitted cherries*
4 oz (125 g) seedless white grapes

Sift the flours and icing sugar together, then rub in the butter until it resembles fine breadcrumbs. Beat the yolks and flower water together then mix with the flour to a firm but fairly soft dough. Knead lightly then cover and chill for half an hour.

Roll out on a lightly floured board to a thickness of a 10p piece and cut out about 24 × 2½″ (7.5 cm) rounds, re-rolling as necessary. Prick the bases and fit into shallow bun tins. Bake at 375°F (190°C, gas mark 5) for 10–12 minutes until pale golden and crisp. Cool on a wire rack, then pack into a rigid air-tight container.

Meanwhile, beat the cream (or cheese for a firmer texture) with the lemon curd, and spoon into a bowl. Chill and cover. Prepare the fruits.

To serve, let your guests spoon lemon cream into the base of each tartlet and top with fruits.
Makes 24. RD

THE GRAND FINALE

Colourful fruit salads, compotes and sorbets
provide a natural and fresh-tasting conclusion to
a meal, while chocolate puddings, ice-cream, cakes
and pastries strike a more indulgent note

CASTAGNACCIO

The Ristorante la Mora is a halt at Ponte a Moriano, on the road from Lucca to the Garfagnana mountains in Tuscany. Sauro Brunicardi and his family are expert restaurateurs, known for the warmth of their reception and their deft cooking of local dishes threatened with eclipse as the region – traditionally a poor one, save for the city of Lucca – grows in affluence.

Castagnaccio, a cake of chestnut flour seasoned with raisins and nuts, is a very old recipe, typically 'lucchese', though also made in other parts of Tuscany; the Ristorante la Mora incorporates walnuts and zest of orange, no sugar – chestnut flour is heavy and sweet – and the hot scent of rosemary. Its dense smokiness is not to everyone's taste, but those who like it tend to be strongly partisan.

The chestnut flour should be found, in London, from the end of October at either of the two Fratelli Camisa shops in Berwick Street and Charlotte Street, W1.

> *Olive oil*
> *14 oz (400 g) chestnut flour*
> *About 18 fl oz (500 ml) water*
> *Pinch salt*
> *1½ oz (40 g) walnuts, coarsely chopped*
> *Handful of raisins*
> *Some freshly-grated zest of orange*
> *1 oz (25 g) pine nuts*
> *Leaves stripped from 2–3 branches of fresh*
>   *rosemary*

Generously oil the sides and base of a 10″ × 1″ (25 × 2.5 cm) circular cake tin or fireproof dish.

Slowly stir water into chestnut flour, working it constantly with a wooden spoon, until the mixture is smooth and liquid enough to pour easily (you may not need all the water). Beat in 3 tablespoons of olive oil, the salt, walnuts, raisins and zest of orange; pour batter into the dish, spread it evenly, strew with pine nuts and rosemary, dribble with oil.

Bake the *castagnaccio* at 440°F (200°C, gas mark 6) for 40 minutes, until the surface has cracked and turned a deep, rich brown. Eat the cake about 15 minutes after removal from the oven.

Serves 6, generously.   AWS

APPLE CAKE MARYROSE

An English recipe from Maryrose Crossman of Somerset, whose summer pudding is admirable and whose apple cake, made in part with wholemeal flour, is unusual, palatable and as rapidly consumed as produced. For apples, you can substitute fresh raspberries in season, or chopped dried apricots (previously rehydrated by soaking and brief simmering in water).

Right *Castagnaccio (in foreground) and apple cake Maryrose*

1 × 14 oz (400 g) Bramley apple
5 oz (150 g) unsalted butter, plus butter for the
*   tin*
2 large eggs
8 oz (250 g) caster sugar
A few drops almond essence
4 oz (125 g) self-raising flour
Pinch salt
4 oz (125 g) wholemeal flour
Icing sugar

Peel, core, and thinly slice the apple; melt and partly cool the 5 oz (150 g) butter. Butter an 8 × 2½″ (20 × 6 cm) circular springform cake tin. Beat the eggs and sugar until thick and well-aerated, whisk in melted butter and almond essence. Sift together self-raising flour and salt, stir in wholemeal flour; beat these well into egg and butter base.

Spread half the mixture over the tin, cover with apples, followed by the remaining batter. Bake the cake at 350°F (180°C, gas mark 4) for something between 1 and 1½ hours; timing varies, but the top should brown to a thick, crisp crust.

Cool cake completely and dust with icing sugar. Slice and serve for tea, or after dinner with chilled sweet muscat wine.

Serves 6.   AWS

LAVENDER AND HONEY ICE-CREAM

Once people have overcome the hesitation of tasting such a fragrant food, lavender ice-cream wins many converts. It is particularly good with fresh strawberries.

1 pint (600 ml) milk
½ pint (300 ml) double cream
8 tablespoons clear honey
2–3 tablespoons caster sugar (optional)
3–4 tablespoons dried lavender flowers
6 egg yolks
2 egg whites
Few drops violet food colouring (optional)

Scald the milk, cream, honey, sugar (if using) and lavender until on the point of boiling. Allow to stand for 30 minutes, then strain and reheat to boiling. Meanwhile, beat the egg yolks in a bowl and slowly pour on the scalded milk, whisking continuously. Pour back into the saucepan and, on the lowest heat possible, stir the custard until it is the consistency of single cream and will coat the back of the spoon. Strain and allow to cool completely. Add a few drops of food colouring if liked, stir well and freeze until nearly firm.

Remove, and beat well until slushy (this can be done in a food processor). Whisk the egg whites and carefully fold into the beaten mixture. Return to the freezer until firm. Allow to thaw for a few minutes before scooping out.

This is nice served in honey snap cups.

Serves 6–8.   RD

HONEY SNAP CUPS

It's not so much the technique that makes these tricky – more the timing. For this reason, it is better to bake them singly.

2 oz (50 g) butter
2 tablespoons clear honey
2 oz (50 g) soft brown sugar
1½ oz (40 g) plain flour
Pinch each ground ginger and salt
Squeeze fresh lemon juice

Melt the butter with the honey, and sugar. Beat in the flour, ginger, salt and lemon juice. Set aside.

Lightly grease a baking sheet, then drop dessertspoons of the mixture, singly, onto the sheet. Bake at 325°F (170°C, gas mark 3) for about 10–12 minutes until golden brown and lacy around the edges. Remove from the oven, allow to cool for a minute, until firm around the edges, then slip off the baking sheet with a palette knife and immediately press over an orange.

When firm, remove and cool completely on a wire tray. Store in an airtight tin until required. Will keep for about 24 hours like this.

Makes about 8.   RD

Pecan and maple pie

PECAN AND MAPLE PIE

A favourite party pie, this is instantly recognizable, popular and lives up to its delicious gooey promise. This version isn't crammed with nuts as some recipes direct because it detracts from the filling and can make the pie rather dry.

PASTRY
3 oz (75 g) butter or sunflower margarine
6 oz (175 g) plain flour
1 teaspoon cinnamon

FILLING
3 eggs, beaten
4 oz (125 g) dark soft brown sugar
¼ pint (150 ml) golden syrup
3 fl oz (1 ml) maple syrup
½ teaspoon vanilla essence
Pinch of salt
4 oz (125 g) shelled pecan nuts

Rub the fat into the flour and cinnamon then mix to a firm dough with a little cold water. Roll out and line into a 9″ (23 cm) flan dish, making sure the sides are quite high so they don't shrink back. Chill for about 30 minutes.

Bake blind at 400°F (200°C, gas mark 6) for 20 minutes, removing the foil and beans for the last 5 minutes of baking.

Beat the eggs, sugar, syrups, essence and salt. Sprinkle the nuts into the pastry shell and pour over the syrup mixture, coating the nuts.

Bake at 350°F (180°C, gas mark 4) for about 40 minutes until slightly risen and firm. Cool and serve with softly whipped cream mixed with a little soured cream.

Serves 6–8.   RD

A VELVETY CURD CHEESECAKE

As smooth and rich as its name suggests, this is a traditional baked cheesecake which has generally been superseded by American desserts set with gelatine. Its success depends on a relatively short baking time which stops the cheese from curdling and the cake sinking when it cools. Serve in moderate wedges with fresh soft fruits.

SPONGE BASE
3 oz (75 g) self-raising flour
2 oz (50 g) butter or margarine, softened
2 oz (50 g) icing sugar
1 egg yolk
2 tablespoons milk

TOPPING
8 oz (250 g) medium-fat curd cheese
8 oz (250 g) quark
1 teaspoon vanilla essence
1 small lemon, grated rind and juice
2 oz (50 g) butter, melted
2 oz (50 g) caster sugar
2 tablespoons cornflour
5 fl oz (150 ml) soured cream
2 eggs, separated

First make the base. Line the base and sides of an 8″ (20 cm) loose-bottomed tin with greased foil or greaseproof paper. In doing this, make sure the edge of the paper overlaps the base so the mixture doesn't leak out on cooking.

Mix all the sponge ingredients together in a blender or processor until smooth, then spoon mixture into the prepared tin. Bake at 375°F (190°C, gas mark 5) for about 25 minutes, until the sponge is firm.

Meanwhile, put all the topping ingredients except the egg whites into a bowl and beat until smooth and well blended.

Whisk the egg whites until forming soft peaks and fold into the cheesecake mixture. Spoon on top of the sponge.

Return to the oven at 350°F (180°C, gas mark 4) for 30 minutes until the cake edge feels firm. Turn off the oven without removing the tin and leave the cake to cool overnight – it continues to cook slowly as it cools. Chill before demoulding and serving dusted lightly with icing sugar.

Serves 8–10.   RD

HONEY AND CINNAMON CREAM

A simple dessert which can be used with any fruit in season – strawberries, soft red berries, cherries, lightly stewed apples and pears or grapes. Without fruit, the mixture makes a delicious alternative to cream for other puddings, especially tarts and pies.

> 8 oz (250 g) fromage frais, low-fat or fat-free
> 2 tablespoons clear honey
> 1/2 teaspoon ground cinnamon
> 8 oz (250 g) grapes, halved and pitted
> A little extra honey and cinnamon

Mix together the fromage frais, honey and cinnamon until smooth, then stir in the grapes.

Spoon mixture into four dishes and trickle over a little extra honey. Sprinkle with cinnamon, and serve the creams chilled.

Serves 4.   RD

HONEYED PEAR AND ALMOND PIE

This is a particularly nice tart for a Sunday lunch or afternoon tea. Serve slightly warm with lightly whipped cream.

> 12 oz (350 g) shortcrust pastry, bought or home-made
> 3 large dessert pears, not too ripe
> 1/2 pint (300 ml) water
> 4 tablespoons clear or set honey
> 2 strips lemon peel
>
> FILLING
> 2 oz (50 g) soft margarine
> 2 oz (50 g) caster sugar
> 2 eggs, separated
> 4 oz (125 g) ground almonds
> 4 oz (125 g) stale cake crumbs (e.g. Madeira or ginger cake)
> 1 teaspoon grated lemon peel
> Pinch ground cinnamon
> Icing sugar, to dust

Roll out the pastry into a 9″ (23 cm) flan tin with a loose base. Trim, and allow to rest while you make the filling. Core the pears and peel thinly. Cut in half then poach in the water with 2 tablespoons of honey and the lemon peel strips for about 15 minutes until just tender. Allow to cool in the syrup if you have the time. Drain, and discard the pear syrup (this can be used up elsewhere as a drink or in a fruit jelly).

Cream the margarine, sugar and remaining 2 tablespoons of honey. Beat in the egg yolks then stir in the ground almonds, cake crumbs, lemon peel and cinnamon.

Whisk the egg whites until stiff, then carefully fold into the cake mixture. Spread this over the base of the flan cases and press down the six pear halves on top.

Bake at 375°F (190°C, gas mark 5) for about 30 to 35 minutes until risen, firm and light brown. Cool until lukewarm and serve dusted with a little icing sugar.

Serves 6–8.   RD

Honeyed pear and almond pie (left) and summer red fruits compôte, decorated with borage flowers

SUMMER RED FRUITS COMPOTE

Raspberries, redcurrants and figs are all fruits that have an affinity with honey. Here they are steeped for several hours in a warm honey syrup, before being chilled and served decorated with the pretty blue flowers of the bee plant – borage. Accompany with thick Greek yoghurt and shortbread, home-made if possible.

1 lb (500 g) redcurrants, de-stalked
3 tablespoons clear or set honey
3 tablespoons water

1 lb (500 g) fresh raspberries, hulled
3 ripe figs, quartered or sliced
Grated rind 1 orange, optional
Borage flowers, to serve

Poach the redcurrants with the honey and water over a gentle heat for about 5 minutes until just cooked and the juice is starting to run.

Place the raspberries and figs in a large bowl and sprinkle with the orange rind. Pour over the redcurrants and juice and leave to steep for 2–3 hours. Chill before serving decorated with the borage flowers.

Serves 4–6. RD

169

Gascony apple and Armagnac tart

GASCONY APPLE AND ARMAGNAC TART

Made with filo pastry, this is easier to make than Normandy apple flan and just as much of a treat to the eyes.

> *6 sheets filo pastry*
> *3 oz (75 g) butter, melted*
> *2 Bramley or 3 Granny Smith apples, peeled and thinly sliced*
> *Icing sugar, to taste*
> *Ground cinnamon or freshly grated nutmeg (optional)*
> *Armagnac (or Cognac), to sprinkle*

Brush the base of a 10″ (25 cm) flan tin liberally with butter. Lay and press in three sheets of filo, brushing well in between with butter.

Trim the edges with kitchen scissors, leaving them slightly ragged. Save the scraps of filo and allow to dry slightly so that they curl a bit.

Scatter half the apple slices on top, brushing with more butter and sprinkling with icing sugar and spices, if using. The amount of sugar you use depends on the tartness of the apples.

Top with the remaining filo sheets, brushing with butter and trimming as before. Scatter the remaining apple on top, sweetening to taste. Casually arrange the pastry scraps on top to cover, and brush or trickle over the last of the butter.

Stand the flan dish on a flat baking sheet and bake at 375°F (190°C, gas mark 5) for about 25 minutes until the pastry is crisp. Check occasionally to see that it doesn't burn. Cool the flan and remove to a serving plate. Dust with a little more icing sugar and, just before serving, sprinkle with plenty of Armagnac.

Serves 4–6. RD

CASSATA SICILIANA

A sumptuous Italian chilled dessert which is best prepared the day before serving. Easy to assemble, it takes advantage of the Italian cakes often seen hanging from the ceiling, in decorative boxes, of delicatessens.

> *1 × 250 g panettone (Italian cake, available from Italian delicatessens)*
> *12 oz (350 g) ricotta*
> *2 oz (150 g) bitter chocolate, cut in small pieces*
> *3 oz (75 g) candied peel*
> *4 oz (125 g) caster sugar*
> *5 tablespoons maraschino*

Slice the top off the panettone in one neat piece, and hollow out the cake as much as possible without piercing the sides.

Put ricotta in a basin and whisk it with sugar until smooth. Add chocolate, candied peel and 1 tablespoon of maraschino, and mix well.

Soak the cake crust with the remaining maraschino, and fill with the ricotta mixture. Replace the top of the cake, wrap in tin foil and refrigerate until ready to serve.

Remove foil and add more maraschino if you like. Sprinkle with icing sugar, and serve in slices. (This dish is best made the day before use.)

Serves 6. PF

FIG AND PLUM ICE-CREAM

For figs and plums at their late summer peak.

13 oz (375 g) very ripe figs
6 oz (175 g) very ripe yellow plums
3 tablespoons white wine
½ pint (300 ml) milk
4 small egg yolks
3 oz (75 g) soft light brown sugar
6 fl oz (175 ml) double cream
Cognac or Armagnac

Stem and quarter the figs, quarter the plums and discard the stones. Put fruits with the wine into a heavy saucepan and barely simmer, covered and stirring often, for 10–15 minutes until the fruits are tender. Purée in a food processor, taking care to leave some texture.

Scald the milk, beat yolks and sugar until very thick, whisk in milk and pour the mixture back into the milk pan. Whisk over a medium heat until the custard *just* boils. Immediately sieve into a bowl, and stir in the fruit purée. Cool and chill.

When the mixture is cold, beat in chilled cream, Cognac or Armagnac as a slight accent, and freeze in your ice-cream maker. Quantities given make 1½ pints (900 ml).

Let the ice-cream soften in the refrigerator for 30 minutes before scooping to serve accompanied by brandy snaps.

Serves 4–6.   AWS

Fig and plum ice-cream

PLUMS AND PEACHES IN SLOE GIN SYRUP

Stewed fruits have never held a great attraction for many of us, but fruits macerated in a hot syrup retain texture and absorb delicious flavours.

November is the month to start assembling the ingredients for this summertime dessert. Found growing in hedgerows on chalky uplands, sloes are best gathered after the first frosts have hit them. The fruit should be pricked all over with a needle, and left immersed in gin, sweetened with a little sugar, for at least 6 weeks. Strain the gin, which by now will be a lovely burgundy colour, and discard the spent sloes.

1½ lb (750 g) ripe plums
2 large peaches

SYRUP
6 oz (175 g) sugar
¾ pint (450 ml) water
2 strips orange peel
1 cinnamon stick
6 tablespoons sloe gin

Halve the plums and peaches and stone. Slice the peaches then put both fruits into a heatproof bowl.

Dissolve the sugar in the water over a gentle heat, stirring occasionally, then add the other syrup ingredients, except for the sloe gin. Bring to the boil, then simmer for about 5 minutes and stir in the gin. Pour the syrup over the fruit, cover and leave until cold. Chill before serving with light, crisp biscuits and lightly whipped cream mixed with natural yoghurt.

Serves 4.   RD

BALTIC FLAT-BREAD TARTS

Flat-bread based fruit tarts are particularly well-suited to a buffet table, as they can be cut and served in bite-sized pieces with none of the worries presented by crumbling pastry or oozing filling.

Yeast and cardamom aromas are a *sine qua non* of festive Baltic baking, and the wide variety of possible toppings allows a colourful display of all that is seasonal, or skilfully preserved for such an occasion.

SWEET YEAST DOUGH
1 lb (500 g) strong, plain unbleached flour
1 teaspoon salt
6–8 pods cardamom, husks removed and seeds ground
1 oz (25 g) fresh yeast
2 tablespoons warm water
1 teaspoon malt syrup
7 fl oz (200 ml) milk
3½ oz (100 g) unsalted butter
2 eggs, beaten, plus 2 yolks (these are optional, but will give a more golden dough)
3½ oz (100 g) caster sugar (preferably light, unrefined)

Sift flour, salt and cardamom into a warmed mixing bowl, and form a well in the centre. Crumble the yeast and blend with the water and malt. Set aside for 10 minutes in a warm place to activate the yeast. Scald the milk with the butter, then cool to room temperature. Beat the eggs with the sugar to partially dissolve the latter, then pour all liquids, including activated yeast, into the well in the flour. Gradually incorporate the liquid into the flour using a wooden spoon, then beat vigorously for 2 to 3 minutes until the dough is smooth and slightly elastic (it will remain slack and 'sticky'). Scrape down the sides, but leave the dough in the mixing bowl. Grease the surface of the dough lightly with unsalted butter or safflower oil. Cover and leave to prove for an hour until almost triple in bulk. Alternatively, the dough may be left to prove slowly in the refrigerator for 4 hours, then a further 4 hours at room temperature.

Fillings, as suggested in the recipes below, may be prepared while the dough is proving.

Knock back the risen dough, which will be too slack to knead on a board; knead it briefly in the mixing bowl, with one hand. Flour a pastry board generously, and tip half the dough out onto the board. With floured hands, flatten the dough a little, dredge more flour onto the surface and roll out to form two rectangles 12″ × 8″ (30 × 20 cm). Alternatively – and this makes for a softer pastry – press the dough without rolling into lightly-greased swiss-roll tins of the above dimensions, using floured knuckles.

Arrange topping over the dough and leave to prove a little more while heating the oven. Transfer the tarts to lightly-greased baking sheets (unless using swiss-roll tins) and bake in a pre-heated, moderate oven (350°F, 180°C, gas mark 4) for 30 to 40 minutes.

Cool the tarts in the tins; if not eating immediately, enclose in plastic wrap as soon as they have reached room temperature. Slice into squares shortly before serving.

Makes 36–48 pieces.

TOPPINGS
Amounts are for each trayful, i.e., half of given quantity of dough.

Wash 14 oz (400 g) young rhubarb, and cut the stems into tiny batons. Pour in a single, but generous, layer over dough. Strew with sugar and cinnamon to taste.

Wash and dry 14 oz (400 g) blueberries, lingonberries or cranberries. Arrange on dough and sprinkle with sugar as before – cranberries will need rather more sugar than blueberries. A traditional treatment of cranberries is to cook until skins are soft with apples reduced to a purée. Sweeten to taste.

Take 14 oz (400 g) flavourful eating apples or firm pears, peeled, cored and thinly sliced into crescent shapes. Arrange in 3 overlapping rows, on the rolled-out dough, and sprinkle with lemon juice, caster sugar and cinnamon to taste. Sprinkle cinnamon crumble topping between rows of apple.

Baltic flat-bread tarts: left, blueberry and cranberry; right, rhubarb, and apple with cinnamon crumble

CINNAMON CRUMBLE

4 oz (125 g) plain flour
2 teaspoons ground cinnamon
2½ oz (65 g) unsalted butter, softened
2 oz (50 g) unrefined, light sugar

Blend all ingredients with fingers until rough crumbs are formed. Use a pressing, rolling action to compact and round the crumbs slightly (unlike the light touch employed when making shortcrust pastry). Either sprinkle over the dough or coat the fruits individually, reducing the quantity of sugar according to taste.   SD

POIRE PARFAIT WITH RASPBERRY SAUCE

A frozen, creamy concoction perfumed with eau-de-vie de poire, and served with contrasting fresh raspberry sauce.

Prepare the parfait the day before, and make the raspberry sauce in advance too, if you like.

FOR THE PARFAIT
2 eggs, separated
3 tablespoons Poire liqueur
1 oz (25 g) sifted icing sugar
¼ pint (150 ml) double cream, lightly whipped

Left to right: Poire parfait with raspberry sauce; yoghurt with apple and raisins; tropical fruit salad

FOR THE SAUCE
8 oz (250 g) raspberries
1 tablespoon sifted icing sugar

TO GARNISH
1 ripe pear
1 tablespoon lemon juice

Whisk the egg yolks with the liqueur until the mixture is pale. Stiffly whisk the egg whites, then whisk in the sugar a teaspoon at a time. Continue whisking, and slowly pour in the egg yolk mixture. Fold in the cream, then turn into a container and freeze for 4 hours or until firm.

There is no need to remove the parfait and beat it further during the freezing process, as the addition of beaten eggs gives a mousse-like consistency. It is, however, advisable to take the parfait out of the freezer 30 minutes before serving, and to leave it in the refrigerator to soften.

Purée the raspberries with the sugar, then sieve to remove all the pips. Peel the pear, core and cut into cubes. Place on a plate, squeeze over the lemon juice and put on one side until required.

Divide the sauce between 4 small plates, then arrange scoopfuls of the ice-cream on top. Decorate each one with a few cubes of fresh pear.

Serves 4.   JR

YOGHURT WITH APPLES AND RAISINS

A simple variation of fruit yoghurt, but one that will prove to be very popular among the large number of Greek yoghurt devotees. Which yoghurt you choose, i.e. cows', goats' or sheep's is a matter of personal choice, although the sheep's yoghurt does tend to be slightly sharper, so is generally better for savoury recipes.

2 oz (50 g) seedless raisins
¼ pint (150 ml) medium-sweet cider
2 dessert apples
2 × 8½ oz (260 g) cartons Greek yoghurt

Put the raisins in a small basin, pour over the cider and leave to macerate overnight. Core the apples and cut into ¼″ (5 mm) pieces. Add to the raisins and mix well.

Divide half the yoghurt between 4 glasses, then spoon a quarter of the raisins and apple mixture into each. Cover with the remaining yoghurt and chill for at least 2 hours before serving.

Serves 4.   JR

TROPICAL FRUIT SALAD

A good tropical fruit salad has a unique scent and taste, but the secret of it is to ensure that all the fruit you use is really ripe. The recipe below is a basic one which you can vary in all sorts of ways, by adding other fruit, such as star fruit, mangosteens and rambutans, or by replacing the lychees and paw paw with some of these fruits.

These fruit salads are best served lightly chilled and look most attractive served in a home-made ice bowl, which is very simple to make. Half-fill a mixing bowl with water and place on a flat surface in your freezer. Suspend a small bowl inside and weight this down to give you the thickness of ice you require.

Leave until the water is completely frozen, then pour a little water into the inner bowl to loosen it and remove this, then pour a little water over the larger bowl and remove it as well. Replace the ice bowl in the freezer until it is required.

6 large passion fruit
1 mango
1 paw paw
6 oz (175 g) lychees

Halve the passion fruit and scoop out the pulp with a teaspoon and place in a bowl. Peel the mango, cut the flesh into as neat slices as possible and add to the passion fruit. Do the same with the paw paw, cutting the flesh into cubes and discarding the seeds. Peel the lychees, cut them in half and remove the stones. Add to the fruit salad, cover and chill until just before serving.

Place the ice bowl on a serving plate and fill with fruit salad.

Serves 4.   JR

PECHE RAFRAICHIE BOURGUIGNONNE

This fruit dessert, illustrated on page 176, is especially welcome in summer months.

1½ lb (750 g) fresh raspberries
9 fl oz (275 ml) good Beaujolais
2 tablespoons icing sugar
8 large peaches
2 oz (50 g) flaked almonds, toasted

Reserve 18 raspberries for decoration, and purée the remaining raspberries through a fine sieve to remove the seeds. Add the Beaujolais and sweeten with a little icing sugar.

Toss the peaches into boiling water for 2–3 minutes to loosen their skins. Slice the peeled peaches into the sauce and leave to chill for 3–4 hours in the refrigerator.

Serve the peaches either on dessert plates or in shallow glass dishes. Decorate with raspberries and toasted flaked almonds. The peaches will keep in the sauce for up to 2 days, improving in flavour.

Serves 6.   SW

Pêche rafraîchie bourguignonne, page 175

Line an 8″ (20 cm) springform cake tin with greaseproof paper. Crush the digestive biscuits in a plastic bag, melt the butter in a saucepan, and stir in the crumbs. Spread the crumbs on to the bottom of the tin, and press firmly with a spoon.

Peel 4 oz (125 g) of the grapes and remove the pips with a clean hair-grip. Soften the gelatine in 3 tablespoons of cold water for 2–3 minutes, then dissolve over a saucepan of hot water.

Loosely whip the cream and blend in the yoghurt. Add the wine to the dissolved gelatine, and stir in the yoghurt-cream mixture.

Whisk the egg whites with the sugar until they form soft peaks, and carefully fold into the now-setting mousse. Add the peeled grapes and pour into the prepared tin. Leave to set in the refrigerator for at least 2 hours. (At this stage it may be frozen for up to 8 weeks.)

Release from the tin and remove the paper. Cut the remaining grapes in half and arrange over the surface. To prepare the sauce, liquidize the apricots in their syrup and pass through a fine sieve.

Serves 6.   SW

WINE AND YOGHURT GRAPE TORTE

Muscat grapes are available during the month of October, so this is the time to take advantage of their delicious perfume, combined here with cream and yoghurt.

BISCUIT BASE
4 oz (125 g) digestive biscuits
2 oz (50 g) unsalted butter

MOUSSE
1 lb (500 g) muscat grapes
3 teaspoons powdered gelatine
5 fl oz (150 g) double cream
5 fl oz (150 g) natural yoghurt
3 fl oz (75 g) dry white wine
2 egg whites
2 tablespoons caster sugar

SAUCE
8 bottled apricots in their syrup

VANILLA AND ROSE CONES WITH RASPBERRY SAUCE

Liqueur de framboise is superb in this dish, but an eau de vie, crème de cassis or kirsch could be substituted, as flavouring for the raspberry sauce. The biscuit cones can be prepared ahead.

VANILLA CONES
2 eggs
3 oz caster sugar
3 tablespoons plain flour (level measuring spoon)
1 tablespoon beurre noisette
½ teaspoon natural vanilla essence

FILLING
8 fl oz (250 g) whipping cream
1–2 teaspoons caster sugar
1–2 teaspoons rosewater
Tiny rose geranium leaves (optional)

RASPBERRY SAUCE
8–10 oz (250–300 g) raspberries
2–3 tablespoons redcurrant jelly
Sugar if necessary
*1–2 tablespoons liqueur de framboise or eau de
vie (optional)*

VANILLA CONES

Break the eggs into a bowl, whisk in the sugar until well mixed then gradually work in the flour. Heat a little butter until it is bubbling and brown and smells nutty and pour into the mixture, leaving the sediment behind. Whisk in the vanilla essence. Place about four tablespoons of the mixture, well apart, on greased baking sheets. Spread with the back of a spoon to even 3″ (8 cm) circles and bake in a hot oven (400°F, 200°C, gas mark 6) for 6–8 minutes when the circles should be pale golden and browning round the edges. Bake any leftover mixture in the same way.

Carefully lift off the baking sheet with the aid of a palette knife and form into cones round your fingers. Stand them for a while in narrow flute glasses to keep their shape but remove and cool on a rack once they have firmed into shape (if you cool them completely standing in a glass, the steam cannot escape and they don't crisp properly). Store in an airtight tin.

FILLING

Whip the cream with light sweetening and rose-water to taste, until firm enough to pipe. Turn into a piping-bag with a large rose nozzle. Keep in fridge until ready to serve.

SAUCE

Set one raspberry aside for each cone, for decoration. Process the remainder with the redcurrant jelly, sugar if necessary and the raspberry liqueur. Sieve to remove pips.

TO ASSEMBLE

Spoon a pool of sauce onto each plate. Pipe some cream into each cone, top with a raspberry and two tiny rose geranium leaves and lay two on each plate. Serve at once.

Serves 4–6.   NC

HONEY AND RAISIN OMELETTE

Accompanied by a sweet, grapey Muscat wine, this makes an elegant and unusual dessert.

3 fresh eggs
½ eggshell of water
Lightweight olive oil
Dessertspoon very thick honey
*3 oz (75 g) washed raisins, soaked overnight in
a little dark rum*
A good pinch of nutmeg

Mix eggs, water and a pinch of salt in a bowl. Heat enough oil in a Japanese *tamago-yaki nabe* pan (available from The Conran Shop, Fulham Road, London SW7) to cover its base. Pour off excess oil.

Pour one third egg mixture into pan, and 'muddle' using a wooden utensil, e.g. the handle of a spoon. Do not use metal. With the aid of a plastic spatula, roll the omelette to the end of the pan which is away from you.

Rolled honey and raisin omelette

177

Pour half the remaining egg into the vacant end of the pan, and muddle it. When nearly set, gently drop the raisins, honey, and nutmeg onto the surface. Using the spatula, roll omelette back to your end. Pour rest of egg into the space, muddle, and roll whole omelette away from you. Tip onto serving dish.

Serves 2.   HDM

BOMBE NOEL

It is very useful to have a homemade iced pudding to hand over Christmas, which can be removed from the freezer and served at just a few minutes' notice when a casual gathering turns into a more formal meal. Made in a pudding mould it also becomes a good alternative to The Pudding.

6 tablespoons demerara rum
4 oz (125 g) stoneless raisins
2 oz (50 g) citron peel, chopped
1 oz (25 g) angelica, chopped
1 pint (600 ml) double cream
½ pint (300 ml) rich milk
2 vanilla pods or 1 teaspoon vanilla essence
6 egg yolks
3 eggs
8 oz (250 g) caster sugar
100 g (3½ oz) bar Menier chocolate, broken

Heat 4 tablespoons of rum and mix with the fruits and angelica. Leave to stand overnight.

Scald the cream and milk with the vanilla pods and leave to steep for half an hour. Remove the pods. (If using vanilla essence, however, steeping is not necessary.)

Whisk the yolks, eggs and sugar, and pour the milk on to the mixture, whisking hard. Return to the stove and, on the lowest heat possible, stir with a wooden spoon until slightly thickened. If the custard looks as if it is starting to curdle, pour it at once into a large cold bowl. It's best to have one at the ready. Allow the custard to cool.

Melt the chocolate in a basin over water that is barely simmering. Do not allow it to overheat or it will go lumpy. Stir until smooth then gradually mix into ¾ pint (450 ml) of custard and remaining 2 tablespoons of rum. Cool, chill and freeze separately, beating occasionally while it freezes.

Mix the rum-soaked fruits into the remaining custard, then chill and freeze, beating occasionally. When firm and nearly solid, spoon the mixture into a 2 lb (1 kg) basin or bombe mould. It helps to have the basin in the freezer half an hour beforehand. Press the ice-cream up the sides to make a hollow. Return to the freezer until firm. Spoon the chocolate ice in the middle then refreeze. Cover, and label if the bombe is to be stored for some time.

Allow to thaw for half an hour in the fridge, before cutting into slices.

Serves 6.   RD

CRANBERRY AND RASPBERRY SHERBERT

A pretty ruby-red, bitter-sweet sorbet.

1 lb (500 g) fresh or frozen cranberries
1 lb (500 g) fresh or frozen raspberries
De-pithed peel and juice of 1 orange
8 oz (250 g) caster sugar
¼ pint (150 ml) ruby or tawny port
2 egg whites

Simmer the fruit with 1 pint (600 ml) of water and orange peel for 15 minutes. Rub the pulp through a sieve with a wooden spoon. Discard the pips and skins. Return juice and pulp to saucepan with sugar. Reheat, stirring until dissolved, then boil – not too fiercely – for 5 minutes.

Cool, then stir in the orange juice and port. Chill, then place in freezer and, when partially frozen, remove and beat until slushy. Whisk the egg whites to soft peaks and fold in. Return to the freezer, cover and seal. Allow to thaw slightly until soft enough to scoop out.

Serves 6.   RD

Right *Bombe noel; cranberry and raspberry sherbert*

HOT CHOCOLATE SOUFFLE

Most of the preparation, up to the point of whisking the egg whites, for this classic pudding can be done in advance. The soufflé can then be assembled and put in the oven as you serve the main course.

4 oz (125 g) plain chocolate
2 tablespoons water
½ pint (300 ml) milk
1½ oz (40 g) butter
1½ oz (40 g) plain flour
¼ teaspoon vanilla essence
4 large eggs
2 oz (50 g) caster sugar
Icing sugar

Preheat the oven to 375°F (190°C, gas mark 5) with a baking sheet placed in the centre of the oven. Thoroughly grease a 2-pint (1.2 litre) soufflé dish with butter and sprinkle with a little of the caster sugar.

Put the chocolate into a pan with the water and 2 tablespoons milk. Stir over a low heat until the chocolate has melted and add the remaining milk. Bring to the boil and remove from the heat.

Melt the butter over a low heat. Stir in the flour and cook over a low heat for 1 minute. Take off the heat and add the hot milk and chocolate. Return to the heat and bring to the boil, stirring well until thick. Add the vanilla essence and leave the mixture until cool.

Separate the eggs and beat the yolks and sugar into the chocolate sauce. (At this point, the mixture may be left for up to 8 hours before the dish is completed.)

Whisk the egg whites to stiff, but not dry, peaks. Fold into the chocolate sauce and pour into the prepared dish. Run a spoon around the edge (this makes the soufflé rise with a 'cauliflower' top). Place on the hot baking sheet and bake in the oven for 40 minutes.

Sprinkle with a little icing sugar and serve immediately with cream.

Serves 4–6.   MN

MOCHA RUM CREAM

Simple to prepare, this chocolate dessert is at once both rich and light.

½ pint (300 ml) whipping cream
½ pint (300 ml) natural yoghurt
3 oz (75 g) plain chocolate
3 tablespoons water
1 tablespoon instant coffee powder
2 tablespoons rum
2 tablespoons dark soft brown sugar

Whip the cream to soft peaks and fold in the yoghurt. Put the chocolate, water and coffee powder into a bowl over a pan of hot water. When the chocolate is melted, remove from heat and stir into the rum with the sugar. Leave until cool, then fold into the cream. Spoon into individual pots and chill before serving.

Serves 6–8.   MN

CHOCOLATE ALMOND PUDDING

There can be nothing more comforting in winter months than an old-fashioned steamed pudding.

4 oz (125 g) unsalted butter
4 oz (125 g) icing sugar
4 oz (125 g) plain chocolate, grated
4 oz (125 g) ground almonds
6 eggs, separated

Well-grease a 2-pint (1.2 litre) pudding basin with butter, and sprinkle with caster sugar. Cream together the butter and icing sugar until light and fluffy and work in the chocolate, almonds and egg yolks. Beat until very soft and light. Whisk the egg whites to stiff peaks and fold into the chocolate mixture. Spoon into the prepared basin. Cover with greased greaseproof paper and foil, and steam for 1 hour. Turn out onto a warm serving dish and serve at once with whipped cream.

Serves 6.   MN

Left to right: Mocha rum cream (in glasses); chocolate cream Sophie; chocolate almond pudding, about to be steamed

CHOCOLATE CREAM SOPHIE

This sumptuous dessert is perfect for serving to chocoholic dinner guests, as it can be prepared in advance and kept in the refrigerator until it is needed.

> *4 oz (125 g) fresh brown breadcrumbs*
> *4 oz (125 g) demerara sugar*
> *8 teaspoons cocoa*
> *4 teaspoons coffee powder*
> *½ pint (300 ml) double cream*
> *¼ pint (150 ml) single cream*

Stir together the breadcrumbs, sugar, cocoa and coffee powder until evenly coloured. Put the creams into a bowl and whip to soft peaks (it is most important that the cream is not whipped too stiffly or it will be impossible to assemble the pudding neatly).

Arrange in layers in a glass bowl, starting with crumbs and finishing with cream, and using three layers of each. Cover with plastic wrap and leave in the refrigerator for at least 4 hours before using. If liked, sprinkle the surface with some grated plain chocolate, or decorate with chocolate leaves, just before serving.

Serves 6. MN

181

PERFECT CHOCOLATE PUDDING

An adaptable chocolate pudding which is equally good hot or cold.

3 oz (75 g) plain chocolate
2 oz (50 g) unsalted butter or block margarine
½ pint (300 ml) milk
2½ oz (65 g) caster sugar
¼ teaspoon instant coffee powder
2 eggs
5 oz (150 g) fresh white breadcrumbs

Put the chocolate and fat into a bowl over a pan of hot water. When the chocolate has melted, remove from the heat. Heat the milk to lukewarm and add gradually to the chocolate, with the sugar and coffee powder. Cool to lukewarm.

Separate the eggs and beat the yolks into the chocolate mixture, with the breadcrumbs. Whisk the egg whites to stiff but not dry peaks and fold into the mixture. Grease a 1½ pint (900 ml) pudding basin and spoon in the mixture. Cover with greased greaseproof paper and foil, and steam for 1½ hours. Leave in the bowl for 5 minutes and turn onto a serving dish. Serve hot with chocolate sauce or cold with whipped cream.

Serves 6.   MN

CHOCOLATE CHEESECAKE

A rich, baked cheesecake from California, with a crunchy chocolate-flavoured base. Make the cake the day before you wish to serve it, as it needs time to set and chill.

14 oz (400 g) semi-sweet dark chocolate
2 tablespoons unsalted butter
1 lb 4 oz (625 g) cream cheese
8 oz (250 g) caster sugar
12 fl oz (350 ml) double cream
1 teaspoon vanilla essence
3 eggs
3 tablespoons cocoa powder

TOPPING
8 fl oz (240 ml) soured cream
2 tablespoons caster sugar
Chocolate shavings

CRUST
8 oz (250 g) chocolate-flavoured-biscuit crumbs
4 oz (125 g) sugar
4 oz (125 g) butter, melted

Combine all the ingredients for the crust, press into the bottom of a greased 9″ (23 cm) springform tin and bake for 10 minutes in the oven at 400°F (200°C, gas mark 6). Allow to cool while you make the filling.

Melt the chocolate and butter in a double boiler and set aside. Cream the sugar and cream cheese together, add eggs, cream, vanilla, cocoa powder and chocolate-butter mixture and blend well. Pour into the prepared crust and bake at 325°F (170°C, gas mark 3) for 1¼ hours. Chill, still in the mould, for 8 hours or overnight.

Next day, unmould the cheesecake, spread top with soured cream blended with sugar, and sprinkle with chocolate shavings.

Serves 10.   CW

CARAMEL FRAPPE

For more than a decade, Robert Linxe has made and purveyed the best chocolates in Paris, and probably the world. At his Maison du Chocolat in the faubourg St-Honoré, and the branch at 52 rue François-I, off the Champs-Elysées, his array of chocolates and exquisite cakes can be tasted with cups of hot chocolate or perfectly-realized spoonsful of sorbet and ice-cream.

To complete the seduction, there are glasses of *caramel frappé* made from ice-cream, cream and caramel, whizzed to the ultimate milkshake. Robert Linxe makes his own *glace de caramel*, but in London Baskin-Robbins' *crème de caramel* ice-cream can be used to good effect; if there is none available near you, substitute the best coffee ice-cream you can find.

Caramel frappé

2 oz (50 g) granulated sugar
Knob unsalted butter
4 large scoops crème de caramel or coffee ice-
    cream
Generous ¼ pint (150 ml) single cream

you are going to make this milkshake often, prepare a larger quantity of caramel and store it for
frequent use.

To produce 2 milkshakes, put ice-cream,
chilled cream, and 1½ tablespoons of the dilute
caramel into the blender and whizz till all is well
mixed. Pour into stemmed glasses and consume
without delay, using fat straws or a spoon.

Serves 2.   AWS

SUMMER PANCAKES

Oven-baked pancakes filled with soft fruit.

> 1 lb (500 g) soft summer fruits; strawberries,
>   raspberries, peaches, kiwi fruit, bananas,
>   black cherries

THE PANCAKES
4 eggs (size 3) separated
2 tablespoons clear honey
2 oz (50 g) caster sugar
2 oz (50 g) wholemeal flour
1 tablespoon cornflour

FILLING
10 fl oz (300 g) natural yoghurt
5 fl oz (150 g) double cream
1 tablespoon clear honey or icing sugar

TO DECORATE
1 tablespoon icing sugar

Make a caramel by melting sugar in a small, heavy
saucepan, then letting it colour to a rich shade. Stop
caramelization by adding the knob of butter, swirling pan as the mixture bubbles. Carefully add
some hot water; the caramel will splutter angrily
and start to solidify, but swirl the pan and set it over
a low heat to liquefy the mixture. Increase the
water by 1–2 fl oz (30–60 ml), and stir the caramel
with a small metal spoon until it is liquid enough to
remain so when cold.

Pour the result into a glass jar and refrigerate,
covered; caramel will keep, thus, for a year, and if

Preheat the oven to 425°F (220°C, gas mark 7).

Put the yoghurt into a coffee filter or muslin
and leave to drain for an hour. Line two baking
sheets with greaseproof paper and put to one side.
Separate the eggs into two mixing bowls. Using an
electric mixer if you have one, whisk the egg yolks
with the clear honey until it is stiff enough to form a
thick ribbon across the surface. With a clean whisk,
beat the egg whites, gradually adding the sugar,
until stiff enough to form peaks. Carefully fold the
beaten egg whites into the yolks with a metal
spoon. Sieve the flour and cornflour together over

183

the eggs, and fold in with a large metal spoon. Spoon the mixture on to prepared trays, putting 3 pancakes on each tray, spreading each one out into a 5″ (13 cm) circle. Bake near the top of the oven for 10–12 minutes. Allow the pancakes to cool on the paper. (At this stage the pancakes will keep in the refrigerator for up to 8 weeks, or can be frozen for later use.)

To make the filling, whip the cream loosely with the honey or icing sugar, and blend with the now firm yoghurt. Put a spoonful of this cream on to each pancake, arrange the soft fruits over the top, and fold in half. To finish, dust with icing sugar and caramelize with a heated skewer.

Serves 6.   SW

CHOCOLATE CHESTNUT CAKE

This is a stylish union, the cake easily-made and not overly sweet. It rises well – falling naturally as it cools – handles amiably, and keeps for several days if left uncut.

> *Butter and flour for cake tin*
> *4 oz (125 g) semi-sweet dark chocolate*
> *1½ oz (40 g) unsalted butter*
> *8 oz (250 g) tinned unsweetened chestnut purée*
> *4 eggs and 1 extra egg white*
> *2 oz (50 g) caster sugar*
> *Icing sugar and double cream to serve*

Butter an 8 × 2″ (20 × 5 cm) circular cake tin, flour sides and line bottom with a round of buttered, floured greaseproof paper.

Melt broken chocolate and butter in a covered pan set into a low pan of just-boiled water; beat smooth. Sieve in chestnut purée and beat again.

Separate eggs, whisk yolks with sugar until thick, and beat in the chocolate mixture. Whisk the 5 egg whites until stiff, beat ⅓ into chocolate base to lighten this, then fold base into whites and pour into tin. Smooth and rap on the work surface to settle contents. Bake at 350°F (180°C, gas mark 4) for 50 minutes or until a trussing needle thrust into

the centre tests clean and hot. Cool cake in its tin on a rack.

To serve, release cake and peel paper from base. Turn right side up and sieve icing sugar across top. Serve sliced, with whipped cream.

Enough for 6–8.   AWS

COCONUT CAKE WITH STRAWBERRIES

Irresistible to children and adults alike.

> *5 oz (150 g) unsweetened desiccated coconut*
> *Butter and flour for cake tins*
> *4 oz (125 g) soft unsalted butter*
> *6 oz (175 g) caster sugar*
> *½ teaspoon vanilla essence*
> *8 oz (250 g) plain flour*
> *Pinch salt*
> *Generous 1½ teaspoons baking powder*
> *Generous 4 fl oz (125 ml) milk*
> *9 egg whites*
> *12½ oz (365 g) granulated sugar*
> *¼ pint (150 ml) water*
> *Almond essence*
> *Fresh strawberries*

Lightly toast coconut in a 275°F (140°C, gas mark 1) oven. Cool.

Butter two 8 × 2″ (20 × 5 cm) circular cake tins, flour the sides, and line the bottom of each with a round of buttered and floured greaseproof paper.

Cream butter in a largish bowl; gradually beat in caster sugar and vanilla. Sift flour with salt and baking powder; sift this into base alternately with milk, beating well after each addition and ending with flour. Beat in 1 oz (25 g) coconut.

In a large bowl, whisk 4 egg whites until stiff, beat ⅓ into the butter base to lighten it, then combine base with the rest of the beaten whites, trying not to knock all air from the mixture. Spoon batter into tins, smooth and spread evenly, and bake at 375°F (190°C, gas mark 5) for 30–45 minutes until risen tops are browning and cakes pull

Clockwise from top: Cherry and mint tart, page 186; chocolate chestnut cake; coconut cake with strawberries

away from sides of tins. They will not rise much. Cool cakes in their tins on a rack.

When ready to assemble, release cakes, peel paper from both bases and turn right side up. Using a serrated knife, carefully split each cake horizontally into 2 equal layers; cut away the rounded top of one to make it flat. You will then have 4 very thin layers, one of them retaining its rounded top.

To make the icing, dissolve granulated sugar in water and boil syrup until it registers 245°F (118°C) on a sugar thermometer.

Simultaneously, use a hand-held electric beater to whisk the 5 additional whites to stiff peaks. When sugar is ready, pour this slowly and steadily into whites, beating them at high speed; continue beating till icing is cold, glossy, and stands again in stiff peaks. Beat in a little almond essence and fold in most of the remaining coconut.

Place a flat layer of cake, cut side up, on a cake stand and spread generously with icing. Assemble the layers, with icing between, ending with the rounded top. Press cake lightly together and cover top and sides with remaining icing – there should be a generous amount for this – swirling the icing attractively. Strew with rest of coconut.

Eat on the day made, with plenty of sliced, fresh strawberries.

Serves 8.   AWS

185

CHERRY AND MINT TART, CHERRY AND MINT SAUCE

The combination of this fruit and herb is deliciously unexpected.

> *10 oz (300 g) rich home-made shortcrust pastry*
> *9 fl oz (generous 260 ml) milk*
> *3 egg yolks*
> *Caster sugar*
> *1 oz (25 g) plain flour*
> *Kirsch*
> *2½ lb (1.25 kg) fresh dark cherries, not too sweet*
> *Small bunch fresh mint*
> *Lemon juice*
> *1 × 12 oz (350 g) jar morello cherry conserve*

Thinly roll pastry to line a 9″ (23 cm) flan ring placed on a heavy baking sheet. Chill.

Make a pastry-cream by bringing the milk to simmer in a small, heavy saucepan while beating yolks, until thick, with 1½ oz (40 g) of sugar. Sift and beat the flour into the yolks. Strain in milk, whisking egg base constantly. Pour all into the milk pan, and whisking continuously over a low heat, bring mixture to the first boil. Raise heat slightly and beat cream vigorously for 2 minutes; there should not be the slightest lump. Whisk in a few drops of kirsch. Scrape cream onto a plate and press cling film across the surface to prevent formation of skin.

Stem and pit cherries. When pastry-cream is cold, spread most of it in a thin layer across base of tart shell. Stew this with 3–4 shredded mint leaves, cover surface with a tightly-packed single layer of cherries and bake at 400°F (200°C, gas mark 6) for 40–45 minutes, until pastry is baked and browning. Cool.

Meanwhile, to make a *coulis* or sauce, purée the remaining cherries in a food processor with just enough mint leaves and lemon juice – and a little sugar if required – to give a well-balanced result.

Briefly simmer cherry conserve with ½ teaspoon of kirsch. Sieve conserve into a bowl (leaving debris behind), and when tart has cooled, lightly spoon what is now warm jelly over the surface to glaze it.

Serve within a few hours of assembling, with spoonfuls of warmed sauce and sprigs of mint on each dessert plate.

Serves 6.   AWS

PORT JELLY

Port jelly is a perennial favourite and hard to beat. The reason it tastes so good is that only half the wine is heated, so it is a pretty alcoholic pudding. If you have an elaborate, old-fashioned jelly mould, this is the time to use it. Serve the jelly with fruit or cream. Any dark red or purple fruit – figs, grapes, plums – looks striking.

> *3 tablespoons gelatine crystals or 10 leaves*
> *1 pint (600 ml) port*
> *2 teaspoons lemon juice*
> *4 oz (125 g) castor sugar*
> *4 cloves*
> *1 stick cinnamon*

Soak the gelatine in a quarter of the port and all the lemon juice or a few minutes until it is soft. Then add another quarter of the wine and the sugar and spices and heat the mixture without allowing it to boil. Stir until the gelatine has dissolved completely then remove it from the heat and allow it to cool. Strain the cool but still liquid jelly into a clean bowl and add the rest of the port.

Pour the jelly into a wetted mould and leave it to set in cool place. Then unmould it, dip mould into hot water, and turn it out on to a plate.

Serves 6.   SCP

FRUIT SALAD WITH LIME AND GINGER SYRUP

This fruit salad will provide a good use for any jar of stem ginger you may be given over Christmas. Combined with exotic fruit and ginger ale, it makes an unusual and most refreshing dessert.

Fruit salad with ginger and lime syrup

1–2 limes, grated rind and juice
3 tablespoons stem ginger syrup
2 tablespoons clear honey
Small knob chopped stem ginger (optional)
½ pint (300 ml) flat ginger ale or boiling water
1 large mango
1 small pineapple, peeled, cored and cut in
    chunks
1 medium-size melon, scooped into balls
2 kiwis, peeled and sliced
1–2 star fruit, sliced
Strips of lime peel (optional for decoration)

Mix the lime rind, juice, syrup, honey, chopped ginger (optional) and the ginger ale or water. Cool, if necessary.

Slice the mango widthways across each side of the stone. Cut the flesh from the skin in chunks. Mix with the other prepared fruits and pour over the syrup. Allow to macerate overnight.

Decorate with strips of lime peel and serve well chilled.

Serves 6.   RD

FIGS WITH CUSTARD AND ARMAGNAC

Figs are a native of southern and southwestern France, so it seems natural to bake them in a slow oven with sugar and a dribble of Armagnac, the distinctive southwestern grape brandy.

The sugar and spirit form a syrup with the fig juice, and the fruit halves are eaten warm with a just-made pouring custard spiked with some more of the liquor.

½ pint (300 ml) milk
1 vanilla pod split down the middle
Armagnac
12 ripe figs
Demerara sugar
3 yolks of very fresh eggs
2 tablespoons caster sugar
8 fresh fig leaves, if available, washed

Scald milk with vanilla and 2 tablespoons Armagnac; remove pan from the heat, cover, and leave to infuse for 30 minutes.

Snip stem tip from each fig, slice all in half from top to base, unskinned, and place halves, cut side up, in a large, flat baking dish (or 2 of these) into which they will fit without overlapping. Sprinkle with demerara sugar and dribble all figs with a thin stream of Armagnac.

After milk has been standing for 30 minutes, place fruit in a 275°F (140°C, gas mark 1) oven. Whisk egg yolks and beat in the caster sugar until yolks are thick. Whisk in milk and sieve the mixture back into the milk pan.

Over a brisk heat, beat egg, sugar and milk until the custard thickens and is just about to boil. Immediately sieve this into a clean bowl and stir to cool slightly.

After the figs have baked for 30–40 minutes, remove from the oven, spoon over them the syrup which has formed, divide the fig leaves – if you have these – among 4 dessert plates, and serve 6 halves per person, cut side upward, with the warm custard passed separately.

Serves 4.   AWS

INDEX

Active

BUSINESS
STUDIES

SUSAN HAMMOND

BECCLES SUFFOLK

CONTENTS

INTRODUCTION FOR TEACHERS

A. Business studies and the national curriculum

In an increasingly complex and interdependent world, a knowledge of the practices and processes of business activity is an important part of the survival kit of any citizen. Business studies can use the experience of students in the core subjects and direct their interests into the 'real' world. It also has the advantage of plenty of 'real life' investigations at hand – from the school or college which they attend, friends and parents who have experience of the working world, supportive local business, to the Saturday job they have found for themselves. Young people are a part of the business world and have their own experience which they can bring to a course. There are few other subjects that can make that claim.

If business studies is relegated to a minority position on the timetable then the teachers of the subject will need to devise strategies to deal with this. Some that come easily to mind are:

* integration with core subject departments:
- the opportunity to explore through creative writing the experience of working within an organisation.
- the impact of science and technology on the individual as both a producer and a consumer.
- the application of word processors, databases and spreadsheets.
- the application of numeracy.
- integration with the study of a modern language through an investigation into its importance in tourism

* the use of supported self study to enable students to progress at their own pace

* modular organisation of courses

* the use of accreditation systems to encourage students and provide them with attainable objectives.

B. About this book

The Units are intended to give students the basic information they require to cover the content of the syllabuses of the different examination boards. This is supported by the Glossary. The decision to collect important definitions into the Glossary was influenced by the desire to make the book as flexible as possible in use.

The suggestions offered in **Finding out** have been attempted in class with different degrees of success. Any exercise intended for active learning supporting a process theory of motivation has to be designed with the needs of the individuals in mind. It would be unrealistic to claim that these exercises will not need modification to be useful for individual circumstances. Appendix B gives further ideas for coursework. Very few suggestions have been made about the way in which students should present their work. Some groups will have a full range of audio-visual resources and information technology with the staff expertise for its use. Others will be limited to A4 and drawing paper.

The **Trying it out** sections are based on examination questions and are intended to test the students understanding of the information they have learnt. They reflect the style of the examination papers. This is taken further with the integrated case studies in Appendix A.

The **Glossary** gives brief definitions of common terms, some of which are also defined in the text. Business dictionaries are useful but can be intimidating to the student.

UNIT 1:
THE INTERDEPENDENCE OF BUSINESS ACTIVITY

What is a business?

Take a careful look at Figure 1.1. It shows things people need to feel that their life is full and happy.

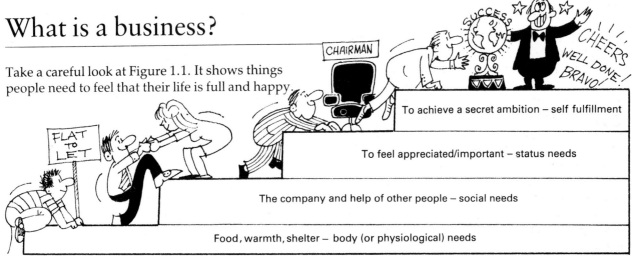

To achieve a secret ambition – self fulfillment

To feel appreciated/important – status needs

The company and help of other people – social needs

Food, warmth, shelter – body (or physiological) needs

Figure 1.1 *What people need*

In our society most people go out to work to earn money. They use the money to buy the goods and services that they think will satisfy their needs. Figure 1.2 shows how they might do this.

Figure 1.2 *How people satisfy their needs*

Businesses exist to satisfy the needs of people. Businesses provide:

* food, clothes and buildings to shelter people and keep them warm

* gas, oil, coal and electricity to keep people warm, clean and to cook their food

* services like restaurants, cinemas, theatres, discos and transport to enable people to enjoy themselves with their friends.

JUST TESTING

Look at Figures 1.1 and 1.2. What goods and services do you buy to help satisfy your needs? Are there any goods and services you get free? Who provides them? Where does the money come from to provide them?

A business is any person or group of people which sells goods or services which keep people alive or make life more enjoyable.

Figure 1.3 shows the relationship between people and businesses.

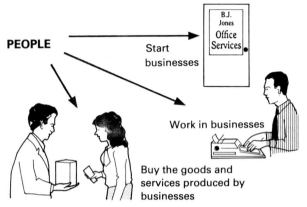

Figure 1.3 *People and business*

What do businesses do?

Figures 1.4 a and b show all the things a business must do if it is to produce goods and services which it can then sell.

a)

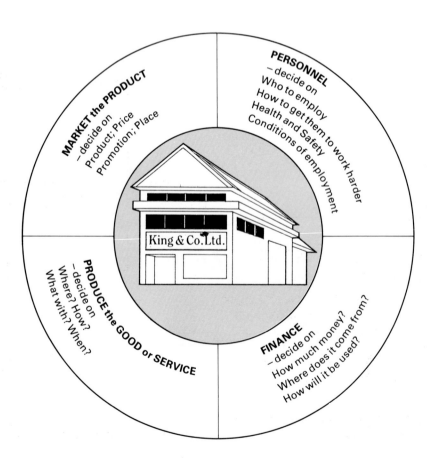

b)

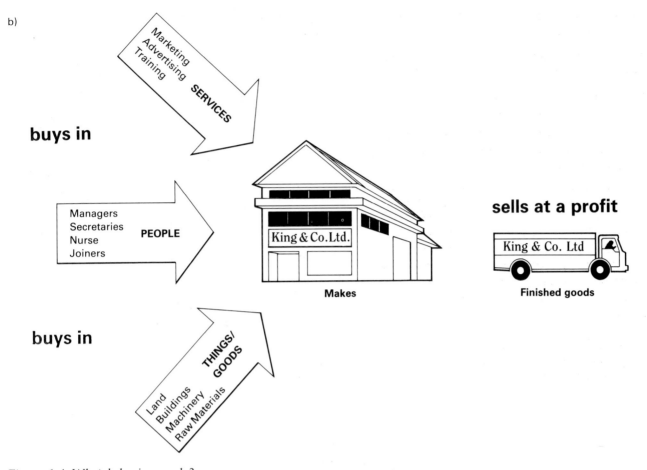

Figure 1.4 *What do businesses do?*

Different types of business

There are many different types of business. To make it easier to know what sort of business we are talking about, it is usual to put businesses which have something in common in the same group.

1. Businesses which mine, quarry, farm, forest, fish or drill to provide raw materials are **primary industries**.

2. Businesses which make goods, for example cars, printing presses, washing machines, clothes and furniture are **secondary industries**.

3. Businesses which offer services to people and other businesses are **tertiary industries**. It is usual to divide the activities of the tertiary industries into two parts: **commercial services**, for example retailing and wholesale; **direct services** (offered directly to people), for example teaching, hairdressing and medical services.

Figure 1.5 shows how the different business activities fit into the classification of industry.

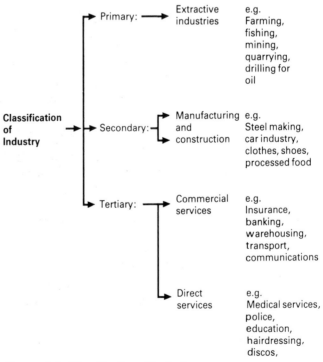

Figure 1.5 *Classification of industry*

3

The chain of production

Some businesses sell the goods and services they produce to other businesses. Figure 1.6 illustrates this **chain of production**. A chain consists of things which are linked together. When we talk about a chain of production we are saying that businesses are linked by what they buy from each other and what they sell to each other.

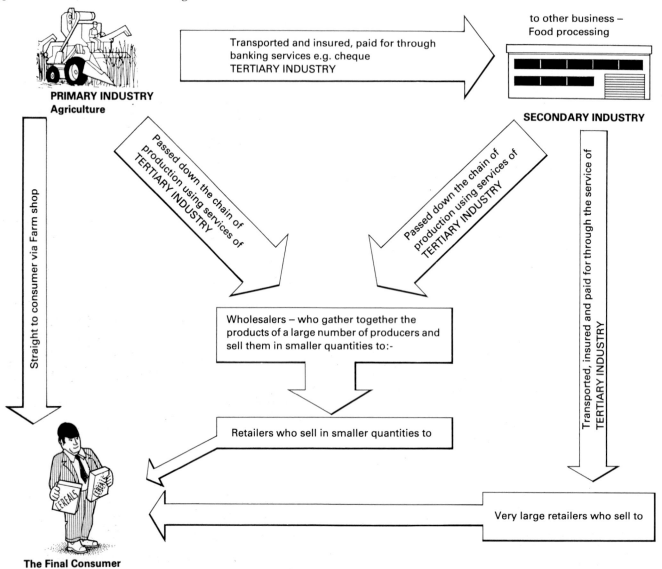

Figure 1.6 *The chain of production*

JUST TESTING

Decide which type of industry (primary, secondary or tertiary) employs the following people:

(a) Miner
(b) Bus driver
(c) Production line worker
(d) Fitter
(e) Waiter
(f) Farm worker
(g) Potter
(h) Nurse
(i) Diver on an oil rig
(j) Diver working for a leisure centre.

Specialisation

By now you should realise that in our society many businesses concentrate on one particular form of production. We say that they **specialise**. The fact that they do so is called **specialisation**. It is sometimes referred to as **division of labour** – the dividing up of the tasks in a production process between separate businesses, parts of a business and different people.

Figure 1.7 shows some of the advantages gained by specialisation. Figure 1.8 illustrates some of the problems associated with it.

Businesses specialising in a product will be able to use machinery to produce more and so reduce costs. Services, e.g. Education, will be offered to industries and thus further reduce costs

People will have more machinery to help them. This will increase the amount they can produce

Countries specialise in activities that either suit their resources or to which they are especially suited e.g. by climate

Regions specialise in industries that suit their resources – so production is cheaper

People do jobs that suit their skill – so learn faster

Countries and regions save time in transport and communications when businesses in one industry are clustered together

Time is saved when people do not have to move from one job to another

Countries and regions will build up a reservoir of skills in the industries they specialise in

Practice makes perfect – doing the same job over and over again increases the skill level

– By increasing skill levels and availability, saving time and increasing output specialisation of countries, regions and people lowers costs
– Quality of goods rises, costs fall so everybody is better off

Figure 1.7 *The advantages of specialisation*

JUST TESTING

Give two advantages and two disadvantages of specialisation for:
(a) a person   (b) a region of a country
(c) a country.

STRIKE IN THE PRESS SHOP
1 500 LAID OFF

A strike by one group of workers affects others. A 'knock on' effect.

UNEMPLOYMENT
PEOPLE DON'T HAVE THE SKILLS WE WANT SAYS MANAGER

Specialised workers can find difficulty in obtaining jobs when their skills are overtaken by changes in technology.

I hate my job. It's boring doing the same thing all the time. Nobody works as hard as us.

People feel no involvement. They do not realise the importance of other people's jobs.

WHEAT CROP FAILS IN USA
– BREAD PRICES SET TO RISE

It is not only weather conditions thousands of miles away that can affect us. Wars and political difficulties can do so as well.

Figure 1.8 *The problems associated with specialisation*

Finding out

1. Survey your local area. Make a list of the different types of business you find. Group them under the headings primary, secondary and tertiary.

(a) Draw a pie chart to illustrate your findings.
(b) Does one type of business appear more often than others? Can you give any reason for this?
(c) Survey a very different area. If you live in a country town survey a similar sized area in a large city. Repeat (a) and (b) for the new area.
(d) Can you see any similarities between the results of the two surveys? Are there any differences? Can you explain the differences between your findings?

2. Figure 1.9 divides all business activity into five major areas called **occupational categories**. Look at the outer circle which gives examples of some of the jobs that are found in each category.

(a) Can you think of five additional jobs which would belong in each category?
(b) Can you discover five local businesses that belong to each category? The yellow pages will help you here.

3. Arrange visits to one business from each of the occupational categories given in Figure 1.9.

4. Interview a local businessman:

(a) What goods does he buy in from other businesses?
(b) What services does he buy in?
(c) What services does he get "free", that is, they are provided by the government or local authority out of taxes and rates?
(d) Compare the chain of production for the goods he buys with that of two services. Can you notice any differences?

Figure 1.9 *Occupational categories*

5. This activity is concerned with finding out about the ways in which businesses satisfy the needs of their customers and the needs of people who work for them. You will need to:

(a) Chose a business that sells its products to the final consumer either directly or indirectly through wholesalers and retailers.
(b) Select somebody who works for that business and ask them to answer your questions.
You may find it easier to ask a friend or relative to help you, provided they work in the right sort of business.
(c) Draw up a questionnaire. It should cover the following points:

(i) What do they like most about the job?
(ii) Do they do the same job all the time or is their work varied?

(iii) Do they work mainly indoors or outdoors? How do they feel about this?
(iv) Do they enjoy going to work or do they go for the money?
(v) Have they made friends at work that they meet socially?
(vi) Which is most important to them – their work, their social life or their hobbies?

(d) Now look at the business that employs them. What needs does its products satisfy in the people who buy them? Be careful about this. A clothing manufacturer could be said to satisfy the basic need of warmth. On the other hand if they are making very fashionable garments they could be said to be giving their customers a feeling of status.

Trying it out

1. Division of labour leads to a better standard of living?

(a) Give two arguments to support this statement.
(b) Give two reasons why this statement might not be true.

2 (a) Give two examples of:

(i) a primary industry
(ii) a secondary industry
(iii) a tertiary industry.

(b) Name a well known business that belongs to each group.

3. Look carefully at the business activities A to C in Figure 1.10a.

(a) Identify a problem for business from each piece of information given and explain why it might have happened.
(b) Now look at the list of business functions D to F. Match them with the business activities by writing the correct letter in the boxes provided in Figure 1.10b.

4. Alison and Lynn were friends at school. After they left school they lost touch and did not see each other for a number of years. Read the following extract from their conversation at

Business activity	Business function
As a result of research a **A** business finds that the number of people in the 16-24 years age group will drop sharply over the next ten years	**D** FINANCE
A business is negotiating **B** a loan when the rate of interest rises sharply.	**E** MARKETING
An advertising campaign **C** does not cause sales of a product to rise.	**F** PERSONNEL

Business activity	Business function
A	
B	
C	

Figure 1.10 *Business activities*

7

a reunion and then answer the questions that follow it.

ALISON: I am the personal assistant to the managing director. The pay is good. I've got my own office and two typists working for me.

LYNN: That's nice for you. I couldn't stand it myself. You have to take too much responsibility. I just get paid according to how many buttonholes I make. When I need extra money there's always the chance of some overtime. Good money and a good social life – that's what I want.

(a) What needs are met by the jobs of:

   (i) Alison
   (ii) Lynn.

(b) Explain what advantages there are for Lynn's employer in organising the work so that Lynn makes buttonholes all day.
(c) Give two reasons why Alison might dislike Lynn's job.

5. Use the pie charts in Figures 1.11a to e to answer the following questions.

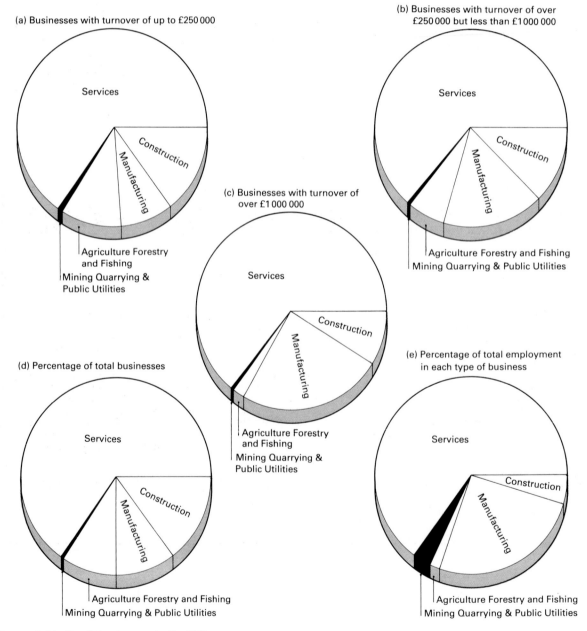

Figure 1.11 *Small businesses in the UK economy*

(a) Which type of industry has the largest number of businesses with a turnover of less than £250 000?

(b) Which type of industry is the most important in the UK economy? Give a reason for your answer.

(c) Which type of business has a turnover of £1m or more and employs a high proportion of the working population?

(d) Which type of industry has the smallest number of businesses with a turnover of £1m or more?

(e) Which of the industries shown in the pie chart belong to the primary sector?

6. Figure 1.12 is an extract from a newspaper article about unemployment in Southside. Read the article then answer the questions.

(a) (i) What are the main types of business mentioned in the article?
(ii) State whether each of these businesses belongs to primary, secondary or tertiary industry.

(b) In the glossary at the back of this book look up the meaning of the word **component** and write down the definition.

(c) What evidence does the article give for:

(i) the chain of production
(ii) the interdependence of business activity.

(d) John Stevens has written to the managing director of the company that runs the new leisure centre at Riverham. His letter is in the same vein as his comments reported in the article. As secretary to the managing director you have to write a reply. Your letter should explain to Mr Stevens the possible advantages to him and his family.

BISCUIT FACTORY TO CLOSE

500 Jobs to go.

CRAYBRIDGE'S FACTORY at Riverham in Southside is to close at the end of the year, with the loss of 500 jobs. This was announced this afternoon by Mr. Albert Johnson, the factory manager.

This factory, which once employed over 2 000 people has had its workforce gradually reduced over the past two and a half years as production was transferred to other plants in the Craybridge organisation. Some of its machinery is over 50 years old where-

as other factories have been re-equipped with up-to-date machines, requiring a smaller number of people to operate them.

The site is to be sold to Getfit Enterprises plc, who plan to demolish the factory and build an extensive leisure centre containing swimming pool, all weather soccer pitch, squash, badminton, and tennis courts, and a sauna. There will also be a car park to accommodate 500 cars.

This may be good news for the

Building and Construction industry and to the thirty to forty people the centre will eventually employ, but it brought little consolation to Mr. John Stevens, a worker at the factory for the past twenty years. 'Where am I going to get another job around here?' he asked. 'I came here when the pit closed down, so what do I know about building sites or leisure activities? Anyway no-one wants to know you once you've turned fifty.'

□

Figure 1.12 *Unemployment in Southside*

UNIT 2:
WHAT A BUSINESS NEEDS TO KNOW ABOUT ITS MARKET

What is a market?

The **buyers** and **sellers** of a good or service make up the **market** for that good or service.

The act of exchanging goods and services for money is called **trade**. People are willing to trade with each other when they can see an advantage in it for themselves. Therefore we can say that trade is the buying and selling of goods and services for a **profit**.

Figure 2.1 shows the different types of market in which a business might buy and sell.

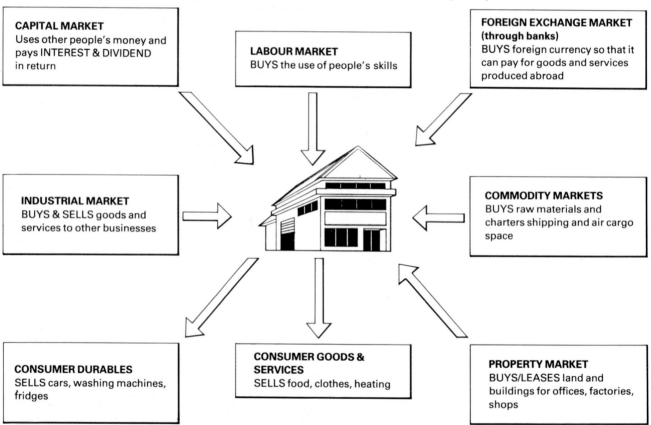

CAPITAL MARKET
Uses other people's money and pays INTEREST & DIVIDEND in return

LABOUR MARKET
BUYS the use of people's skills

FOREIGN EXCHANGE MARKET (through banks)
BUYS foreign currency so that it can pay for goods and services produced abroad

INDUSTRIAL MARKET
BUYS & SELLS goods and services to other businesses

COMMODITY MARKETS
BUYS raw materials and charters shipping and air cargo space

CONSUMER DURABLES
SELLS cars, washing machines, fridges

CONSUMER GOODS & SERVICES
SELLS food, clothes, heating

PROPERTY MARKET
BUYS/LEASES land and buildings for offices, factories, shops

Figure 2.1 *The market in which a business buys and sells*

JUST TESTING

1. Look at Figure 2.1. What markets do you and your family:

(a) buy and sell in now?
(b) remember buying and selling in in the past?

Draw a diagram similiar to Figure 2.1 to illustrate your answer.

2. The different markets in Figure 2.1 can be subdivided into more specialist markets. For example, the market for labour can be divided into the markets for plumbers, teachers, shop assistants, doctors, bus drivers and so on. List ten different markets that might come into the market for consumer goods.

What do you need to know about the market?

All markets differ but sometimes only slightly. Somebody buying jeans for leisure wear will be looking for different qualities in those jeans than someone who is buying them to work in. This is another subdivision of a market. Businesses try to find their **niche** in the market. This is when what they produce fits in very closely with what the customer wants. To do this the business needs information.

Before you look at Figure 2.2, make sure you understand the meaning of the terms **product launch** and **target market**:

* **product launch**: the process of introducing a new product onto the market – the most obvious part of this for the potential customer will be the advertising campaign

* **target market**: the people the business is trying to sell to, described in terms of their interests, income, where they live and so on.

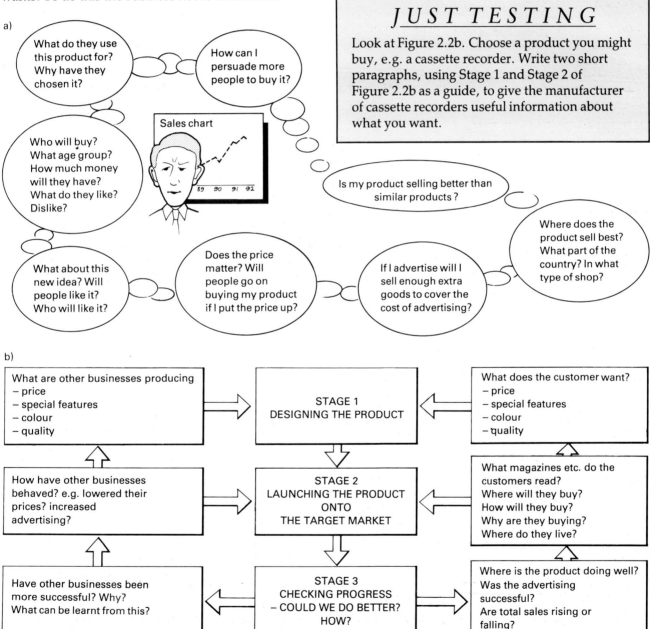

a)

What do they use this product for? Why have they chosen it?

How can I persuade more people to buy it?

Who will buy? What age group? How much money will they have? What do they like? Dislike?

Sales chart

89 90 91 92

Is my product selling better than similar products?

Where does the product sell best? What part of the country? In what type of shop?

What about this new idea? Will people like it? Who will like it?

Does the price matter? Will people go on buying my product if I put the price up?

If I advertise will I sell enough extra goods to cover the cost of advertising?

b)

What are other businesses producing
– price
– special features
– colour
– quality

STAGE 1
DESIGNING THE PRODUCT

What does the customer want?
– price
– special features
– colour
– quality

How have other businesses behaved? e.g. lowered their prices? increased advertising?

STAGE 2
LAUNCHING THE PRODUCT ONTO THE TARGET MARKET

What magazines etc. do the customers read? Where will they buy? How will they buy? Why are they buying? Where do they live?

Have other businesses been more successful? Why? What can be learnt from this?

STAGE 3
CHECKING PROGRESS
– COULD WE DO BETTER? HOW?

Where is the product doing well? Was the advertising successful? Are total sales rising or falling?

Figure 2.2 *What a business needs to know about its market*

JUST TESTING

Look at Figure 2.2b. Choose a product you might buy, e.g. a cassette recorder. Write two short paragraphs, using Stage 1 and Stage 2 of Figure 2.2b as a guide, to give the manufacturer of cassette recorders useful information about what you want.

What does the customer want?

It is important for a business to know who will want to buy its products and why. This is so that it can decide on the design of the **product**, its **price**, how to **persuade** people to buy and **where** to sell the product.

This mixture of **product**, **price**, **promotion** and **place** is called the **marketing mix**. Every product has one, but each mix is different from that of another product. Think of it as a cake mix. The ingredients might be the same but the way in which they are put together will appeal to different people.

1. People buy goods and services because they *need* them. Everybody needs food, warmth and shelter to stay alive – so people buy food, clothes, gas, electricity, pay rent, buy houses and so on.

2. People also buy goods and services for pleasure, e.g. restaurant meals, compact discs, package holidays.

3. Apart from needing and wanting something, the final choice might depend on seeing the item displayed, or on the availability of the goods. Figure 2.3 shows some of the reasons why people might buy goods and services.

Figure 2.3 *Why people buy goods and services*

The way in which people buy.

The way in which people decide to buy its product is important information for a business.

1. Where does the customer learn about the product? From friends? From advertisements or – once they have decided they are interested – by reading reports in magazines, e.g. the Consumers' Association magazine *Which?*.

2. How often does the customer buy the product?

3. Do the customers buy the same brand every time or do they chop and change?

4. Do the customers take a long time to make their decision – or do they buy on impulse? Supermarkets often put items that they know customers buy on impulse near the check out desk. When a business knows that its product is bought on impulse it will pay particular attention to the packaging and display – it will want to catch the customer's eye.

Figure 2.4 shows a report on walking boots published by the Consumers' Association in *Which?*.

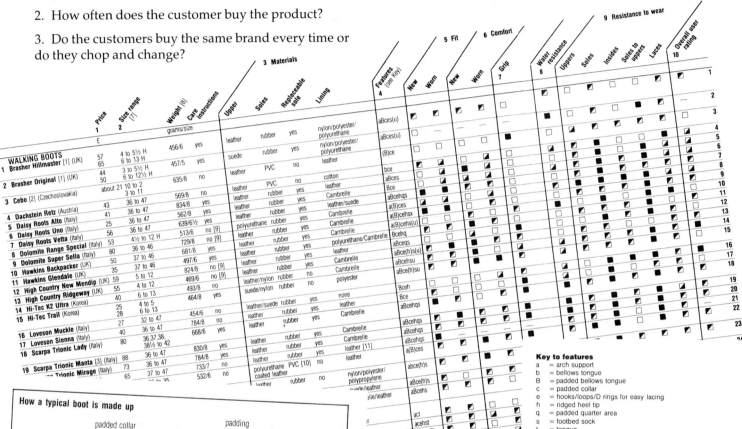

Key to features

a = arch support
b = bellows tongue
B = padded bellows tongue
c = padded collar
e = hooks/loops/D rings for easy lacing
h = ridged heel tip
q = padded quarter area
s = footbed sock
t = tongue
T = padded tongue
u = padded upper
x = padded back
Note: letters in brackets mean 'partly' or 'slightly'

How a typical boot is made up

- padded collar
- padding
- bellows tongue
- quarter area
- counter
- ridged heel tip
- midsole or throughsole
- footbed sock (often removable)
- outsole with cleats or ridges
- hooks/loops/D rings for easy lacing
- mudguard

JUST TESTING

1. What features does the Consumers' Association think are the most important in a pair of walking boots?

2. You have been given £40 to buy a pair of walking boots. Which pair would you buy and why? What did the rest of your group decide? How did the buying decisions of the group differ?

3. Explain how a manufacturer of walking boots might find this report useful.

Who will buy?

The business needs a description of the sort of person it is trying to sell to. This description will include things like age, sex, occupation, interests, income and where they live. Figure 2.5 shows the way a business might group its customers according to their occupation and income.

Class 1 A	**PROFESSIONAL: Top income earners** Doctors, lawyers, company directors	
Class 2 B	**MANAGEMENT and TECHNICAL: including** Teachers, nurses, managers, librarians. (Education rather than income places some people in this group)	
Class 3 C1	**CLERICAL and SUPERVISORY: non-manual** Shop assistants, clerks, police constables	
Class 3 C2	**SKILLED TRADES: manual** Carpenters, bricklayers, tool setters, cooks, electricians, train drivers	
Class 4 D	**SEMI-SKILLED: including** Fitters, store-keepers, etc.	
Class 5 E	**UNSKILLED: including** Labourers, porters, cleaners	

Figure 2.5 *Occupational and income categories (socio-economic groups)*

What are other businesses doing?

1. How many other businesses make the same product? In what ways are their products different?

2. What is the size of these businesses? If they are bigger, richer and more powerful a small business might find it difficult to compete against them.

3. What is their marketing mix? Knowing how competitors price, promote and distribute their products can often give a business good ideas to use with their own products.

When do people buy?

Some goods, for example bread, are bought throughout the year. If demand goes up before Christmas or other holidays it is followed by a time when people are likely to buy less bread than they did before. The customers might over-order – just in case they run out when the shops are closed – but it will not be by any great amount.

There are other goods that have a sharp rise in the number sold at certain times of the year. Christmas trees and Easter eggs are obvious examples of seasonal goods. Toys and chocolates are bought in larger quantities at Christmas and ice-cream sales rise in summer, particularly if it is hot.

Demand for goods and services that changes depending on the time of year is called **seasonal demand**.

When does a business need this information?

Businesses need information about the market when:

* they are just starting up

* they are intending to offer a new product

* they intend to spend money on advertising

* they are entering a new market, for example, selling their products in a different part of the country or in a different country altogether.

Businesses also need market information to make sure that they are succeeding in what they are trying to do. Is the new advertising campaign working? Do people like the new design?

A business that looks carefully at what the market wants before deciding on its marketing mix is said to be **market oriented** (that is, facing towards the market). Businesses that make the product and then go out to find a buyer are said to be **product oriented**. It does make sense to find out what you can sell before going to the expense of making it.

Finding out

1. A business and its markets

Your research for this exercise should include an interview with the owner or manager of a business. It will make some of the tasks easier if the business you are studying sells directly to the consumer. The questions you ask can include:

* what supplies of raw materials, semi-finished goods and finished goods does the business buy in?

* how does the business decide on a supplier?

* what different types of skills does a business employ?

* are any of these skills bought in from another business? (e.g. rather than employ an accountant, the business might buy the services of a firm of accountants),

* where does the money used in the business come from?

* does the business have more than one product? If so, what are these products?

Task A   As a result of group discussion about the findings of your research, make a list of the different types of market in which the business buys and sells.
1. Draw a large chart to show the different markets.
2. On an outline map of (a) the United Kingdom and (b) the world, show the different areas from which the business draws its supplies.

Task B   When deciding on suppliers, a business is likely to have a choice.
1. Choose three markets the business buys in.
2. List the criteria (reasons) the business might give for selecting one supplier rather than another.

Task C   Using the list of criteria you have drawn up in Task B, select one market in which the business buys and for this market put the list of criteria in the order you think would be the most important. Give reasons for your answer.

Task D   You are the owner of a small shop selling tobacco products, newspapers, a range of tinned goods, cold meats and pies, and other goods including a small range of stationery and medical supplies (elastoplast, aspirin). You are the only person working full time in the business. If you have to leave the premises during business hours you have to employ another person. You can get your supplies from the following sources:
(a) A large cash and carry wholesaler, ten miles away. The goods are cheap but you have to collect them yourself and pay in cash. It can provide supplies for the whole range of your goods, apart from newspapers.
(b) Specialist wholesalers who deliver and offer credit but are more expensive than the cash and carry. You have to use a specialist wholesaler for your newspapers and magazines.
(c) A bakery and delicatessan in a nearby town who will supply you with their high quality goods (which your customers like), but you must collect and pay cash.
(d) A large bakery that will deliver but the goods are not of the same quality as the smaller bakery.
Take part in a group discussion and decide which supplier or suppliers you would use and why. Write a report outlining the decisions you made and give your reasons.

Task E   Review the whole exercise.
(a) What contribution did you make to the group discussions?
(b) How could you improve your contribution?
(c) What have you learnt about the buying decisions of businesses?
(d) What problems did you find when doing these tasks?
(e) What additional information would help you in completing these tasks?

2. Looking at the marketing mix

Choose one product from each of the following lists:
List 1: chocolate bar, magazine, baked beans, cosmetics, bread, detergent.

List 2: carpet, personal computer, personal stereo, car, continental holiday, washing machine.

Task A   Working as a group, collect as much information as you can about each of the products. Organise your information under the headings **price, promotion, place**.

Task B   Compare the information you have collected about the product in group 1. For example, if you chose baked beans you will be comparing the price, promotion and place of Heinz baked beans with the price, promotion and place of other brands. Repeat this exercise for the product you chose in group 2.

Task C   Working alone and using the information you have gathered in the previous tasks, write a report comparing the marketing mixes of the products. Your report should point out both similarities and differences. Illustrate your report with examples. Can you think of any reasons to explain your findings?

Trying it out

1. Look carefully at the photographs in Figure 2.6 before answering the questions below.

Figure 2.6 *The market for mugs*

(a) List the different types of market the pottery sells in.

(b) Who is the customer in each market?

(c) In what ways might the requirements of each customer be different from the others?

(d) What effect do you think each of the following would have on the orders for mugs from this pottery:

(i) the football team wins the FA cup and comes top of the League in the same season?
(ii) another pottery opens ten miles away producing the same type of mug?
(iii) there is a Royal Wedding?

2. Ros Evans owns a small business producing made to measure dresses for the middle price range in the market. She has a small shop with workshop above, in a prosperous suburb of a large town. Ros consults very closely with her clients to make sure they get exactly what they want. If a client produces a rough sketch of the dress she wants Ros will design it for her.

(a) What is Ros Evans's product?

(b) Look at the following list of price ranges for a simple woollen dress. A dress of this type can be bought in a major chain store for about £35. How much do you think Ros would charge?

£10–25, 25–50, 50–75, 75–100, 100–125, 125–150, 150–175.

(c) (i) Give three reasons why a woman might be prepared to buy one dress from Ros rather than spend the money on two or three cheaper dresses from a chain store.
(ii) The prices charged by Ros Evans are very similar to the prices of the more expensive ready-made dresses. Ros's customers, however, have to wait a month on average for the delivery of their dress. Give three reasons why a woman who can afford the more expensive ranges of off-the-peg dresses would prefer to buy from Ros.

(d) Explain why a shop in "a prosperous suburb of a large town" is a good place for this business.

When Ros Evans looked at the orders she had received for evening and wedding dresses in 1988 she found that these varied from month to month.

Orders for evening and wedding dresses
January 1989–December 1989

January	0	July	2
February	3	August	0
March	5	September	1
April	6	October	3
May	5	November	4
June	3	December	0

(e) Draw a graph to show how the sales of these dresses varied throughout the year.

(f) Explain why the orders might vary in this way.

3. In a recent newspaper article, a businessman explained his success in the following words:

"My first thought is for my customer. What does he want? What price is he prepared to pay? Then I go away and find out if I can satisfy his requirements at a cost I think is reasonable. In other words, can I sell him what he wants, at a price he will pay and still make a profit. It is the only way to sell."

(a) Is this business man:

(i) product oriented?
or (ii) market oriented?

(b) Explain your answer, using evidence from the quotation.

4. When Jimmy Chan left school he went to the local technical college and completed a two year course in cabinet making. Although he was very successful in the final assessments, Jimmy could not get a job when he had finished the college course. He was unemployed for twelve months before approaching his father with the idea of setting up his own business.

Mr Chan owned some property in the town which included a disused barn that was ideal for conversion into a workshop. Jimmy proposed that his father should finance the conversion and lend Jimmy the money to buy the tools and machinery he would need. To Jimmy's surprise his father did not agree immediately. Instead he sat his son down and presented him with a list of questions he had to answer.

(a) Draw up the list of questions Mr Chan asked Jimmy about the market for craftsman-built furniture in the district.

(b) Choose six of the questions from the list and explain why each one is important.

17

UNIT 3:
HOW DO BUSINESSES FIND OUT ABOUT THEIR MARKETS?

Businesses find out about their markets by collecting together all the information that is available to them. This activity is known as market research. Figure 3.1 outlines some of the sources of information open to a business and the uses to which that information can be put.

Information about the market can be found both inside the business, **internal sources**, and outside the business, **external sources**.

JUST TESTING

Make a list of the type of information, useful to marketing, a business might find in its own records.

a)

b)

c)

d)

e)

Figure 3.1 *Sources and uses of market information: survey, internal records, trade associations, government reports, research organisations*

18

Methods of collecting information

Primary data

This is information collected specifically to answer a particular question about the market. There are several ways of doing this.

1. *Questionnaires.* The business decides what information is needed and prepares a list of questions which are then given to people to answer. The questions can be asked in a face-to-face situation by an interviewer (see photograph a) in Figure 3.1), over the phone or posted to the chosen people.

Questionnaires can provide a great deal of useful information about attitudes, past purchases and the sort of person who buys the product, but they do have a number of disadvantages, see Figure 3.2.

There are nearly 57 million people living in the United Kingdom. It would take a long time and cost a great deal of money to question all of them to find the information wanted. Besides, the business will not be interested in many of these people because they are unlikely to want to buy its products.

To save time and money and to make sure that they reach the right people, businesses select the people to be questioned very carefully. The people who are chosen to answer the questions are known as the **sample**. Figure 3.3 shows the different types of sampling that may be used.

Figure 3.2 *Disadvantages of questionnaires*

Random:	Everybody in the population has an equal chance of being surveyed e.g. every 10th person	1 Difficult to do accurately 2 May include people who do not use the product 3 Expensive – but used for government surveys
Stratified random:	The population is divided into groups according to age, income, area, job etc. Then the groups are sampled randomly	1 Cuts down on the number of people to be interviewed and so on the expense 2 Could miss out on important information. How do you know 15-25 year olds will not be interested in your product?
Area:	This takes people in groups e.g. all the people in one school are interviewed	Very good and cheap if you are **sure** you know your market
Convenient:	Who are the easiest people to interview? If you wanted to know what people thought of your restaurant you could ask the first 100 customers in the day	Useful if you want to check that things are going well
Judgement:	The interviewer decides who to approach	Useful for limited information for a known market

Figure 3.3 *Examples of sampling methods*

Although surveys can give the business a great deal of valuable information about their markets, they are expensive and a great deal of care has to go into organising them. Figure 3.4 outlines the stages in designing and organising a survey.

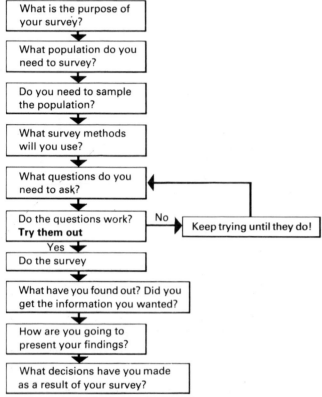

Figure 3.4 *Designing and organising a survey*

2. *Observation.* Watching people can tell the business a great deal about how people behave, but not why they behave in that way.

3. *Testing and tasting.* Groups of people, sometimes known as **consumer panels**, are asked to try the product out and report on it. Tastings sometimes take place in public places, e.g. supermarkets.

JUST TESTING

You are a manufacturer about to launch a new chocolate bar, Scrumpo Xtra. Which method of primary research do you think would be most suitable to answer the following questions?

(a) What do people think of the taste of Scrumpo Xtra?
(b) What price are people prepared to pay for it?
(c) Why do people buy chocolate bars?
(d) How do people buy chocolate bars? (After careful thought? On impulse?)

Secondary data

This is information that has been collected for other purposes but which contains information useful to the business.

A business has to be very careful when using secondary data:

* the information might be out of date. It takes time to publish reports and people and situations change

* the people who gathered the information might have held something back when publishing. Perhaps they thought some of the facts reflected badly on them!

* it is difficult to judge the efficiency and experience of the people who collected the information without knowing them. The report might be inaccurate because the people who produced it did not do a very good job.

The problems of market research

Market research is necessary – even for the smallest business. It is also expensive, time consuming and, except on the smallest scale, needs special skills.

The problem of finding out about the market becomes more difficult if a business is selling to other countries. There are the additional problems of different language, customs and culture. The British Overseas Trade Board and the Department of Trade provide information about overseas markets to businesses that want to sell abroad.

Finding out

1. Studying a business

You can complete the tasks in this assignment by either:

　(a) a visit to a business
or (b) a talk from a manager or owner.

Task A　List the different types of information the business will need (e.g. what other businesses supply the same goods or services). Give a brief explanation as to why each is important.

Task B   From the results of your research, list each type of information in the order of its importance to the business you have studied. Write down the reasons (criteria) for the order you have selected.

Task C   How does the business find out about its market? Explain each method and give reasons for its use.

Task D   As the marketing manager, write a report outlining the strengths this business has, compared with its competitors. Your report should include products, where the business is situated, and so on.

2. To complete this assignment you can either:

(a) conduct a market research survey for a small business you know
or (b) conduct a market research exercise before setting up your own mini-enterprise.

Task A   Make a list of all the different types of information you will need. This should include a description of the type of person you think you will sell to.

Task B   1. As a group, draw up a questionnaire designed to find out what your customers want from your product, how much they are prepared to pay, where and when they will buy your product.
2. Test your questions on the other groups in your class. Did they find the questions hard to answer? Did they misunderstand any questions? If the answer to either of these two questions is 'Yes', re-design the questions.

Task C   Using your questionnaire, survey your market. Write up your findings using graphs and charts to illustrate them.

Task D   What have you found out about your market as a result of this survey? Will you have to change any of your original ideas as a result of it? Did you find any problems? How can you avoid these problems in the future? Give reasons for your answer.

Trying it out

1. Ros Evans owns and runs a business making dresses to meet the individual needs of her clients. Several of her clients have suggested that she should stock a range of hats, gloves, shoes and other accessories. If Ros did this, her clients would be able to chose a complete outfit on one visit.

Ros is tempted by this idea. If it was successful it would bring in more business and increase her profit. On the other hand, her present shop is small. There is no room on the premises for storage. Ros had still made no decision when the shop next door came on the market. She knew it was ideal for her purpose, but was still determined to be cautious.

(a) Give two advantages and two disadvantages to Ros in expanding her business.

(b) (i) List the things Ros would need to find out before deciding whether or not to lease the shop next door.
(ii) Select three of the things Ros needs to find out and explain what method of market research would be most suitable in each case.

2. Write a short report outlining the way in which you would organise the market research for a product. Your report should include:

(a) the stages in organising market research

(b) your reasons for including each stage in your report.

3. Mr and Mrs Webster own a village shop. They are considering adding services in shoe repairs and dry cleaning to their list of products. The clothes and shoes would be taken by them to specialist businesses in the nearest town.

(a) List three ways in which Mr and Mrs Webster might have become aware that there was a market for these services.

(b) What other information would they need before offering these services to their customers?

(c) How could they find this additional information? Give reasons for your answer.

UNIT 4:
FINDING OUT ABOUT FINANCE

Finance is the word used to describe:

* the money a business uses

* the ways in which a business raises money

* how the business uses that money.

Why does a business need money?

A business will need money:

* when it is being set up

* when there are plans for expansion and/or diversification

* when, for some reason, the money it is getting for selling its products does not cover its expenses.

Figure 4.1 shows some of the different reasons why a business needs money.

JUST TESTING

Sanjay Rustgi wants more money to put into his business. The following extract is part of a conversation Sanjay had with his bank manager:

"The furniture I make is getting more popular all the time. I've had a 10% increase in orders this month. I could do with a bigger workshop and someone to help me. My machinery is pretty old too. With more modern tools I could take on jobs that are impossible for me now".

What are Sanjay Rustgi's reasons for wanting more money? Explain your answer.

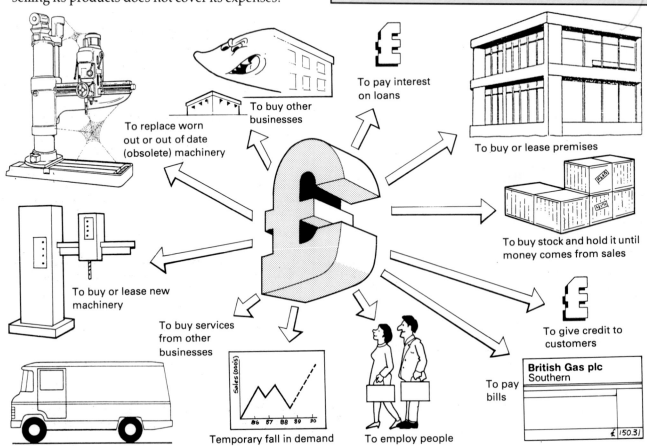

To replace worn out or out of date (obsolete) machinery

To buy other businesses

To pay interest on loans

To buy or lease premises

To buy stock and hold it until money comes from sales

To buy or lease new machinery

To buy services from other businesses

Temporary fall in demand

To employ people

To pay bills

To give credit to customers

British Gas plc
Southern
£ 150.31

Where does the money come from?

A business gets money from four main sources:

1. the owner or owners

2. borrowing

3. credit

4. government grants.

Money from the owners

1. The owner or owners of a business will put money into the business:

* at the birth of the business. This is called **start-up capital**

* when the whole or part of a business is bought.

Figure 4.2 outlines the different ways in which people can put money into a business.

As a partner
– can be up to 20 partners
– share the decisions
– share the profits
– share the risk

As a shareholder in a company
– can be a very large number of shareholders
– vote for directors to take decisions on behalf of shareholders
– very little control for many, one share gives one vote
– receive dividends (profit) according to the number of shares held
– risk of loss limited to the money invested in the business

As a sole proprietor
– owns the entire business
– takes all the major decisions
– takes all the profit
– takes all the risk

Retained profits
– owners decide not to take profits out of the business to built up a fund to replace worn out equipment or to expand
– directors decide on behalf of shareholders to keep money in the business

Figure 4.2 *Putting money into a business*

2. The profit (i.e. the amount of money received from sales minus the costs needed to produce the goods for sale) a business makes belongs to the owners of the business. If it is left in the business it is called **retained profit**.

3. Sometimes the owners of a business will put extra money into it:

* when they want the business to grow larger

* when the business cannot pay its way for some reason.

Owners' capital is the cheapest and safest way of financing a business. It still costs the owner the use of the money – either to spend or to lend to somebody else at a profit.

Figure 4.3 shows some of the reasons why a business cannot pay its way.

Figure 4.3 *Why a business may be short of money*

JUST TESTING

What is the difference between start-up capital and retained profit? Who do the retained profits belong to?

Borrowing money

When a business borrows money, (unless it borrows it from trusting relatives or friends) it enters into a legal agreement (known as a **contract**) with the people who are lending the money. This usually states:

* the length of time for which the loan is made

* the **interest** which will be paid by the borrower

* the date on which the loan will be repaid

* the **security** the borrower is offering. Security is something the borrower owns which the lender can sell if he needs to recover the cost of the loan because it has not been repaid on time.

The terms of the contract are drawn up to suit the needs of the borrowers and lenders. If the borrower is a small business without much security the terms of the loan will, if granted, be more severe. For example, if the level of interest is usually 11%, small businesses might be charged 16%. On the other hand very large businesses, such as ICI or Unilever, could get a loan at the same time at 9% interest.

1. A *bank loan* is a fixed sum of money lent for a fixed period of time at a fixed rate of interest by one of the banks.

2. A *bank overdraft* is permission for the business to draw more money from its bank account than it has in it. The rate of interest varies according to general changes in the interest rate and each time the business pays in some money the amount owed, and therefore the amount of interest to be paid, goes down.

3. *Debentures* are loans to a company. Debentures have a fixed rate of interest for a fixed period of time – usually a long time.

4. *Mortgages* are loans for a fixed period of time with some form of property as the security.

5. *Hire purchase* is an agreement to hire goods for a certain length of time. At the end of this time, the person hiring the goods has the right to buy them for an agreed amount (usually very small). Until they have paid this amount they do not own the goods.

Borrowing does have disadvantages:

1. Lenders sometimes put conditions on the loan that interferes with the way in which the owner or owners want to run the business. There is a loss of **control**.

2. The interest on the loan must be paid regularly which can be a heavy burden on a business if times are hard.

3. If, for any reason, the business cannot pay the interest or repay the loan when it matures, the lenders can sue the business and force it into **bankruptcy** (sole proprietors and partnerships) or **liquidation** (companies).

JUST TESTING

1. What is the difference between a bank loan and a bank overdraft?

2. What four things will be included in an agreement between a borrower and a lender? Explain why you think each is important.

Credit

Credit is used to describe business transactions where no money changes hands at the time. A potter, for example, might buy clay on the 1st June but does not pay for it until the end of the month. He has received one month's credit. This is sometimes called **trade credit** to distinguish it from the credit used by consumers. Creditors can also sue for the repayment of any money owed to them.

Goverment grants

The government gives grants to businesses who meet certain conditions. The map of the United Kingdom in Figure 4.4 shows the Assisted areas and Urban Programme areas.

These are the parts of the country that have higher than average levels of unemployment. Small firms and businesses that are just starting can apply for regional enterprise grants. These are available for:

* **investment** – 15% of the cost of buildings and equipment to a maximum of £15 000

* **innovation** – 50% of the cost of improving production methods, product or developing a new product to a maximum of £25 000

* **consultancy** – businesses that employ consultants to improve their marketing, design, quality, information and financial systems will have two thirds of the cost paid for them. In other parts of the country this money is still available but only half the costs of consultancy fees will be paid.

Contact Points

1 Scotland
2 DTI North-East
3 DTI Yorkshire and Humberside
4 DTI North-West *(Manchester)*
5 DTI North-West *(Liverpool)*
6 DTI East-Midlands
7 DTI West-Midlands
8 DTI South-East *(Cambridge)*
9 DTI South-East *(London)*
10 DTI South-East *(Reading)*
11 DTI South-East *(Reigate)*
12 DTI South-West
13 Wales

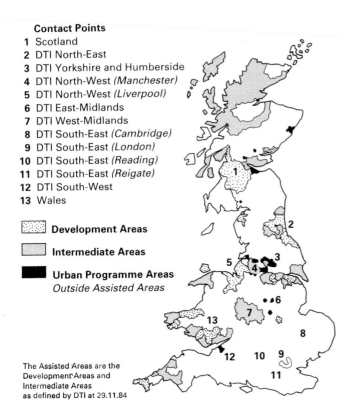

Development Areas

Intermediate Areas

Urban Programme Areas
Outside Assisted Areas

The Assisted Areas are the
Development Areas and
Intermediate Areas
as defined by DTI at 29.11.84

Figure 4.4 *Assisted areas in England, Scotland and Wales*

Businesses of any size in the Assisted areas can apply for grants to help with investment provided the project:

* will create or protect employment

* will make a profit

* offers distinct national and regional benefits.

The government also offers a **loan guarantee scheme**. Under this the government covers 70% of any loan a bank makes to a small business. This guarantee reduces the risk a bank takes in lending to small businesses.

Major complaints about financial help from the government are:

* there is not enough available

* government departments are too cautious. Time is wasted filling in forms and waiting while civil servants investigate the claim.

JUST TESTING

State two ways in which the government tries to help small businesses. Give reasons to explain why the government gives this help.

Which method shall I use?

The method of raising money used by a business will depend on the answers to the following questions:

* For how long is the money needed?

* How much control am I prepared to give to other people?

* How much risk am I prepared to accept?

Time

Money is used by the business to buy things it needs. Factories and machinery will stay with the business for as long as it exists or, in the case of machinery, until it wears out. Raw materials, on the other hand, will be used up quickly. It is usual to divide the type of finance needed into three parts:

1. Long-term finance that will stay in the business for at least five years.

2. Medium-term finance that will stay with the business for one to five years.

3. Short-term finance that will be available for up to one year.

Figure 4.5 shows the different sorts of finance suitable for each length of time.

Time	Sources of Finance	Use of money
Over five years (long term)	Owners' capital Long term loans Debentures Mortgages	Anything that is expected to stay in the business for longer than five years: – property – machinery
1-5 years (medium term)	Owners' capital Loans negotiated for less than 5 years e.g. bank loans Leasing Hire purchase	Anything that is expected to be useful to the business for at least five years: – smaller items of machinery – office equipment – motor vehicles
Less than 1 year (short term)	Owners' capital Bank overdraft Trade credit	Useful to help the business over temporary problems: – buying in stock to prepare for the Christmas rush – sudden increase in the price of stock This money is cheaper in the short term but expensive for longer periods

Figure 4.5 *Money and time*

How much control?

When a business is owned by one person, that person makes all the decisions. As soon as more people are involved the amount of control the original owner has is less. Some people want to keep control more than others. Rather than take on partners or become a company they will use their own money, plough back profits or borrow to finance the business.

How much risk?

If you have £5 000 to start a business and the business fails, you have lost all your money. If you start the business with a partner, then you would have lost £2 500. People take this sort of risk into account when they decide how they will finance their business.

Figure 4.6 shows how a business person might decide on the form of finance to use.

JUST TESTING

What are the three main things a business has to take into account when deciding on its method of finance? Why are these important?

Figure 4.6 *Finance in the balance*

Finding out

1. You are about to start a small business in your local area. You might find it more efficient to organise yourselves in groups to find out the information in Tasks A–C. You should produce your own report on the information for Task D.

Task A   Invite a representative from one of the High Street banks to talk to you about the financing of a small business. You will find the Banking Information Service useful in arranging this visit.

Task B   Contact a local wholesaler. What credit terms do they offer their customers? Do all customers get credit? How does the wholesaler decide to whom he will give credit?

Task C   What financial help does the government offer small businesses in your area? You can start your enquiries for this task by phoning the Enterprise Initiative (Freephone Enterprise).

Task D   Write a report based on your investigation. It should include the following points:
(a) What are the main sources of finance for a small business?
(b) What problems face a new business trying to find finance?
(c) Which methods of finance would you chose and why?

(d) What problems did you experience in finding out the information and writing the report? How can you try to avoid these problems in the future?

2. You decide that you will need a small van in your business.

Task A (a) Select the type of van you need and calculate the cost of buying it:

> (i) using your own money
> (ii) on hire purchase
> (iii) with a bank loan.

(b) Draw a graph to show the total amount of money you will have to pay out each year using each method. Comment on your findings.

Task B Contact a business that leases vans. What are the advantages to you of leasing rather than buying a van? Which method would you choose and why?

Task C What are the costs of running the van for one year? How would you expect to finance them?

Task D Using the information you have collected, decide which method might suit you best if you are in the following situations, giving reasons for your decisions.

(a) You have enough money to buy the van outright but there is a chance that an important piece of equipment used in your business will need replacing in the near future.

(b) Your bank manager is willing to give you a loan but he wants a bigger say in the way in which you run your business. You have not got the money yourself.

(c) You are not sure if you are making the right choice of van. It may not be large enough for your purposes.

Trying it out

1. In 1980 Paula Bowe, machinist, set up a small workshop making clothes in Liverpool. Paula had just been made redundant and had received £4 000 in redundancy money from her former employers.

Paula had worked in the clothing trade for fifteen years and was highly thought of by larger businesses who were prepared to promise to give her enough orders to keep the business going for the first six months of its life. With these guarantees, Paula was able to negotiate a loan from her bank to cover the rest of the cost of setting up her business. She was also able to offer her house as a security for the loan.

In setting up her business Paula made one mistake. Her six machinists had to be paid and it would be a month before she received payments for her first orders. Paula had forgotten to take this into account when working out how much money she would receive from the bank.

By 1986 Paula's business was doing very well. She was now employing twenty machinists. She knew she could expand the business but lacked the capital to do so. Paula's sister suggested that she should come into the business as a partner. She also pointed out to Paula that she could get help from the government.

(a) Paula had to offer the bank security for the loan she negotiated with them.

> (i) What is **security**?
> (ii) What security did Paula offer the bank?
> (iii) Why did the bank insist on having security for the loan?

(b) Paula had forgotten she had to pay her employees for the first month.

> (i) Where could she go for financial help?
> (ii) What type of financial help would be most suitable?

(c) Paula hesistated when her sister suggested she joined the business as a partner.

> (i) Give one advantage to the business of the proposed partnership.
> (ii) Give one reason why Paula might be reluctant to take on a partner.

(d) Give three examples of the help Paula might get from the government.

c)

a)

b)

d)

Figure 4.7 *How a business spends money*

2. Figure 4.7 shows some of the different ways in which a business spends money.

(a) Look at each photograph in turn and decide which goods or services would stay with the business for:

  (i) less than one year
  (ii) between one and five years
  (iii) over five years.

Give reasons for your answers.

(b) Name one suitable method of finance in each case and:

  (i) say why you chose that method of finance
  (ii) give a possible disadvantage of using that method of finance.

3. By the time she was 21 Mal Jones had saved £5 000 towards realising her ambition of owning a general store. A small shop had come onto the market near her home. It was in a short row of shops, which included a sub-post office, on the major bus routes to the city and within easy walking distance of a large hospital. Mal thought it was an ideal site for a general store. After some careful enquiries she came up with the following list of things she would need to open her shop.

Cost of shop	£30 000
Fixtures and fittings	£ 1 000
Second hand van	£ 4 000
Opening stock	£ 2 000

Mal's bank was prepared to offer her a **mortgage** on the property of £25 000.

(a) Answer the following questions using the information given in the passage above.

  (i) Give three reasons to explain Mal's belief that the shop was in a good position for a general store.
  (ii) What is the total amount of finance needed by Mal?
  (iii) What two types of finance are available to Mal? Give one advantage and one disadvantage of each.

(b) How might Mal finance the purchase of:

  (i) the van
  (ii) the fixtures and fittings
  (iii) her opening stock.

(c) Outline and comment on some of the problems Mal might meet in financing her general store.

UNIT 5:
KEEPING CONTROL

Keeping control of money is part of life. Is there enough money in the bank to pay the electricity bill? What food is there in the freezer? What do we need to buy? Can we afford that expensive holiday?

Efficient people keep records that allow them to answer these questions quickly and easily. The less efficient have to spend time rummaging through the freezer, looking for bank statements, requesting statements, and so on. If they don't bother, they find out, sometimes too late, that they are running short of food or money.

The same principles apply to business. Keeping records provides information that:

* gives early warning of the problems the business might be facing. The business can then take action to avoid the problems

* saves time (and therefore money) when information is needed

* makes it easier for the business to stay within the law. All businesses have to keep accounts for tax purposes.

Records communicate information to the owner and managers of a business that can be used to make decisions and spot problems before they become too serious.

JUST TESTING

1. Give two reasons why a business needs to keep records.

2. Explain two problems which inaccurate and/or out-of-date records can cause for a business.

Book-keeping

This is the most basic part of any system of accounts. It is a record of all payments by the business and the money it receives. Small businesses can buy books already set out for use. Figure 5.1 is a sample page from such a book.

Larger businesses will use a computer–based system. As computers become more powerful and their software more sophisticated, they can give managers a great deal of help in controlling the business. Not only will computers store the basic information they can also answer questions of the "What if . . . ?" type by drawing on the information already stored in them.

Figure 5.1 *Book-keeping*

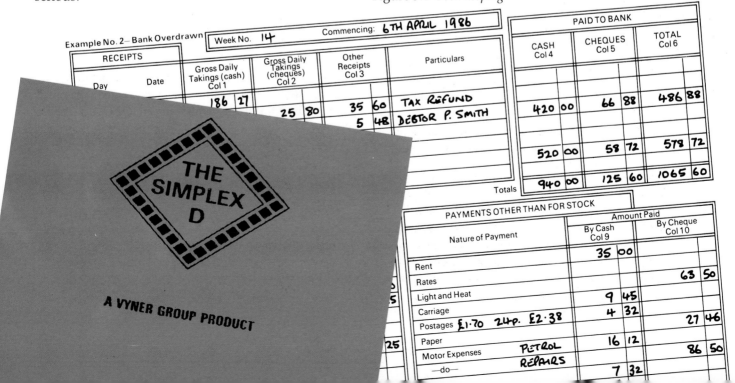

THE
SIMPLEX
D

A VYNER GROUP PRODUCT

Example No. 2— Bank Overdrawn	Week No. 14	Commencing: 6TH APRIL 1986				PAID TO BANK		
RECEIPTS		Gross Daily Takings (cash) Col 1	Gross Daily Takings (cheques) Col 2	Other Receipts Col 3	Particulars	CASH Col 4	CHEQUES Col 5	TOTAL Col 6
Day	Date							
		186 27						
			25 80	35 60	TAX REFUND	420 00	66 88	486 88
				5 48	DEBTOR P. SMITH			
						520 00	58 72	578 72
				Totals		940 00	125 60	1065 60

PAYMENTS OTHER THAN FOR STOCK		Amount Paid	
Nature of Payment		By Cash Col 9	By Cheque Col 10
		35 00	
Rent			
Rates			63 50
Light and Heat		9 45	
Carriage		4 32	
Postages £1·70 24p. £2·38			27 46
Paper		16 12	
Motor Expenses	PETROL		86 50
—do—	REPAIRS	7 32	

JUST TESTING

List four items of information a business needs to record. Figure 5.1 will help you with this.

Budgets

A budget is a short-term plan of action outlining what the business wants to achieve, what it needs to do to reach its goal and how much it will cost. The steps in budgetary control are outlined in Figure 5.2.

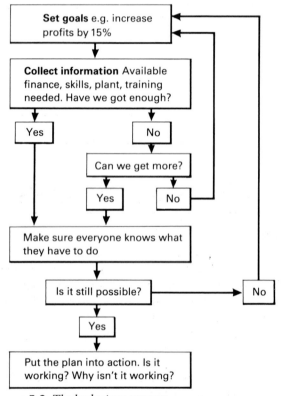

Figure 5.2 *The budgetary process*

Budgets act as a control for the business because they set targets and the people running the business can check to see if they are reaching these targets. If a budget is to be successful in controlling a business:

* the targets have to be realistic. A salesman is likely to be discouraged if he has to sell £1 000 worth of goods in a month when he knows he will be lucky to sell £700 worth of goods

* people have to be involved in drawing up the budget. If management announce that the production target is so many items a month, the workers on the production line could ignore it

* there should be some incentive for reaching the target – perhaps a bonus for all output over the target level.

JUST TESTING

1. Peter Lee has just been appointed finance manager for a fast growing business. He wants to introduce a budgetary system. Write down the main points he would put in his report to his managing director to persuade him of the advantages of this course of action.

2. You have a piece of coursework to complete for GCSE Business Studies. Your teacher wants to set a deadline for the work to be in, to make sure you complete all the work required by the date set by the examining board. What steps can your teacher take to encourage all students to work towards that target? What could go wrong?

Cash flow forecast

A cash flow forecast is the cash budget of the business. It sets out what the business expects to receive in payments over a future period of time and how much it will have to pay out. Figure 5.3 shows a cash flow forecast for a small business over a period of six months.

Look at Figure 5.3. There are two columns for each month. The first column is the cash budget. This is what the business thought might happen. The second column contains the actual figures for each month. By comparing what happened with what they thought would happen the owners and managers spot problem areas and take action to remedy them.

1. *Orders*. This figure represents the number of days work for which the business has received orders. Note that Webster's Wires expected orders to fall in November. If orders fall unexpectedly it could mean that there is something wrong with the marketing of the product – or perhaps a competitor is taking custom away from the business. An increase in the amount of work the business has could be a sign that it should expand.

2. *Sales* and *receipts* are very important. Sales are the number of customers who have been sent an **invoice**. Too high a level of sales can cause problems for a business. When sales increase, the business has to buy in more raw materials and possibly pay overtime to

Time	August		September		October		November		December	
	Budget	Actual	Budget	Actual	Budget	Actual	Budget	Actual	Budget	Actual
Orders	Quantity 2 000	Quantity	Quantity 4 000	Quantity	Quantity 3 000	Quantity	Quantity 1 000	Quantity	Quantity 1 500	Quantity
Revenue:	£	£	£	£	£	£	£	£	£	£
Cash sales	20 000		25 000		28 000		22 000		6 000	
Debtors	5 000		2 000		3 000		2 000		2 000	
Total Revenue (A)	25 000		27 000		31 000		24 000		8 000	
Payments:										
Materials	8 000		10 000		7 000		5 000		5 000	
Wages	5 000		5 000		5 000		5 000		5 000	
Rent/rates	1 000		1 000		1 000		1 000		1 000	
Insurance	200		200		200		200		200	
Heat/light/power	2 000		2 000		2 000		2 500		2 200	
Transport	500		500		600		700		200	
Repairs	500		1 000		200		200		2 000	
Creditors	4 000		3 000		2 000		2 000		1 000	
HP interest	800		800		800		800		800	
Total payments (B)	22 000		23 500		19 800		17 400		17 400	
Balance at end of previous month (C)	1 000		4 000		7 500		18 700		25 300	
Balance at tne of this month (A–C+B)	4 000		7 500		18 700		25 300		15 900	

Figure 5.3 *A cash flow forecast for Webster's Wires*

employees. The business has to find the money for this extra expense until the customers pay their bills. If receipts are low then the business must chase up its customers and persuade them to pay.

3. *Purchases* are the money the business has paid out for raw materials and other items it needs to make its product, that is, its **stock**. The secret here is to have just enough stock to keep the business running smoothly. Any extra stock is tying up money – and there is the chance it might deteriorate. Wires can go rusty, food can be past the "sell by" date written on the package.

4. *Payments.* Businesses will often offer a reduction in the price of goods (a **cash discount**) for prompt payment. If the business has enough cash it should take advantage of this. On the other hand, if it does not have the cash it might have to borrow money from the bank. The interest paid is likely to be greater than the discount. **Trade discount** is a reduction in the **retail price** of the good (what the ordinary customer is expected to pay) when it is sold to a business.

JUST TESTING

What is meant by cash flow? Give one reason why it is important to a business.

Creditors and debtors

Creditors are the people and businesses to whom a business owes money. **Debtors** owe money to the business. Creditors can sue the business if their money is not paid to them and, when the situation is serious, force the business into bankruptcy. Debtors who do not pay reduce the receipts of the business and perhaps force it to take out expensive overdrafts to keep going.

A business can encourage its customers to pay cash or pay its debts promptly by:

* offering a **cash discount**. In this case the price quoted by the business is the price for credit customers. If a customer pays cash he will be offered a lower price. This is usually offered in percentage terms. For example, with a cash discount at 2.5%, a bill for £100 at the quoted price would then be:

$$\frac{£100 \times 97.5}{100}$$

The business would pay £97.50

* by keeping careful records of which customers owe money and by sending out regular letters to remind them to pay

* when collecting debts takes too much of a business's time and money, selling them to another business which specialises in collecting debts. The debts are sold at a lower price than their value. The specialist business covers its costs and makes a profit from the difference between the amount it paid for the debt and the money it collects from the debtors. The specialist business is called a **debt collecting agency**. When it offers other financial services to its customers it is called a **debt factor**.

Figure 5.4 shows how a small business might keep check on creditors and debtors.

Debtor list

Customer	Length of time credit agreed	Invoiced January (£)	Invoiced February (£)	Invoiced March (£)	Total (£)

Creditor list

Supplier	Length of time credit agreed	Supplied January (£)	Supplied February (£)	Supplied March (£)	Total (£)

Figure 5.4 *Creditor and debtor lists*

JUST TESTING

1. Joe Martin is running into cash flow problems with his delivery business. His customers are not paying him on time. Suggest two ways in which Joe could encourage his customers to pay him more promptly.

2. A Builders Merchant offers building material to contractors at 20% trade discount. If the bill is paid within seven days there is a 3% cash discount. How much would a contractor pay for goods valued at £500 if he paid within two days?

Working capital

Working capital is the money available for the day to day running of the business. It is calculated in the following way:

(Cash + Debtors + Stock) − (Overdraft + Creditors)

Cash, debtors and stock are known as the **current assets** of a business. These are items the business holds to allow it to keep on working. Creditors and a bank overdraft are known as the **current liabilities** of the business, that is, the money owed to people and other businesses.

Figure 5.5 shows the working capital for Webster's Wires over a period of six months. Notice that the amount has gone up from month to month. Unless the business has bought any new equipment in that time it should have retained profits of £10 000 at the end of the six month period.

Working capital is not the same as the cash available to a business. It is possible to increase the amount of cash by a bank overdraft. If you look at the formula given for calculating working capital you can see that a bank overdraft for £1 000 would increase the cash available to a business by that amount – but it would also increase the overdraft by the same amount. Working capital would stay the same.

To improve working capital a business can:

* get more money from the owners

* sell unwanted property, machinery and vehicles

* make the existing money work harder.

JUST TESTING

Joe Martin is also worried about the amount of working capital he has in his business. "Another £5 000 would make a big difference", he told his wife.

1. What is working capital?

2. Give two ways in which Joe could increase the working capital in his business.

	January	February	March	April	May	June
Current assets						
Money in bank	£ 2 000	£ 1 000			£ 1 000	£ 2 000
Debtors	£ 5 000	£ 6 000	£ 5 000	£ 7 000	£ 8 000	£ 8 000
Stock	£ 3 000	£ 4 000	£ 10 000	£ 11 000	£ 10 000	£ 10 000
Total current assets	£ 10 000	£ 11 000	£ 15 000	£ 18 000	£ 19 000	£ 20 000
Current liabilities						
Overdraft			£ 2 000	£ 1 000		
Creditors	£ 4 000	£ 4 500	£ 6 000	£ 8 000	£ 9 500	£ 10 000
Total current liabilities	£ 4 000	£ 4 500	£ 8 000	£ 9 000	£ 9 500	£ 10 000
Working capital	£ 6 000	£ 6 500	£ 7 000	£ 9 000	£ 9 500	£ 10 0

Figure 5.5 *The working capital of Webster's Wires*

Finding out

1. Arrange a visit to three businesses which sell the same type of good or service, e.g. retailing. The purpose of your visit is to investigate the type of records each business keeps.

Task A   Working in a group compare the results of your investigation. What records were kept? Were there any differences between the businesses? What reasons can you give for any differences you have noted?

Task B   You intend to set up a mini-enterprise in your school or college. You have been offered a loan of £100 to help start the business provided you can show that you expect to be able to pay it back in three months time. How would you do this? Draw up samples of the documents you think would be relevant.

Task C   In order to pay off your loan in three months time you need to keep track of the progress of your business. What records would you need? Explain how they can help you reach your goal.

Task D   From the results of your research write a report. Outline the importance of accurate records to a business and explain some of the problems that might arise if accurate records are not kept.

2. This assignment is concerned with the use of information technology in keeping business records. To complete the tasks you will need to:

(a) know how to use a simple spreadsheet and database
(b) find out the price of several computer software packages designed to help the financial management of a business and discover what they offer a business
(c) watch a software package being demonstrated.

Task A   As a group draw up the main advantages of using a computer software package in the financial management of a business.

Task B   You have only a simple spreadsheet and database for use in a small business. What records could you use this software for? Set up samples of each type of record and explain why you made this choice.

Task C   Using the information you have collected from businesses selling business software, draw up a chart showing the special features of each package. Design a questionnaire for the owner of a small business. It should contain ten questions which will help you discover what he wants from a software package.

Task D   You are the only clerical worker employed in a small business. Part of your job is maintaining all the records of the business. Write a report to your employer outlining the advantages of investing in a computerised system for record keeping. From the results of your research recommend a package and explain why you have chosen it.

Trying it out

1. D.I. Wright is a small building contractor. At the end of 1988 Mr Wright drew up the following data about the state of his business.

D.I. Wright: Building Contractor

Current assets		Current liabilities	
Stock	£ 100	Creditors	£1 000
Debtors	£15 000	Overdraft	£5 000
Cash	£ 8 000		

(a)   In the above data what is meant by:

(i)   Creditors
(ii)   Debtors

(b)   Mr Wright does not carry large amounts of stock. He prefers to buy it during the course of a job rather than risk losing it through theft. Name one item of stock that might be held by this type of business.

(c)   The debtors figure is causing Mr Wright some concern. When he looks up his records he discovers five separate accounts that are three months overdue. Together they add up to £4 500. What can Mr Wright do to improve the speed at which his debtors pay?

(d)   From the figures given above, state the working capital of the business.

(e)   Mr Wright believes that he will have cash flow problems in the next three months.

(i)   What is meant by the phrase "cash flow problems"?
(ii)   What method could Mr Wright have used to discover this fact?
(iii)   Give three things Mr Wright could do to improve the cash flow of his business.

2. Cathy Pierce bought a telephone answering machine for her small cleaning business. The retail price of the machine was £150. Cathy was offered the machine on the following terms:

Either (i) two months credit with a trade discount of 15%
or   (ii) a cash discount of 2% with a trade discount of 15%.

(a)   What is meant by the following terms:

(i)   two months credit?
(ii)   trade discount?
(iii)   cash discount?

(b)   Cathy decided to buy the answering machine on credit. How much did she have to pay?

(c)   Was Cathy a creditor or a debtor of the company selling the answering machine? Explain your answer carefully.

(d)   How much would Cathy have had to pay if she had decided to pay cash?

(e)   Give one reason why Cathy decided on credit rather than cash payment.

(f)   At the end of the two months Cathy could not afford to pay the money she owed.

(i)   How could she have forecast the amount of cash she would have available in two months time?
(ii)   Give two actions the business who sold the answering machine might take as a result of this.
(iii)   Give two ways in which Cathy might find the money to pay her debt.

3. The Fancy Fayre Gift Shop is located in a popular seaside resort. The shop specialises in high quality souvenirs for the summer visitors. Jane Draper, the owner of the shop, has also found a profitable business in acting as a wholesaler for smaller gift shops situated in the surrounding countryside. Sales to these shops are usually on credit terms.

Figure 5.6 shows the cash flow, and working capital of Fancy Fayre Gift Shop.

(a) Answer the following questions using the data given in the Figure.

(i) How much cash was held by the business at the end of June?

(ii) What is the total value of the debt owed to the shop at the end of April?

(iii) Draw a graph to show the changes in the business's working capital over the six months.

(b) What are debtors? Give one reason why the Fancy Fayre Gift Shop might allow debts.

(c) Have the profits of the business increased or decreased over the six months? Explain your answer.

(d) Draw a graph to show the changes in cash flow into the business between January and June. Give one reason to explain why these changes should have taken place.

Figure 5.6 *Records of the Fancy Fayre Gift Shop*

	January	February	March	April	May	June
Revenue						
Sales	£10 000	£8 000	£8 000	£16 000	£35 000	£50 000
Debtors	£15 000	£9 000	£1 000	£1 000	£1 500	£2 000
Total revenue	£25 000	£17 000	£9 000	£17 000	£36 500	£52 000

	January	February	March	April	May	June
Payments						
Cash purchases	£10 000	£12 000	£25 000	£30 000	£30 000	£40 000
Creditors	£5 000	£1 000	£1 000	£2 000	£2 500	£3 000
Wages	£1 000	£1 000	£1 000	£1 500	£1 500	£1 500
Heat/light	£100	£100	£100	£100	£70	£70
Rent/rates	£1 000	£1 000	£1 000	£1 000	£1 000	£1 000
Transport	£50	£70	£100	£150	£200	£200
Total payments	£17 150	£15 170	£28 200	£34 750	£35 270	£45 770

	January	February	March	April	May	June
Bank balance previous month	£25 000	£32 850	£34 680	£15 480	–£2 270	–£1 040
Change in bank balance in current month	£7 850	£1 830	–£19 200	–£17 750	£1 230	£6 230
Total bank balance at the end of month	£32 850	£34 680	£15 480	–£2 270	–£1 040	£5 190

	January	February	March	April	May	June
Current assets						
Money in bank	£32 850	£34 680	£15 480			£5 190
Debtors	£10 000	£4 000	£5 000	£10 000	£6 000	£7 000
Stock	£12 000	£17 600	£38 500	£20 300	£22 600	£24 700
Total current assets	£54 850	£56 280	£58 980	£30 300	£28 600	£36 890

	January	February	March	April	May	June
Current liabilities						
Overdraft				£2 270	£1 040	
Creditors	£1 000	£2 000	£5 000	£5 000	£2 000	£20 000
Total current liabilities	£1 000	£2 000	£5 000	£7 270	£3 040	£2 000
Working capital	£53 850	£54 280	£53 980	£23 030	£25 560	£34 890

UNIT 6:
GETTING ORGANISED

What is an organisation?

Figure 6.1 *A football team*

1 Central defender. Defence of centre of pitch plus support for central mid-field.
2 As 1. above.
3 Goalkeeper. Self explanatory. Also should control and manage his penalty area, and feed the ball to other members of the team.
4 As 3. above.
5 As 1. above.
6 Utility player. Fits in where needed.
7 Coach. Member of backroom staff. As well as coaching players, he is available for advice and consultation on tactics on and off the pitch.
8 Right side mid-field. Support for attack and assist right side defence when necessary.
9 As 6. above.
10 Left back. Defence of left side of field and support for left side midfield in attack.
11 As 1. above.
12 Forward. Attacking player. Also assists in defence when necessary.

13 Right back. Defence of right side of field and support for right side midfield in attack.
14 Trainer. Similar to coach, also treats injuries on the field of play.
15 Left side mid-field. Support for attack and assist right side defence when necessary.
16 Right back/Central defender. See 1. and 13. above.
17 As 1. above.
18 Player/Manager. Most responsible job and probably the most important. Needs to:
    liaise with Directors/Chairman/Secretary/playing and coaching staff.
    decide on tactics after consultation with playing and coaching staff.
    decide on the best player for each position.
19 Central mid-field. In charge of the "engine room". Supports and feeds forwards in attack, and fellow mid-fielders in attack and defence.
20 As 19. above.
21 As 12. above.

Figure 6.1 shows the members of a football team labelled with their jobs in the team. Each player must do his job if the team is going to score goals.

It is the Manager's task to select players who have the skills the team needs. It is the Manager who tells the players what they are expected to do and trains the team to work together so that they can score goals. The Manager **organises** the team.

An **organisation** is a group of people, each one of whom has a definite task which must be completed if the group is to achieve its goals. All businesses are organisations. Every business has goals it hopes to reach. These are called the **objectives** of the business.

36

Business objectives

Business objectives differ according to who owns the business. There are two basic types of business ownership:

* the **private sector**. This includes all businesses owned by individuals, either on their own or in groups. In the private sector the owners set the objectives of the business

* the **public sector**. Businesses in this sector are owned by the State or by local authorities. The objectives of these businesses are set by the government or the local council for the benefit of the whole community.

Private sector objectives

1. *To make a profit.* Profit is what the business has left after it has paid all the costs of producing its goods and services. It is important for a business to make a profit so that it can:

* pay wages, buy raw materials and pay its bills

* borrow money when it needs it. People who lend money want to be sure they will be paid back, so how profitable a business is plays an important part in the decision to lend

* have a reserve of money to replace machinery when it wears out or becomes out-of-date

* judge how efficiently the business is being run.

Profit, especially in smaller businesses, can make people work harder. You might find it useful to look at the descriptions of profit sharing, profit related wages and worker participation in the glossary to see how this idea is used by some businesses to persuade employees to work harder.

2. *Survival.* This objective speaks for itself. Sometimes a business may have to take lower profits for a time to make sure it survives.

All businesses want to make a profit and survive. In addition to this a business may add one or more of the following to its list of objectives.

3. *A good public image.*

4. *To grow larger.*

5. *To increase its sales* at the expense of its competitors, that is to increase its share of the total market, (**market share**)

Public sector objectives

Businesses in the public sector are not necessarily expected to make profits. The objectives of these businesses emphasise the good of the whole community. Frequently these firms were taken over by the government (**nationalised**) because it was felt that the profit motive was not in the best interests of the community.

Publicly owned businesses do not escape from the need to make a surplus (profit). They are expected to:

* at least break-even, that is they should be able to pay all they owe out of the money they earn

* make enough profit to buy new equipment and to replace worn-out machinery

* make a target return on capital employed, for example, the government sets a target of 5%. This means that if a business uses £1m in land, machinery and so on:

$$\frac{£1\,000\,000 \times 5}{100}$$

it needs to have £50 000 after it has paid all its costs.

Of course, for a business to reach its goals each part of the business must do its share. Figure 6.2 shows some of the targets a business must achieve if it is to make a profit.

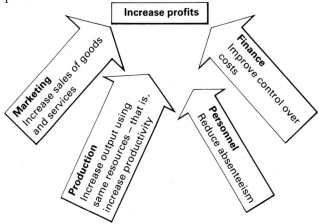

Figure 6.2 *The goals of a business*

JUST TESTING

1. What is an organisation?

2. Give two ways in which the objectives of a business in the private sector are different from those of a business in the public sector.

Sharing out the jobs

The jobs a business needs to do to reach its objectives are known as the **functions** of the business. In a very small business all the tasks may be done by one person. As the business gets larger the work becomes too much for one person. Some jobs will have to be **delegated**. The owner of the business will give another person the right (**authority**) to do a job on his or her behalf. The person delegated is **responsible** for that job and must **account** to the owner for the way in which it is done.

As businesses get larger the number of people required to perform one function gets larger. The groups of people working together to perform one function are known as **departments**.

The main departments found in a business are shown in Figure 6.3.

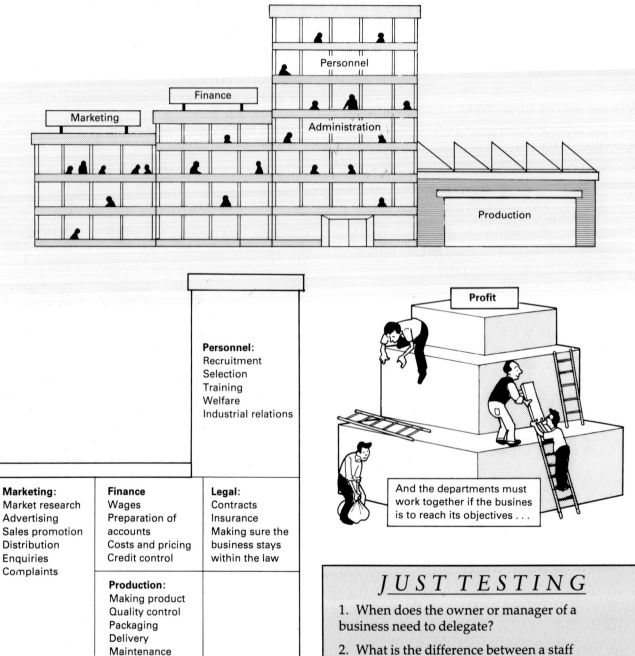

Personnel:
Recruitment
Selection
Training
Welfare
Industrial relations

Marketing:
Market research
Advertising
Sales promotion
Distribution
Enquiries
Complaints

Finance
Wages
Preparation of accounts
Costs and pricing
Credit control

Legal:
Contracts
Insurance
Making sure the business stays within the law

Production:
Making product
Quality control
Packaging
Delivery
Maintenance

Profit

And the departments must work together if the busines is to reach its objectives . . .

Figure 6.3 *Departments of a business*

JUST TESTING

1. When does the owner or manager of a business need to delegate?

2. What is the difference between a staff department and a line department?

Delegation

Delegation means that a manager:

* gives a task to someone

* gives them the authority to do that task

* helps the person realise what their responsibilities are and their accountability to the manager for the successful completion of the task.

Centralisation and decentralisation

When a senior manager is very involved with the decisions made by managers at lower levels in the hierarchy, authority is said to be **centralised**. In other words not a great deal of delegation is taking place.

When managers at lower levels in the hierarchy are given the authority and responsibility to take decisions that are important to the business we say that authority is **decentralised**.

Advantages of centralisation

1. Decisions can be made quickly.

2. Senior managers have more experience of decision making and are less likely to make mistakes that could prove expensive to the business.

3. Senior managers have an overall view of what the business needs.

Disadvantages of centralisation

1. There can be delays in decision making, particularly if the decisions have to pass through a number of levels in the hierarchy.

2. Senior managers may not be able to cope with the number of decisions to be made.

3. Managers lower down in the hierarchy do not gain experience in making decisions.

4. Senior managers may not be aware of local problems or problems in a particular department.

The structure of a business

Figure 6.4 shows how the jobs might be divided up in a medium sized manufacturing company.

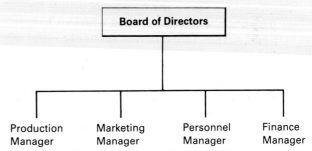

Figure 6.4 *The structure of a medium sized manufacturing company*

This type of diagram is called an organisation chart. It shows some of the principles of organisation.

1. *Chain of command.* This is the path the instructions follow from the person making the decision to all the people concerned with putting it into practice. The dotted lines in Figure 6.5 show a possible chain of command.

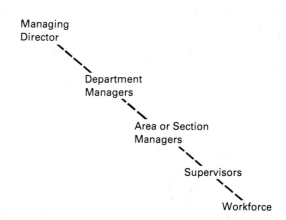

Figure 6.5 *A chain of command*

2. *Levels of hierarchy.* The employees at each level in the organisation chart carry more authority and responsibility than the employees on the level below. These levels are called levels of hierarchy. The organisation chart in Figure 6.6 has three levels of hierarchy.

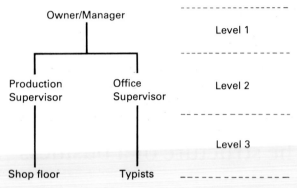

Figure 6.6 *Levels of hierarchy*

3. *Span of control.* This is the number of people for whom a manager is responsible and who look to him for help and advice. Two different spans of control are illustrated in Figures 6.7.

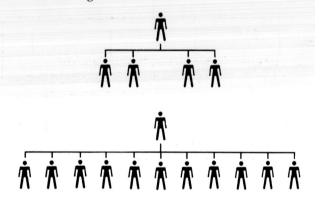

Figure 6.7 *Spans of control*

The number of people a manager can control effectively depends on:

* the type of job. The more complex the job the more supervision that might be required. When people are doing simple jobs that do not need a great deal of skill a supervisor might have a span of control of fifty. The production manager has a span of control of four

* the ability of the manager. An able person will be capable of controlling more people than one of less ability

* the ability of his subordinates. The more skilled people are at their jobs, the less the supervisor has to do, therefore the larger the span of control.

JUST TESTING

Look at Figure 6.3

1. To which department do you think the following people would belong?

accounts clerk, fitter, laboratory assistant, lorry driver, typist, industrial relations manager, salesman.

2. How many levels of hierarchy are there in the business?

3. What is the chain of command from the managing director to the secretary of the production manager?

What is the best type of organisation?

There is no 'best' type of organisation. Every business is different and has different needs. Figure 6.8 shows the main ways in which a business might be organised.

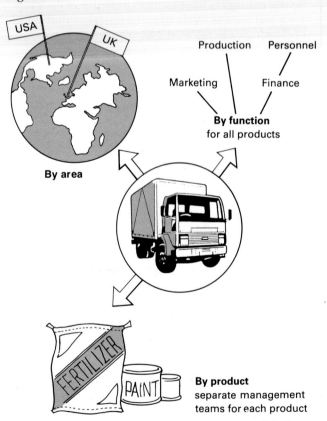

Figure 6.8 *Different ways in which a business might be organised*

The choice made by a business will depend on:

1. The size of the business. A firm producing a number of different products might find that it makes more sense to divide the work into groups according to products.

2. The type of business is also important. Retailing, for example, can often be organised on a geographical basis. This makes it easier for the managers of shops to meet the needs of their own particular customers.

3. The type of technology used. When a business has a very specialised piece of equipment it can make sense to organise the business so that the equipment is used all the time.

JUST TESTING

Why might it be better for a chain of shops to be organised on a regional basis?

Formal and informal groups

This unit has been about formal groups, that is, people who come together as a result of organisational decisions.

When people are working together they will also form informal groups. These are groups based on friendships, similar ideas and interests.

Informal groups can be useful to a business. When people know each other they tend to work well together. On the other hand, when an informal group does not agree with the objectives of a business they can work against them.

Finding out

1. Arrange an interview with the owner of a small business. You should also ask if it is possible to "shadow" that person for a day.

Task A Before the interview draw up a questionnaire to cover the information you will require. Use the stages in designing a survey on p20. Your questionnaire should cover:
    (a) the objectives
    (b) the business functions
    (c) delegation
    (d) who makes the decisions
    (e) span of control.

Rehearse your interview before you go. Owners of small businesses tend to be very busy so you do not want to waste their time.

Task B When you visit the business observe the way in which it is run. What sort of jobs are delegated? Why are they delegated? Keep a record of what you see.

Task C Write a report on the organisation of the business. Give reasons for the organisational decisions the owner of the business has taken. What problems had to be solved?

2. Arrange visits with two businesses. The businesses should be medium sized to large and, if possible, use different production methods. Make sure you have your questions ready before you go. It may be easier to work in two groups for the research. Each group would visit a different business and share their findings.

Task A Describe the businesses in terms of product, size, location, type of technology used and history.

Task B Write a report comparing the organisational structure of the two businesses.

Task C In small groups discuss the differences between the organisation of the two businesses. What reasons can you suggest for these?

Task D As a result of the whole exercise write a short essay commenting on the factors influencing business organisation, illustrating your points with evidence from your research.

3. This is a practical activity based on some event in your school or college. You might be running a stall at a Christmas Fair, organising a school trip, starting a mini-enterprise. You should work in groups.

Task A   Make a list of all the jobs that need to be done. What skills will be needed to complete the jobs successfully?

Task B   Now put the jobs in order of importance. Why have you decided on that order?

Task C   Decide who will do each job. Who is going to organise the activity? Explain why you came to these decisions.

Trying it out

1. Figures 6.9a and b are examples of organisation charts.

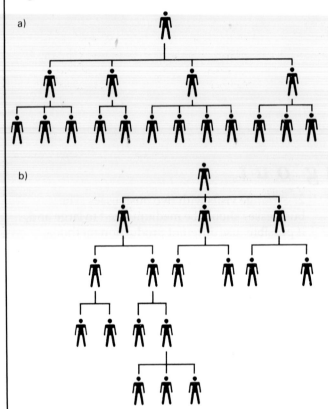

Figure 6.9 *Organisation chart*

(a) What are the main differences between the charts? In your answer you should refer to:

   (i) levels of hierarchy
   (ii) span of control
   (iii) chain of command.

(b) If the business moves from the type of organisation shown in Figure 6.9a to that shown in 6.9b, what might it mean for the people employed in the business?

2. Ali Imam is the sales manager for a manufacturing business. He arrived home one evening in a very bad temper.

"The trouble with the boss is that he does not know how to delegate," he complained to his wife when he had calmed down a little. "I know he is in charge of marketing but he keeps trying to do my job as well. We've just lost a big order because he made the first contact, decided he would see it through himself and then forgot about it. He just will not realise that he can't do everything these days. The business is too big."

His wife was soothing. "I suppose he finds it difficult to get used to the size of the business. Don't forget, when he started he had to do everything. At least he does not interfere with your department."

"Oh yes he does. Two of my best salesmen are threatening to leave. They say they are tired of being treated like errand boys. Just because they have company cars he thinks they should do any odd messages he has."

(a) Explain briefly what is meant by:

   (i) delegate
   (ii) responsibility
   (iii) chain of command.

(b) (i) What is the chain of command outlined in the passage?
   (ii) For each role in this chain of command give an example of the type of decision the person might make.

(c) State two basic problems of this business. How could the situation be improved?

42

3. Sweeney's Ltd is a business manufacturing a wide range of footwear. It employs 2 000 people. In 1988 it bought a small chain of retail shops. The chart in Figure 6.10 shows the existing organisation of the business. The chart is not complete.

(a) What is meant by the terms:

(i) span of control?
(ii) level of hierarchy?

(b) (i) To whom is the production manager accountable?
(ii) For whom is the production manager responsible?

(c) At the moment the business is organised on a functional basis. Since Sweeney's acquired the chain of shops the managing director does not think that this is the most efficient method of organisation.

(i) Explain what is meant by the phrase organised on a functional basis.
(ii) Explain why this might not be the most efficient method of organisation since they bought the retail chain.
(iii) In what other way might Sweeney's Ltd be organised? Draw an organisation chart to illustrate your suggestion.

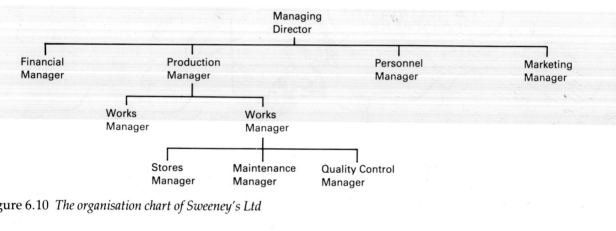

Figure 6.10 *The organisation chart of Sweeney's Ltd*

UNIT 7: GETTING THE MESSAGE RIGHT

What do we mean by communications?

The act of communicating is very simple. Look at Figure 7.1.

Figure 7.1 *The process of communication*

The **sender** has a message that he wants people to know about. This might be:

* information, i.e. facts the sender wants the receiver to know

* an attitude, e.g. "I do not approve of that."

* an emotion, e.g. "I am very happy."

The **medium** (the plural is media) is the way in which the message is sent.

The **receiver** is the person or people the message is intended for. The receiver can want to receive the message, be indifferent to it or be hostile to it.

The receiver lets the sender know the message has been received and how it has been received. This is called **feedback**.

If the receiver is satisfied with the feedback the message ends. If the sender is not satisfied with the feedback then the message is likely to be repeated – perhaps in a different way.

JUST TESTING

Look at Figure 7.1. Who is the sender? What is the medium? What is the message? What is the feedback to the sender?

Communications media

1. *Orally* – use of the spoken word in conversation, giving instructions, meetings, tape recorders, radio, tannoy systems, telephone.

2. *Written* – the use of the written word and numbers in memos, reports, the agenda and minutes of meetings, letters, telex and fax.

3. *Visually* – posters, advertisements, charts, graphs, computer graphics, television, facial expression, use of the body.

4. *Electronically* – radio, television, cassette recorders, telex, fax and computer networks.

A person needs skills to communicate. A very young baby communicates by facial expression and sounds, e.g. crying when it is uncomfortable. As the child grows older it learns to talk. This means that it can communicate more efficiently. Instead of crying, the child can say, "I am hungry".

Schools develop other communication skills. Reading, writing and numeracy are also important if you are to receive and transmit information. Class discussions and giving talks help to develop oral skills. If you have to interview people as part of your coursework, you will probably have practised interview techniques in class.

There are some communication skills that you possess that you do not think of as a skill. Unless you can use radio, television and stereo equipment you cannot get the messages that are being sent – there are some old people who are frightened of this equipment and have never learned to use it.

J U S T   T E S T I N G

1. Make a list of the different types of activity you do in school or college. What type of communication skill does each one help develop.

2. Make a list of your communication skills.

Barriers to communication

Not all messages get through from the sender to the receiver. When this happens we say there is a barrier to communication. The main barriers to communication are illustrated in Figure 7.2.

1. The sender lacks the skill to explain the message clearly or does not want to send the message. Perhaps he does not want to tell his boss that something has gone wrong in case the boss blames him.

2. The receiver lacks the skill to understand the message. This can happen because the receiver:

* does not understand the non-verbal signs of the sender

* cannot speak the language

* does not understand the technical language used

* does not have the technical skill to use the means of communication, e.g. cannot operate the telex machine

* is afraid of the machinery used.

3. The receiver does not want to get the message. This can happen because the receiver:

* does not like the sender

* is not interested in the message

* does not want to receive the message – perhaps the receiver wants to avoid a job.

4. The message is passed through too many people. Each person changes the message slightly so that it becomes distorted.

5. Either the sender or the receiver might have physical disabilities that make it difficult for them to communicate.

6. There are physical barriers to communication, e.g. distance, noise, poor visibility.

7. The equipment breaks down or there is a postal strike.

J U S T   T E S T I N G

What barrier to communication is illustrated by each of the following:

* "I can't stand our supervisor. He's always nagging. In the end I just don't listen."

* The Met Office warns about fog in the English Channel

* "These instructions are useless. What's a three core alternator?"

Channels of communication

Channels of communication are the **routes** a message takes from the sender to the final receiver and back

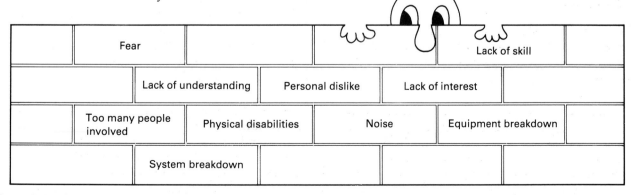

Figure 7.2 *The main barriers to communication*

again. Some channels of communication are given in Figures 7.3a to d.

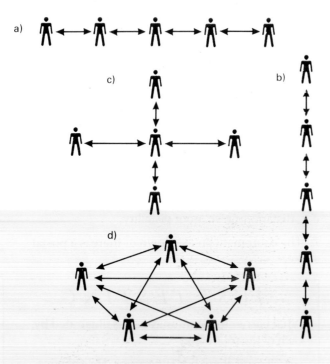

Figure 7.3 *Channels of communication*

The arrows show the directions in which the communication can flow.

(a) This is **horizontal** communication. All the people concerned are on the same level of hierarchy in the business.

(b) This is **vertical** communication. The messages are passing up and down the chain of command.

(c) This pattern of communication can be both horizontal and vertical:

  * the production director communicating with his works managers in different parts of the country (vertical)

  * a supervisor collecting information from other supervisors at the request of the production manager (horizontal).

(d) Horizontal communication and vertical communication are illustrated here:

  * the managers of a business should be in touch with each other all the time if the business is to run smoothly

  * in a small business people will be able to communicate freely.

These patterns of communication are the official routes laid down in the business. There is also the **grapevine**. This word is used to describe unofficial channels of communication based on personal relationships. Figure 7.4 outlines the route taken by the news that there is trouble in the maintenance team from the shop floor to the production manager.

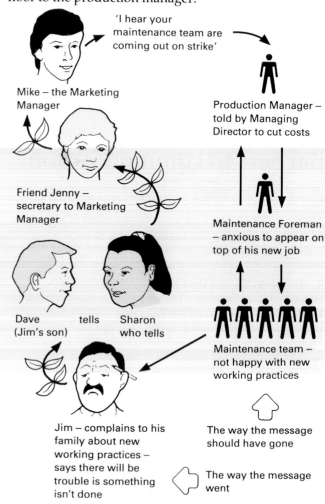

Figure 7.4 *A grapevine*

JUST TESTING

1. Think of a lesson you have had which involved group discussion followed by a written report that had to be handed in to your teacher. What patterns of communication did you use? What methods of communication did you use?

2. Look at Figure 7.4. Why do you think the foreman was reluctant to tell the production manager about the trouble brewing in the workshop?

Who does a business communicate with?

Communications in a business are both internal and external. The internal communications are those that take place between the people engaged in running the business. The external communications are with groups such as customers, suppliers and government departments. Figure 7.5 gives some of the external contacts of a business, why it needs to communicate with them and the methods used.

Orders, invoices, delivery notes

Demonstration

Government department

Meetings, local government

Media reports

Suppliers

Figure 7.5 *The external communications of a business*

The importance of good communication

The most important thing about good communication is that if it does not exist the job will not get done. Some of the problems that might develop in a business with poor communications are given in Figure 7.6.

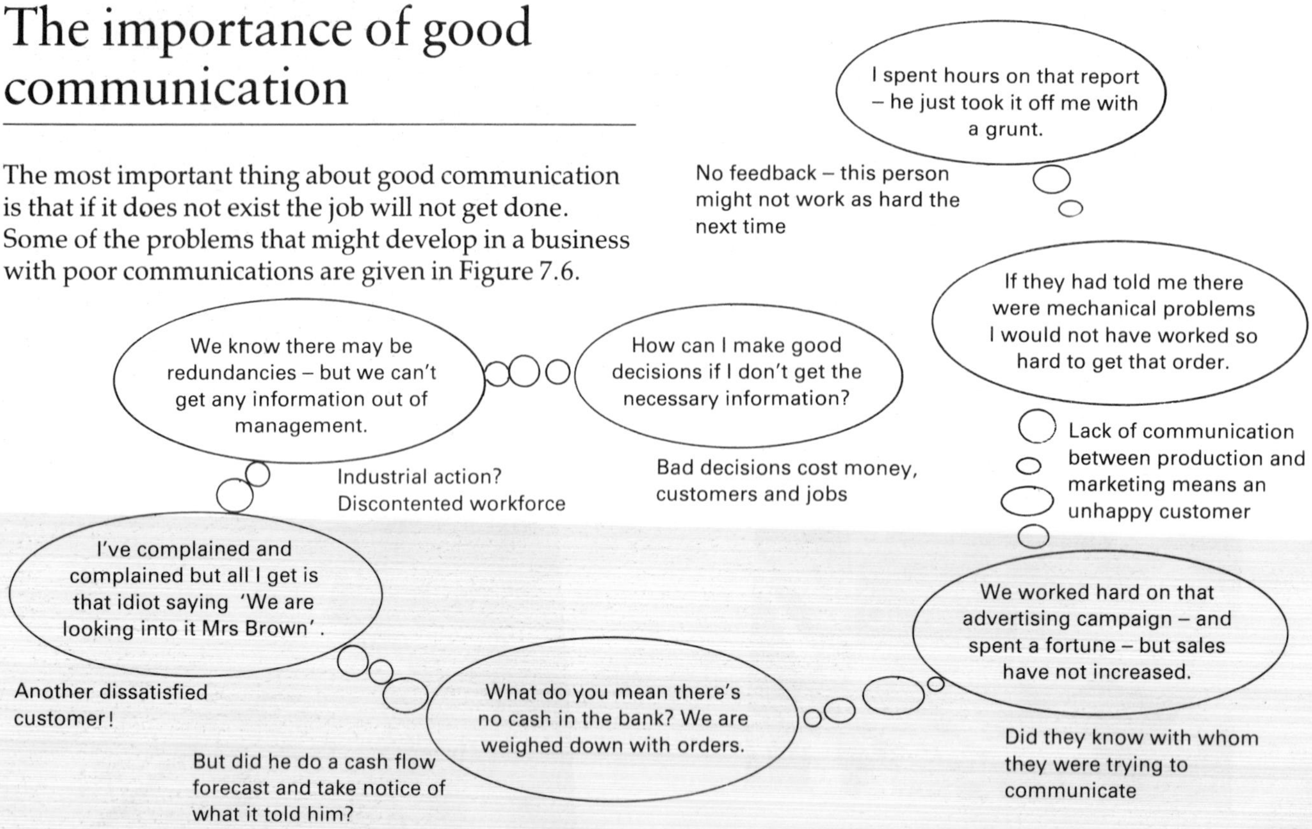

I spent hours on that report – he just took it off me with a grunt.

No feedback – this person might not work as hard the next time

We know there may be redundancies – but we can't get any information out of management.

How can I make good decisions if I don't get the necessary information?

If they had told me there were mechanical problems I would not have worked so hard to get that order.

Industrial action? Discontented workforce

Bad decisions cost money, customers and jobs

Lack of communication between production and marketing means an unhappy customer

I've complained and complained but all I get is that idiot saying 'We are looking into it Mrs Brown'.

Another dissatisfied customer!

What do you mean there's no cash in the bank? We are weighed down with orders.

We worked hard on that advertising campaign – and spent a fortune – but sales have not increased.

But did he do a cash flow forecast and take notice of what it told him?

Did they know with whom they were trying to communicate

Figure 7.6 *Problems arising from poor communications*

Rules for successful communication

If communication is so important, how do you make sure you get it right? The principles for good communication are outlined in Figure 7.7.

Methods of communication in a business

This section is concerned with some of the methods used to communicate in a business. It will outline:

* the direction in which the message can move in the hierarchy of the business (up, down, horizontal)

* some advantages and disadvantages of each method,

when this is appropriate.

Non-verbal communication

The faces and figures in Figure 7.8 tell you something about the way in which people are feeling. People tend to droop when they are tired or miserable, smile when

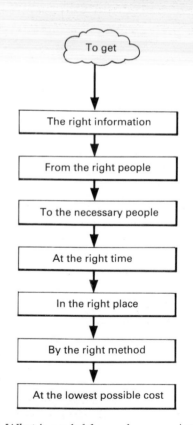

To get

The right information

From the right people

To the necessary people

At the right time

In the right place

By the right method

At the lowest possible cost

Figure 7.7 *What is needed for good communications*

Figure 7.8 *Non-verbal communication*

they are happy, frown when they are annoyed or puzzled. This type of communication goes on all the time. It is a very rare person who does not betray the way they are feeling in the way they move or walk. Actors and actresses use our familiarity with these signals about the way in which we feel to build up the character they are portraying.

Unfortunately, these signals can be misinterpreted. The boss might be frowning because the traffic was bad on the way to work. Her assistant could interpret this as displeasure with the work he had done. People such as politicians realised the importance of this when they started to appear on television. The viewers made judgements on the appearance, facial expressions and mannerisms of the politician rather than on the spoken message.

JUST TESTING

Look at Figure 7.8. What feeling do you think each face and figure is trying to express?

Oral communication

Oral methods of communication include meetings, face-to-face, for example in giving instructions, interviews and telephone conversations. They can be vertical or horizontal depending on the positions of the people concerned.

The advantages of oral communication are:

  * speed

  * the receiver can question any point that is not clear

  * the sender gets instant feedback.

Not all methods of oral communication have these advantages. A tannoy system in a large factory can give messages but there is no opportunity for instant feedback. A manager addressing a large number of people in his department could find people reluctant to ask questions because of the size of the meeting.

49

The disadvantages include:

* no written record. This can lead to misunderstandings going uncorrected and disputes over who said or did not say what

* if the same message is passed through a large number of people it can get distorted. It only needs each person to change the message slightly for it to become nonsense.

JUST TESTING

One person in the group thinks up a sentence, writes it down but allows nobody else to see it. This sentence is whispered to the next person in the group who writes down the message received and again allows nobody else to see it. This is repeated until the message has been passed through the whole group.

* Compare the message received by the last person in the group with the original message. How does it differ?

* What is this an example of?

* Using the written record of every person in the group trace the stages by which the message changed. Would the result have been different if the group had been (a) larger? (b) smaller?

Written communication

Written communications can use words and figures or a combination of both.

One of the disadvantages of oral communication is the fact that there is no written record to refer back to. Businesses often take advantage of the speed and flexibility of oral communication but include a written record for the main advantage of **permanancy**. Unless it is lost, destroyed or stolen a written record can be used to check on what was said which can help to resolve disputes. This can be done by:

* taking **minutes** at meetings. These are a record of the main items discussed and the decisions that were made. The minutes must be agreed as a true account of the meeting with all the people who attended the meeting

* **letters** or **memos** confirming agreements reached or instructions given in face-to-face conversations or by telephone. Both letters and memos can be used to pass on information both vertically and horizontally. There are examples of both in Figure 7.9.

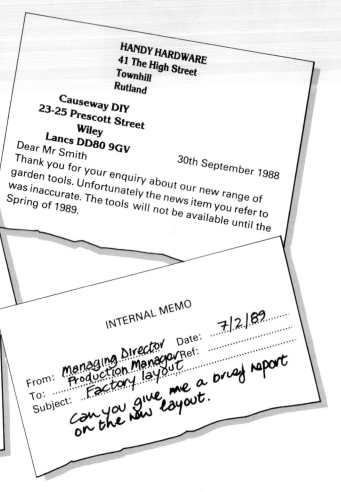

Figure 7.9 *Letters and memos*

Written records provide:

* a permanent record of instructions given or decisions reached

* an opportunity to give detailed instructions

* the ability to reach a large number of people.

Written records can also:

* be lost, destroyed or stolen

* be ignored

* give no chance for the receiver to ask for an explanation.

Other examples of written communication include:

1. *Instruction manuals*. These can give detail about the way in which a machine or an organisation operates. Their usefulness depends on the skill of the writer in judging what the reader can understand.

2. *Notice boards* can be very useful to reach a large number of people with urgent instructions. Their impact is less if they are untidy and the notices stay up too long. There may be no feedback so you do not know whether or not people have got the message. Notice boards tend to be vertical and downwards – although notices advertising the Christmas party can be both vertical and horizontal.

3. *Reports* keep management informed about how the business is going and the results of research.

4. *Circulars* are written messages sent to all the people who need to know that information. Feedback can be a problem so circulars frequently have a slip attached which the receiver has to sign.

5. *Newsletters* are vertical and downwards in direction, particularly when they are used by management to give the information they want people to receive. Some newsletters are both vertical and horizontal, and so give the people on the shop floor a chance to air their views.

6. *Suggestion schemes* allow the people who are doing the job to make suggestions for improvements. Suggestions can cover technical details about the job or the way in which the job is organised. The direction of communication is vertical and upwards. Businesses that run these schemes usually offer a variety of awards for ideas that are adopted, the value of these is usually related to the amount of money saved by the suggestion.

7. *Forms* are used by all businesses to keep a record of transactions. The main forms used in buying and selling are described in Unit 11 (p86). Forms are used by a business for activities that have to be repeated a number of times.

Visual communication

Photographs, diagrams, videos and the layout of documents and notice boards are all used to convey information. Visual communication attracts people's attention, gives impact to the information and, by simplifying it, makes it easier to understand. Figure 7.10 shows how a business uses a picture in advertising to communicate with potential customers.

In Figure 7.11 you can see some methods of visual communication used to make figures easier to understand.

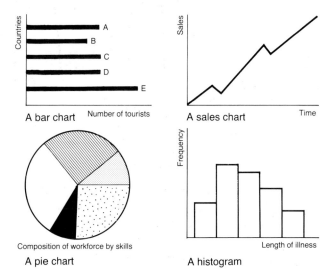

Figure 7.11 *Presenting numerical data*

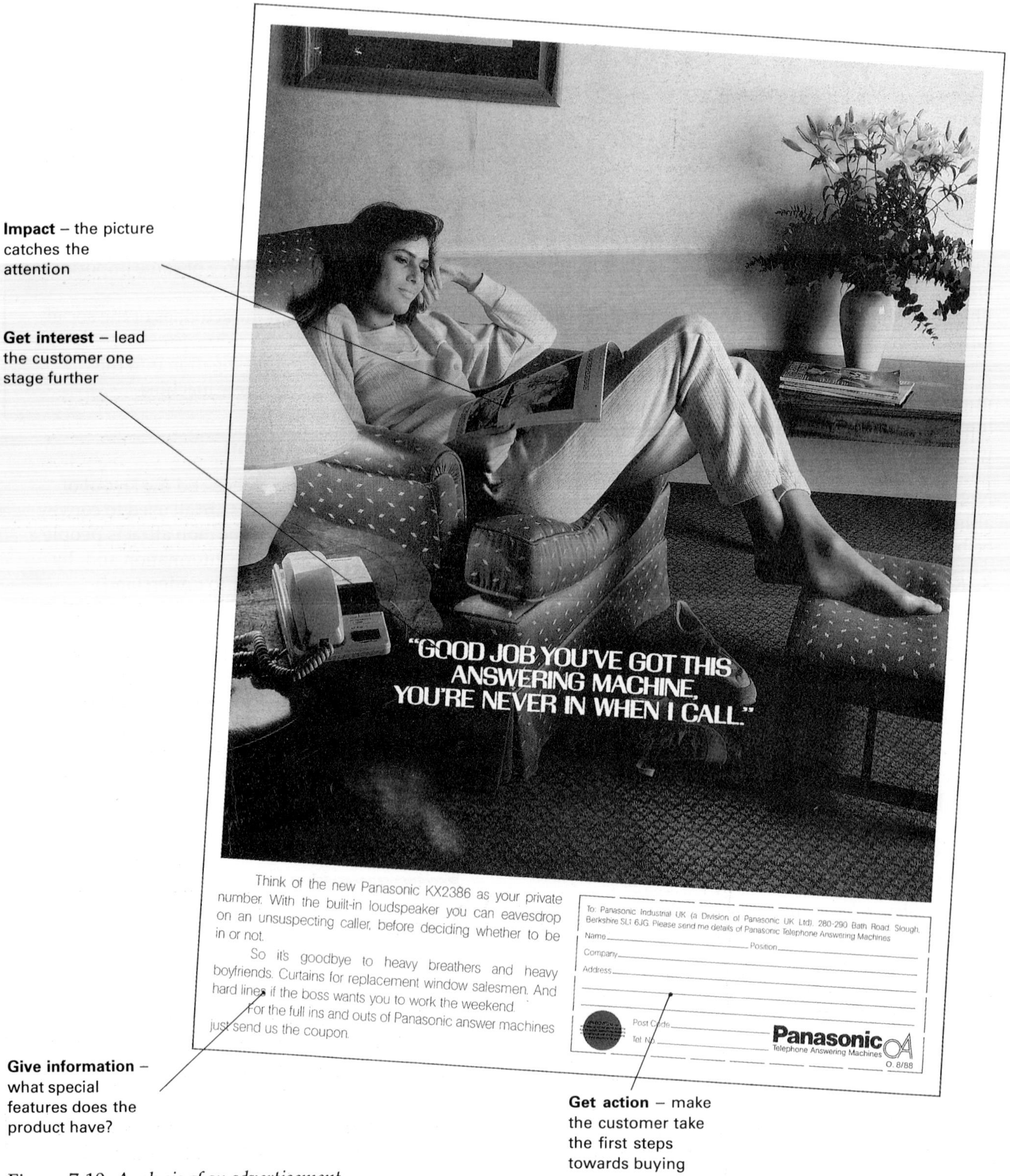

Impact – the picture catches the attention

Get interest – lead the customer one stage further

"GOOD JOB YOU'VE GOT THIS ANSWERING MACHINE, YOU'RE NEVER IN WHEN I CALL."

Think of the new Panasonic KX2386 as your private number. With the built-in loudspeaker you can eavesdrop on an unsuspecting caller, before deciding whether to be in or not.

So it's goodbye to heavy breathers and heavy boyfriends. Curtains for replacement window salesmen. And hard lines if the boss wants you to work the weekend. For the full ins and outs of Panasonic answer machines just send us the coupon.

To: Panasonic Industrial UK (a Division of Panasonic UK Ltd), 280-290 Bath Road, Slough, Berkshire SL1 6JG. Please send me details of Panasonic Telephone Answering Machines

Name_____

Company_____ Position_____

Address_____

Post Code_____
Tel No_____

Panasonic OA
Telephone Answering Machines
O. 8/88

Give information – what special features does the product have?

Get action – make the customer take the first steps towards buying

Figure 7.10 *Analysis of an advertisement*

Visual communication is usually used with spoken and written communication.

Information technology

In the past thirty years there has been a major revolution in the technology available for communications. This has had a far-reaching effect on many aspects of society and not just business. The development of computers, the invention of the microchip and optic fibres has increased the range of information available and the speed and ease with which it can be stored and used.

1. All businesses need to keep information in a way that means it can easily be found when it is required, that is, retrieved. Folders, filing cabinets, card indexes are still the main ways of storing information and are necessary for documents. Information on customers, e.g. a mailing list, can be kept on a **database**. This is a piece of computer software that allows the storage of information in an easily accessible form. The information can be sorted and presented in the way in which it is required at any one time. For example, if the business wants the addresses of all its customers living in the south-east the database can sort the information and select the customers very rapidly compared with searching through written information by hand.

2. **Telecommunications**. The telephone provides fast communication within a business and also with suppliers and customers. Improvements in technology mean that the telephone system can be used for a variety of other purposes:

* **Fax** (facsimile) machines which can transmit documents electronically over long distances

* **Teletex** transmits written messages from one typewriter (or word processor) to another, using the telephone system

* **Prestel** is a very large database which is constantly updated. It contains information such as stock exchange prices, commodity prices and advice to importers and exporters. A business pays for this service and can then use this information. It is transmitted on the telephone system and seen on an adapted television screen. Prestel and similar services can also be used to transmit information from the business to other businesses.

3. **Information technology** can also help managers by giving them information to help in decision making and the control of the business. Information can be stored in a computer system. If a manager wanted to compare the level of sales in different geographical areas the computer will select the information and present it in a useful form – perhaps using computer graphics to do so.

The rapid development of information technology has led to some problems:

* people need training to use the new machines

* there are a wide variety of different systems in use. Information stored using one type of system cannot be transferred easily to another system

* there are fears that personal information held on a computer could be used against the people concerned.

To overcome the last problem the government passed the **Data Protection Act** in 1984. This limits the amount of information a business can hold about one person, gives individuals access to information held about them and lays down security measures that must be followed to make sure the data is not changed. Businesses and public authorities storing information about people on a computer have to register with the **Data Protection Registrar**. Disputes about the storage of information are settled by the **Data Protection Tribunal**.

Finding out

1. Schools and colleges are organisations and make a good starting point for the study of communications in organisations.

Task A   Draw up an organisation chart of your school or college. Select one member of staff from each level of the hierarchy. Note that in schools and colleges this is unlikely to be as clear cut as it is in many businesses. The headteacher

could be an assistant teacher in one of the departments. Make a careful note of any differences between the organisation of your school/college and the typical business organisation described in Unit 6.

Task B   Arrange interviews with a member of staff from each level of the hierarchy. You want to know which groups they communicate with and why. Prepare your interview carefully. In the course of the interview take a careful note of any problems you meet in getting the information you require.

Task C   Working in groups and using the information you have collected, draw up examples of patterns of communication within the organisation.

Task D   Write a report on your findings. This should cover the following points:

(a) who communicates with whom and why
(b) problems of communication experienced by the organisation
(c) the patterns of communication
(d) the methods of communication.

Give explanations of all the statements you make.

2. This is a group exercise on how people communicate.

Task A   Divide the class into two groups. Group 1 will attempt to solve the following problem.

Problem:

The headteacher has decided that the business studies facilities in the school need to be improved and has made £5 000 available for this purpose. At the moment the business studies department has three classrooms equipped with chairs, tables and built-in cupboards. The head of department has made a list of some possible equipment and has asked you, the customer, to decide which equipment is most important. The list contains prices of single items. You can have as many as you like of each item, provided you spend no more than £5 000.

Computer with software including database and spreadsheet   £1 200

Electronic typewriter   £250

Telephone (installation and equipment)   £75

Switchboard   £700

Filing cabinet   £150

Copier   £400

Office desk   £250

System of integrated office furniture including desks, storage space and filing cabinets   £3 000

Individual study carrels   £150

As a group decide how you will spend the £5 000.

Group 2 will observe the decision making process.

(a) How did they communicate?
(b) Did a leader emerge from the group? If so, how did the leader take over?
(c) What was the pattern of communication in the group? Which members of the group spoke most frequently? Who did people talk to?
(d) Watch carefully for facial expressions, body language. For example, was anybody bored by this exercise? How could you tell?

When this exercise is finished the groups should reverse roles.

Task B   Working in smaller groups discuss what you have learned from this exercise. Did the second group have an easier task in solving the problem than the first group? Did the groups work well together? How could you improve this group work?

Task C   Still working in groups, work on the following problem.

The owner of a business has decided to improve the office/reception area of his factory. He considers:

(a) making all the decisions himself
(b) asking the two men and three women who work in that area to advise him on what they need.

What type of communication patterns are involved in these two options? From your experience explain the advantages and disadvantages of both.

Task D   What problems did you and the group as a whole experience in this exercise? How could you avoid them in future?

Trying it out

1. Look at the patterns of communication illustrated in Figures 7.12a and b.

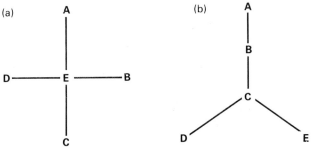

Figure 7.12 *Patterns of communication*

(a) What do the arrows show in these diagrams?

(b) Describe a situation in which each pattern of communication might be suitable.

(c) Give one disadvantage of each of these patterns of communication.

(d) In Figure 7.12a which person is likely to have the most power? Give one reason for your answer.

2. C & CF plc owns a chain of retail furnishings shops situated on the outskirts of large towns. Each shop consists of a well laid out showroom from which the customers select the furniture. The order is placed on a form signed by the customer who then presents it at the desk. The salesperson enters the details on a computer, which stores the information. The computer also transfers the information to the warehouse on the same site. In the warehouse the staff assemble the order at the customer service hatch. This gives direct access to the car park so that there is as little handling as possible.

(a) What is the pattern of communication outlined in the above passage? Draw a diagram to illustrate your answer.

(b) State two things that could go wrong with this pattern of communication.

The head office of C & CF plc receives computer print-outs of the stock delivered to each store and print-outs of the number of orders. One store had been regularly ordering 500 kitchen units per week but only selling 250. One of the staff at head office spotted this difference and became suspicious. He sat in a car outside the customer service hatch and counted the number of kitchen units that were sold in a week. He could do this because the boxes containing the units had an identification mark and number printed on the outside. He counted 550 being sold in that week.

(c) What methods of communication are used in the above passage?

(d) The member of staff from head office suspected a fraud. Give one other possible explanation for the number of units delivered to that site and the number sold.

(e) Give two reasons why a business with more than two sites might experience communication problems.

3. Read the illustrated story overleaf and then answer the questions that follow.

(a) Give two methods of communication used in the illustrated story.

(b) List three barriers to communication in the illustrated story.

(c) For each of the barriers to communication you have chosen explain one way in which it could have led to lower profits and bookings.

(d) Why is an untidy desk evidence of poor communications?

(e) List and explain three ways in which communications at Rodgers' Hotel might be improved if Mary spent less time in her office.

Figure 7.13 *Communication problems in Rodgers' Hotel*

UNIT 8:
ORGANISING FOR PRODUCTION

What is production?

Production includes all the activities a business needs to make the goods and services it sells.

The organisation chart of the production department of a manufacturing company is given in Figure 8.1.

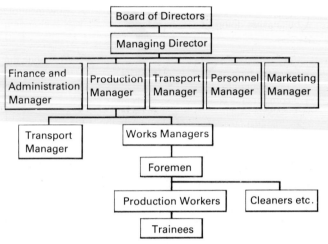

Figure 8.1 *Production organisation chart in a manufacturing business*

The main activities involved in production are:

* locating and siting the business

* purchasing and stock control

* organising the work

* quality control

* work study.

The production department will work with the other departments in the business in designing the product and deciding on the scale of production (the number of a product it will make in one year). The production department will also set objectives that support the overall objectives of the business. In a business that has prestige as an important objective, quality control will be given more importance in the production process.

This unit will concentrate on production organisation in manufacturing. You should remember that manufacturing accounts for only 30% of all production in the United Kingdom in one year. Figure 8.2 is a simplified organisation chart of a business running a chain of retail shops.

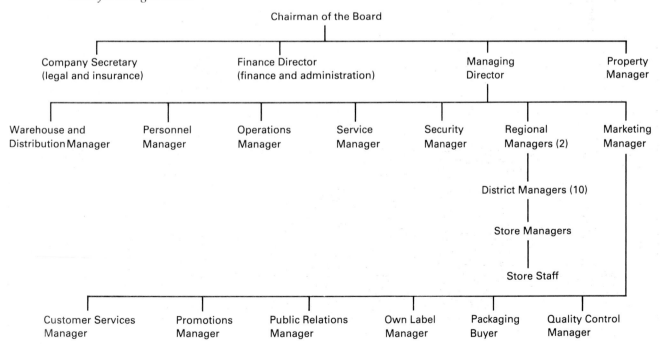

JUST TESTING

1. What is production? Give three activities that are included in the organisation of production.

2. Look at Figures 8.1 and 8.2. What major differences can you see in the production organisation of the two businesses?

What will sell?

Before a business can start organising for production it must know what it is going to make. Eighty per cent of all new products **launched** on the market fail because people do not want them. This costs the business time and money. Figure 8.3 outlines the information a business needs before it can begin to design its product.

Businesses that design their product to fit in with the needs of the market are said to be **market oriented**. Businesses that design their product and then try to sell it are said to be **product oriented**.

The needs of customers do not change very rapidly. For the last hundred years businesses have demanded fast, accurate methods of calculating. The photographs in Figure 8.4 show some of the ways in which these needs have been satisfied.

Figure 8.3 *Information from within the business and information about the market*

Figure 8.4 *Satisfying the need for calculators*

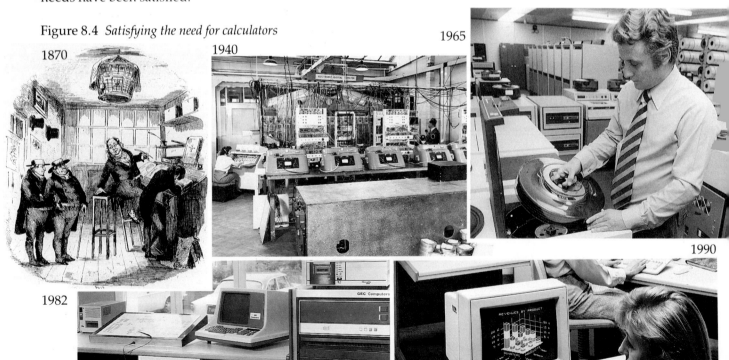

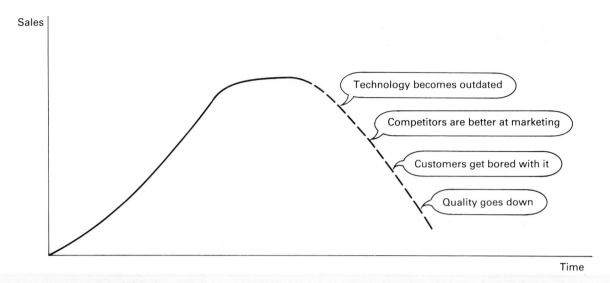

Figure 8.5 *Why products stop selling*

Although the customers needs may not change very rapidly, the way in which they are satisfied will change. Look at Figure 8.5. It shows some of the reasons for people to stop buying some goods and services.

It is the job of the **research and development** department to keep up with changes in technology. **Market research** provides information about people's changing tastes and fashions, as well as information about what competitors are doing.

When designing a product a business will be concerned with four major things:

1. *Safety* – the work of consumer groups and legal requirements mean that people are becoming more aware of the dangers in ordinary products. This covers obvious goods such as cars and electrical equipment. It also includes such things as the fire resistance of materials used in furniture and children's clothing.

2. *Efficiency* – is it cheap and easy to operate? Advertisements for cars and goods such as washing machines often emphasise the cheapness of operation. Badly placed controls can cause tiredness in industrial machines. An efficient machine can also be safer to operate.

3. *Appearance* – goods have to keep up with fashion if they are to sell. Attractive design can also be important in goods sold to industry. People work harder if the appearance is attractive.

4. *Repairs and servicing* – this can add to the cost of a purchase. How long before the first service? A car that needs servicing every 20 000 miles will be cheaper to run than a car that needs servicing every 6 000 miles.

Of course the business also has to take into account how much the ideal design will cost to produce, whether it can afford that cost and whether the good will sell at a price high enough to cover the cost.

JUST TESTING

1. What are the main stages in designing a product?

2. Give three reasons why a market oriented business might be more successful than a product oriented business.

3. Match what people said in Figure 8.5 with the reasons why people stop buying a product given below.

(a) fashions change
(b) technical changes
(c) a similar but improved product comes onto the market.

Finding the place

Location is the general area in which production takes place. The **site** is the actual piece of ground on which production takes place.

In general, businesses will locate in an area that will keep their production costs as low as possible. Some types of production have less choice than others. Some crops will only grow in a certain climate, mining can only take place where the minerals are present in the ground. Other types of business have much more choice. All they need is a good communication system and electricity. These industries are sometimes called **footloose industries.**

Figure 8.6 shows some of the things a business will take into account when deciding where to locate.

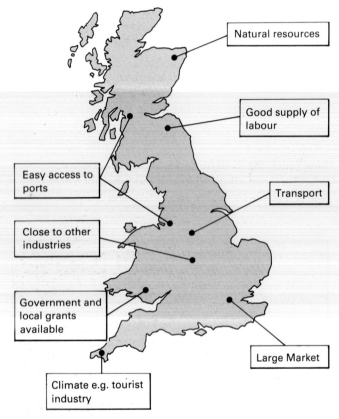

Figure 8.6 *Factors affecting location*

Purchasing and stock control

Purchasing

Businesses buy in:

* raw materials

* components

* finished goods.

Components and finished goods can be bought by the business or made by it. These **make or buy** decisions vary from business to business. Before deciding, a business will ask itself the following questions:

* is it cheaper to buy than make them ourselves?

* are the supplies safe? Can we be sure of getting what we need, when we need it?

* how many do we need? The more important the component, the more likely the business is to produce it itself.

Of course some business, e.g. retailers and wholesalers, buy in large quantities of finished goods. Very large retailers and wholesalers may produce some goods themselves.

When deciding on a supplier a business will take into account the **price**, the **quality** of the goods offered and the **service** (e.g. delivery times) of the supplier.

Stocks

At any time a business will have more raw materials, components, semi-finished goods and finished goods than it needs. This is necessary so that the business can:

* carry on production if, for some reason, supplies dry up

* continue to supply customers if demand for the product rises unexpectedly

* take advantage of discounts (lower prices) offered for buying in large quantities

* buy when prices are low and so keep the cost of production down.

On the other hand, if the business has more stock than it needs, it is wasting money:

* perishable goods, e.g. food, might deteriorate if they are kept for too long

* the cost of wages for warehouse staff and security staff

* loss through stealing

* insurance premiums against fire, other damage and theft

* the market might change, people may no longer want to buy the product

* money used to buy stocks can be used in other parts of the business.

Because the cost of holding stock is high, stock control is a very important activity for a business. A good stock control system will make sure that it has enough stock to meet its needs, but that the costs of holding stock are kept as low as possible. Figure 8.7 is a graph which shows the ideal pattern of stock holding and ordering in a business.

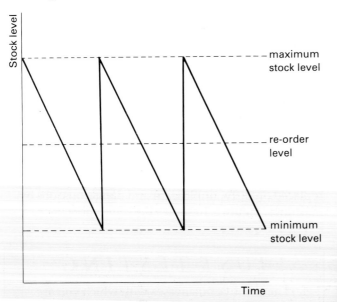

Figure 8.7 *A stock control graph*

The **maximum stock level** indicates the highest level of stock a business is willing to hold after taking into account its need for stocks and the cost of holding them.

The **minimum stock level** is the lowest amount of stock the business is prepared to hold. Below this level there is a danger of production stopping because there is a shortage of materials. The business may not be able to meet orders because it has not got enough finished goods. The **re-order level** is the point at which the business will order new stocks to make sure the amount held does not fall below the minimum level.

Computerisation of stock control systems has cut costs by improving efficiency. It is possible for a business to have a much clearer picture of the stock level and how rapidly or slowly it is being used. This allows a business to be more flexible in its ordering.

JUST TESTING

1. What is a make or buy decision? Give two reasons why a business might decide to make rather than buy a component.

2. Give two reasons why a business might decide to reduce the level of stocks it is holding.

Types of production

Job production

This term is used when:

* goods are made individually

* no single product of the business is exactly alike

* the product is made when the customer orders it. It is not made for stock – that is made in the hope that someone will want to buy it

* the equipment and machinery used will not be specialised.

The photograph in Figure 8.8 shows a cabinet maker working on a piece of furniture. He will have discussed the design with the customer and is making it to fit the customer's personal requirements.

Figure 8.8 *Job production*

Batch production

This is used:

* when there are a number of orders for a special product

* when the number of sales means that only a small number are needed

* when the technology or type of product makes it necessary.

Figure 8.9 is an example of batch production in which the technology used and the type of product dictates the use of batch production. The large vats contain cultures of bacteria which are being fed and kept at a certain temperature. The activity of the bacteria in the vats will eventually produce a batch of anti-biotics.

Figure 8.9 *Batch production*

Flow production

In this type of production the machinery is arranged in lines in the order in which it is needed to make the product. The products are moved from machine to machine, travelling to the next machine as soon as an operation is complete. Flow production is used when identical products are needed in very large numbers.

Because flow production breaks down the work needed to make a product into a number of simple operations it is easy to replace people by machines. Simple operations can be performed by robots. This has increased over the last few years as the advantages of improved quality and reliability have been realised. Although it has reduced the number of jobs in manufacturing it has also meant that people are being replaced on dirty, unpleasant and dangerous jobs by machines. Figure 8.10 shows the differences.

JUST TESTING

1. Think of five businesses with which you are familiar. You can use businesses that you pass on your way to school each day, e.g. the local garage, a shop. What type of production does each business use.

2. Look at the photographs showing the different types of production. Make a list of all the differences you can see between the photographs.

Figure 8.10 *Then and now in flow production*

What quality?

It is important for a business to decide the quality it is aiming for. Figure 8.11 shows why the quality of the product is important to a business.

Figure 8.11 *The importance of quality to a business*

The product life cycle

The length of time that people will continue to buy a product is called the **life** of the product. The life of a product has four main stages.

1. *Introduction.* This is when the product is first put on the market. It is an expensive time for the business launching it. Money has had to be spent on research and development. Advertising and promotion costs are high – the product is not earning any money yet.

2. *Growth.* People are starting to buy the product, and money from sales starts coming into the business.

3. *Maturity.* Sales are unlikely to go any higher without some help. Some ways in which the business might do this are:

   * more advertising

   * changing the image of the product

   * finding a new market.

4. *Decline.* Sales have started to go down.

Figure 8.12 shows the pattern of the life of a product. This is called a **product life cycle**.

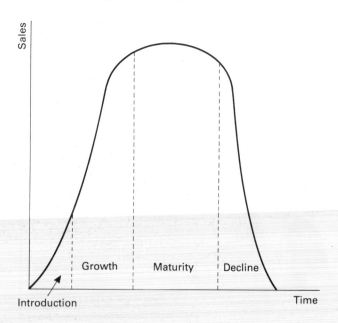

JUST TESTING

What are the main stages in the life of a product? Why do you think the life of a car is longer than the life of a dress fashion?

The product mix

There is an old saying: "Do not keep all your eggs in one basket." If you drop the basket you can lose all your eggs. If you keep your eggs in two baskets and drop one you will only risk half your eggs. Businesses try to protect themselves against the sales of one product falling by having a number of products. The larger the business the more products there are likely to be. Figure 8.13 shows the different products of a very large business. This group of products is called the **product mix**. A business with a wide range of different products is known as a **conglomerate**.

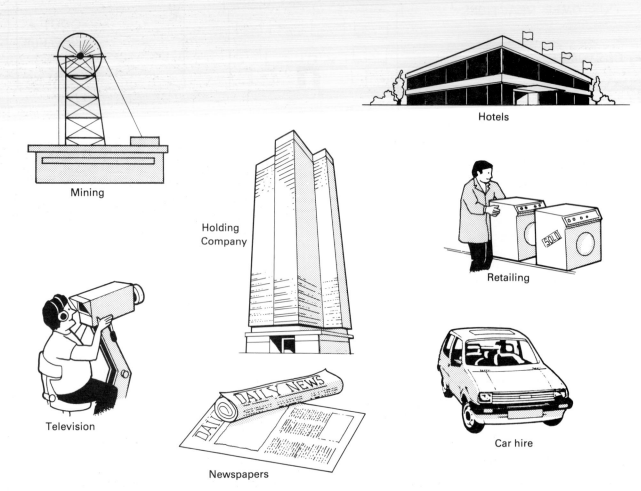

Figure 8.13 *The product mix of a conglomerate*

Another approach to this problem is to introduce a new model every few years. The new model will have design changes or some change in technology. The car industry offers a good example of this.

Figure 8.14 *The changes in the Ford Cortina*

Finding out

1. Visit three different businesses. The businesses you chose can be:

* small, medium and large businesses offering the same type of product. For example, three businesses of different sizes which make clothes

* businesses of the same size making different products.

Task A   Draw up a list of questions you will want to ask and things you should look out for on your visits. When you have drawn up your own list, get into small groups, compare your lists and draw up a final list. If you are not sure what you should be looking for, the major headings in this unit will give you some help.

Task B   Write a brief, factual report on what you have found out. Share your results with other members of the group. What differences and similarities did you notice? List all the reasons you can think of for your observations.

Task C   Draw a plan of the working area of the businesses you have visited. Make a note of where each process takes place and the way in which work moves from one process to the next.

Task D   As a result of your research write a report on the criteria a business takes into account when deciding how to organise production.

2. Select a product that has just been launched onto the market. You should chose a product of general interest to make sure you have a wide range of evidence available. Products designed for the gardener will be advertised in specialist magazines and in the gardening sections of newspapers and other magazines. It can take several months before your evidence is complete in these cases.

(a) Survey television, newspaper and magazine advertisements for the product. Note how often they appear, what appeal each advertisement makes to the customer and any similarities between advertisements in each section of the media.

(b) Discover the cost of advertising space.

Task A   Draw up a chart analysing the results of your research.

Task B   Using the findings of your research, list the main concerns of the producers. Why do you think these things are important to them?

Task C   Which type of advertising was used most frequently? What reasons can you give for the producers making this decision? You can use your knowledge of the costs of advertising to help in this. Did the pattern of advertising change during the period you were studying this product?

Task D   Write a report on the way in which the producers introduced the product to the customers.

Trying it out

1. Sawyers Ltd manufactures garments. The business employs thirty people: a cutter, two pressers and twenty-six machinists. Jane Sawyer, who started the business eight years ago, is responsible for overall management. She also sees to quality control.

Sawyers is employed by other, larger, garment manufacturers who negotiate orders with major chain stores. Sawyers has little say in the design of the garments they make, the materials used and delivery dates. The chain stores make these decisions, and the materials, patterns, buttons etc, are supplied to Sawyers when an order is negotiated.

(a) What do you understand by the terms:

   (i) product oriented business?
   (ii) market oriented business?

(b) Is Sawyers Ltd a product or market oriented business? Give reasons for your answer.

Jane received an order for 200 dresses of a particular design. She followed her usual practice of having the dresses cut out; each machinist was then given the pieces for a given number of complete dresses which they had to make up. Buttonholing was done by two machinists who specialised in this work. The dresses then went to the pressers who checked for quality as they worked. Jane made the final check for quality before the order was dispatched.

(c) What type of production is used by Sawyers Ltd?

(d) Give one reason why Jane Sawyer does the final check on quality.

(e) All the production processes in Sawyers Ltd take place in one large room. Draw a diagram showing the flow of work through Sawyers. Explain the decisions you have made.

2. A large mail order company wants to open a warehouse in the North West. It has the following requirements:

* easy access to the motorway system so that orders will get to customers quickly

* a large piece of flat land to build the warehouse on. This is to make the handling of goods easier and also to provide plenty of parking space.

(a) List three other factors the business might take into account when deciding where to locate its warehouse.

(b) Look at the map in Figure 8.15. Which town do you think would make the best location for the warehouse? Give one reason for your answer.

3. Figure 8.16 shows the stock levels of components held by a business over six months.

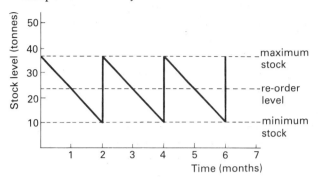

Figure 8.16 *Graph to show stock levels*

(a) What is meant by the following terms:

(i) minimum stock level?
(ii) re-order level?
(iii) maximum stock level?

(b) Give two reasons why the business decided on the minimum re-order level.

(c) What was the level of stock held by the business at the end of the third month?

(d) How long did it take from ordering to delivery?

(e) Explain why the business might have decided to hold higher stock levels at the end of the fourth month than at any other time.

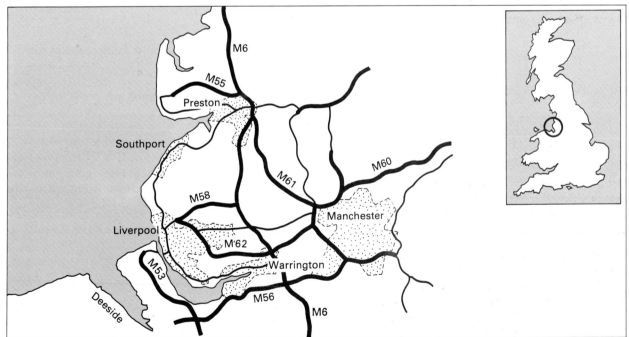

Figure 8.15 *Possible locations for the distribution warehouse*

UNIT 9:
GETTING THE PRICE RIGHT

There are four main things a business must take into account when deciding what to charge for its products:

* the goals (objectives) the business is trying to reach

* how much the product costs to make

* the price charged for the same type of products by other businesses

* how much the customers are prepared to pay.

Figure 9.1 illustrates some of the things a business will need to take into account when deciding on a price.

We are aiming for an 11% increase in profits this year.

Wages are rising – we'll have to put the price up to get our profit.

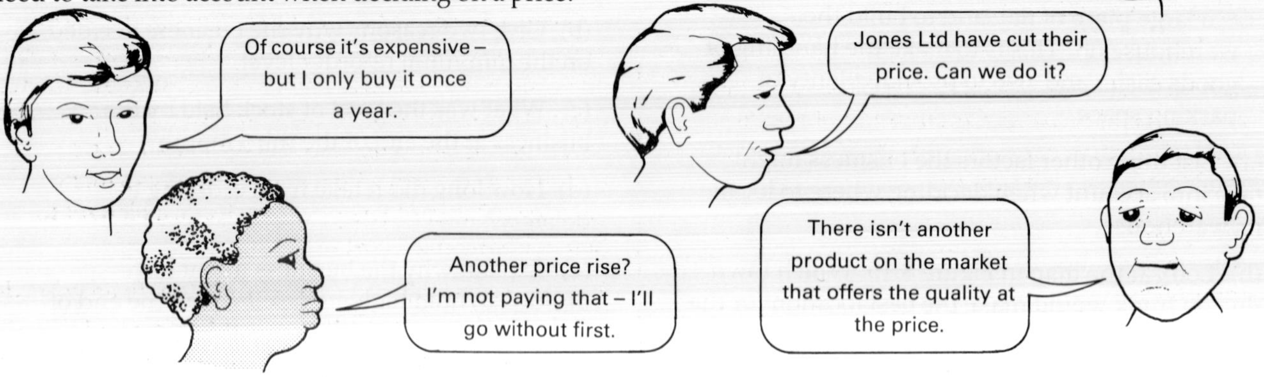

Of course it's expensive – but I only buy it once a year.

Jones Ltd have cut their price. Can we do it?

Another price rise? I'm not paying that – I'll go without first.

There isn't another product on the market that offers the quality at the price.

Figure 9.1 *Deciding on a price*

JUST TESTING

Look at figure 9.1. Which of the statements refer to:

(a) costs?
(b) prices charged by other businesses?
(c) what the consumer is prepared to pay?
(d) the objectives of the business?

Pricing goals

Some pricing goals are:

* getting a certain percentage profit

* holding or increasing the market share

* reducing competition, for example by selling at a low price for a time.

Pricing goals will depend on the objectives of the business.

How much does it cost?

A business has to buy in goods and services from people and other businesses so that it can make the product. The money it pays for these goods and services are its costs of production. There are two main types of costs:

1. *Fixed costs.* These are the costs a business cannot avoid and include buildings, machinery, rates. A business might have a factory capable of producing 100 000 hairdryers a year. The basic costs of that factory will be the same if it produces 100 000 hairdryers or 5 000 hairdryers. The **total fixed costs** of the factory stay the same for a certain period of time.

2. *Variable costs.* These costs change (vary) depending on how many hairdryers (or whatever) the business

68

produces. Variable costs include the materials, components and energy used. They also include certain types of labour.

Variable cost per unit is calculated by dividing the **total variable costs** by the number made.

Example: A business manufactures 1 000 trays in a month. The total variable costs are £2 000. The variable cost of each tray (unit) will be £2 000/1 000 = £2.

JUST TESTING

1. Calculate the variable cost per unit for each of the following sets of data:

(a) Total variable cost – £5 500
     Output – 100
(b) Total variable cost – £9 000
     Output – 1 000
(c) Total variable cost – £100 000
     Output – 20 000

2. The total fixed costs for a business in one year are £20 000. The maximum number of goods it can produce in that year is 10 000. What are its total fixed costs if it produces:

(a) 2 000
(b) 5 000
(c) 9 000

3. What is the main difference between the fixed and variable costs of a business?

Using costs to decide on a price

All businesses must take costs into account when deciding on a price. Sometimes cost is more important than at other times.

Mark-up on costs

All types of business can use this method but it is particularly used by wholesalers and retailers. A small shopkeeper buys in twelve packets of a breakfast cereal. They cost £9.60. Each packet of breakfast cereal the shopkeeper sells has to:

* cover the cost of buying it

* contribute to the running costs of the shop

* make a profit.

The shopkeeper decides she will add 40% of the cost of the breakfast cereal to the cost and sell at that price.

40% of the cost = 40% of £9.60

£9.60 × 40/100 = £3.84

Add it onto the original cost

£9.60 + £3.84 = £13.44

The shopkeeper bought twelve packets, so to find out the selling price of each packet it is necessary to divide £13.44 by twelve.

£13.44/12 = £1.12 or 112p

Contribution pricing

A contribution is something given to something else. In the case of contribution pricing it is what the price can give to fixed costs.

A manufacturer has enough machinery to make 5 000 items in a month. At the moment he is only making 4 000. A customer offers him an order for another 500 items at a price that is below the full cost of producing them. The manufacturer calculates that this price will cover the **variable** costs, that is the extra labour, materials and energy he will have to buy to make another 500 items. The price will leave a bit over to help with the fixed costs.

The important thing to remember is that fixed costs do not go away so every little helps. Of course the manufacturer would not accept the order if somebody else offered him a price that covered all the costs.

Tenders

A tender is an offer. A local authority, for example, which has decided to build a new school will invite tenders from builders for the job. A building firm will work out how much it thinks the job will cost, decide on the profit they want and work out a detailed document stating what they will do and for what price. The local authority will receive a number of these tenders and chose the one it thinks offers the best deal.

JUST TESTING

Why does a business have to take costs into account when deciding on a price?

Costs and size

Some businesses find that when their output rises, their cost of production per unit falls. These businesses are said to be enjoying **economies of scale**.

Because businesses enjoying economies of scale can produce at a lower cost, they can also sell at a lower price. As a result, large businesses are usually more **competitive** than small businesses.

The main economies of scale enjoyed by large businesses are:

1. *Purchasing economies.* When a business is buying a large quantity of raw materials, components or finished goods it can often negotiate a lower price than a smaller business. By getting rid of a large amount of stock in one transaction, the seller will save on storage costs. Some of these savings are passed on to the buyer in the form of lower prices. Very large businesses buying from smaller businesses have more power than their suppliers. They can use this power to negotiate a lower price. The difference between the usual price and the price charged for large orders is known as **bulk discount**.

2. *Financial economies.* Financial institutions such as banks and insurance companies are more prepared to lend money to large businesses than small ones. Often they are prepared to lend money to large businesses at a lower rate of interest. Financial institutions want to be sure that their loans are secure. A large business has more to offer in the way of land, buildings, machinery and other investments than a small business.

3. *Marketing economies.* Marketing is very expensive with high fixed costs. The more products the business makes the lower the marketing costs for each unit it sells. If you do not understand this, look up the definition of fixed costs on p68.

4. *Technical economies.* There can be a number of different machines that perform the same industrial process. The more expensive machines are likely to work faster, producing high quality goods with less waste. The more of a product the business makes, the smaller the cost of the machine that has to be counted into the cost of each product. Large businesses can also use flow production methods (p62) if they are suitable. Again this cuts down costs.

5. *Managerial economies.* A very small business – just one person owning it and doing all the work – lacks specialist skills. As the business grows larger, the owner can employ people with expertise in, for example, finance. Experts can be under-used. As the business grows in size the cost of their salary gets smaller compared with the total costs of production.

Businesses do not have to be very large to enjoy some economies of scale. It is a continuous process as businesses develop from very small to large firms. Managers have to be careful to make sure that growing larger does not increase their costs by:

* adding to communication difficulties between departments

* increasing the number of rules and so slowing down decision making. If this happens it will take the business longer to respond to change

* making employees feel that they are 'just cogs in a machine'

* giving people dull and limited jobs that give them no interest (job satisfaction).

JUST TESTING

1. Give two advantages and two disadvantages of a business growing larger.

2. Growlarge PLC gives the following advantages of growing larger. What type of economy of scale is it talking about in each case?

(a) "Advertising costs per unit are down by 15%."
(b) "As managing director I felt I had too much time to play golf."
(c) "We get a much better deal from our suppliers. 20% discount is a big improvement on 10%."
(d) "The new Walleys machine provides Walleys for all our factories – and fifty per cent per Walley cheaper."
(e) "We got the loan at 10%. Five years ago we would be paying 3% above the going rate."

What do other people charge?

Of course a business has to cover its costs, but it also has to look at what other businesses are charging for the same or similar products.

1. The market price. A farmer taking his lambs to market cannot decide on his own price. He will have to

accept the price that is being offered for lambs of the same size, weight and quality as his. The same is true of a manufacturer producing goods for a market in which there are a number of other businesses all charging about the same price. The producer must sell at the market price and keep an eye on the costs to make sure of a profit.

2. The price of similar products. Biggin PLC has invented a new form of man-made fibre. This fibre can be used instead of other man-made fibres. When pricing its new product Biggin will have to take into account the prices of other man-made fibres, that is the **substitutes** for its own product.

3. If a business charges a very high price for a new product, it may make a lot of profit – but it can also give other businesses the chance to creep into the market with a similar product sold more cheaply.

Figure 9.2 shows some of the ways in which businesses that sell similar products can charge a higher or lower price than their competitors.

What will the customer pay?

1. Sometimes customers get used to paying a certain price for a product. They see anything higher as being too expensive and anything lower as being suspect. When this happens, producers will stay with that price and alter the quantity sold. They might offer "15%

extra" instead of lowering the price. Reductions in quantity (raising the price) are not usually so well advertised.

2. Customers have an idea of what a product is worth to them. This is the highest price they are prepared to pay. Of course, all customers will put a different value on a product but there is often a top price, if the producer goes above this his sales fall rapidly.

3. Customers often judge a product by its price. A product that has always sold at a high price will be looked at with suspicion if it is offered at a much lower price.

4. The sales of some products are more sensitive to changes in price. People are more likely to stop buying a luxury good when the price goes up than something that they need to survive.

JUST TESTING

1. Give two reasons why a business takes note of what its competitors are charging.

2. You are going to buy a gold locket as a birthday present for your mother. You visit a number of jewellers and find that their prices are all very similar. However, one jeweller is selling a gold locket at half the price of his competitors. Would you buy the cheap locket? Give reasons for your answer.

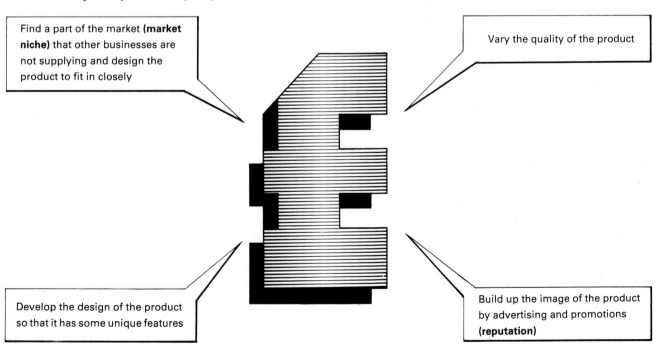

Find a part of the market (**market niche**) that other businesses are not supplying and design the product to fit in closely

Vary the quality of the product

Develop the design of the product so that it has some unique features

Build up the image of the product by advertising and promotions (**reputation**)

Costs and revenue

Once a business knows the costs of production and has some idea of the price it can charge, it can work out how many it needs to sell in order to cover its costs.

The minimum number it has to sell to cover its costs is called the **break-even point**. This can be worked out using a **break-even chart**. An example of a break-even chart is given in Figure 9.3.

The revenue is calculated by:

Selling price × number of sales

In this example:

Fixed costs for one year = £1 000

Variable cost per unit = £1

Maximum capacity = 5 000

Selling price = £2

JUST TESTING

What would be the break-even point in the example shown in Figure 9.3 if the selling price was raised to £2.50?

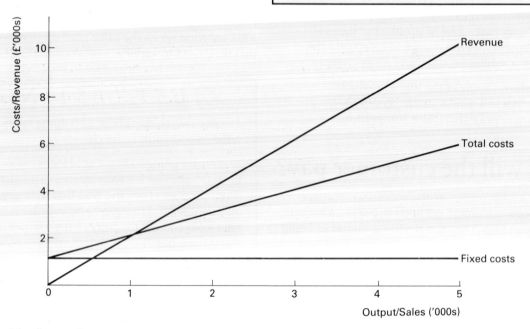

Figure 9.3 *A break-even chart*

Finding out

1. This is an investigation into the costs of setting up a small business. You will need:

* a large number of copies of your local newspaper

* Yellow pages

* the friendly owner of a small business.

There is a lot of research in this so you would be advised to work in groups.

Task A Select a small business. Keep it simple! If you choose a business that carries a large amount of stock, the costing will get out of hand. A small hairdressing salon or a gardening service are good possibilities. Now make a list of all the

things you will need to start the business and keep it running for six months. Find out the cost of all the items on your list.

Task B Sort out the costs into fixed and variable. Any costs that you will have to pay for more than six months are fixed. Using Figure 9.3 as a guide draw a graph to show your fixed and total costs for a period of six months.

Task C How much can you charge for your product? Draw in the revenue line on your graph.

Task D As a result of your research comment on the importance of fixed costs to the business. Would it have a better chance of survival if costs were lower? How much control did you have over the prices you charged? Could any of the costs have been reduced? What problems did you experience in deciding whether costs were fixed or variable.

2. This is an investigation into the different prices charged for upholstered furniture. You can substitute another product but be careful to keep it simple.

Task A   Collect as many advertisements for upholstered furniture as possible. Take your examples from a wide range of newspapers and magazines. Make sure you take a note of the name of the newspaper or magazine and the price. Survey local furniture shops. What prices are they charging for upholstered furniture?

Task B   Sort the furniture into groups according to price. You might have 3-piece suites for less than £300, less than £600, less than £900 and so on. Has the furniture in each price group got anything in common?

Task C   Now, taking into account the type of magazine the businesses advertised in, the style of the furniture, the quality of the furniture and any services that were offered (e.g. wide range of covers, type of service in the shops) build up a picture of the sort of consumer. Think of it in terms of age, income, traditional ideas, likes modern furniture, etc.

Task D   Write a brief report on the way in which costs of production (quality and service), competitors and customers influence the price of upholstered furniture.

Trying it out

1. Asha Khan runs a small coffee shop. The data given below is a summary of her income and expenses in 1988.

Revenue from sales	£10 000
Cost of sales	£ 2 000
Average unit selling price	£ 1
Rent and rates	£ 1 500
Wages	£ 5 000
Heat/light	£ 200
Insurance	£ 300

(a) Which of the costs in the information above are fixed and which are variable?

(b) Give an example of a fixed cost which is not included in the list above.

Asha calculated her unit selling price as an average.

(c) How many snacks did she sell?

(d) What was Asha's profit?

2. Les Parr was made redundant in 1988. He decided to set up in business as a jobbing gardener working from home. This would keep his fixed costs low. Les made a list of the second hand equipment he would need to start his business.

Hand tools	£ 50
Lawnmower	£ 150
Rotavator	£ 200
Van	£2 600

(a) (i) What are fixed costs?
(ii) What are Les's fixed costs in starting his business?

In addition Les estimated that he could charge £2.50 for an hour's work. He hoped to pay himself £60 per week. He calculated that petrol would be 50p for every hour's work.

(b) What are Les's variable costs?

(c) How may hours a week will Les have to work in order to cover his variable costs?

(d) What information would Les need before deciding to charge £2.50 for an hour's work?

Les decides that he will work a forty hour week for forty-five weeks in the year.

(e) (i) What are the total number of hours Les will work in a year?
(ii) How much is Les paying himself per hour?
(iii) What are Les's variable cost per hour?

(f) Calculate the number of hours Les will have to work in order to break even.

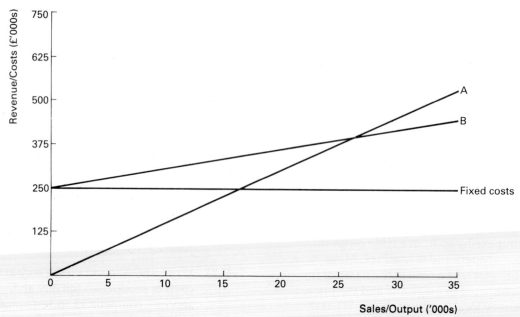

Figure 9.4 *Hogan's break-even chart*

3. Hogan's makes picture frames which it sells to a number of wholesalers. Michael Hogan was not satisfied with the level of profits in 1989 and drew up the break-even chart in Figure 9.4 to give himself some information.

(a) Which line on the graph shows:

  (i) revenue?
  (ii) total costs?

(b) Explain what is meant by:

  (i) variable costs
  (ii) fixed costs.

Michael Hogan decided that the break-even point was too high and, as a result, the level of profits was too low.

(c) Use the graph to find:

  (i) the break-even level of revenue
  (ii) the profit earned in 1989
  (iii) the level of fixed costs.

Michael Hogan did not expect his costs to change in 1990. He decided to increase the cost of his frames to £20.

(d) Using the information on the break-even chart, calculate:

  (i) the 1989 selling price of the picture frames
  (ii) the expected profit in 1990 after the increase in price.

4. Eileen Taylor was planning to set up her own business hand painting china plates to order. She also intended to build up a small stock of decorated plates that she could sell to interested customers. Eileen calculated how much money she would need to start her business and went along to her bank to ask for a loan of £500.

The bank manager shook his head. "You intend to sell the plates at £80. How did you decide on that price?"

Eileen looked puzzled. "I worked out my costs very carefully, then I added on how much money I needed to live."

The bank manager sighed and began to explain.

As the bank manager, explain to Eileen the importance of each of the following when deciding on her price.

(a) Costs
(b) Competitors
(c) Customers

UNIT 10:
COMMUNICATING WITH THE CUSTOMER

Good communications

Good communications depend on getting

* the right message

* to the right people

* at the right time

* in the right place.

The right message will depend on who a business is trying to communicate with, when it is communicating and where its customers are when they are in a mood to listen.

1. The customer and the message. The message a business wants to get across to its potential customers is that they will get more benefits if they buy its products rather than those of its competitors.

The way in which the message is presented must appeal to the customer. The business must know its target market – the age, income, interests and attitudes of the people it wants to sell to.

* some goods are obviously designed to appeal to a certain age group

* expensive goods are more likely to appeal to high income groups or people without other responsibilities such as children and a mortgage

* there are goods that will only appeal to people with certain interests. Gardening tools and fishing tackle would not be of much use to a non-gardener or a non-angler

* people have a wide variety of attitudes to the goods they buy. They might buy a car for transport– but they might also want a car to give them a good image with their friends.

2. The message and time. The message to the customer will also change with the time it is given. The product life-cycle in Figure 10.1 shows the way in which the advertising message changes according to the position the product is in its life-cycle.

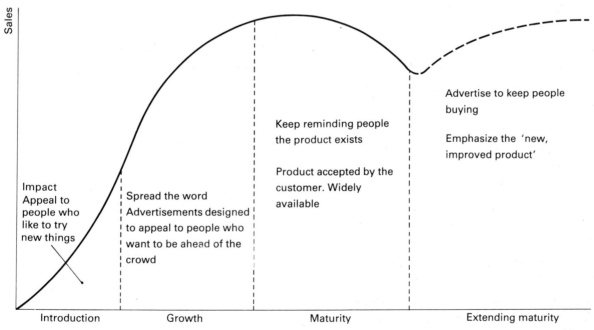

Figure 10.1 *The product life cycle and advertising*

This must also take into account the type of customer the business is trying to reach. In the early part of its life the customer is likely to be the adventurous type – the sort of people who like trying something new, or perhaps just people who have the money to take the risk. Some products never get beyond this stage because the advertising never convinces more cautious people that the product is worth the money.

Timing is important for goods that have a seasonal pattern of sales. Toy companies advertise more before Christmas than at any other time in the year.

3. The customer and place. There are products that are bought on impulse. The message is best at the place the customer buys – **the point of sale**. Customers read different magazines – the business must decide which magazines will be read by its target market. Newspapers, magazines and television companies help with this by researching their readership and publishing information about their ages, incomes, interests and attitudes.

4. The method and the message. There are three methods that all businesses use to get their message across to the customer:

* sales staff in shops or visiting the customer personally. Sales staff can give immediate answers to any queries that the customer might have. (Look up the advantages of oral communication on p49). To do this they must have a good knowledge of their product. The more complicated the product, the more expertise the sales staff must have. A person selling industrial machinery is likely to have a degree in engineering

* advertising describes the product and gets the customer interested in it

* sales promotion offers the customer other advantages. Competitions and two for the price of one offers come into this group.

JUST TESTING

A business is about to launch a new product.

1. What are the main things it must remember if its communications with its customers are going to be successful?

2. What sort of customer is likely to buy the product?

3. What are the ways in which it can communicate with the customers?

What is advertising?

What advertising does

When you advertise something you make it generally known. A business advertises its products for the following reasons:

* to **tell** the customer about the product. Look for advertisements that give a Freephone number or a Freepost address for examples of this

* to get people **interested** in the product. An eye catching headline is often used for this purpose

* to **persuade** people to buy the product. Special offers, competitions and other methods are used to persuade people to give a product a chance. The advertiser hopes that once people have tried the product they will like it and go on buying it

* to give the business a good **image**. British Nuclear Fuels advertises to counteract the poor image of nuclear energy portrayed by the anti-nuclear lobby. Esso and Shell advertise their own conservation efforts.

A good advertisement will attract **attention**, draw **interest**, create **desire** and get **action**. Figure 10.2 demonstrates how an advertisement tries to do this.

Figure 10.2 *Analysis of an advertisement*

"I'm glad we can still enjoy our little trips to the coast Mum."

If you'd like to drive a stylish hatchback, and still be able to afford the other good things in life, take a look at a Yugo.
A Yugo has everything you'd expect from a new car. Except a big price tag.
Positive front wheel drive and light handling, together with a Yugo's compact hatchback design, make parking a cinch.
And a nippy, responsive engine means when you really want to go places, you can. Yet fuel consumption remains low.
Better still, both for you and the environment, all new Yugo's run on unleaded petrol.
Four adults (even more kids) can travel in comfort or fold the rear seats down and you've a useful 27.5 cu. ft. of loadspace.
So go on, treat yourself to a Yugo.

Your nearest Yugo dealer is listed in Yellow Pages. Or contact Yugo Cars Zastava (GB) Limited, Worcester House, Basingstoke Road, Reading. RG2 0QB.
Telephone: Reading (0734) 866921. Car illustrated 65, GLX £5,295 excluding number plates and delivery).

Yugo cars

Advertising methods

1. *National newspaper*

For: – reach a large number of people daily or weekly

– know their readership very well in terms of age, sex, income, interests, opinions – they have to do this to sell the newspaper!

– advertisements can be placed within days so advertisers can change quickly if necessary.

Against: – advertising is expensive.

2. *Local newspaper*

For: – often have a wide circulation in a small area

– relatively cheap

– good for local businesses or branches of a big business that wishes to increase sales in a certain area

– knows the readership. Local newspapers often have a wider readership than the national newspapers in terms of age, income and interests.

Against: – limited to one area.

3. *Magazines*

For: – most magazines are aimed at people with special interests or for a certain age group, e.g. women's magazines, DIY, computers, gardening. This helps advertisers to get directly to the people who will be interested in the sort of things they have to sell. People who buy these magazines often read the advertisements with more care than usual.

4. *Trade and technical journals*

These are publications directed towards people working in certain jobs or certain types of business. They have the same advantage as magazines given above but they are directed to producers rather than consumers. Suppliers might advertise in these magazines. So might employers.

5. *Direct mail*

This has become more important over recent years. The development of word-processing technology has meant that advertising material is addressed to individuals.

For: – people can read it at their leisure.

Against: – some people do not like getting advertisements through the post and throw it into the bin without reading it.

6. *Television*

For: – gets to a large number of people, especially if the advertisement goes out at the same time as a popular programme.

Against: – no way of knowing if people are watching it

– expensive

– reaches everybody whether they are interested in that type of product or not.

JUST TESTING

1. What is the difference between advertising and sales promotion?

2. What are the main methods of advertising?

Sales promotion

Sales promotion is used for only a limited period of time – "Offer closes on the 31st December 1990". Businesses use these methods of communicating with the customer when it wants to:

* persuade the customer to buy at a certain time of the year. For example, a business whose products sell better in winter than summer might run a sales promotion in summer. It may not sell *more* goods in the year but the sales will be more spread out. This is shown in Figure 10.3

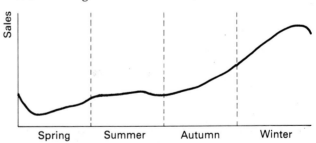

Before the promotion campaign. High sales for Christmas

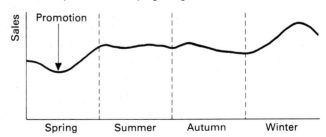

After the promotion campaign

Figure 10.3 *Sales promotion and changing sales pattern*

* persuade people to try a new product line. In this case it might offer a free trial pack

* persuade people to buy its product rather than those of its competitors.

Below are the methods used in sales promotions. These are illustrated in Figure 10.4.

1. On-pack offers, e.g. free seeds with a gardening magazine, free sachets of shampoo

2. Free gifts

3. Coupons

4. Competitions

5. Exhibitions and demonstrations

6. Short-term price cuts.

Figure 10.4 *Methods of promoting sales*

JUST TESTING

Look at Figure 10.4. Match up the pictures with the methods of sales promotion given above.

Communicating with other businesses

1. Manufacturers often support the people who sell their goods to the final consumer or try to persuade wholesalers and retailers to stock their goods by:

  * point of sale material, e.g. special units, shelf strips

  * manufacturers putting their own staff into the retail shop to demonstrate and answer questions about the product

  * catalogues

  * special discounts.

2. Businesses that sell to other businesses will advertise in newspapers and magazines. They will use more specialised salespeople than businesses selling to the final consumer.

Figure 10.5
Cosmetics packaging

Packaging

Packaging is important to keep products clean and safe and to make handling easier. It also communicates a message to the customer. Look at the photograph in Figure 10.5.

Cosmetics packaging tries to convey a variety of messages – luxury, cleanliness and purity of product are just a few. The packaging reflects the advertising used – in fact it will link up with the advertising in colour and style. Whatever the message, the packaging of cosmetics tends to be luxurious.

RESTRUCTURE
EYE CONTOUR GEL

THE BENEFITS:
CRYSTAL CLEAR

THE LOOK:
PURE VICHY

Specially formulated for the delicate eye area, Restructure from Vichy is a dual action gel that actively combats wrinkles, dark shadows and bags caused by ageing or fatigue.

Active moisturisers instantly soothe tired eyes and tone the epidermis. Liquid crystals, suspended in the translucent gel, are enriched with vitamins A and E, renowned for their anti-ageing benefits.

As a result, Restructure refreshes, revives and rejuvenates for a younger, fresher look.

Restructure has been tested under ophthalmological control on contact lens wearers and sensitive skin. Fragrance free, it is wonderfully light, non-greasy and easily absorbed, allowing make-up to be applied immediately.

VICHY

AVAILABLE AT LEADING BOOTS AND CHEMISTS.
Vichy UK Limited, 15 Nuffield Way, Abingdon, Oxon OX14 1TJ.

The Body Shop came up with a different approach. The emphasis is upon attractive, cheap simplicity. It has proved to be a very successful message.

The corporate image

The image customers have of a business depends on such things as:

* the reliability of its products

* the size of the business

* the quality of the after sales service

* value for money

* the business's role in the community, for example its attitudes to conservation.

Some businesses give themselves a recognisable identity by having a company colour, providing uniforms for their employees, having a uniform style of furnishing and using a **logo**.

A logo is a simple symbol used on all the company's products. When it is first introduced, advertising will be used to make customers aware of it. A business that uses a logo on all its products will be very careful about quality control. A great deal of money has to be spent on building up a corporate image and one bad product could affect the sales of the rest of the business's product mix.

Conglomerates are careful about the use of a logo. You must remember the image customers have of themselves. The buyers of airline tickets, hotel rooms and hire car services may want a jetset image. If the conglomerate that provides these goods and services also manufactures baby foods it will not attract that sort of person.

JUST TESTING

1. How does packaging help promote products? Give two other purposes of packaging.

2. What is meant by the term "corporate image"?

3. Give one advantage and one disadvantage of a business having a logo.

Does promotion work?

The answer to that is "Not always". If the product satisfies the needs of the customer, is a good product

and if the promotion has been well planned it will.

A poor promotion campaign can lead to more sales – but unless the amount of money from these sales exceeds the amount of money spent on promotion it is a failure.

Because all promotion activities carry the risk of being an expensive failure, businesses often use specialist firms to plan and carry them out. Specialist firms have a number of advantages. They have:

* the expertise. This is very important in radio and television advertising

* highly skilled people working for them. Highly skilled salespeople do not come cheap. If they are spread out over a number of products, the cost is lowered. (Look up the definition of marketing economies on p70)

* a specialist knowledge of other businesses that can do a job. They will know the best director for a certain type of TV commercial

* an outsider's view of the product. People who have been working on a product for a long time are likely to have ideas about its advantages and disadvantages. If these are too rosy the outsider can throw cold water over some ideas.

These specialist firms are **agencies**. In law, an agent has the right to sign a contract on behalf of another person. Figure 10.6 outlines this process.

Figure 10.6 *What an agency does*

The agencies used by a producer for communicating with the customers are:

* **advertising agencies** who specialise in advertising

* **marketing agencies** who have a specialist knowledge of the whole market for a particular product. Marketing agencies are concerned with product, price, promotion and place. They might employ an advertising agency to do the promotion work for them. This type of agency is often used when a business wants to sell abroad or the businesses producing a product are very small and the market is geographically widespread.

The work done by marketing and advertising agencies can overlap but both have their specialist areas.

JUST TESTING

1. What is an agency?

2. A business advertised its product. At the end of the campaign it found it was out of pocket. Give one reason why this happened.

3. Give two reasons why a business should use an agency to communicate with its customers.

Finding out

1. Write to the manager of a local business. This should be a retail shop because it will give you a wider range of examples of communications methods. You should ask for permission to study the shop and interview some of its customers.

Task A   Visit the shop and write down all the ways in which the shop attempts to communicate with its customers. Do not forget that the appearance and layout of the shop are also important. Make a note of any particularly successful or unsuccessful methods of communication.

Task B   Prepare a *short* questionnaire to ask the customers what they think of the shop's ability to communicate with them. You should send copies of the questionnaire to the manager of the shop for comment. You should also arrange for a suitable time in which to conduct the interview. What sort of people are you going to ask?

Task C   Working in groups, devise a suitable advertisement for the shop. Explain carefully the decisions you made in drawing up the advertisement. What method of advertising would you use and why? (Remember that advertisements can use a number of methods: videos, audio tapes as well as newspapers and magazines.)

Task D   As a result of your investigations write a report on the use of customer communications in the retail trade. To what extent do you think the business you have studied makes effective use of the available methods in communicating with its customers?

2. This exercise is a study of magazines. You should work in groups.

Task A   As a group select a type of magazine that you are going to study. You might, for example, chose women's magazines. Each member of the group should select a different magazine of that type and read it from cover to cover. Draw up a chart to show the different goods and services that are advertised in that magazine. What percentage of advertising is on cars?

What are the interests of the people who read the magazine? You could count the number of pages devoted to cookery. What are their attitudes? Is there a strong emphasis on the importance of the family?

Task B   Compare the results of your research with that of the rest of the group. In what ways are the magazine you have studied similar to and different from the magazines studied by the rest of your group? Working on your own, write a brief description of a typical reader of your magazine under the headings of age, sex, occupation, possible income, interests and attitudes. Use the results of your research to show why you think this is a reasonable description.

Task C   Your teacher will give you a list of products. Select one that would be suitable for advertising in one of the magazines studied by your group. As sales manager of the magazine, prepare a presentation to persuade manufacturers of that type of product that they should advertise in your magazine.

Task D   What problems did you meet with in this exercise? Would a manufacturer about to start national advertising meet the same problems? How could the manufacturer overcome them? Give reasons for your answer.

Trying it out

1. Peter and Jane Makin own a shop selling accessories for the home: ornaments, plant pots, lamps and the like. Although the shop is doing reasonably well Jane is convinced that if they advertised they could do even better. Peter is not so sure. "All our customers come from this area," he argued. "They know about us already. Why waste money on advertising?"

(a) List the ways that Jane and Peter could communicate with their customers other than by advertising.

(b) Select one of the methods of communication you have given and explain the advantages and disadvantages of this method to a small business.

(c) Give three methods of advertising that Jane and Peter might use.

(d) Peter suggests that advertising is a waste of time. Writing as Jane, list the arguments to convince him that they should advertise.

(e) Explain the situation in which Peter could be right.

2. The following advertisement was seen in the window of a high street electrical shop.

(a) Advertising can be both informative and persuasive. Using the advertisement in Figure 10.7 give one example of the way in which it is:

(i) informative
(ii) persuasive.

(b) Explain how the advertisement in Figure 10.7:

(i) has impact
(ii) arouses interest
(iii) gives information
(iv) gets action.

The advertisement states that people who buy a cooker before Christmas will not have to pay until the following March.

(c) (i) Of what is this an example?
(ii) Give two advantages to the consumer of this offer. Explain your answer.
(iii) Give one advantage to the business of making this offer.

3. Figure 10.8 shows the sales pattern of a business over the period of a year.

Figure 10.7 *A new cooker for Christmas*

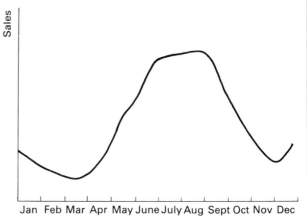

Figure 10.8 *The sales pattern of a business*

(a) Using the information given in Figure 10.8 describe the sales pattern of this business.

(b) List two disadvantages to the business of this pattern of sales.

The sales manager decides to launch a sales promotion.

(c) List four methods of sales promotion that might be used. Give an example of each method.

(d) Over what months of the year should the sales promotion take place?

(e) Assuming that the sales promotion is successful, will it necessarily increase the sales of the business?

4. Easyfix plc is a business manufacturing a range of electrical tools for the DIY handyman. It has just introduced a new power drill to the market. Figure 10.9 shows the expected life-cycle of this power drill.

(a) Between, approximately, which years is the drill at the:

   (i) introductory   (iii) maturity
   (ii) growth   (iv) decline

stages of its life?

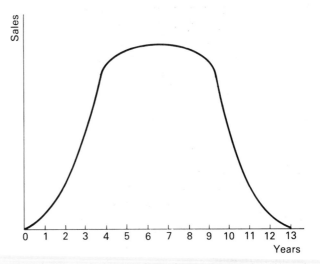

Figure 10.9 *The expected life cycle of a power drill*

(b) How would the business's advertising change at each stage?

(c) Give two other ways in which a business must take account of time when deciding how to communicate with its customers.

UNIT 11:
GETTING THE PRODUCT TO THE CUSTOMER

Distribution is all about **place** in the marketing mix. The customer wants:

* the right goods

* in the right place

* in the right quantities

* at the right time.

If you do not believe this, think of how many times you have walked out of a shop because they did not have what you wanted in stock. When that happens a business has lost a sale. If you take something else in place of what you wanted, a business may still have lost a sale. A competitor got it instead!

To make sure it can produce the right product, in the right place, at the right time – and still make a profit – a business has six main problems:

* the number of warehouses and machines it will need

* the amount of stock it will have to carry

* the communications it uses

* other types of business involved

* the type of transport to use

* the way in which it packages large quantities of its goods.

Warehouse and machinery

Look at Figure 11.1.

The business is located in the Midlands. To serve its customers it has warehouses at all the points marked W. At each warehouse there will be people employed, and insurance to be paid, in addition to the cost of the land, the buildings and their maintenance.

The business in this example could have other problems as well. In Figure 11.1 most of the warehouses are in the north. If the demand in the north falls then there are the problems of closing existing warehouses and opening up new ones.

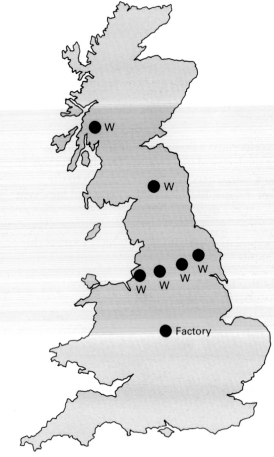

Figure 11.1 *Distribution in the UK*

Transport costs will be lower because the business can send goods in large quantities to each of the warehouses. This will happen if the business employs a separate transport firm (bulk discounts) or has its own fleet of vehicles (the loads can be organised more efficiently).

JUST TESTING

Give one advantage and one disadvantage of a business having warehouses in different parts of the country. Do you think this would be a good idea for small and medium sized businesses?

84

How much stock?

On p60 you will find a list of the advantages and disadvantages of a business holding stock. The business has to hold enough stock of finished goods to satisfy its customers. In some types of business this is not very important. When the customer orders something to be made specially for him, then he will expect to wait. We expect most of the things we buy to be waiting for us on the shelves. This costs the business money. A business must balance the cost of holding stock with giving the customer the best possible service.

JUST TESTING

Look at the captions under the photographs in Figure 11.2. If you were in the situations described, would you want to buy the goods immediately or would you be prepared to wait? How would your answers affect the business?

Made to fit your own requirements

Would you try another shop or chose another brand?

Out of stock. Would you be prepared to wait a month?

An impulse buy . . . ?

Figure 11.2 *How much stock?*

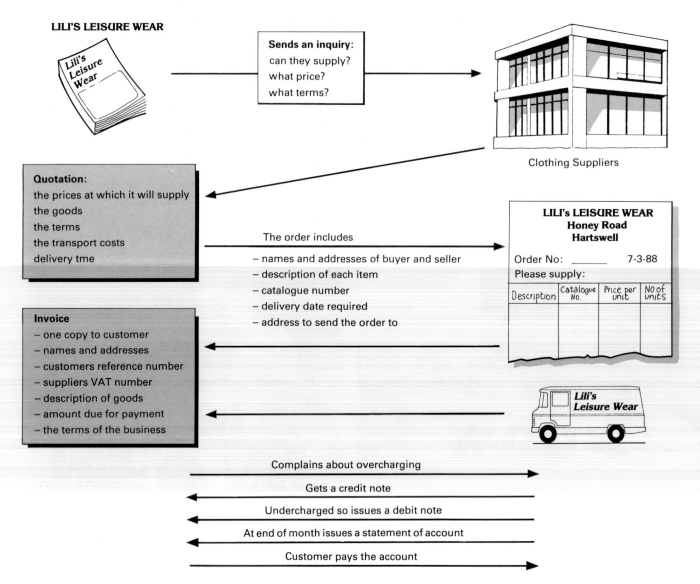

LILI'S LEISURE WEAR

Lili's Leisure Wear

Sends an inquiry:
can they supply?
what price?
what terms?

Clothing Suppliers

Quotation:
the prices at which it will supply
the goods
the terms
the transport costs
delivery tme

LILI's LEISURE WEAR
Honey Road
Hartswell

Order No: _____   7-3-88
Please supply:

Description	Catalogue No.	Price per unit	No of units

The order includes

– names and addresses of buyer and seller
– description of each item
– catalogue number
– delivery date required
– address to send the order to

Invoice
– one copy to customer
– names and addresses
– customers reference number
– suppliers VAT number
– description of goods
– amount due for payment
– the terms of the business

Lili's Leisure Wear

Complains about overcharging

Gets a credit note

Undercharged so issues a debit note

At end of month issues a statement of account

Customer pays the account

Figure 11.3 *Documents used in ordering and delivery*

Communications

Figure 11.3 outlines the documents used in the ordering and delivery of goods.

If a business is not very careful with its records of orders and deliveries a number of problems can arise:

* orders do not arrive on time – there is a dissatisfied customer. This can lead to a loss of custom

* the business might have to send out the order by special delivery. This is likely to cost more money

* the production department will find it more difficult to organise its work if it keeps having to meet rush orders because the original order was lost

* if invoices, credit and debit notes are inaccurate, the record of creditors and debtors a business keeps will also be inaccurate. The business will have payment problems.

Other types of business

Businesses can:

* sell direct to the customer

* sell to wholesalers. Each wholesaler in turn sells to a number of retailers

* sell direct to the retailer

* sell to an agent who sells direct to the customer

* sell to an agent who then sells to a wholesaler.

Figure 11.4 shows the different channels of distribution.

What does the wholesaler do?

1. Buys goods in large quantities from the manufacturer and sells in smaller quantities to the retailer.

2. Takes on the costs and risks of storing the goods for the manufacturer and retailer.

3. Pays the manufacturing business so it has the money to carry on with production without waiting for people to buy the goods.

4. Gives credit to the retailer. This is not true of all wholesalers. Some describe themselves as **cash and carry**. The retailer has to pay for these goods. Some cash and carry wholesalers also provide credit. This usually works like the credit cards offered to their customers by the larger stores.

5. Gives the retailer a wide choice of brands of the same product.

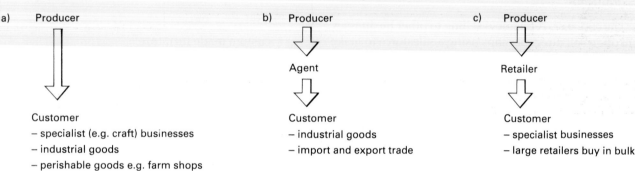

a) Producer → Customer
  – specialist (e.g. craft) businesses
  – industrial goods
  – perishable goods e.g. farm shops

b) Producer → Agent → Customer
  – industrial goods
  – import and export trade

c) Producer → Retailer → Customer
  – specialist businesses
  – large retailers buy in bulk

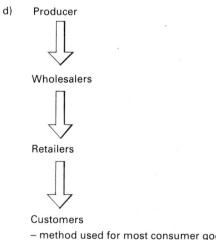

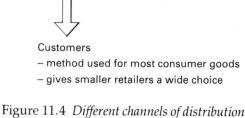

d) Producer → Wholesalers → Retailers → Customers
  – method used for most consumer goods
  – gives smaller retailers a wide choice

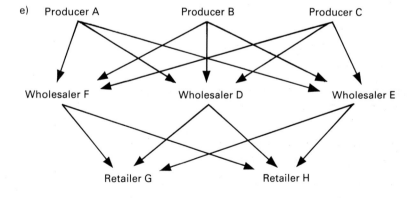

e) Producers A, B, C → Wholesalers F, D, E → Retailers G, H

Figure 11.4 *Different channels of distribution*

What does the retailer do?

1. Buys in larger quantities from the wholesaler so the customer can buy in the quantities needed.

2. Offers credit and advice to the customer.

3. Provides delivery for larger items.

4. Makes goods locally available to the customer.

A business might use more than one channel of distribution. A business producing soap powder will:

  * sell direct to a large retailer because the order will be large enough to make it worthwhile

  * sell to wholesalers so that their product gets into the smaller shops.

Which channel of distribution?

A business will select its channel of distribution according to:

1. The *customer*. A business selling to other businesses will often sell direct perhaps using a salesforce to make contact.

2. The *product*. The more specialised the product, the fewer the stages it will go through before reaching the final consumer. This is also true of perishable goods.

3. The *geographical spread* and *size* of its market. A small number of customers spread over a wide area can be served by selling directly to the customer using mail order. A large number of customers over a wide area will result in the use of wholesalers.

4. *Frequency* of purchase. Goods which are not bought very often can reach the consumer through mail order or the use of a salesforce (particularly for expensive goods). When people need to buy them frequently the manufacturer will try to get them into as many shops as possible.

5. The *image* of the product. Luxury products are sold in luxury settings.

6. The *complexity* of the product. When a product needs to be demonstrated or it requires technical after sales service the manufacturer might sell direct or use agents.

JUST TESTING

What channel of distribution would be suitable for each of the following? Explain your answer.

  * cornflakes

  * a car

  * custom made furniture

  * expensive perfume

  * petrol.

What type of transport?

Figure 11.5 shows some forms of transport.

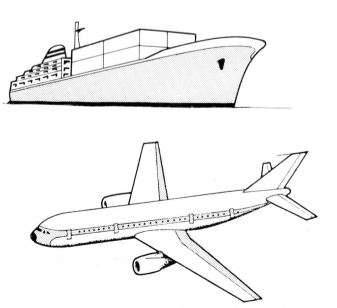

Figure 11.5 *Different types of transport*

The United Kingdom is a small country. Businesses find that the advantages of road transport are greater than those of rail for a wide variety of [...]

Although the advantages and dis[...] of each type of transport hold in most [...] sometimes they are ignore[...] [...]haps an emergency, results in [...] [...]uld normally be sent by sea be[...] [...]e most likely to see examples of this wh[...] [...]eing sent abroad when there has been an earth[...] or other natural disaster.

Figure 11.6 gives the transport used by a consignment of goods for another country. At the end of each stage in the journey the goods have to be unloaded and stored for a while before being loaded into the next type of transport. This increases the risk of spoiling and loss through pilfering. If the goods are in small packages then a great deal of labour is needed for the loading and unloading, with a greater chance of damage. To avoid these problems many goods are now loaded into very large containers. These can be

lifted from one form of transport to another very easily with the help of machines. Pallets are another way in which the cost of distribution can be reduced.

JUST TESTING

1. Give two advantages and two disadvantages of road transport.

2. What type of transport would you use for the following? Give reasons for your answer.

(a) A very large piece of machinery travelling from Glasgow to Manchester. It is an awkward shape and very heavy.
(b) A standard heavy load travelling from Birmingham to Liverpool for export.
(c) A businessman who wants to get from Glasgow to London for a meeting.

3. Give three advantages of containerisation.

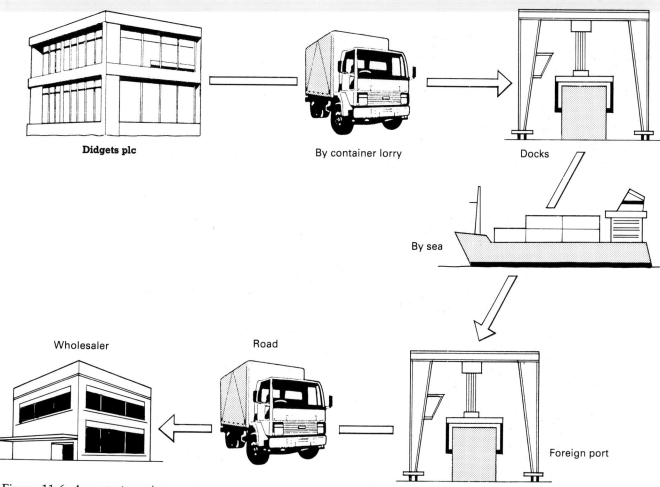

Didgets plc   By container lorry   Docks   By sea

Wholesaler   Road   Foreign port

Figure 11.6 *An export consignment*

Exporting

Selling goods at home is not enough. Businesses in the United Kingdom also need to sell goods abroad. This earns additional income from other countries which can then be used to buy goods from abroad.

Figure 11.7 shows why this is necessary.

Gives the customer a wider choice of design

Climate not suitable for certain goods e.g. bananas

Raw materials that are not found in the UK

Goods we can produce but other countries can make them more cheaply

Countries can specialise – so wider range of goods for everyone

Figure 11.7 *Why we import*

Problems of exporting

Exporting has special marketing problems.

1. Market research is more difficult. Cultural differences mean that what is acceptable in one country may be considered insulting in another part of the world.

2. Governments do not always encourage trade. They may say that only a certain amount of a product may be imported in a year (**quota**) or they may put a tax on goods imported (**tariffs/import duties**). This could raise the price of the imported goods so that people are less willing to buy them.

3. Some governments make it difficult to export to their country by making the customs organisation complicated and time consuming. It is difficult to know when this is done deliberately and when it is the result of the natural development of that country.

4. Electrical goods, cars and other technical products have problems. The electrical power supplied by the national system varies from country to country. Safety regulations introduced for cars means that foreign manufacturers may have to change their models or leave that market. Which course of action they take will depend on how important the market is.

5. Different countries have different currencies and banking systems. The value of one currency compared with another can change. When the value of the United Kingdom's currency (sterling) increases (**strengthens**) compared with that of another country, e.g. the USA, then British goods exported to the United States become more expensive. Look at the following example:

   January: £1 buys $1.50

So a British car manufacturer selling a car costing £8 000 to a dealer in the United States would be selling at $12 000.

   June: £1 buys $2

The pound has strengthened so more dollars are needed to buy £1. Now the same car, still priced at £8 000 in the UK will cost the American dealer $16 000.

6. All the above difficulties of exporting mean that the risks of selling abroad are greater than selling in the United Kingdom. This can cause problems with insurance – particularly if wars also complicate the situation.

Help for exporters

Very large businesses will employ experts in the different branches of exporting knowledge. Smaller businesses cannot afford this. They will employ specialist businesses and use government help when they want to export.

1. *Specialist businesses*

   * marketing agencies know the exporting market. They can give market information to the manufacturer and deal with all importing and financial transactions on his behalf

   * merchants know overseas markets. They buy goods from the manufacturer and then export them. This takes away all exporting problems for the manufacturer.

2. *Government help for exporters*

   * trade fairs or shows are large exhibitions in another country. The Department of Trade will organise the time, place and publicity. British firms will hire stands to display and explain their goods. Trade fairs organised by a government are usually limited to the products of that country. Trade fairs organised by private industry will usually be devoted to one type of product

   * British Weeks are a promotional technique organised by the government in co-operation with local traders. Shop displays and exhibitions with the emphasis on British goods are a way of bringing products to the attention of people.

JUST TESTING

1. Give three reasons why we need to import goods.

2. If the value of the pound goes up will this help UK exporters?

3. Give two ways in which the government offers help to exporters.

Finding out

1. This is an investigation into how goods reach the customer.

Task A Choose a local producer. It will have to be a business selling goods – businesses selling services are in direct contact with their customers most of the time. To whom does it sell its produce? Be careful! A farmer might sell his free range eggs to private customers (direct) and to the local shop, but he might also sell his livestock in a market. Now find out as much as you can about the path the goods take to the customer. This could involve writing a lot of letters.

Task B Draw a diagram to show the different paths the goods take to the market. Make a list of all the possible reasons why the business chose these channels of distribution.

Task C Select a product with which you are familiar. Outline and explain the channel of distribution *you think* it took from the manufacturer to you. Were you right? Explain why you were right or wrong.

Task D Explain why businesses choose different channels of distribution for the same product. Give examples from the results of your research.

2. You need a friendly local business for this one! You are going to study the ordering of supplies for the business and the way in which the business processes the orders it receives.

Task A On a visit to the business find out the way in which a business orders goods it needs. Whom does it order from? How does it know when it needs to re-order stock? What path does the order take from the time the business realises it needs more stock until the order is sent out? What happens to stock when it arrives in the business?

Repeat this for the way in which the business processes orders it receives. What documents are used in both cases. If possible get samples of the documents.

Task B Draw a large chart showing the ordering of goods and a chart showing the processing of an order within the business. Give a brief explanation of why each stage is important to the business.

Task C In what ways does the business you are studying differ in its methods from the outline given in Figure 11.3 (p86)? Explain why these differences exist.

Task D Using the results of your research explain the importance to a business of maintaining good communications with its suppliers and customers.

3. You are going to compare the goods and services offered by two different shops. You might compare a hypermarket with a supermarket; a department store with a specialist shop; a small travel agent with a firm such as W.H. Smith.

Task A How do the two businesses differ in terms of:

(a) range of goods?
(b) display of goods?
(c) prices?
(d) convenience of location?
(e) total size of business?
(f) size of store you are studying?
(g) additional services offered?

Task B List the advantages and disadvantages of each type of shop for the customer.

Task C Conduct a survey of customers of the shops. Why do they shop there? What advantages do they find. Draw up a chart showing the most popular features of each shop.

Task D From your research explain the advantages to a manufacturer of distributing his goods to both types of retail outlet.

Trying it out

1. Josie Metcalfe started "For Your Children" two years after she left Art College. Ten years later it is a thriving business making high quality ornaments and plates in hand-painted china. Retail prices range from £75 to £150. At first Josie sold her ornaments through mail order. She inserted small advertisements in glossy magazines aimed at the woman's market. Later she began to sell direct to large department stores.

(a) (i) Using the information given in the passage, draw a diagram showing the channels of distribution Josie used for her products.
(ii) Give one reason why Josie selected short channels of distribution.

(b) Give two advantages to Josie of selling her products to the department store.

Because her products are fragile Josie has always taken special care in their packaging and transport. She uses road transport. "For Your Children" owns one van for local deliveries and uses specialised parcel delivery businesses (e.g. BRS) for longer distances.

(c) Give three reasons why Josie always uses road transport.

Recently an American friend of Josie's came to visit "For Your Children". He was very impressed with the products and suggested that Josie tried marketing them in the United States. Josie laughed at the idea. "Far too much risk" was her immediate reply. Later she began to think about this idea and found it tempting. She decided to find out more about exporting.

(d) Explain why exporting is more risky than selling in the United Kingdom.

(e) Where could Josie go for advice on exporting?

(f) When Josie began to consider exporting to the United States the exchange rate was £1 to $1.50. Eighteen months later it was £1 to $2.00.

(i) What effect would this have on the price of one of her ornaments which would have sold in the United States for $150? Show how you worked out your answer.
(ii) What effect would this change in the exchange rate have on Josie's sales in the United States?

2. Joseph and Molly Cearns have just inherited a substantial amount of money. After some thought they decide to open a shop selling high quality, high fashion clothes for men and women in their local market town. The shop will also carry a small range of accessories such as shoes, bags and belts. Some of these can be supplied by craft workshops in the surrounding area.

(a) List three advantages to the Cearns of buying from a wholesaler rather than a manufacturer.

(b) (i) What are the main documents that would be used when the Cearns ordered and bought goods from the wholesaler?
(ii) Explain the purpose of four of these documents.

The local authority begins to promote the town as a tourist resort. As a result a large clothes chain opens a store in the town.

(c) State two ways in which this could affect the Cearns' business.

(d) Give three things the Cearns could do to keep their trade? Explain the reasons for your choice.

3. Maddox Ltd is a manufacturing business making a range of metal products, for example central heating radiators, which it sells to both wholesalers and large building contractors. You work in Customer's Enquiries. One morning you look at your in-tray and find the following problems:

(a) a customer has been overcharged on an invoice.

(b) a customer is claiming that he has not received the goods that should have been delivered a week ago.

(c) the accounts department has sent you a memo to point out that a customer has not been invoiced for the total amount of the goods delivered.

(d) a customer is complaining that the radiators ordered from you are faulty.

In each of the above cases state what action you would take and why.

UNIT 12:
PEOPLE WORKING

What do people want?

Ask people why they work and most will say "for the money". A few might give other reasons such as "company" or "I want to help people", even fewer would admit that they love the work and would do it for nothing if necessary.

Figure 12.1 shows the wide range of reasons for why people go out to work.

OF COURSE I DON'T NEED TO WORK, BUT IT IS SO BORING BEING IN THE HOUSE ALONE ALL DAY!

WE HAVE A LOT OF FUN IN THE OFFICE — IT'S MORE LIKE A CROWD OF FRIENDS.

I WAS GOING TO START MY OWN BUSINESS — BUT IT IS VERY RISKY — SO I TOOK THIS JOB. IT'S BORING BUT SAFE.

IF I WON ON THE POOLS I WOULD HAND IN MY NOTICE AT ONCE!

THERE IS SO MUCH SATISFACTION IN SEEING PEOPLE RESPOND — I WOULD ALMOST DO THE JOB FOR FREE.

A SENIOR FINANCIAL MANAGER HAS A GREAT DEAL OF RESPECT IN THE COMMUNITY. LOOK AT MY HOUSE AND CAR!

What do businesses want?

In modern industrial society there are many different jobs, each of which has its own needs in terms of educational level, aptitudes (talents people possess), skills, training, qualifications and experience. The photographs in Figure 12.2 illustrate some of the different types of job needed to run one business.

When there are a large number of jobs in a business the personnel department keeps a statement of what each job entails. A general statement – the title of the job, a broad description of what is involved, who the person should report to and who will report to them – is called a **job description**. A more detailed statement about the job is called a **job specification**. This is sometimes called a **personnel specification** because it describes the personal qualities that would be most

Scientific and technical skills

Specialist management skills

Wide range of job skills

Clerical and administrative skills

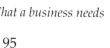

Figure 12.2 *What a business needs*

useful in that job. The job specification will include:

* the physical activities
* the mental activities
* the amount of contact with other people
* the type of contact with other people
* the type of technology used.

Figure 12.3 illustrates some of the uses of a job specification in a business.

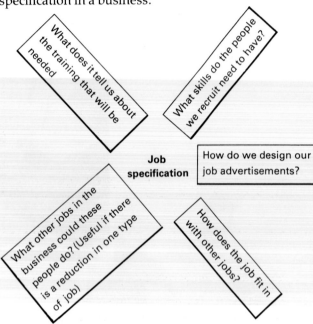

Figure 12.3 *Uses of a job specification*

JUST TESTING

Select one of the photographs in Figure 12.2. Write a description of the job using the information given in the photograph.

Finding the right person

Attracting people

The business needs to find a person who has the right qualities for the job. There may be someone in the business who can do the job. If so the vacancy will be filled from within the business:

* it will be quicker and cheaper. Advertising costs money
* the person will be known so it is safer

* the person knows the business, so does not have to settle in. There is more chance of them staying

* if the job means promotion the person will feel appreciated. Other people employed by the business will feel that there is a chance for their own promotion.

When there is nobody suitable already employed by the business, then it can advertise the job through job centres, careers service, schools/colleges, employment agencies and in newspapers. It can also ask existing employees to suggest people. This has some of the advantages of appointing an existing employee, e.g. it costs very little and the person applying for the job will probably know a great deal about the business already.

The way in which a business advertises the job will vary according to where the job is advertised and how much money it has to spend. For example, in the job centre it will be a type-written card on a notice board. Wherever the advertisement appears, and in whatever form it appears, it should contain enough information to give people who apply for the job a clear picture of what they will have to do.

Narrowing the choice

One newspaper advertisement for a receptionist had 500 replies! Which of these is the right person? This is the problem facing the personnel manager. The task of reducing the list to the one person for the job can be broken down into stages, as shown in Figure 12.4.

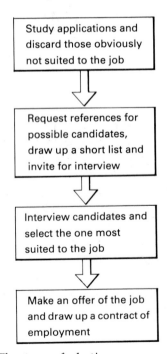

Figure 12.4 *The stages of selection*

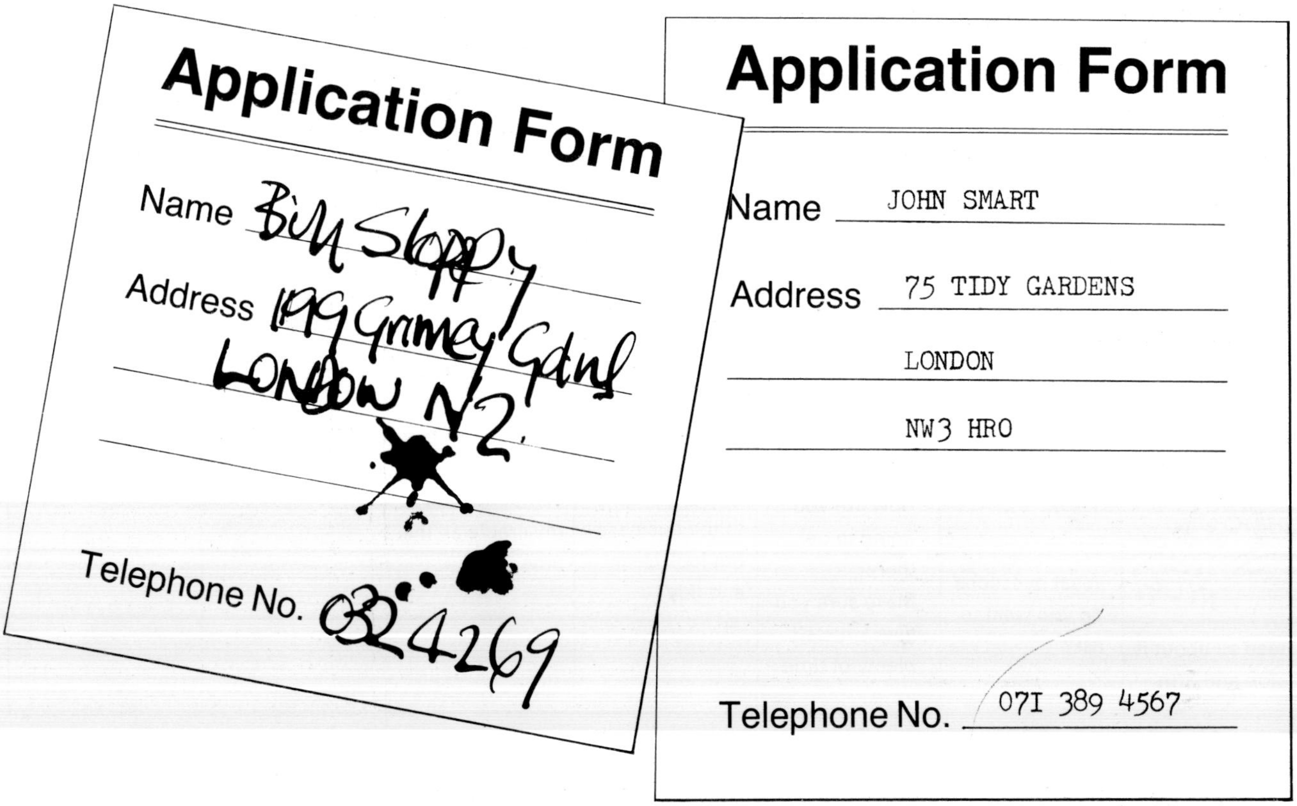

Application Form

Name Bill Sloppy

Address 199 Grimey Gdns

LONDON N2

Telephone No. 824269

Application Form

Name ___ JOHN SMART ___

Address ___ 75 TIDY GARDENS ___

___ LONDON ___

___ NW3 HRO ___

Telephone No. ___ 071 389 4567 ___

Figure 12.5 *Comparison of two application forms*

The first stages may seem very hard on people applying for the job but a receptionist must be a neat and tidy worker otherwise phone messages, for example, might be lost or misunderstood. Look at Figure 12.5. Which form can you read most easily?

Note the information asked for on the application form. This one is reasonably straightforward. More complicated jobs will have a more complicated application form.

Using the evidence given by letters of application and application forms, the personnel manager will draw up a short list of people who seem to be suitable for the job. These people will then be invited for interview.

Making the choice

Some people see an interview as an ordeal – a make or break situation over which they have no control. A good interview needs a lot of preparation on both sides. Even if the interview goes well the job position may not be filled! After all, the person being interviewed might not like the look of things when they see the business.

Interviews are useful because they:

* allow the interviewer to ask more detailed questions than is possible on the application form

* allow the interviewer to meet the applicant and form an opinion about his or her personality. Personality can be very important in a job. A very well qualified person can be very quiet – not much use in a selling job where there are a lot of people to be met

* allow the interviewer to give more information about the job. This is very important. The person applying for the job wants to know what they are letting themselves in for! If they think they have been misled they will be resentful – and a resentful person is not likely to work hard

* allow the person being interviewed (the interviewee) to ask questions about the job – things that were not in the advertisement or in any other information the business has sent them

* allow the person applying for the job to see where they will be working and the people they will be working with. Some people, for example, do not like working in a job where most of the people are a lot older or younger than they are.

An interview is a chance for both sides to find out more about each other. If it is going to be used to its full advantage both sides must put in a lot of preparation. Figure 12.6 shows some of that preparation.

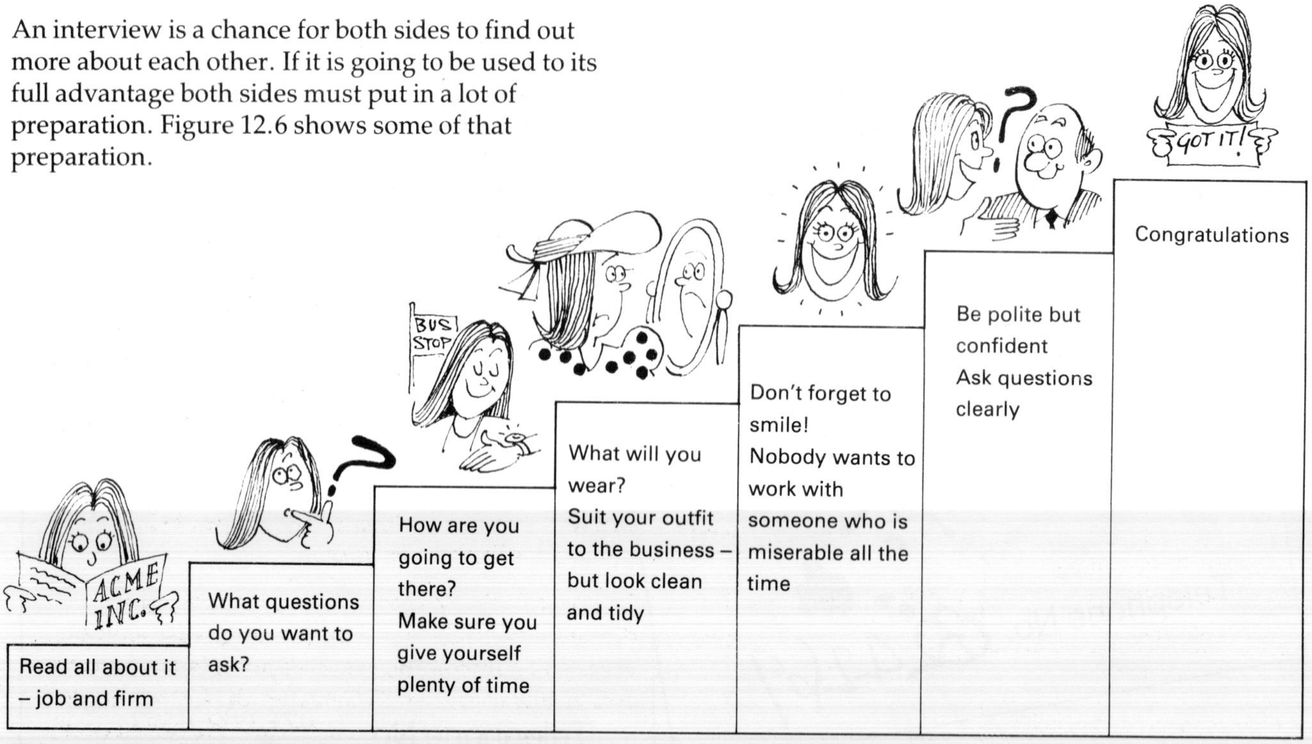

Read all about it – job and firm

What questions do you want to ask?

How are you going to get there? Make sure you give yourself plenty of time

What will you wear? Suit your outfit to the business – but look clean and tidy

Don't forget to smile! Nobody wants to work with someone who is miserable all the time

Be polite but confident Ask questions clearly

Congratulations

Figure 12.6 *Preparing for an interview*

JUST TESTING

Abe Simon owns a small garage. He wants to employ a part time office worker to do some typing and keep his records in order.

(a) Give two ways in which he might find the right person.
(b) Joe draws up a job description. How will this help him select the new employee?

Training

Training takes place at a number of times during a person's working life:

* when they start to work for a business

* when they are learning a skill

* when they are preparing for promotion

* when changes in technology mean they have to learn new skills because their old ones are no longer needed.

Businesses also train people so that they will have the right attitudes to the job, the skills they need for the job and the knowledge required by the job.

Types of training

1. *Pre-vocational education* takes place in schools and colleges. It helps bridge the gap between school and work by allowing students to learn something about the type of job they are interested in, while at the same time continuing with their general education. The Foundation Course offered by the City and Guilds of London Institute and the Certificate of Pre-Vocational Education are examples of this type of course.

2. *Youth Training* (YT), started by the government in 1983, the scheme aims to give training to unemployed young people improving their chance of finding a job. Trainees divide their time between the firm and college and are paid a small allowance. Many businesses use the YT scheme as part of their selection process when looking for employees.

3. *Induction* is the short training period a new employee receives. It will vary from business to business but might include lectures about the history of the business, information about the benefits it offers its employees and a chance to get to know the different types of work done by the business.

4. *Skill training* involves teaching and developing skills, e.g. the ability to type, the skills of a joiner, electrician or carpenter. Skill training can also reduce the need for supervision – so cutting the costs of the business.

5. *Staff development* is concerned with identifying the abilities of employees and providing them with training opportunities that will prepare them for promotion. It can also be used to increase the efficiency of the workforce. Figure 12.7 shows the stages that are normally built into a staff development programme.

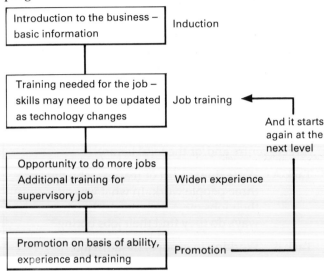

Figure 12.7 *Stages in staff development*

Methods of training

The section on types of training describes the aims of a business or other organisation, while methods of training shows how it achieves the training aims. They can be divided into two areas.

1. *On job methods.* These include watching people who are experienced at the job, working on the job and developing the skill by practice. On job methods allow the trainees to develop skills quickly. They get used to the conditions of the job – which can be very important if they will be required to work in dirty, noisy surroundings or under pressure to get the job finished on time. The disadvantage is that the trainees might pick up bad habits from older workers. At first they will waste a lot of materials. The range of skills they can learn is likely to be limited.

2. *Off job methods.* These include lectures, group discussions, problem solving through case studies, visits and simulations, e.g. computer business games and in-tray exercises. In the latter the trainee is given a pile of documents related to his job. He has to decide what to do in each case.

Most training programmes are a combination of on job and off job methods. This allows the training officer to put together a package that avoids the major disadvantages of both. Sometimes this causes confusion for the trainees, particularly when they are taught the ideal way of doing a job in the training school or college, and then see short cuts being taken on the shop floor.

Figure 12.8 relates the type of training needed by business to the methods used.

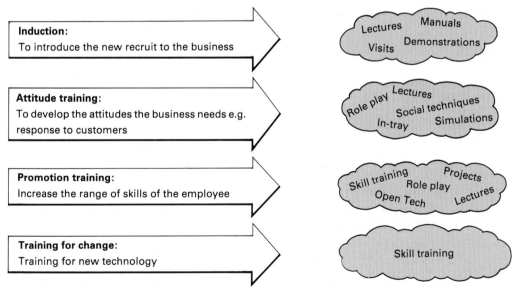

Figure 12.8 *Types and methods of training*

JUST TESTING

What type and method of training do you think would be most suitable in each of the following cases:

(a) An eighteen-year-old starting his first, unskilled, job?

(b) A civil servant who wants promotion to the next grade?

(c) A sixteen-year-old school leaver who wants to train as a car mechanic?

(d) A school teacher who wants to change from teaching 11–16 year-olds to teaching 7–10 year-olds?

Finding out

1. This is an investigation into what employers are looking for.

Choose ten types of jobs for which advertisements appear regularly in your local newspaper. Over a period of time, collect as many advertisements for these jobs as you can.

Task A   Make a list of the personal qualities, skills, qualifications and experience that the advertisers want. Draw up a chart to show how often these qualities appear in the advertisements. Using your chart list the qualities under the following headings: *Essential, Desirable*.

Task B   Choose five of the original ten jobs you selected. Find out as much as you can about the activities involved in each job. In the light of this research, explain why the qualities you have listed as essential and desirable are useful in this job.

Task C   Select one of the jobs. In the role of an applicant for that job:

(a) Write a letter of application for the job.
(b) Write a curriculum vitae that shows your suitability for the job.

If possible, use a word processor for this task.

Task D   As a result of this exercise, write a report explaining the importance of a job description in recruiting staff. Why are a wide variety of skills and aptitudes essential to business?

2. Interview three people about their jobs. Find out as much as you can about each job using your careers centre and/or the local library.

Task A   Write down a list of reasons why the three people work. In what ways do their jobs meet their needs? In what ways do they find their jobs boring?

Task B   Working in groups, design a job description for each job. What qualities would you consider essential for the job? What qualities would you consider desirable? Explain your answers with reference to the evidence from your interviews.

Task C   As the personnel manager of a business, draw up an advertisement for one of the jobs you have studied. Where would you advertise the job and why?

Task D   What type and methods of training would be suitable for each job? Give reasons for your answer.

Trying it out

1. Figure 12.9 shows a range of advertisements for a salesperson.

BEAUTY BASE

We have a vacancy for a cosmetics consultant in Jason's Department Store. We are looking for a confident and highly motivated person with experience for this position. The rewards are high – a good salary, excellent commission and generous holidays are part of the package.
Contact: Mr Smith . . .

If You've Got The Drive We've Got The Customers

Central Heating salesperson required for well established local firm. The successful applicant will have the drive and confidence to earn £ 12 000 (commission) in their first year. Training given.

THE KITCHEN KORNER

is opening a new shop and is looking for sales personnel.
The people we appoint will be articulate, confident and have a genuine interest in our stock.
Experience is not essential.

Figure 12.9 *Salesperson wanted*

(a) What qualities are the advertisers looking for?

(b) What does a business need to consider before employing another person?

These advertisements were not successful.

(c) Give two other methods the business could use to recruit new staff. Explain why these methods might be more successful than advertising in the local newspaper.

(d) What sort of training will the business give the successful applicant?

2. Sandra Williams has worked in the head office of the Star Insurance Company since she left school four years ago. She now has a chance of promotion to section supervisor. This would require her to allocate work to members of her section, make sure the work was done to a good standard, order the necessary stationery and other materials and make sure all equipment was kept in good repair. She would also be expected

to cover for absent staff, e.g. in the use of word processing and reprographic equipment, filing and record keeping as it related to the work of the section.

(a) Using the information given in the passage, write a job description for the post of supervisor.

(b) The personnel manager has made a list of the qualities she requires for the post of supervisor:

Well groomed	Persuasive
Manual dexterity	Good health
Ambitious	Dependable
Intelligent	Sociable
Punctual	Wide experience of office work
Numerate	Sense of humour
Self reliant	GCSE (grade A-C) in three subjects
Respected	Good attendance record

(i) Which of the qualities listed above would you consider:

* essential

* desirable

for the post of supervisor?

(ii) Explain briefly why you have chosen the essential qualities.

(c) Using the qualities listed in (b), draw up a job specification under the following headings:

* physical requirements

* attainments

* general intelligence

* special aptitudes

* interests

* disposition.

Under each heading distinguish between the qualities that would be considered essential and those that would be considered desirable.

Sandra is an internal candidate for the post of supervisor. She is told by the personnel officer that she does not need to fill in an application form but should write a letter in support of her application. The personnel officer points out that Star Insurance already knows a great deal about her work.

(d) Sandra decides that sociability and self reliance are two important qualities for the post. What additional evidence can she give in her letter of application to support her claim that she possesses these two qualities?

(e) Give three reasons why Sandra thinks she will enjoy the job as supervisor.

3. The photographs in Figure 12.10 show different types of training in progress. Study the photographs carefully before answering the questions.

Figure 12.10 *Different types of training*

(a) Which photograph illustrates:

(i) induction?
(ii) basic skill training?
(iii) staff development?

Give a brief explanation of your choices.

(b) What method of training is being used in each case? Give one advantage and one disadvantage of each method.

You are the training officer of a manufacturing business that is about to introduce new technology. You decide that you will need to introduce training programmes for each of the following groups of workers:

* management

* supervisors

* skilled workers.

(c) Explain why each of the above groups will need training as the result of introducing the new technology.

(d) Select one of the above groups and outline a training programme for it. You should:

(i) Give the types and methods of training you think appropriate.
(ii) Explain why you selected the types and methods of training.

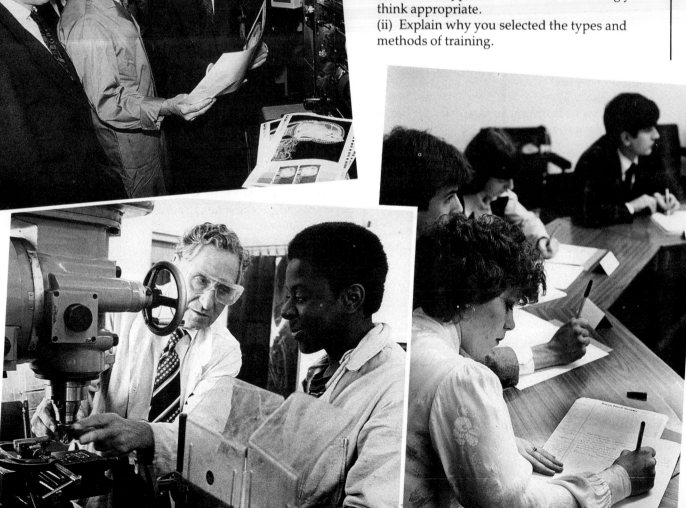

UNIT 13:
GETTING THE BEST FROM PEOPLE

Businesses have objectives. So, too, do the people who work for them. Figure 13.1 shows what happens when the objectives of the business and those of its employees are not the same.

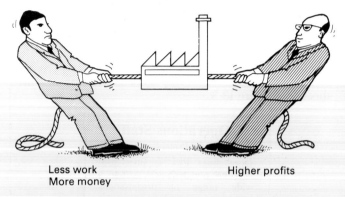

Less work
More money

Higher profits

Figure 13.1 *Conflicting objectives*

When the goals of the business and its employees are in conflict then neither side wins. Profits fall, the business starts to lose money, people are made redundant, so they too do not attain their goals.

Of course, that is the extreme case. Some businesses paddle along happily. Others set out to work with their employees and to persuade their employees to work with them. These businesses try to **motivate** the people who work for them. That is, they try to give them a reason to work hard and efficiently. A motivated workforce will produce high quality goods and services, on time and in sufficient quantities, to satisfy the customer.

It is worth noting that "employees" are all the people who work for the business no matter how much money they earn. Poor motivation is not the monopoly of the people working on the shop floor.

JUST TESTING

Joe is annoyed. His supervisor has just asked him to work overtime on a Saturday morning. There is an order due out on Monday and it is not ready. The customer has already been let down twice by the firm and is threatening to take his business elsewhere. Joe plays football on Saturday mornings. His team are doing well in

the league. He would also like the extra money he would get from working overtime. He knows that the production manager does not like working in the evenings because travelling is difficult.

1. What conflicting objectives can you find in the passage?

2. Should Joe do the overtime? Give reasons for your answer. Did everybody in your group give the same answer?

Money and motivation

Money is used for other things than buying food and keeping warm. Somebody who is not very interested in the job itself might work much harder for the money to help them have a better social life or to buy a new car that will impress their friends and make them feel important.

1. *Time rate*. This is paid according to the number of hours worked. For example a job might be advertised at £152 for a 38-hour week or £4 an hour. This is called the **basic rate** for the job. When time rate is paid weekly it is known as **wages**. When it is paid monthly it is called a **salary**.

Any additional work the employee might agree to do is called overtime. This is usually paid at a higher rate than basic, e.g. basic plus an extra half. The amount extra often depends on when the overtime is done. Weekend overtime can pay "double time", that is, twice the basic rate.

The advantages of time rate are:

* the pay is simple to calculate

* people are not rushing to finish a job so quality can be better

* it is useful in jobs where it is difficult to work out how much work someone has done during the day or week

* it gives people security. They know the minimum amount of money they will receive each week to pay their bills.

Time rate does not give people an incentive to work harder. Because of this many businesses employ other forms of payment to reward extra effort.

2. *Piece rate*. This is sometimes known as **payment by results**. Under this method, people are paid for the amount of work they do – by the piece. The harder people work, the more efficient they are at the job, the more money they are able to earn. Some people enjoy this type of payment. It gives them the opportunity to earn money according to their skill. For these people piece rate can act as a motivator. It does mean there is a lack of security. If the work does not come in or the management do not get the materials needed on time, then the money in the weekly wage packet goes down. This can lead to conflict in the workplace. People might also be tempted to work too fast to the detriment of safety standards and quality.

Figure 13.2 is a graph showing the relation between work and earnings in a simple piece rate system.

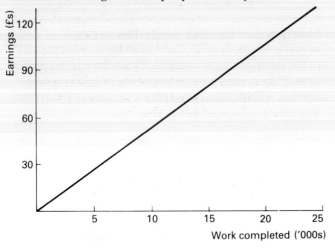

Figure 13.2 *A simple piece rate system*

Because of the insecurity of the piece rate many businesses pay a basic rate with additional payments for any work done over an agreed minimum.

Industries in which some form of piece rate is used include construction, garment manufacture and car sales. In the latter case it is known as **commission**.

3. *Bonuses*. These are another form of payment by results, but are related to the output of a group of people rather than one person as in piece rate. They are sometimes referred to as **productivity deals**. They do provide an incentive for extra work but have been criticised in industries such as mining on the grounds that they reduce safety.

4. *Profit related pay*. Under this type of payment the amount people are paid is related to the profit made by the business employing them. If the profit goes up, so do wages. If the profit goes down, so do wages. The idea behind profit related pay is that people should be made aware that the money they earn depends on the success of the business employing them rather than what other people with their qualifications earn in other businesses. This, it is argued, will motivate them to work harder to make a success of the business.

The idea of profit related pay is relatively new. People who are against it argue that high profits do not necessarily come from hard working employees. They can also come from luck.

5. *Fringe benefits*. Many businesses offer additional financial benefits to their employees. Some of these are shown in Figure 13.3.

> ### Operations Staff
> #### A Career with Promotion Prospects
> Doodlebugs Ltd. supplies professional and technical staff to a wide range of organisations requiring engineers or computer operators on a contract and temporary basis.
>
> The successful candidate will work as a member of a team, recruiting staff and matching them to customer requirements.
>
> In addition s/he will be expected to develop sales in the UK (a company car is provided), Europe and possibly the Middle East.
>
> All staff are members of BUPA. Those stationed abroad have generous living/accommodation allowances and there is provision for the education of children at any chosen school.
>
> Applicants should write to . . .

Figure 13.3 *Job advertisement showing fringe benefits*

Although fringe benefits are taxed they can be of great value to the people receiving them.

JUST TESTING

1. What is the difference between piece rate and a bonus?

2. Using the information given in the graph in Figure 13.2, calculate how much the business pays for each piece of work completed.

3. Why is it argued that people paid by time rate might work less hard than people paid by piece rate?

Analysis of a pay slip

Pay and allowances		Deductions (R = Refunds)	£	Department
	(R = Refund)			REASEARCH AND DEVELOPMENT

Pay and allowances	Deductions	
BASIC PAY 1522.00	NATIONAL INSURANCE	96.10
ALLOWANCE 23.00	SUPERANNUATION	92.70
	INCOME TAX	318.00

Department: REASEARCH AND DEVELOPMENT

MS. J.M.SMYTHE

Tax Code 215	Identity No. C-9546-13

MONTH 02 PAYABLE
31 MAY 1989

Taxable pay	Non-taxable pay
1545.00	
Deductions	**Net pay**
506.80	1038.20

Figure 13.4 *Analysis of a pay slip*

1. *Basic pay* or *Gross pay*. This is the total amount of money the employee has earned in a week or a month.

2. *Superannuation*. A contribution to a pension fund.

3. *National insurance*. A compulsory payment to the government to help pay for sickness, unemployment and retirement benefits.

4. *Income tax*. Earned income is taxed once it is above a certain level. For most people the tax is deducted before they receive their pay. This is known as **pay as you earn (PAYE)**.

5. *Net pay* or *Take home pay*. This is gross pay minus superannuation, national insurance, tax and other deductions (e.g. loss of pay for lateness).

What determines pay?

Figure 13.5 shows some of the factors that determine the rates of pay for a particular job.

People can get very annoyed if they think they are being paid less than they are worth. Charges of sexual and racial discrimination can be made against employers who pay different rates for what appears to be the same job. To avoid this, businesses give a value to the different jobs according to the conditions of work, the skill, experience and responsibility involved. This process is called **job evaluation**.

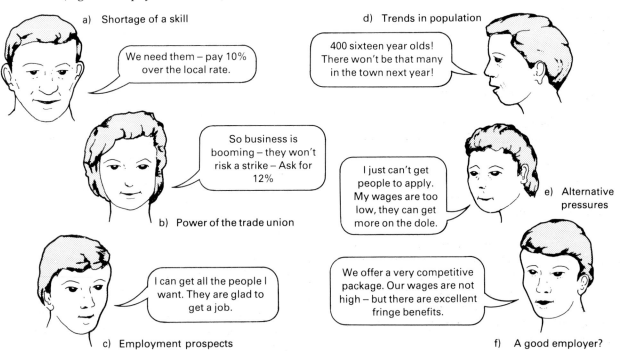

Figure 13.5 *Determination of pay*

Motivation and organisation

People work hard for reasons other than money. Listed below are some of the reasons why people enjoy their jobs:

* they like the people they are working with

* they have responsibility

* they feel they have accomplished something

* the job gives them a feeling of importance or power

* there is plenty of variety in the job so they don't get bored

* there is the possibility of promotion

* a good training is offered which will help in their future career

* they like the job itself, e.g. the possibility of travel, working in an office, working with animals.

Some businesses try to organise the way in which people work so that they enjoy these motivators.

1. *Job enlargement*. More tasks of the same skill level are included in the job. People are not repeating the same tasks over and over again and so are less likely to make mistakes out of boredom. Job enlargement can prevent boredom. People will need additional training and will want more money.

2. *Job enrichment*. A person is given more responsibility for their own work which can give them a feeling of importance.

3. *Job rotation*. The jobs people do are changed at regular intervals. Again there is a need for more training although the business will benefit from having a workforce that is capable of more than one job.

Although job rotation can be a motivator, some businesses introduce **flexible working practices** because of the advantages they offer in the more efficient use of the workforce. People can be moved to another job when there is insufficient work in their section. This usually meets with opposition from the trade unions.

JUST TESTING

Read the advertisements in Figure 13.6. Make a list of all the things about the jobs advertised that might motivate people. Give reasons for your answers.

Hilo Slumber Co. Ltd.

Come and join us. As a fast growing company we offer excellent chances for promotion to managerial positions.
Self motivated applicants need have no fear!
At the end of 12 months you should have earned £15K.
For details phone Karen on . . .

Person Friday Wanted

Man Friday looked after Robinson Crusoe.
Can you look after us?
We are a small team of highly talented designers who need someone to take care of our paperwork/accounts and bring us coffee when our muse deserts us.
The salary is not high, but we can offer you a superb West End office, the chance of world-wide travel, and the knowledge that you will be developing your managerial skills by keeping us on the straight and narrow.
Phone Michael on . . .

JENSONS (Solicitors)

This well-established firm of Solicitors is seeking a mature person to be secretary to the senior partner. The successful applicant will possess excellent social and business skills.
The remuneration may justly be described as very competitive. Flexi-time, luncheon vouchers and independence are offered as additional incentives.
Write to Mr J. R. Jenson . . .

Figure 13.6 *Job advertisement*

Unilox Goes Flexible

J. R. ADAMS, managing director of Unilox Ltd., said bluntly, 'We had to do it. The market for our product is contracting in this country. We are competing on the world market with the Germans and Japanese. They were undercutting our prices every time. The only costs we could reduce were labour costs.'

Mr Adams was referring to the major reorganisation of working practices in the business. Skilled and semi-skilled labour now take their share of general maintenance and cleaning jobs when necessary.

'This means we can hold on to skilled labour when orders are low. They benefit by having a job. We benefit because we do not have people sitting idle when there are jobs to be done. We employ 50% less unskilled workers than we did two years ago. We are leaner, fitter, more competitive, and moreover our orders are going up and the horror of declaring redundancies has receded. Not that we did not have our problems.'

Unilox did have problems. The skilled workers objected to being put on semi-skilled jobs and on the 'pool'. The pool does everything that needs to be done, from painting to brushing up the rubbish and keeping the rose beds outside the factory free from litter. Their union objected but took a close look at the figures, and the high level of unemployment in the area brought a reluctant agreement. Since then, one of the most highly skilled men has said, 'I really hated the idea, but the pool isn't that bad. It makes a change, and you meet different people. I suppose it has to be done anyway.'

Figure 13.7 *Flexible working practice at Unilox*

4. *Good working conditions.* A pleasant place in which to work, good lighting, rest rooms and sports facilities will not necessarily persuade people to work harder but they do show that the managers of the business value the workforce.

5. *Good communications.* These can also help improve the motivation of the workforce. When people do not know what is going on they tend to imagine the worst. Good communications are particularly important when things are changing. Rumours of redundancy will mean that people will be afraid for their jobs. Frightened people do not work well. They will become resentful. As a result they may see no point in trying.

Improving the job satisfaction and motivation of a workforce costs money for, among other things, re-organisation of the workplace, training and meeting times. Businesses spend this money because they expect to save money and make more profit from a more contented workforce. Some of the possible benefits are listed below:

* less waste from poor quality goods or bad service because people take more pride in their work

* greater customer satisfaction so there is more chance of a customer repeating the order

* more success in recruiting well-qualified people

* people are more likely to stay in the job, so cutting down recruitment and training costs

* less absenteeism, greater punctuality

* better industrial relations

* business has a good public image.

JUST TESTING

1. Using the information given in the newspaper article in Figure 13.7, outline the advantages to the business of job rotation. What problems did the business encounter when it tried to introduce this type of organisation?

2. Look at the list of advantages a business hopes to get by spending time and money on motivation. For each advantage give one reason why it might happen.

Motivation and leadership

Leadership is getting other people to cooperate with you in achieving objectives. People obey a leader either because he or she is the boss or because the leader has the sort of personality that people want to follow. Figure 13.8 illustrates the different styles of leadership that can be found in business.

Autocratic: tells people what to do. Very much concerned with the job to be done.
* Excellent when there is need for immediate urgent action at time or the group is inexperienced.
* Useless for developing self-reliance.

Laissez-faire(let them do what they like):
* Not so good. * Subordinates need some help and will feel stressed if they do not get it.

Democratic: encourages people to think and make their own decisions.
* Excellent in an expert situation.
* Not so good when they do not know.

Figure 13.8 *Different styles of leadership*

The style of leadership used depends on the personality of the manager (some people are naturally more bossy than others), the business (some are more authoritarian than others), the type of job and the conditions of work.

Figure 13.9 outlines how different circumstances need different types of leadership.

Autocratic – over the top
Danger, unwilling workforce

I refuse to answer any more silly questions!!!

Expertise: The leader may not know as much as his workforce. "Tell me what you think"

Figure 13.9 *Jobs and leadership*

Finding out

1. Arrange to interview three people about their jobs. Your friends and relatives may be willing to help you.

Task A   In a group, make a list of the questions you will ask. Use the list of factors that motivate people on p106 to give you ideas. Conduct your interviews individually.

Task B   Draw up a chart to show the differences between the jobs covered by your group. You could put the job titles down the left-hand side of the paper and the motivating factors across the top.

Task C   Prepare a presentation on the data you have collected, explaining what appears to be the most important motivating factor. From your knowledge of the

people and the jobs, explain why these differences exist.

Task D   What difficulties did you experience in carrying out this exercise? Would a change in your original questions help?

2. Working as a group choose five jobs you want to study.

Task A   On your own, find out as much as you can about the jobs. Your careers centre or local library will help you with this.

Task B   From the information you have gathered, decide which job you would find most interesting and motivating. Give reasons for your choice.

Task C   Compare your choice with those of the rest of the group. Did their choices vary a great deal from yours? Why did they make their choices?

Task D   Write an essay explaining how your activities have given you an insight into:

* the importance of good selection procedures in motivation

* the variety of human needs

* the problems a business can experience in trying to motivate its workforce.

Trying it out

1. The following conversation took place between the managing director of a business making sports equipment and the sales manager.

Managing director: Look at these sales figures. They are appalling. Half way through the year and well below target.

Sales manager: I lost three of my best salespeople to Springers. The rest of the team do not have much experience. They find the pressure hard to take.

Managing director: Do Springers pay that much more commission than us? I thought we paid the highest rates.

Sales manager: We do. But Springers pay a basic wage plus commission. The area their reps cover is smaller than ours and they provide bigger cars. They get more freedom in planning their own work as well.

Managing director: When I was selling I thought nothing of driving down to the south coast and up to Scotland the next day. What do they want us to do? Wrap them in cotton wool?

Sales manager: When you did that you were building up your own business.

(a) From the information in the passage, outline the reasons why the sales force might be discontented with their jobs.

(b) What effect is the discontent having on the business?

(c) Give two reasons why the managing director was prepared to work harder than his sales staff.

(d) What needs do you think the sales staff are satisfying by joining the Springers' team?

(e) Write briefly about the managing director's style of leadership and its possible effects on the motivation of the employees.

2. The photographs in Figure 13.10 show different types of working conditions.

Figure 13.10 *Different types of working conditions*

(a) Study the photographs carefully. From the evidence they offer suggest:

(i) Two conditions which might motivate the workforce.
(ii) Two conditions that might lead to less job satisfaction in the workforce.

Give reasons for your answer.

(b) Which job do you think would give the greatest job satisfaction and why?

(c) For each photograph decide what type of leadership is being demonstrated. In each give two reasons why that style of leadership might be appropriate.

3. Figure 13.11 shows a pay slip.

Study it carefully and answer the questions below:

(a) What is meant by the terms:

(i) gross pay?
(ii) net pay?

(b) Calculate the net pay due to this worker.

(c) How was the figure for income tax arrived at?

(d) What type of payment system is used by this business? Use examples from the pay slip to explain your answer.

(e) The trade union negotiates a 10% pay rise. What effect will this have on the workers' take home pay, assuming superannuation and national insurance stay the same?

Figure 13.11 *A pay slip*

4. Julie Goh, a director of Allframes, is concerned about the high costs of production. At a Board meeting she points out to her fellow directors that the wage bill for twenty now stood at £3 000 for a 40-hour week, before the business had paid national insurance contributions. "On top of that," Julie pointed out, "every employee works five hours overtime at time and a half. Output is only one hundred frames per week."

(a) What are:

(i) national insurance contributions?
(ii) overtime?

(b) What is the average wage of each employee without overtime?

(c) How much does each employee earn in overtime per week?

(d) Calculate the labour cost of one frame.

Julie suggests to the Board that the company introduces a piece rate system of payment, paying each worker £25 for each completed frame.

(e) What is meant by the term piece rate?

Calculate:

(i) how much a worker would earn each week if 5 frames were completed.
(ii) the difference to the total wage bill if the piece rate system of payment was adopted, assuming the output stayed the same.

(f) Write a paragraph as an employee of Allframes explaining:

(i) why you welcome the introduction of the piece rate system.
(ii) what you do not like about it.

Pay and allowances		Deductions		Department	MARKETING AND SALES
BASIC PAY	1200	NATIONAL INSURANCE	98		MR R.J.ALCOCK
COMMISSION	509	SUPERANNUATION	96	**Tax code**	217
		INCOME TAX	350	**Month payable**	JUNE 1988
				Gross pay	£ 1709
				Deductions	£ 544
				Net pay	

UNIT 14:
INDUSTRIAL RELATIONS

The owners of a business and the people who work for it have a common interest in the survival and prosperity of the business. After all, it provides both groups of people with their living.

The interests of both groups are not exactly the same. On the simplest level the business will want to buy its labour as cheaply as possible while the employees will want to get the maximum amount of money for the work they put in.

The relationship between the different groups of people engaged in business is known as **industrial relations**. Trade unions are the best known organisations that try to resolve the conflict that exists between the interests of employers and employees.

Trade Unions

Do we need trade unions?

In the past there were very few restrictions on the way in which employers treated the people who worked for them. Long hours, low pay, dangerous working conditions were all part of the experience of the worker. One person alone could not get better conditions, but combined in a union there was a chance for improvement.

The functions of trade unions are to negotiate and put pressure on employers, the government and other unions to protect the interests of their members in the areas listed below:

* pay and fringe benefits

* training and promotion

* security of employment. This will include negotiating on behalf of its members and giving advice to them when there is any threat of redundancy

* conditions of work, e.g. hours worked, number and length of breaks

* health and safety

* dismissal of members

* providing benefits for their members, e.g. health care.

Methods of trade unions

Figure 14.1, overleaf, shows some of the methods used by trade unions to achieve their objectives.

Although the drama of strikes and picketing gets the most publicity they are only a small part of a trade union's work for its members. Other activities include:

* collective bargaining when the trade union represents the interests of its members in negotiation with representatives of employers

* writing for the press, giving interviews on radio and television to put the members interests in any current debate that affects them

* presenting evidence to government committees when there is legislation planned that will effect its members

* putting pressure on the government through members of parliament when it has identified problems for its members that legislation could improve

* negotiating with other unions when the members have a conflict of interest.

Not all strikes are backed by a trade union. Strikes that have union backing are known as **official strikes**. When the workers in a business go on strike without union backing the strike is said to be **unofficial**.

Unofficial strikes can occur when union members feel that they are not getting enough back-up from their officials – or when they act on impulse. Unofficial strikes are converted into official strikes when the problem cannot be resolved quickly. When this happens skilled union negotiators can take over to argue the case.

Negotiate

Put their case through the media

Strike

Demonstrate

Advertise

Figure 14.1 *Methods used by trade unions*

The different types of trade union

1. *Craft unions* represent skilled workers. These are one of the oldest types of trade union. Craft unions tend to be small and this limits their power when negotiating with employers. As a result many craft unions have now amalgamated to form one of the larger general unions.

2. *General unions*, e.g. the Transport and General Workers Union, have members from a wide range of skilled, semi-skilled and unskilled occupations. They are usually divided into sections, each one of which will represent a different type of skill.

3. *Industrial unions* represent all the workers in a particular industry whatever their skill. An example of this type of union is the National Union of Mineworkers (NUM).

4. *White collar unions* (e.g. the Manufacturing, Science and Financial Union) are the most recent type of union to appear. They represent scientific, clerical and managerial staff. Traditionally this type of work is referred to as "white collar jobs". People working in jobs that require manual skills are often referred to as "blue collar workers". The names come from the type of clothing worn to work. White collar work is clean. Blue collar work needs the protection of overalls. As technology makes more and more jobs clean, this distinction is becoming blurred.

5. *Professional associations* are not registered as trade unions but they perform the functions of a trade union. In addition they are also concerned with laying down entrance requirements to the profession and the establishment of professional standards. The Institute of Cost and Management Accountants (ICMA) and the Institute of Chartered Accountants (ICA) are two professional associations whose decisions affect businesses.

JUST TESTING

1. State one way in which improvements in technology can lead to the decline of blue collar unions.

2. In what ways are professional associations similar to trade unions?

The organisation of a trade union

Like businesses, trade unions have organisations designed to suit their own needs. The organisation outlined in Figure 14.2 is only a general guide to the organisation of a typical trade union.

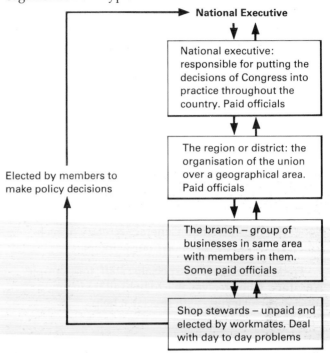

Figure 14.2 *Organisation of a typical trade union*

Some of the officials of a trade union work part time and are unpaid. Others are full time officials who are paid for their work and have a contract of employment like other workers.

1. A **shop steward** is elected by the workforce each year and deals with the day to day problems his members bring to him. If the business employs a large number of people, spread out among different parts of the factory, there will also be a senior shop steward in each union. Senior shop stewards are elected by the shop stewards of their union.

2. The senior shop steward acts as a **convenor** for that union. A convenor brings together all the problems of the shop stewards and negotiates with senior management about them. The convenor of a union in a large organisation will represent his union on a **Joint Consultative Committee**. This is a committee which consists of the convenors of all unions employed by a business, and representatives of management. It meets to discuss and negotiate solutions to problems that have arisen before a dispute starts.

3. A **branch** of a union consists of all the members of that union in an area. The area covered by a branch differs from union to union. It depends on how the union decides to split the country up. At branch level, union officials start to be paid.

4. All the branches in one geographical area (e.g. the North West) are combined into **districts**. Each district has a committee which covers problems that affect the whole district or are too complicated for branch officials to sort out.

5. The district committees nominate people to serve on the **National Executive**. This group of people is responsible for running the finances of the union and dealing with national strikes. It is the national executive which puts pressure on the government concerning such matters as trade union legislation.

6. Once a year each union has an annual general meeting, or **congress**. At this meeting the members of the National Executive Committee have to account for their running of the union to delegates from the shop floor. The President and General Secretary of each union is elected by the shop floor workers.

7. Trade unions employ specialist staff, for example solicitors, who are available to help all trade union officials, at all levels, with specialist help.

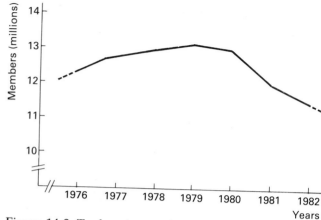

Figure 14.3 *Trade union membership*

J U S T   T E S T I N G

1. Why are joint consultative committees necessary?

2. As a member of a trade union, what personal qualities would you want your shop steward to possess?

The Trades Union Congress (TUC)

The TUC is a federation of most of the trade unions in the United Kingdom. The TUC can discipline unions, for example expel them, if they break the rules agreed by member unions. Although the member unions have a great deal of freedom in how they conduct their affairs, resolutions passed by the TUC at their annual congress can have a big effect on the way in which they behave. The Trades Union Congress also represents the view of all trade unions on matters of union law and offers various educational services to the members of unions.

Are trade unions too powerful?

In recent years the number of people who belong to a trade union has declined. This trend is illustrated in Figure 14.3.

This has happened for a number of reasons:

* the rapid increase in unemployment in the late 1970s and early 1980s

* the number of people employed in industries in which the trade union was particularly strong fell as a result of changes in demand for the product and the introduction of modern technology

* the rise in employment in the mid 1980s was in occupations where trade unions had never been strong. There was also an increase in the amount of part-time jobs and in the employment of women.

There are still many people who argue that trade unions have too much power. This power works against both the employers and the members of the union:

* people who do not belong to a union still enjoy the pay increases and improved conditions the unions negotiate for their members. This is considered unfair. To avoid this some industries have a **closed shop** agreement. This means that to get a job in that industry a worker must be a member of the union

* large trade unions, like large businesses, can lose touch with the ordinary worker. Critics of the trade union movement say that the national officials do not know what their members want. Recent strikes undertaken after a secret ballot of the members suggest that the members can be more militant than the leaders

* unions in industries such as power and in public service such as the Department of Health and Social Security can cause disruption and hardship to large numbers of the population if they go on strike

* unions bid up the wages of their members. It is argued that this is unfair to the unemployed. An increase in wages can lead to redundancy

* wages that are too high increase the costs of the business and make it less competitive.

The power of trade unions is not unlimited. In Figure 14.4 you can see some of the things that curb their power.

> The amount of money the business will lose if there is a strike. The more successful the sales, the more power to the union

> Legislation: the government can increase or decrease the power of unions by the laws it passes

> Number of members. The more members the more disruption industrial action will cause

> Is management determined to win?

> Are the members militant? Or would they prefer a quiet life?

> What do the newspapers say?

Figure 14.4 *Limits on the power of trade unions*

Employers' Organisations

1. Employers' associations represent the employers in an industry. Like trade unions they are concerned with putting the point of view of their members to the government and to the public through press, radio and television. When negotiating pay and conditions of service for a trade or industry it is representatives of the employers' associations concerned who meet with the national officials of the trade unions involved.

2. The Confederation of British Industry (CBI) is the employers' equivalent to the TUC. Like the TUC it gives advice and puts pressure on the government to act in the interests of its members.

JUST TESTING

In what ways is the TUC similar to the CBI?

Getting an agreement

What happens if the union and management involved in an industrial dispute cannot reach an agreement? Disputes are expensive for both sides. During a strike, workers lose their wages and run up debts. The business loses money from lost orders – and some customers may never return. To stop this sort of situation carrying on for too long, in 1974 the government set up the **Advisory, Conciliation and Arbitration Service (ACAS)**.

1. *Advice.* ACAS offers advice on a wide range of business activities concerning the management of the workforce. These include recruitment, selection, induction, training, payment policies, legislation and setting up procedures to deal with disputes before they get out of hand.

2. *Conciliation.* ACAS provides conciliation in disputes. Conciliation describes the process of trying to find a solution that satisfies, as far as possible, the different goals of the workforce and management.

3. *Arbitration.* ACAS provides an arbitration service. Arbitration goes one step further than conciliation. The arbitrator examines the evidence offered by both sides of the dispute and decides on an award.

Both conciliation and arbitration are voluntary. They are used when management and unions feel that they can get no further with their own discussions and the dispute is costing both sides too much money.

JUST TESTING

1. What is the difference between conciliation and arbitration?

2. Why do you think conciliation and arbitration are voluntary?

Finding out

1. Using newspapers, periodicals, radio and television reports, collect as much information as you can on an industrial dispute involving a large business. If you know somebody involved in this dispute, ask them what they think of it.

Task A   Working as a group analyse the information you have collected.
(a) What were the causes?
(b) How did it develop?
(c) What methods did the unions use?
(d) How did management react?
(e) Did any other parts of the economy suffer as a result of the dispute?
(f) How was the strike reported by the media?

Use any charts or diagrams you think appropriate to illustrate your findings.

Task B   Study one stage of the dispute closely.
(a) What are the objectives of the management and unions?
(b) What arguments does each group use?

Divide into three groups: *Management*, *Unions* and *Observers*. The management and unions will attend a meeting to attempt to find a solution to the dispute that will satisfy both sides. The observers should take notes on the following:

* which side was most successful?

* what methods did the successful side use to win its arguments?

* how important was personality, knowledge of arguments, ability to communicate in achieving success?

Was the outcome of your group discussion the same as the real life outcome?

Task C   As the public relations officer representing either the management or the union, prepare a presentation for a press conference arguing your case in the dispute.

Task D   What have you learnt about industrial disputes as a result of this exercise?

2. Arrange interviews with an official in (a) a trade union, and (b) a chamber of commerce. In the course of your interview find out as much as you can about the jobs of the two people and the organisations for which they work.

Task A   Draw up an organisation chart for both organisations. Indicate the role of the people you have interviewed on the chart. Explain who and what they are responsible for and to whom they are responsible.

Task B   Prepare job descriptions and job specifications for both people. Explain your reasons for including each item.

Task C   You work for a central heating firm as a plumber. The business has recently taken on a contract to fit central heating into local authority housing as part of a refurbishing scheme. In the course of the work asbestos is discovered. This can be a serious health hazard. You are not happy with the reassurances of your employers that there is no danger in this case. Explain how the trade union official you interviewed could help you and at what stage. Why would the qualities you listed in the job specification be important?

Task D   From the results of your research, describe the main advantages of belonging to a trade union. What are the implications for appointment of officials to the trade union?

Trying it out

1. Study the banners shown in Figure 14.5 carefully.

(a) From the evidence of the banners in Figure 14.5 state the objectives of each group of people.

(b) Explain why employees might feel strongly about the issues on the banners.

(c) Explain how each of the two disputes might effect:

   (i) the general public
   (ii) the business involved
   (iii) other businesses.

(d) You are a reporter for a newspaper. Write a brief article about one of the disputes:

   (i) in favour of the dispute
   (ii) against the dispute.

The article should be no more than 200 words long and contain the appropriate headline.

Figure 14.5 *Campaigning*

2. There had been grumbling on the production line at Donegan's for several months. There were complaints about safety, the attitude of the management ("Treat us like children – do this, do that. Never occurs to one of them to say 'Please'."), the working conditions and low pay. A large minority of the women did not belong to a trade union.

The shop steward did what she could about the complaints but made little headway with the management. Unemployment in that area was high. The production manager was firm. "If they don't like the job they can leave. I'll have no trouble getting replacements."

(a) Explain why the women were dissatisfied with their job.

(b) Give two reasons why the managers were not particularly worried about the complaints from the shop floor.

The time for the annual negotiation on pay and conditions was approaching. The shop steward consulted with her local branch officials. She told them that if something was not done about Donegan's she would resign. The union agreed to mount a campaign to persuade more women to join the union.

(c) Why was it necessary to get more women to join the union?

(d) Design a poster to advertise the advantages of belonging to a union.

(e) How might the management react to this campaign and why?

3. Study the following passage.

In 1980 a large British company began a reorganisation of its workforce with the co-operation of the trade unions. The aim was to improve efficiency and reduce the costs of production. In this they were successful. The number of different job titles was cut from 500 to 45 – so the workforce could be moved more easily from one job to another, productivity increased by 45%.

The foreign competitors of the business were still more efficient. The company wished to reduce the workforce and introduce more labour-saving working practices.

The problem came to a head when the business made its pay offer. The offer was above the average being offered at that time, but the workers and their unions felt that it was not enough. As a result of the changes in working practices the business was making big profits. The workers felt that as they had co-operated in the changes they deserved a share in the higher profits. Although the company had been free of strikes for three years, in the early stages of the pay negotiations it began to suffer a fall in production.

A convenor commented: "If they want more work from us they are going to have to make a better offer. We have given a lot over the past three years, now its their turn. The lads are in a militant mood, if there is a vote they will go for a strike. No one wants it, but no-one is prepared to settle for less. So far there is nothing official. There soon will be."

(a) What is the meaning of the terms:

(i) strike free
(ii) convenor.

(b) What are the objectives of:

(i) the management
(ii) the unions.

(c) The business lost production before the strike was called. What methods might the workers have used to show how they felt about the company's pay offer before they went on strike?

(d) Do you think this strike was entirely about pay? Explain your answer.

(e) The market for the goods produced by the business was booming at the time of this dispute. What other factors could influence the success of the unions in achieving their goals?

(f) At what stage in the negotiations might the management and unions agree to go to arbitration? Explain your answer.

UNIT 15:
PROTECTING THE WORKER

Working can be a dirty, dangerous and unpleasant way of spending a large part of your life. The photographs in Figure 15.1 illustrate some of the different environments people have to work in if we are to enjoy our present standard of living.

It is not only the conditions people work in that can cause problems. Much of the machinery that is used can also be dangerous. Employers too, determined to get the best possible profit, can contribute to the dangers by spending insufficient money on safety,

Figure 15.1 *Where people work*

forcing the employees to do too much so that they have no time to take proper safety precautions – or are too tired or too busy trying to keep up with their production quotas to bother.

A single worker lacks power. Trade unions can do something to help but their power is also limited. Since the beginning of the nineteenth century the government has passed laws regulating the treatment of workers by their employers.

> ## *JUST TESTING*
>
> Divide the hazards given in Figure 15.3 into those that cause immediate injury and those that will damage health in the long term.

Things that cause long-term damage to the health of employees come under the heading **health**. Things that cause immediate injury come under the heading **safety**.

What does the law say?

The Health and Safety at Work Act 1974 lays down a general framework for health and safety. Employees are responsible for the safe use of equipment, following safe practices and wearing any protective clothing that is needed. The Act also set up two bodies:

* the **Health and Safety Commission** which reviews health and safety legislation and makes suggestions for improvement

* the **Health and Safety Executive (HSE)** which is responsible for enforcing the Act. HSE Inspectors visit workplaces to make sure the regulations are being obeyed.

Figure 15.4 shows who the business has a responsibility to.

> ## *JUST TESTING*
>
>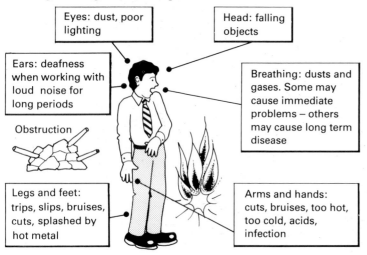
>
> Figure 15.2 *Nineteenth century working conditions*
>
> Compare the conditions in the nineteenth century with conditions in the present day industry in Figure 15.1. Make a list of all the improvements you can see. How many of the improvements do you think came from advances in technology? How many from changes in the law?

Health and safety

In Figure 15.3 you will find some of the things that can go wrong in the workplace.

Eyes: dust, poor lighting

Head: falling objects

Ears: deafness when working with loud noise for long periods

Breathing: dusts and gases. Some may cause immediate problems – others may cause long term disease

Obstruction

Legs and feet: trips, slips, bruises, cuts, splashed by hot metal

Arms and hands: cuts, bruises, too hot, too cold, acids, infection

Figure 15.3 *What can go wrong*

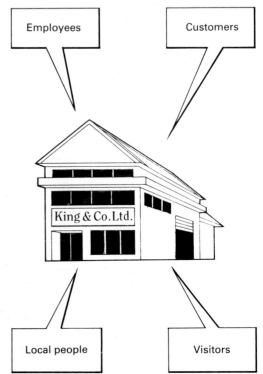

Employees

Customers

King & Co. Ltd.

Local people

Visitors

Figure 15.4 *Who the business is responsible to*

As a result of these responsibilities the business is required by law to make sure certain jobs are done. These are shown in Figure 15.5.

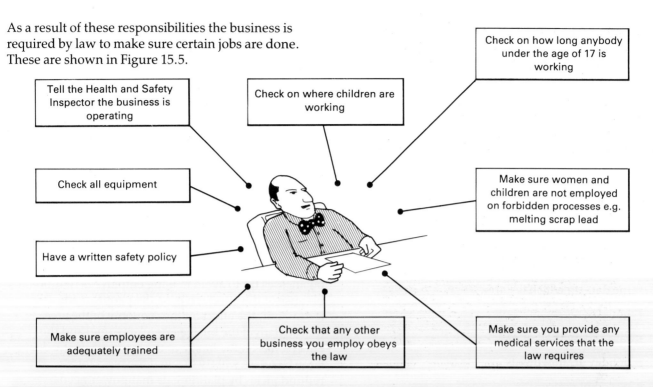

Tell the Health and Safety Inspector the business is operating

Check on where children are working

Check on how long anybody under the age of 17 is working

Check all equipment

Make sure women and children are not employed on forbidden processes e.g. melting scrap lead

Have a written safety policy

Make sure employees are adequately trained

Check that any other business you employ obeys the law

Make sure you provide any medical services that the law requires

Figure 15.5 *Employers' responsibilities*

JUST TESTING

Look at Figure 15.6. What possible safety problems can you see? How can the business help prevent them?

Figure 15.6 *Safety problems*

Dismissal and redundancy

The Contract of Employment Acts 1972–1982 state that an employer and employee have entered into a legally binding agreement (that is a **contract**) when:

* the employee accepts the job

* the employer agrees to pay a wage for the job.

The law also states that the employee must receive a written statement of the terms of the contract within thirteen weeks of starting the job. This must contain:

* the name and address of the employee

* the title of the job

* the date on which it starts

* hours of work

* rate and method of pay

* holiday arrangements

* period of notice

* terms of any pension scheme

* trade union rights

* the disciplinary rules of the business.

By making the conditions of employment clear from the start and by making them legally binding for employers and their employees, the possibility of industrial disputes as a result of misunderstandings is reduced. This does not mean that they disappear altogether.

When a dispute arises it can be taken before an **industrial tribunal**. The tribunals consist of a legally qualified chairman and two other people. Anybody appearing before a tribunal can be represented by a solicitor, a trade union official, a representative of an employer's association – or any other person of their choice.

The idea of a contract of employment leads to the idea of **fair** and **unfair dismissals**. An employer can fairly dismiss an employee:

* for misconduct

* for being unable to do the job

* when the employee is no longer needed, that is **redundant**

* when it would be illegal to continue employing that person.

The employee must be given reasonable warning of dismissal. This is usually taken to mean:

* a verbal warning. If the problem continues over a further period of time the verbal warning should then be followed by a written warning. Again the employee should be given time to improve before the final stage

* dismissal.

In certain circumstances instant dismissal is possible. Stealing, fighting on the premises of the employer, refusal to obey reasonable instructions, repeated drunkenness at work and failure to observe safety regulations can all lead to legal instant dismissal.

Redundancy is a special form of dismissal. Many businesses try to avoid making employees redundant because of the effect it has on the people made redundant, the effect on the economy of the area (particularly if the business is a large one) and the effect it has on the image of the business. Instead, a large business will try to avoid the need for redundancies by planning its manpower needs carefully. When the number of people it needs is likely to fall it will cut back on recruitment and, if possible, re-train its existing workforce for new jobs within the business (**redeployment**). When this is not possible the business will prefer to cut its workforce by encouraging early retirement and voluntary redundancy.

When making people redundant an employer has a responsibility to give as much notice as possible and select the people to be made redundant fairly. In addition, an employee who has worked for the business for longer than two years for more than 21 hours per week is entitled to a minimum redundancy payment. Higher payments may be made when an employer is hoping to encourage voluntary redundancy.

JUST TESTING

1. What is the difference between fair and unfair dismissal?

2. Give three things an employer could do to avoid making some of the workforce redundant.

3. What is the difference between dismissal and redundancy?

Racial and sexual discrimination

Discrimination is noticing the differences between people and treating them differently as a result. For an employer to treat the workforce or the people who apply for jobs differently because of race, colour or sex is illegal. Discrimination can occur when people are refused employment, promotion or are paid lower wages than people doing an equal job because of their race, colour or sex.

Racial discrimination was forbidden by the **Race Relations Act** 1976. The **Commission for Racial Equality** was set up to enforce the Act. Sex discrimination was made illegal by the **Sex Discrimination Act** 1975 which also established the **Equal Opportunities Commission** to investigate cases that went against the Act. People who feel that they are being discriminated against on any of the above grounds can also take their case to an Industrial Tribunal. These Acts also apply to job advertisements.

JUST TESTING

From your experience of the business world, state four ways in which an employer might infringe (go against) either the Race Relations Act or the Sex Discrimination Act.

The law and trade unions

Since 1980 there have been a series of Acts passed which affect the way in which trade unions behave:

* the **Employment Act** 1980 stated that picketing was only lawful if it took place outside the person's place of work. Other picketing (known as **secondary picketing**) is now illegal. The Act also reinforced the right of a person not to join a trade union. This affected the **closed shop** – i.e. when a person had to be a member of a particular trade union to get a job with a firm

* the **Trade Union Act** 1984 introduced the **secret ballot**. Unless there was a secret ballot of all members before a strike started the union concerned could be sued for loss of revenue caused by the strike. The governing bodies of the trade unions were also to be elected by secret ballot. Where trade unions collected funds from their members for

political purposes the members had the right to vote at intervals to say whether or not their union should have a political fund.

JUST TESTING

1. Give one disadvantage and one advantage to the employer of the right of people not to join a trade union. Which Act reinforced this right?

2. The members of trade unions are sometimes more militant than their officials. In what way might a secret ballot lead to more strikes?

Finding Out

1. Over a period of time, collect as many newspaper cuttings as possible relating to cases brought before an industrial tribunal. If you find this difficult work as a group and pool your findings.

Task A   From the information you have collected make a list of the subject of the cases. What evidence was offered in each case? What was the verdict? What reasons were given for reaching that verdict? Under what laws were the cases brought? Might the result have been different if they had been brought under other laws?

Task B   Draw charts/diagrams to illustrate the material you have gathered together in Task A. Write a short report commenting on the most interesting points you can see in the charts and diagrams.

Task C   Select one way in which the law protects the worker. As the personnel officer of a business draw up a plan to make sure that all the managers in the business are aware of the law. Your plan can include meetings, posters and other useful methods of communication. Explain why you decided on this course of action.

Task D   As a result of this exercise explain how the laws protecting employment can increase the costs of a business. How can these costs be justified from the point of view of the employer and the employee?

123

2. Arrange a visit to a business to investigate how health and safety legislation affects that business.

Task A Prepare a questionnaire on the responsibilities of the business and what they have to do to meet these responsibilities. Figure 15.4 will help you in this.

Task B Working in a group and using the information you have collected, make a list of the ways in which the law affects the business. Put your final list in order of importance. Why did you make these decisions?

Task C Select one way in which the law can affect the business. Design a poster to bring it to the attention of the workforce. What other methods could you use to reinforce the message on the poster?

Task D Why are these laws necessary? Do you think the business would do anything about these problems if there were no laws? Give reasons for your answer.

Trying it out

1. Read the following extract from a local newspaper before answering the questions.

DEATH CLOUD DRIFTS OVER BADSEA

At 3pm today a poisonous yellow cloud of gas escaped from the chemical works of Sulpho PLC.

Immediately a huge emergency operation was set in operation. Ambulances and fire engines were rushed to the scene. The police mounted road blocks to keep motorists clear of the area and stood by ready to evacuate householders in the nearby estate.

Fortunately the gas was blown out to sea before a major incident developed. Fifteen employees of Sulpho were taken to hospital for emergency treatment.

A spokesman for Sulpho said that the emergency procedures had worked well. The leak was quickly found after the first alarm and the company was not aware of any casualties other than the workmen. A team of technicians was touring the area taking samples of air to make sure all was clear.

(a) (i) What did Sulpho do as soon as the leak was discovered?
(ii) The leak was a health risk. Which groups of people were at risk?

(b) As a result of their investigations, Sulpho found the leak was the result of carelessness by one of its employees. He was immediately dismissed. Was the company within its rights to do this?

(c) The worker claimed unfair dismissal on the grounds that Sulpho had given him inadequate training for the job. The case went before an industrial tribunal.

(i) What is an industrial tribunal?
(ii) What are the responsibilities of the business with respect to training?

(d) The incident caused a great deal of anxiety in the surrounding district. What do you think would be the attitude of:

(i) a school leaver about to apply to Sulpho for a job?
(ii) a householder living near the plant?

(e) Sulpho's public image was badly damaged by this incident. What steps could it take to improve it?

2. Michael Pearson works on the assembly line in a large factory. He has strong objections to trade unions and has never been a member of one. Recently the company who owns the factory has negotiated a closed shop agreement with the trade union. In spite of considerable pressure, Mr Pearson still refuses to join a union.

(a) (i) What is meant by the term "closed shop"?
(ii) Which Act would support Mr Pearson in his determination not to join a union?

(b) What arguments could Mr Pearson's workmates use to try to persuade him to join a trade union?

UNIT 16:
OWNERSHIP OF BUSINESS

Some businesses are owned by just one person. Others are owned by groups of people. Businesses can be owned by:

* private individuals either alone or in groups

* groups of people who co-operate together

* the state and local authorities.

The state and local authorities are part of the **public sector**. The other groups are part of the **private sector**.

How a business is owned affects:

* the way in which it is financed

* who makes the decisions – that is who controls the business

* who is responsible for the actions of the business, for example, who is responsible for the debts of the business

* the goals of the business.

The private sector

The sole proprietor

The sole proprietor (sometimes called the sole trader) is a person who owns an entire business.

Sole proprietorship is the most popular form of business ownership in the United Kingdom. Because of the advantages of this form of business organisation new businesses often use it. It is therefore found in all types of business activity.
The advantages are:

* it is cheap and easy to form

* the owner can make all the decisions

* the owner can make decisions quickly because there is no need to consult another person

* because the business tends to be small, the owner is likely to have close contact with the workforce and customers

* the finances of the business remain private. The amount of profit a business makes is known only to the owner – although people lending money to the

business will want to see the accounts – and so will the tax man.

The sole proprietor does suffer disadvantages:

* because the business is the property of one person it is taxed when the owner dies (capital transfer tax). If there is not enough money to pay these taxes the business will have to be sold

* sole proprietorships tend to be small. For this reason and because the business relies on one person, sole proprietors find it more difficult to borrow money from banks than other types of business

* sole proprietors are responsible for all the debts of the business. If there is not enough money in the business to pay the debts, the owner has to use his own money to pay them. The **liability** of the sole proprietor is **unlimited**.

Figure 16.1 gives the objectives of the sole proprietor and the way in which the business is owned, controlled and financed.

The sole proprietor

owns

the entire business

controls

the decision making

receives

all the profits

is responsible for

all the debts

raises money from

his own capital
retained profit
borrowing

aims (possible)

to make a profit
grow larger
keep control
security
independence

Figure 16.1
The sole proprietorship

Partnerships

A partnership consists of between two and twenty people who jointly own a business and work in it together. The rights and duties of each partner are ruled by the Partnership Act 1890. Amongst other things, this Act states that the profits and losses of the business are divided equally among the partners. A **deed of partnership**, that is a legal agreement drawn up by the partners, can change the rules of the partnership so that they differ from those of the Act. When a partner dies or leaves the partnership a new agreement has to be drawn up.

The advantages of a partnership include:

* more finance from the personal capital of each partner, from loans and from ploughed back profits, because the business can grow to a larger size

* a wider range of skills. Partnerships are often found in business activities which require a wide range of skills and expertise. A plumber will find it an advantage to go into partnership with a bricklayer and an electrician. A solicitor experienced in property transactions might need a partner with experience in divorce cases

* partnerships, like sole proprietors, do not have to publish their accounts.

Partnerships do have disadvantages:

* they have unlimited liability

* there is a limit on the size to which they can grow

* there may be disagreements among the partners about the control of the business

* the decisions of each partner are binding in law on the rest. This can cause problems if a partner makes a mistake.

JUST TESTING

Draw a diagram similar to Figure 16.1 showing

(a) who owns a partnership
(b) who controls a partnership
(c) who is responsible for the debts of a partnership
(d) where the finance comes from in a partnership.

Limited Companies

A company is a group of people who have joined together to carry on business. In this it is similar to a partnership. However, the use of the word company means that the owners have gone through the legal processes necessary to make their business a **separate legal entity** from them. This means that the business is a person in law. If a company is involved in any criminal activity, it is the company that is sued – if it is found guilty it is the directors who go to jail.

Although companies can be very small, the minimum number of people who can form a company (**shareholders**) is two, there is no limit on their size. In a company whose shares are held by several thousand people there is no way in which all the shareholders can take part in the running of the company. The shareholders elect a **Board of Directors** who run the business on their behalf. In turn the directors employ managers to see to the day-to-day business of running the company. Look at Figure 16.2. You can see that in a large company the people who own the business have very little control over the way it is run. This situation is known as the **divorce of ownership and control**.

Shareholders
(can be very large numbers all with different goals)

elect

The Board of Directors
(who make the policy)

who appoint

Managers
(whose goals may be very different from the shareholders)

who appoint

the rest of the workforce
(whose goals might be different from those of both shareholders and the management)

Figure 16.2 *The divorce of ownership and control*

126

> ## JUST TESTING
>
> 1. Explain why the managers' goals might be different from those of the shareholders and the directors.
>
> 2. What happens when a business becomes a separate legal entity?

There are two types of company:

* the private limited company whose shares cannot be bought by the general public. This means the shareholders are able to keep control of the company while enjoying the advantages of more capital and limited liability. A private limited company will have LTD in its official name

* the public limited company which must have a minimum capital of £50 000. The shares of a public limited company can be sold to the general public. The official name of a public company will include the letters PLC.

If the company is financially sound, the shares can be traded on the **Stock Exchange**. The functions of the Stock Exchange are given in Figure 16.3.

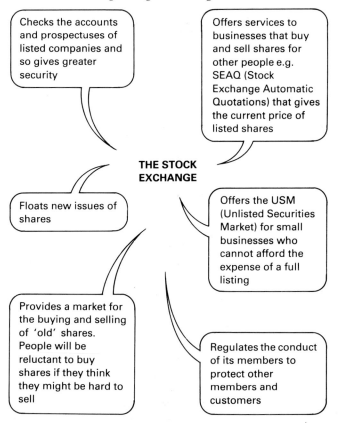

The word limited in the name tells people that a company has **limited liability**. The shareholders are only required to pay the debts of the business to the limit of the amount of money they invested.

Companies are controlled by the Companies Acts 1948–1981. This increase in legal control is the result of:

* limited liability

* the size of the company

* the divorce of ownership and control.

The legal process involved in setting up a limited company is outlined in Figure 16.4

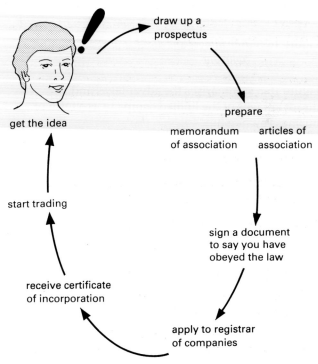

Figure 16.4 *The setting up of a limited company*

Setting up a company is expensive and takes time. Smaller businesses wishing to become a company often buy one "off the shelf". These are companies which have already been formed but which, for some reason, have either never started to trade or have ceased trading.

Because they can grow to a very large size, companies have the possible advantage of large amounts of owners capital. To protect the shareholders from mismanagement and so that prospective shareholders can see what they are buying into, companies have to publish their accounts.

Limited liability

More capital for growth

Can sell shares and the business still goes on

Can buy in expertise

Divorce of ownership and control

Can lose control

Expensive to form, especially plc s

Can grow too large so lose economies of scale

Figure 16.5 *Advantages and disadvantages of a limited company*

Figure 16.5 summarises the advantages and disadvantages of the limited company as a form of business ownership.

Companies that own more than half the shares in other companies (and can appoint the Board of Directors) are known as **Holding Companies**. The companies in which they hold shares are their **subsidiaries**.

JUST TESTING

1. What are the differences between a private and a public limited company?

2. Explain how limited liability protects the shareholders of a business? Why is this important when the company is so large that the shareholders have very little to do with the day-to-day decisions?

Co-operatives

Co-operatives, like partnerships and limited companies, are groups of people combining together to own and run a business. Co-operatives differ from other forms of business ownership in the following ways:

* the **workforce** controls the objectives and management of the co-operative

* the workforce owns the assets of the enterprise. If this is not possible at the beginning, every effort should be made to acquire ownership

* there is a voting system so the workforce can make their wishes known about decisions

* profits are divided amongst the workforce

* at the start of the life of the co-operative it should be agreed *how* decisions will be made, e.g. if some members of the co-operative want it to close down, will a simple majority vote be sufficient?

Co-operatives give the workforce control over the objectives of the business, the way in which it is organised and their own working environment. Co-operatives do have some disadvantages:

* the members must put in capital to enjoy full voting rights. Not everybody can afford this

* it may be difficult to leave. A member would have to find somebody to buy him or her out

* if the co-operative is unsuccessful the members lose the money they put in

* voting takes time. People may not like the idea of staying on when the working day is finished to attend meetings

* the members may disagree on important policy issues. This can lead to bad working relationships during the day

* votes may go against decisions that the members working in management think are sensible. The management team might feel there are too many restrictions placed on them.

In any enterprise that involves a group of people it is as well to draw up some legal documents that lay down the "rules of the game". The legal agreement can be used to decide any future disagreements between members.

Co-operatives can register as a co-operative society under the Industrial and Provident Societies Acts 1965–1975. To do this there must be at least seven members. The **Industrial Common Ownership Movement** (ICOM) has model rules that can help in the formation of a co-operative.

Co-operative societies can be used in every type of business. The size tends to be small or medium. Perhaps the most common in the United Kingdom are the Co-operative Retail Societies that can be found in all parts of the country.

Franchising

A **franchise** is a business idea that has been developed by one business and is then leased to another business for use. The business providing the franchise (the **franchisor**) has a product, either a good or a service, and a way of packaging that product that has been successful. The **franchisee** pays for the use of the idea and agrees to maintain the standards. The franchisor will often provide training, advertising and materials as part of the agreement. Figure 16.6 shows some of the well known names that are franchise operations.

Figure 16.6 *Franchises*

JUST TESTING

1. An unemployed bricklayer hears of a building co-operative that is looking for members. What problems might be encountered in attempting to join.

2. Give three ways in which a co-operative differs from a limited company.

3. Give one reason why people prefer to buy shares that are quoted on the Stock Exchange.

The public sector

1. *Central government*. Voters elect Members of Parliament. The political Party with the most MPs forms the government which is then responsible for setting the objectives of the country and making sure they are put into practice. Central government employs civil servants and other people in a wide variety of jobs to carry out its policies and provide us with services.

2. *Local government*. Elected councillors make decisions about matters that affect their own community. They employ people to put these decisions into practice.

3. *Nationalised industries*. These are businesses wholly or partly owned by central government. They provide goods and services for sale.

4. Organisations such as the British Broadcasting Corporation which are not owned by the government or local authorities but are not owned by private individuals.

Figure 16.7 shows some of the goods and services supplied by the public sector.

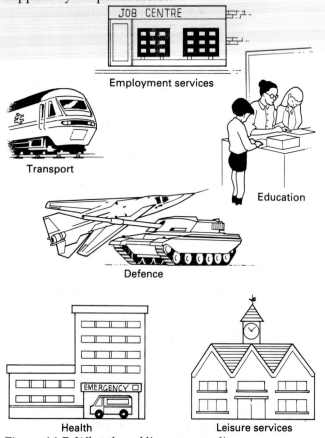

Figure 16.7 *What the public sector supplies*

Public corporations

The public corporation is the type of business ownership used in the United Kingdom for nationalised industries. In 1987 nationalised industries employed 800 000 people and produced 5.5% of the total output of the United Kingdom.

Nationalised industries:

* are separate legal entities

* are owned by the State

* have a Board of Managers who are responsible for the running of the business. The managers are appointed by the Minister responsible for the industry

* produce annual reports and statements of accounts

* are financed by the government, not by the sale of shares

* do not have to make a profit. They are expected to earn 5% of the value of any new investment (**target rate of return**).

Nationalisation or privatisation?

Figure 16.8 outlines the arguments for and against nationalisation.

To nationalise . . .
* Nationalised industries can take expensive safety precautions when there is risk to the public.
* Nationalised industries can provide services in uneconomic areas e.g. rural post and transport.
* Some nationalised industries are natural monopolies – the size at which their costs are lowest is monopoly size – it is better for these industries to be accountable to the State.
* Nationalised industries can be used to manage the economy – by keeping their prices low to beat inflation.

. . . or not to nationalise?
* Nationalised industries cannot pay the high wages to top managers that are paid in the private sector so they do not get the best people.
* Nationalised industries have no incentive to be efficient because of the lack of competition.
* Nationalised industries do not offer the customer choice.
* Nationalised industries suffer from government attempts to use them to manage the economy.

Figure 16.8 *To nationalise or not to nationalise*

Nationalised industries at the end of 1988

British Coal
Electricity (England and Wales)
North of Scotland Hydro-Electric Board
British Steel Corporation
Post Office
Girobank
British Railways Board
British Waterways Board
Scottish Transport Group
British Shipbuilders (Merchant)
Civil Aviation Authority
Water (England and Wales)
London Regional Transport

Nationalised since 1979

British Telecom
British Gas Corporation
British National Oil Corporation
British Airways
British Airports Authority
British Aerospace
British Shipbuilders (Warships)
British Transport Docks Board
National Freight Company
Enterprise Oil
National Bus Company

(Adapted from Economic Progress Report December 1987)

Figure 16.9 *The progress of privatisation*

In the end the decision as to whether or not to nationalise is a political decision. Some people believe that too much government interference with business and too much government ownership leads to inefficiency. Other people argue that if business is not controlled then people with lower incomes suffer and this is socially wrong.

Since 1979 a number of industries have been **privatised**. This means that either the industry has been converted into a public company or privately owned businesses have been allowed to compete with suppliers in the public sector. This is sometimes called **deregulation**. The changes are listed in Figure 16.9.

The arguments for and against privatisation are summarised in Figure 16.10.

State owned business are responsible to the people through Parliament, Local government

Private enterprise follows the profit motive

Figure 16.10 *For and against privatisation*

Finding out

1. This exercise can be carried out as part of setting up a mini-enterprise.

Task A   Select a form of business ownership and find out as much as you can about the way in which it is set up and the necessary legal requirements.

Task B   Working in groups make a list of stages you will need to go through to set up your enterprise and the problems you might encounter.

Task C   Working on your own, draw up an action plan to decide the rules of your enterprise. Do your ideas differ from those of the rest of the group? Can you come to an agreement? What is the final action plan? Why was it chosen?

Task D   Put your plan into action. Make a careful note of any problems that arise. This task should be continued throughout the life of your enterprise.

Task E   How successful was your plan? What problems did you meet? Were they the problems you expected? Would a different type of organisation have been more successful? Has this activity helped your understanding of the problems businesses face, if so how? Explain your answers.

2. Using newspapers, magazines, radio and television reports, collect as much information as you can on the flotation of a private company on the stock exchange.

Task A   From the material you have collected, prepare an account of the situation you have studied. Draw up a time scale of the flotation and the advantages and disadvantages.

Task B   Select one problem for the business concerned. Working in groups decide on the consequences the business might experience as a result of this problem. What could the business do about this?

Task C   Plan a promotional campaign for floating the company. This could include the prospectus, a video presentation of the advantages of buying shares in the company, a television advertisement for the company's products designed to attract investors as well.

Task D   From the information you have collected did you expect the flotation to be successful? Give reasons for your answer. Was it successful? What did the experts say? How did their views differ from yours? What has this exercise taught you about the problems of share buying?

Trying it out

1. In 1979 Angela McDonald opened a health food shop in her local market town. The food was bought in bulk and sold in the quantities the consumer required. Herbs were a popular line and this led to Angela making contact with the local producers. By 1981 Angela knew she could expand into the nearby town but she did not have the capital.

Angela considered going to her bank and asking for a loan. She decided against that. Instead, she took her sister as a partner. They signed a deed of partnership and Alice, the sister, took over the management of the new shop.

(a) (i) What is a deed of partnership?
(ii) Why did the partnership solve the problem of finance?
(iii) Give two advantages to Angela of taking her sister as a partner.

The business continued to expand. Angela and Alice had hit on the combination of goods and service that people wanted at that time. In 1983 the business became a private limited company – Wot-u-need Ltd. There were eight shareholders. Angela owned 51% of the shares, Alice 30%.

(b) (i) Draw a pie chart to show the percentage of shares held by Angela, Alice and the other shareholders.
(ii) What is meant by the letters LTD after the name of a business?
(iii) Explain why you think Angela and Alice decided to form a private limited company when they expanded.

Wot-u-need became on outstanding success. There were suggestions that it should go public. Both Angela and Alice were against the idea. They wanted to keep control.

(c) (i) What is meant by "going public".
(ii) State three advantages of going public for Angela and Alice.
(iii) How might Angela and Alice lose control by going public?

The McDonalds decided to franchise their idea.

(d) (i) What is meant by "franchise"?
(ii) Give two reasons why the McDonalds preferred to franchise their business rather than go public.

2. Look at the pictures in Figure 16.11.

(a) State the type of organisation of the businesses shown in Figure 16.11.

(b) Using the information given in the drawings explain why that type of organisation is suitable for each business.

(c) Explain why a small business might wish to register as a private limited company.

(d) Write a short account of the role and responsibilities of the Registrar of Joint Stock Companies when a business becomes a public limited company.

3. Four solicitors have formed a partnership. Two friends, in partnership in a catering business, have decided to form a private limited company as part of their expansion plans.

(a) State four reasons why the solicitors might have chosen the partnership form of legal organisation.

(b) Give three reasons why the caterers chose to form a private limited company as part of their expansion plans.

(c) What legal document would be drawn up for:

   (i) the partnership?
   (ii) the private limited company?

(d) What effect would the death of:

   (i) a partner
   (ii) a shareholder

have on their business?

(e) The catering business grows rapidly. It is suggested that it becomes a public limited company. What problems might it face?

a)

b)
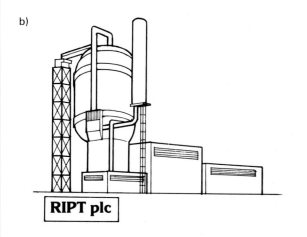

c)

Figure 16.11 *Different types of business organisation*

UNIT 17:
GROWING LARGER

Large businesses have a number of advantages:

* they can make more use of division of labour for greater efficiency

* they can use the latest technology

* they can offer employees better training and services such as health care, social clubs and, sometimes, better pay

* they can afford expensive advertising and so increase their market share

* banks are more willing to lend money to them because they are more secure – and employees are less likely to be made redundant because of a temporary fall in demand

* they can employ specialist managers

* they can afford the research and development costs that discover new products and techniques. This helps to keep them competitive and makes it more difficult for other businesses to break into that market.

Why do businesses grow larger?

Businesses grow in order to:

* make more profit

* have a wider range of products and so increase their security

* take advantage of discounts for bulk buying

* make sure of their supplies of raw materials or components by buying the firms that supply them

* make sure they have an outlet for their products by buying the firms they sell to

* make sure that their supplies meet their quality requirements

* stop their competitors getting supplies or selling in a particular market

* take advantage of the special skills (e.g. marketing) or assets (e.g. land) owned by another business

* make more use of underused resources it already possesses.

The way in which a business grows depends on why it wants to grow. Look at Figure 17.1. It shows the different patterns of growth a business might use.

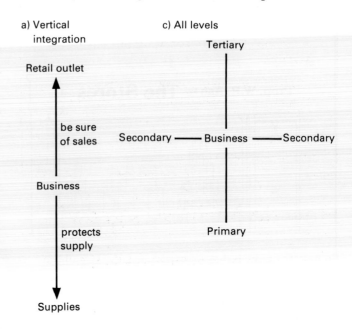

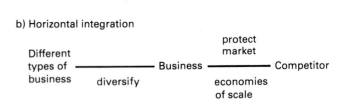

Figure 17.1 *Patterns of growth*

JUST TESTING

1. Look at the list of reasons why businesses grow given at the beginning of this Unit. Which ones do you think would be most likely to lead to:

(i) vertical integration?
(ii) horizontal integration?
(iii) either horizontal or vertical integration, depending on the circumstances of the business?

Give reasons for your choice.

---

2. State one reason why a person might prefer to work for a large business rather than a small business.

3. What type of integration is each of the following:

  * a package holiday business buys a car hire firm

  * a large business manufacturing goods in steel buys a steel works

  * a wholesale business buys a chain of retail shops

  * a chain of department stores buys a carpet factory

  * a business making dairy products (cheese, yoghurt, etc.) expands into the production of health foods?

For each case give one reason why the business made that decision.

How do businesses grow?

Businesses grow either by expanding the size of the existing business or by taking over other businesses.

1. *Internal expansion*. This is expanding the size of the existing business. It is also known as **organic growth**. An example of this might be a supermarket chain that increases the number of shops it owns. The continuing expansion of Sainsburys and Marks and Spencer are examples of organic growth.

2. *Mergers*. A merger happens when two or more businesses join together to form a new business. They are usually agreed by the businesses concerned to improve the efficiency of both. When a merger takes place there is very little change in the ownership of the business. The shareholders stay the same but exchange their shares in the original company for the same value of shares in the new company.

3. *Take-over bids*. Shareholders vote for the Board of Directors who, in turn, control the company. It follows that if one company buys enough shares in another company to vote in a Board of Directors of its choice, then it will control the company.

The shares in public companies can be bought by anybody. At the same time anybody who is interested can find out who owns shares in a public company.

When one company begins to collect a large number of shares in another company, this can lead to rumours of an intended take-over bid. The shares of both companies can go up in price if it is thought that the company considering a take-over is likely to offer good terms.

Take-over bids offer the opportunity for a lot of sharp practice – not quite illegal but still unfair. A number of institutions such as insurance companies, the banks, the Stock Exchange and the CBI got together and drew up the **City Code on Take-overs and Mergers**. This is not a legal document and there are no penalties for companies who do not keep to it. The Code is concerned with making sure that everybody who is likely to be affected by a take-over bid knows about it and that all shareholders are treated in the same way.

Both mergers and take-over bids can cause problems for everybody concerned:

  * there may be resentment and fear among the employees of the business that has been taken over which can lead to less job satisfaction

  * in the new business there may be more than one person for each job. There may, for example, be two Purchasing Managers. This will lead to redundancies or retraining for some people

  * the businesses will have the same objective – profit – but the way in which they try to achieve it is likely to be different.

JUST TESTING

1. What is the difference between a merger and a take-over bid?

2. Give two advantages of organic growth over mergers and take-over bids.

3. Give one reason why a business might go for a merger rather than wait for organic growth.

Who has the power?

Successful organic growth, mergers and take-over bids create large businesses that serve a larger and larger part of their market. This can work against the interests of the customer. If a business manages to buy up all the firms that supply a raw material it can force all its competitors out of existence. The ordinary consumer would have even less power.

For	Against
Some businesses are 'natural monopolies' – that is, the size at which they enjoy economies of scale is a monopoly size	Because the monopolist is the only supplier it can charge a higher price than businesses in competition. This increases the income of the monopoly at the expense of the customer
It is sometimes argued that only very big businesses can afford the cost of research and development	Because there is no competition there is no incentive for a monopoly to improve efficiency

Figure 17.2 *Advantages and disadvantages of monopolies*

Businesses that own all the means of supplying a good or service are called **monopolies**. Figure 17.2 outlines some of the advantages and disadvantages of monopolies.

The disadvantages of monopoly power have been realised by governments since 1945. Some industries were nationalised because the advantages of large scale, monopoly production were greater than the disadvantages (**natural monopolies**). It was felt that it was better for these businesses to be under the control of the State.

In industries where there are only a few companies it is easy for them to get together and agree on such things as prices. This reduces competition and is against the interests of the customer. All these practices, known as **restrictive practices**, are controlled by law.

JUST TESTING

1. Look at Figure 17.2. Give reasons why you think:

(i) the railways in the United Kingdom
(ii) electricity generation in the United Kingdom

have been considered natural monopolies.

2. Explain why a business that has control of 50% of the outlets for the product of the industry it belongs to would have an advantage over its competitors.

The Monopolies and Mergers Commission

Between 1948 and 1973 a number of Acts were passed to control the activities of large businesses. The **Fair Trading Act** 1973 created the **Director of Fair Trading** and the **Office of Fair Trading (OFT)** whose job it is to investigate any suspicious practices and refer them to the **Monopolies and Mergers Commission**.

The Commission is a group of people whose job it is to decide whether or not any merger or take-over bid is in the public interest. They are also concerned with price fixing agreements or any other activity on the part of businesses that are considered to be to the disadvantage of the customer. When a merger or take-over bid could lead to an investigation by the Commission (as a result the business will have a market share greater than 25%) it may be cleared with them before it takes place. The Commission will allow greater power to a business if:

* the failure of the merger/take-over bid would lead to a large increase in unemployment

* it would lead to greater competitiveness in the export market

* the customer would have to pay higher prices if the merger did not go through.

JUST TESTING

Do you think the criteria used by the Monopolies and Mergers Commission for allowing a merger or a take-over bid are reasonable? Explain your answer.

Protecting the consumer

The Director of Fair Trading is not only concerned with preventing businesses taking advantage of their market position. The Office of Fair Trading also has the job of protecting the consumer. It does this by:

* encouraging industry to develop codes of practice

* giving information to consumers and retailers about the law

* devising new laws on control of industry and trade to encourage fair trading

* prosecuting businesses that break existing laws.

Protecting the consumer by law has a long history dating back to the middle ages. Suppliers who break the law can be prosecuted under the **criminal code** or under the **civil code** of laws:

* when the criminal code is used the suppliers can be fined or sent to prison. The State prosecutes them

* when the civil code is used the consumer takes the supplier to court. The consumer takes the chance of paying the legal costs (if the case is won the supplier usually has to pay). The consumer is awarded compensation if the case is won.

The main Acts protecting the consumer are:

1893 *The Sale of Goods Act*

* products must be fit for the purpose for which they are sold

* they must be suitable for the purpose for which they are sold. For example, a pair of boots designed for wearing in bad weather must keep out the wet. On the other hand "fashion boots" are not expected to take rough treatment

* they must fit the supplier's description.

1955 *Food and Drugs Act* (Criminal code)

* food and drink must be suitable for human consumption

* food and drink must be correctly described.

1963 *The Weights and Measures Act* (Criminal code)

* it is an offence to give short weight or measure

* certain goods can only be sold in stated quantities, e.g. pints.

1968 & 1972 *The Trades Descriptions Acts* (Criminal code)

* it is an offence to give a false description of goods

* sale prices must be genuine. To advertise a price reduction, a retailer must have offered to sell the goods at the higher price for at least 28 days (in one block) in the previous six months

* the country of origin must appear on the labels of imported goods.

1971 *Unsolicited Goods and Services Act*

* suppliers cannot send goods to people and demand payment for them unless the customer has asked for the goods.

1974 *Consumer Credit Act*

* businesses offering credit services must have a licence to do so

* the businesses supplying credit are responsible (with the retailer) for the quality of the goods and services sold

* people buying on credit have a "cooling down" period after they have signed the contract. During this time they can change their minds

* people buying on credit must be told how much the credit is costing them.

1978 *Consumer Safety Act* (Criminal code)

* this act deals with the construction, materials, labelling and packaging of any goods that could cause actual physical injury to the user.

JUST TESTING

1. What is the difference between criminal and civil law? Why do you think two of the acts given above come under the criminal law?

2. List five goods that you think would come under the Consumer Safety Act. Give a reason for each of your choices.

Finding out

1. Collect information on the history of a take-over bid. If it is being resisted – so much the better.

Task A   Draw up a chart to show the timescale of the bid. Show what happened at each stage of the bid and the actions of both the attacking and defending businesses.

Task B   What reasons were given for the take-over bid? Which, in your opinion, were the most important reasons? What evidence can you give for your choice?

Task C   You are the managing director of a company threatened by a take-over bid. Plan a campaign to convince all the interested parties that a successful take-over would not be in their best interests.

Task D   What changes occurred in the organisation and structure of the business as a result of the take-over bid?

If the bid was not successful, why did it fail?

2. Arrange a visit to your local Trading Standards Department. Find out as much as you can about the work of the department.

Task A   Write an account of the work of the department. What powers do Trading Standards Officers have? Why are they necessary?

Task B   Visit a large retail shop. Make a note of everything that could infringe consumer law, for example, advertisements, labelling and packaging. Make sure that you check first with the manager of the store that he does not mind, and explain what you are doing and why you are doing it. How many different problems have you found?

Task C   Prepare a presentation arguing the case for more money for your local Trading Standards Office.

Task D   As a result of your investigation explain the importance of consumer legislation.

Trying it out

1. Looking at the photographs in Figure 17.3.

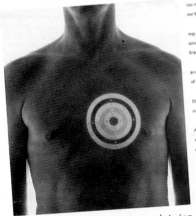

Figure 17.3 *Appeals to the consumer*

(a) Using the information given in the photographs, list three ways in which the consumer might be misled.

(b) What Acts of Parliament protect the consumer in each case?

(c) Why is it necessary for the government to protect the consumer?

2. The following passage is adapted from an article in the *Guardian* (12/12/87) and deals with a proposed take-over bid.

Another independent oil company became the target of a takeover bid yesterday when the French government-controlled Elf Aquitaine launched £134.7 million offer for Tricentrol.

The City concluded the group was worth more because of the bid fever in the oil industry. It also suspects that Elf sees great attractions in Tricentrol's stake in new finds which may be linked to the Wytch farm oil field in Dorset. These could prove a great moneyspinner in the 1990s.

The shares closed over 20p above the 145p offer price, at 165.5p . . . .

But Elf later revealed that it had persuaded Trafalgar House, the construction and shipping group, to part with its 5.5 per cent stake, which with other holdings made a total of 7.6 per cent.

Elf is one of France's largest companies, and the French government owns 54 per cent of it, though the group is on the list for privatisation.

Mr Pierre Moussel, Elf's UK managing director denied that Elf's hands had been forced by the BP move on Britoil, which he describes as an "inconvenience".

Elf had invested £1 billion in the UK in oil and gas exploration in the last five years and Alwyn field is now coming on stream. Tricentrol has a complementary portfolio which provided an opportunity to reinvest in the UK the returns from its oil and gas investments.

Tax advantages were not the reason for the bid, he added.

(a) (i) How much did Elf offer for Tricentrol?
(ii) By how much did the price of Tricentrol's shares rise above the offer price?
(iii) What percentage increase was this?

(b) List and explain the possible reasons given in the extract for Elf launching a take-over bid for Tricentrol.

(c) What did Mr Moussel give as the reasons for the take-over bid?

(d) The take-over bid could go before the Monopolies and Mergers Commission. Give one reason why Elf gaining control of Tricentrol could be an advantage to the British economy.

3. Pastor's Holdings is a property company with interests in commercial and residential developments. Over the past five years Pastor's has grown rapidly.

(a) What advantages might Pastor's enjoy from the growth?

(b) Give three problems Pastor's might experience as a result of the growth.

One of the major restraints on the growth of Pastor's Holdings was finding sufficient land for property developments. In 1987 the business began to buy shares in an engineering company which, as a result of technological change, now had a number of large factory sites that were very much underused. These sites were all within or near major cities.

(c) Why was the location of the sites important for Pastor's Holdings?

(d) If Pastor's Holdings is successful in its bid for the engineering company what organisational problems might it face?

(e) What pattern of integration is this take-over bid?

UNIT 18:
RENDERING AN ACCOUNT

Businesses keep records to:

* help with decision making

* show the owners of the business and people who have lent money to the business how that money has been used

* satisfy the tax authorities and other government departments that they are obeying the law.

Records contain all the information a business needs but they can be confusing to use. To make the financial information of a business more useful it is summarised. The two main summaries are:

* the profit and loss account

* the balance sheet.

The profit and loss account

	£	£
Sales		10 000
Less: Cost of sales		6 000
Gross profit		4 000
Less: Overheads		
Wages and salaries	2 000	
Heat and light	500	
Rent and community charge	600	
Insurance	100	3 200
Net Profit		800
Tax		200
Net Profit after tax		600
Payment to shareholders		300
Reserves		300

Figure 18.1 *A profit and loss account*

The profit and loss account contains the following information:

* how much the business earned from selling the goods and services it produced in a certain period of time, that is, the **sales** or **turnover** of the business.

* how much it cost the business to produce those goods and services

* how much profit the business made

* how the business used its profit.

Look at Figure 18.1. The definitions below refer to terms used in the profit and loss account.

1. *Cost of sales.* The amount of money paid for stock.

2. *Gross profit.* Sales minus the cost of sales.

3. *Net profit.* Gross profit minus the total costs.

4. *Net profit after tax.* The business has to pay tax on the money it earns.

5. *Distributed profit.* The Board of Directors of a company decide how much of the profit will be distributed to the shareholders. This is the shareholders' **dividend**.

6. *Retained profit.* This is the part of the profit that stays with the business to finance future growth and development.

JUST TESTING

Use the information in Figure 18.1 to answer the following questions.

1. What was the gross profit of the business? Show how it was calculated.

2. Calculate the net profit of the business.

3. What proportion of the net profit after tax was distributed to the shareholders?

The balance sheet

The balance sheet shows:

* where the money the business is using has come from, that is, the **liabilities** of the business

* how this money has been used, that is, the **assets** of the business.

	£		£
Land and property	20 000	Proprietors' funds	25 000
Fixtures and fittings	5 000	Bank loan	1 000
Cash at bank	2 000	Creditors	1 000

Figure 18.2 *A balance sheet*

1. The left hand side of the balance sheet lists the assets of the business. These are divided into:

* fixed assets

* current assets.

Fixed assets stay with the business until they wear out, are sold or the business closes – which is why they are called fixed. Fixed assets include land, buildings, machinery and equipment, vehicles and things like goodwill, patents and trademarks:

* goodwill covers the reputation a business has built up

* a patent is a legal document that gives the inventor of a machine the exclusive right to use that invention for twenty years. If anybody else wishes to use that invention they have to pay for the right to do so

* trademarks and brand names help to identify a product and build up consumer loyalty.

Current assets are those that are ''used up'' in the day to day running of the business. Current assets are easier to turn into cash if the business needs it. They include stock, debtors, money in the bank and cash.

2. The right hand side of the balance sheet lists the liabilities of the business.

The money put in by the owners always comes at the top of this list. If the business is a company this money is called the **shareholders' funds**. In other types of business organisation it is called **proprietors' funds** or, more simply, **owners' capital**.

The loans the business has received are listed in order of their life. At the bottom of the list are creditors and bank overdraft. These are known as the **current liabilities**.

The balance sheet shown in Figure 18.2 is in the 'T' form. Another way of setting out the assets and liabilities of the business is the columnar form of the balance sheet. This is shown in Figure 18.3. This type of balance sheet is said to be easier to understand.

The Companies Act 1985 states that the accounts of all limited companies must be examined every year by

	£	£
Assets employed		
Fixed assets		
Land and property		20 000
Fixtures and fittings		5 000
Current assets		
Cash at bank		2 000
Deduct		
Current liabilities		
Creditors		1 000
Net assets		1 000
Net assests employed		26 000
Financed by		
Proprietors funds		25 000
Bank loan		1 000
		26 000

Figure 18.3 *A columnar balance sheet*

accountants who are not employed by the company. These accountants are known as **auditors** and the inspection of the records and accounts of the business is called the **audit**. The auditors produce a report that is attached to the annual report that the directors of the company give every year to the shareholders. The auditor will say if there is anything unsatisfactory in the way in which the finances of the business are being run. For example, the auditor may not have had enough information or may not be satisfied with the explanations given by the business.

The auditors' report is a protection for the shareholders and for people who have lent money to the business. It is necessary because of the divorce of ownership and control.

JUST TESTING

1. What names are given to the two different forms of balance sheet?

2. Put the following list of assets into the order in which they would appear on a balance sheet: cash, vehicles, machinery, land, debtors.

3. In what way does an auditors' report protect the shareholders of a company?

What the accounts can tell you

By comparing one piece of information given in the accounts with another, managers, investors, trade unions and lenders can learn something about the state of the business. This is called **ratio analysis**.

The current ratio

Current assets : current liabilities

This ratio tests the ability of the business to pay its debts. A current ratio of 2:1 is usually thought to be about right. Assets are twice as high as liabilities because they include stock which might be difficult to sell in a hurry.

The acid test ratio

Liquid assets : current liabilities

This also tests ability to pay debts. The acid test ratio should be 1:1. This shows that the business has enough money either in cash, at the bank or coming in from debtors to pay all the money it will have to repay in the short term. A business that cannot pay its debts might be forced into liquidation by its creditors.

Investment ratios

These ratios are useful to people considering buying shares in a business. They are usually expressed as a percentage.

1. *Return on equity.* "Equity" is the capital of a business owned by the shareholders.

$$\frac{\text{Net profit after tax} \times 100}{\text{Shareholders funds}}$$

This ratio shows how well the business is using the capital it possesses.

2. *Dividend yield ratio.* Not all the profit made by a business is distributed to the shareholders. Some is kept in the business for future investment. Investors want to know the income they will get from their shares. They can compare this information with, for example, the interest they would get from a deposit account at a bank – with far less risk of loss attached.

$$\frac{\text{Dividend per share} \times 100}{\text{Share price}}$$

3. *Price earnings ratio.* This tells the investor how long it will take for the earnings of a share to cover the price of the share. By dividing the price of the share by the earnings, the investor will find out how many years it will be before the earnings from the share repay the price paid for the share.

$$\frac{\text{Market price of share}}{\text{Earnings per share}}$$

Gearing ratio

This compares the amount of money the business has raised from borrowing with the total amount of money it is using.

$$\frac{\text{Long term borrowing}}{\text{Net assets employed}}$$

Borrowed money is paid for at a fixed rate of interest. When the profits of a business are rising, interest payments take a smaller and smaller proportion of the income of the business. When the revenue of the business is falling the interest payments can be a burden to the business.

Return on capital employed

This shows how well the business is using the money. It is not enough to know how much profit a business makes, the amount of capital needed to make that profit is also important.

$$\frac{\text{Net profit} \times 100}{\text{Assets}}$$

Ratios on their own can give very little information about a business. If they are compared with the same ratios for the past few years they can show if the business is improving its performance – or if the performance is worsening. Compared with the same ratios for other businesses it gives some indication about the performance of the business.

Ratios are based on the records of the business. There are a number of other things that have to be taken into account. These are illustrated in Figure 18.4.

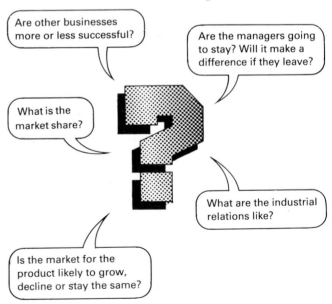

Figure 18.4 *What you need to know about a business*

JUST TESTING

1. Look at the profit and loss account and the balance sheet in Figures 18.1 and 18.2. Calculate the current ratio and the acid test ratio for the business. Show your workings.

2. Do you think the business has anything to worry about? Give reasons for your answer.

Finding out

1. This activity could be completed as part of the running of a mini-enterprise. This will probably be a group activity so keep a written record of your contribution and the contributions of other members of the group.

Task A   Go through all the records of your enterprise. Collect all the information you need to make up a profit and loss account and a balance sheet.

Task B   Draw up a profit and loss account and a balance sheet for your business. Using ratios analyse the performance of your business. How well is it doing? What problems have you discovered? What can you do about them? Use your results to draw up an action plan for your next month of trading.

Task C   Repeat Tasks A and B at the end of another month of trading. Has the performance of your enterprise improved? How far did your preparation of accounts help you?

Task D   What problems did you encounter in drawing up the accounts of your business? Were the records accurate? Were they complete? If you had been an auditor would you have been satisfied with the way the managers of the business could account for the way in which the business had been run? Give reasons for your answer.

2. You will need the annual report of a large public limited company for this activity. You will also need to collect all the information you can about the industry of which the company is part. For example, if you choose a property company you might collect information about house buying, the cost of materials, a shortage of brick-layers and so on. You should also find out the market value of the shares of the company.

Task A   Using ratios analyse the accounts of the business. What percentage return would a shareholder get on an investment of approximately £100?

Task B   Examine the report closely. What explanations are given in the report for the performance of the company. Make a list of the reasons. Explain how each one could affect the company.

Task C   From your knowledge of the industry to which the business belongs, explain the problems the business is facing. How many of these problems can the business control? What action could it take?

Task D   You have sent for this report because you are considering investing £1 000 in the company. As a result of your investigations would you do so? What additional information do you think you need before making your decision?

Trying it out

1. Metalcraft Limited produces a wide range of household fittings in a variety of metals. The business was founded in 1982 to satisfy the demand for fittings in keeping with the period of older houses. Below is the turnover of the company since its foundation.

Year end	Turnover
1982	£ 10 000
1983	£ 12 000
1984	£ 25 000
1985	£ 40 000
1986	£ 70 000
1987	£ 90 000
1988	£120 000
1989	£135 000

(a) What is meant by the "turnover" of a business?

(b) Draw a graph to show the changes in turnover between 1982 and 1989.

(c) What was the percentage increase in turnover between 1987 and 1988? Show your workings.

When the business was founded it was a partnership. It was registered as a private limited company in 1986 as part of a planned expansion. There are now twelve shareholders in addition to the original two founders of the business.

(d) Give three pieces of financial information a person investing in the business would want to know before making a final decision about buying shares. Explain why the investor would want each piece of information.

(e) What other information might the investor find useful in making a decision?

2. Sharon Daley drifted into party planning almost accidentally. She prepared the buffet for a friend's wedding and received several bookings as a result of this. Within two years the business had outgrown her own kitchen and Sharon decided to look for premises to work from. She moved into her new premises on November 1st 1987 and advertised her business under the name Party Plan.

Party Plan's Profit & Loss Account year ending 31st October 1988

	£	£
Sales		26 000
Cost of sales	15 600	
Gross profit		10 400
Less costs:		
Rent & rates	3 000	
Wages	4 000	
Light & heat	1 000	
Maintenance	200	
Insurance	500	
Advertising	300	
Transport	1 000	
Total		
Net profit		

(a) Calculate Sharon's net profit at the end of 1988.

(b) Calculate:
   (i) the ratio of gross profit to sales
   (ii) the ratio of net profit to sales.

(c) What do these ratios tell you about the business? Explain your answer.

Sharon is not pleased with the results of her business expansion. She complains to her husband that although her turnover has increased by £6 000 her net profit has fallen by £1 000.

(d) Calculate the percentage increase in Sharon's turnover.

(e) Give two reasons why Sharon's net profit has fallen. What can she do about this?

144

3. Joe Large is a small farmer who is beginning to think he would do better to sell up and invest his money in a building society. Given below is his balance sheet on 31st March 1988.

Large's Farm

Balance sheet at 31st March 1988

Assets	£	Liabilities	£
Land & buildings	140 000	Proprietor's funds	160 000
Machinery	30 000	Mortgage	40 000
Vehicles	10 000	Bank loan	34 000
Stock	50 000	Bank overdraft	5 000
Cash at bank	10 000	Creditors	1 000

(a) Explain what is meant by:

  (i) assets
  (ii) liabilities.

(b) Joe Large is always worried about not being able to pay his bills. Calculate:

  (i) his current ratio
  (ii) his acid test ratio.

Do you think he has any need to worry? Explain your answer.

(c) Joe calculates that in 1989 he will earn £12 000 net profit from his business. If he sold the farm and invested the money in a building society account paying 7% interest, would he be better off? Explain your answer and show any workings you think necessary.

UNIT 19:
OTHER ORGANISATIONS AND BUSINESSES

A business is an organisation. That is, it is people, working together, each with a job to do (their roles) to achieve the objectives of the business.

Businesses are not the only type of organisation in our society. When a business sets an objective, how it reaches that objective will be affected by the decisions of other organisations. A business has to take the law into account when employing or dismissing its workforce. The laws are the result of the decisions of the central government.

The people who work in a business can also have an influence on its decisions. Not everybody is convinced that their employer and the management knows best.

Formal and informal groups

When people come together in groups as the result of organisation the groups are called **formal groups**. People who work together will have different interests and needs. They will tend to get together with other people with whom they have something in common. This sort of group is called an **informal group** because it is not part of the organisation.

Informal groups can both help and hinder the business in reaching its goals.

1. People who enjoy working together and are friends will often be a very efficient team. They will set their own high standards and work towards the goals of the business. If a group like this becomes unhappy the management would be wise to take notice.

2. The same group of people might become dissatisfied if the way in which the business is run changes drastically. In that case, their strength as a team could lead to lower production. It could also lead to workers leaving the business. This would lead to extra expense in recruiting new workers.

3 When people have worked for the same business for a long time they will often have informal contacts in other departments. They can use these contacts in an emergency to get a job done quickly. If they always

rely on their informal contacts it can cause problems for the business in organising the work. Too many rush orders put through by a department to help friends can lead to more important orders being late. The business might lose valuable customers.

4. Unofficial strikes are the work of informal groups. The workers on strike are not acting as members of a trade union. These strikes can often be very difficult to resolve because the real reasons for the strike may be hidden. It might seem to be about low pay. Underneath the workers may be protesting about the way in which the work is organised.

Informal groups that stand in the way of the business reaching its goals often develop because the workers feel they have no power in the business – they feel that they are just cogs in a machine. Management tries to handle this by getting the workforce more involved with the decision making of the business. They try to make the workforce feel that the objectives of the business are important to them. They can do this by:

* improving communications. When people know what is going on they are more likely to work to a common goal

* encouraging employees to buy shares in the business so that they have an interest in high profits and the success of the business

* organising suggestion schemes and rewarding people with money for ideas that improve the efficiency of the business

* involving the workforce in the decision making of the business – perhaps by having worker directors on the Board that are voted on by the workforce

* organising quality circles where groups of workers involved with the production of a certain good meet with management to see how the work could be improved. Quality circles are based on the ideas that the people doing the job often have a better idea of what is going wrong than management who are more divorced from it. If quality circles are to succeed then the management must take notice of the workforce and work with them to improve the system.

146

JUST TESTING

Figure 19.1 shows a number of situations in a business.

Figure 19.1 *Events in the daily life of a business*

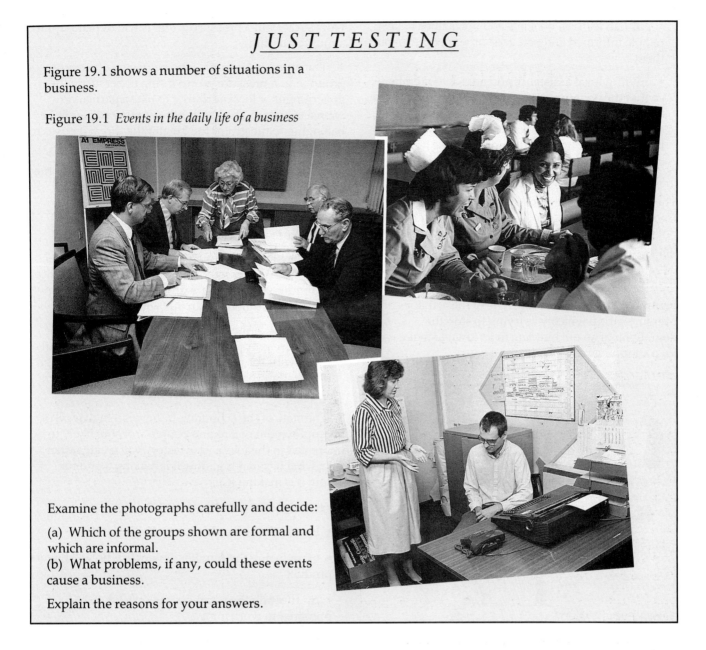

Examine the photographs carefully and decide:

(a) Which of the groups shown are formal and which are informal.
(b) What problems, if any, could these events cause a business.

Explain the reasons for your answers.

Pressure groups

A pressure group is a group of people who try to persuade a business or other organisation to act in the way they think is right. They bring pressure to bear on other organisations by:

∗ **lobbying** Members of Parliament and Councillors. The **lobby** in the House of Commons is a very large hall, open to the public, where they can meet their Member of Parliament (MP). The word "lobbying" is now used to describe all meetings with MPs and Councillors and the writing of letters to them in an attempt to persuade them to take action

∗ **advertising** in newspapers. This is to make sure that as many people as possible who might support you know what you are trying to do. We will see how important this can be when we look at the ways in which pressure groups win their campaigns

∗ **persuading** the editors of newspapers and magazines to publish articles supporting their campaign or interviews with a representative of the pressure group

∗ **demonstrating** to show how strongly they feel. Strikes, sit-ins, and marches can all draw attention to the cause

* **publish** leaflets, booklets and magazines to keep people informed and persuade other people to join them

* offering **legal** assistance and advice to members so that the government becomes aware through the Courts of the problems its laws are causing. Legal assistance can also force businesses to take note of laws they were hoping to ignore because it would cost their customers too much to sue them for compensation.

The purpose, size and life of a pressure group can vary from the very large and powerful who try to change, not just what happens in one country, but what is happening in the world, to the residents of a road who join together to try to stop the building of a factory at the end of their road.

Figure 19.2 has examples of some of the activities of a pressure group which was trying to stop the demolition of an old building in its town to make way for a shopping mall.

Figure 19.2 *The activities of a pressure group*

How successful a pressure group is will depend upon a number of things.

1. The number of people who belong to a pressure group, e.g. a pressure group trying to persuade the government or local authority to take a particular course of action. The greater the number of people belonging to the group the greater the threat it poses to MPs and local councillors in elections.

2. The more people belonging to a pressure group the more wealthy it is likely to be. The more money a pressure group has the more it can advertise, pay people to work for it full time or pay for specialist advice, for example, in legal matters.

3. The political situation in the country or in the area. If the political party in power is in general agreement with the aims of a pressure group it is more likely to listen to its arguments than one which is not.

4. The image of the pressure group. If the leaders of the pressure group are seen as a bunch of cranks, out of touch with the real world, people will tend to laugh at them rather than join them. Violence will also turn most people against a pressure group.

5. The state of the economy. If there is a high level of unemployment in a region people are more likely to be interested in the jobs a new factory will create rather than what it is making, how it is making it and for whom it is making it.

Pressure groups can affect business:

* by increasing production costs

* by reducing the number of people who will buy its product

* by affecting the number of people who are prepared to work for it

* by forcing them to pay more attention to the way in which the public sees them. This will cost money in advertising and for such things as guides to show people around the factory.

The **Consumers' Association (CA)** is an important pressure group working to improve the safety of goods sold to consumers, the value for money of goods and services and the protection offered by the law to consumers. It tests consumer goods and services, publishing a report on the results of its tests in its monthly magazine *Which?*. In addition it prepares evidence to put before Parliament when there is any legislation proposed that might affect consumers. It presses Parliament to take action when it identifies a problem and offers legal advice to its members.

The Consumers' Association does not limit its interest to goods and services. It is also very concerned about pollution and has worked hard for such issues as a clean water supply and lead free petrol.

Voluntary codes

When the law does not give enough protection to the customer, businesses might get together to lay down standards of behaviour that their members agree to follow. An example of this is the British Code of Advertising Practice. This was set up in 1962 and is run by the **Advertising Standards Authority (ASA)**. The ASA is a separate organisation to any of the businesses involved and has a great deal of power.

The code itself is a very detailed document. It sets out to make sure that all advertisements are "legal, decent, honest and truthful".

Other industries set up separate organisations to protect the consumer if a member business fails to give good service. The **National Housebuilders Register (NHBR)** and the **Association of British Travel Agents (ABTA)** offer this type of service to customers. Member firms subscribe to a common fund which is used to pay compensation when, for example, a travel firm ceases trading and leaves holiday makers stranded.

JUST TESTING

What is the difference between a voluntary code and an organisation such as ABTA? How might membership of ABTA affect a business?

Finding out

1. ASH, CBI, NSPCC, BMA, TUC, CND, FoE, Oxfam are all pressure groups or act as pressure groups at times.

Task A (a) What are the full names of these organisations?
(b) What are they trying to do?
(c) How do they go about it?

Task B How successful are these organisations? Collect information on them over a period of time and make a note of some of their successes and failures.

Task C Working in a group, draw up a plan to organise a campaign that you feel strongly about. There might be a piece of waste ground near you that could be better used as a garden. You might want to get a controlled crossing installed. Include in your plan a presentation arguing your case.

Task D As a result of this exercise write an account of the problems facing pressure groups. The difficulties you may have experienced in finding information for Task C could help you with this. Were all the members of your group enthusiastic, for example?

2. Choose a product that has been the subject of a recent *Which?* report. You will need a copy of the report and as many advertisements as you can collect that advertise different brands of that product.

Task A Look closely at the *Which?* report. Which qualities did it consider most important in the product? How many of those qualities appear in the advertisements?

Task B Select four of the advertisements. Do you think they are "honest, legal, decent and truthful"? Explain your answers.

Task C Draw up your own advertisement for one of the products. Your aim is to persuade people to buy the product without going against the Code of Advertising.

Task D Explain how both the Consumers' Association and the Advertising Standards Authority can influence the behaviour of a business. Give as much detail as possible. For example, how could they influence production, marketing and finance.

Trying it out

1. Read the story in Figure 19.3 carefully and then answer the questions.

Figure 19.3 *Campaign for a crossing*

(a) Anne's first meeting was a failure. Explain how each of the following reasons might have contributed to the failure:

(i) not enough publicity
(ii) meeting held in the evening
(iii) no written information about the meeting
(iv) people did not believe the campaign could be successful.

(b) Make a list of the methods Anne and her friends used to apply pressure. Can you think of any other things they might have done?

(c) Why was the second councillor concerned about the coming elections?

(d) Why do you think the shopkeepers would want to support Anne and her friends? Is there any evidence in the story to show that local businesses might have benefitted from the crossing?

2. A waste reclamation plant has been established on a derelict site on the edge of a dock estate. To the north of the plant the land is used for industrial purposes. To the south, however, there is a large marina and leisure centre. This area is mainly residential. The people living there are protesting about the noise and dirt created by the plant. The businesses involved in the marina and leisure centre claim that the plant has reduced the value of their property and limited their takings.

(a) Explain why:

(i) the owner of the waste reclamation plant
(ii) the owners of businesses in the marina and leisure centre
(iii) the householders

each feel that they have a justifiable case.

(b) Plan a campaign on behalf of the householders.

(c) List all the things that might stop the householders' campaign being successful.

3. The advertisements in Figure 19.4 below and overleaf are for popular food products.

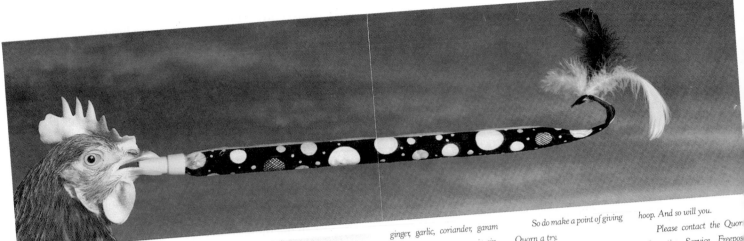

Good news for chickens.
A Korma made with Quorn.

Why good news?

Because there isn't a chunk of chicken in it.

But before you turn up your nose, this vegetarian Korma without a word of a lie, is every bit as mouthwatering as the curry house original.

It's prepared with Quorn, a remarkable new wholesome food.

One that's vegetable, com-pletely natural in origin and grown from a tiny, tiny plant.

It's reassuringly low in fat yet surprisingly high in protein.

It contains just as much dietary fibre as fresh green vegetables.

And Quorn makes past alternatives to meat taste like poor alternatives to meat.

The reason is an uncanny ability to draw flavour from the delicious herbs, spices and sauces it's cooked with.

Qualities which have cer-tainly curried favour with Tesco.

For the Kashmiri Korma in question is now part of the Healthy Eating range available from the Tesco chilled cabinet.

A dish prepared with pieces of Quorn, onion, ground almonds, ginger, garlic, coriander, garam masala, cardamon, turmeric, cin-namon, cloves and sour cream.

If you're fond of healthy eating, dull it isn't.

And fattening it isn't either. Under 400 calories, the lot.

So do make a point of giving Quorn a try.

(There are more and more dishes around with Quorn in them, so it's easy enough. Tesco have a Bombay Bhagia too.)

Chickens will be cock-a-hoop. And so will you.

Please contact the Quorn Information Service, Freepost London SW1P 1YZ if you'd like to know more about Quorn. **Quorn**

GOOD FOOD. GOOD HEALTH

TESCO KASHMIRI KORMA

Figure 19.4 *Advertisements for food products*

In recent years people have become increasingly concerned about their diets. Health experts say that we should cut down on fats, sugar and salt, and increase the amount of fibre we eat. Some people claim that there are too many additives in food and that these can cause ill-health.

(a) Explain why the manufacturers advertise in this way.

(b) Do you think these advertisements fit in with the code of the Advertising Standards Authority? Give reasons for your answer.

(c) Give two examples of how pressure groups have persuaded manufacturers to change their products. What methods did they use?

UNIT 20:
BUSINESS AND THE ECONOMY

Population and unemployment

There are approximately 57 million people in the United Kingdom: men, women and children. They provide between them the market for all the goods and services sold and the workforce to make goods and services.

Changes in the population

The population of a country changes over time. It can:

* grow larger – an **increasing population**

* become smaller – a **declining population**

* change its **age structure**, that is, the proportion of the population contained in each age group. When there is a growing number of older people the population is said to be ageing

* change the areas in the country where most people live.

Figure 20.1 shows the age, size and regional distribution of population in the United Kingdom.

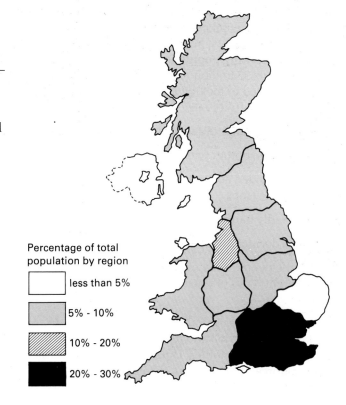

Percentage of total population by region

☐	less than 5%
▨	5% - 10%
▤	10% - 20%
■	20% - 30%

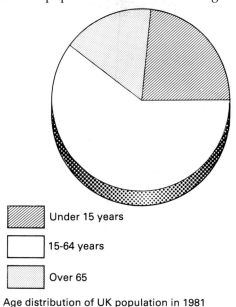

Under 15 years

15-64 years

Over 65

Age distribution of UK population in 1981

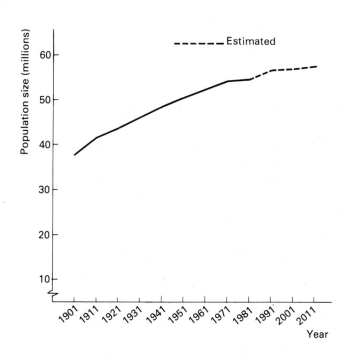

153

Unemployment

Not all of the population can work – or want to work. Laws put restrictions on the employment of anybody under the age of sixteen and over the age of sixty-five. These people are the **dependent population**. The money they receive comes from their parents, the State, or occupational pensions. In the United Kingdom the people who are considered available for work – the **working population** – numbers approximately 33 million. Of those only 26 million or so are employed or looking for employment. This is known as the **activity rate**.

The 7 million unaccounted for might be:

* too rich to bother with paid work

* have decided against working for their own personal reasons

* too badly handicapped to do any work

* have decided to retire early.

Not all the people who want a job can get one. There are different types of unemployment with different causes.

1. *Frictional unemployment.* This happens when a worker leaves one job and registers as unemployed while looking for another. Unless the State directs all the workforce, this is almost inevitable. How long people remain unemployed depends on how much unemployment benefit they receive, how many jobs are on offer and whether they have the skills other businesses want.

2. *Seasonal unemployment.* People employed in the tourist, building, and farming industries may be laid off at certain times of the year. Seasonal unemployment is usually highest in the middle of winter and lowest in the middle of summer.

3. *Structural unemployment.* Demand for goods and services decline, so the firms that make them go out of business or reduce their workforce. There is also less demand for that type of skill. This can cause high unemployment in regions of the country that depend on a particular industry.

4. *Technological unemployment.* Changes in technology can lower the demand for certain skills and lower the demand for labour overall. As machinery gets more sophisticated it can do jobs that were once done by people – so fewer people are needed. The same effect is seen when machinery gets more efficient.

5. *Cyclical unemployment.* For reasons no one has yet managed to totally explain, industrialised economies have periods of boom (when there is high demand and high employment) and slump (low demand and low employment). This pattern is known as the **trade cycle**. Figure 20.2 shows the trade cycles of England and Wales since 1800.

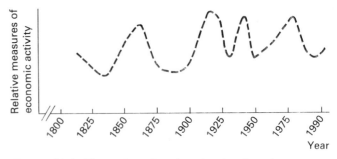

Figure 20.2 *The trade cycles of England and Wales 1800–1989*

6. *Regional unemployment.* Certain parts of the country tend to experience higher unemployment levels than others. The cause can be a combination of seasonal, structural and cyclical unemployment. When this happens over a long period of time the economy of the area becomes depressed, people get disheartened and it becomes less attractive as a place to live. As a result businesses are less inclined to set up in those areas. The map in Figure 20.3 gives the differences in unemployment levels in the United Kingdom.

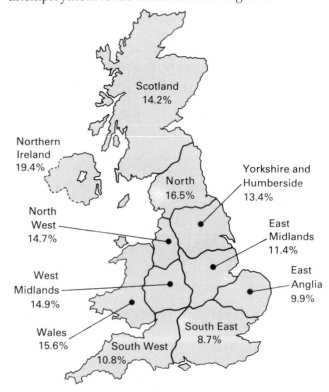

Figure 20.3 *Regional unemployment in the UK*

154

Figure 20.4 *Fred's problem with unemployment*

One person's unemployment can be a combination of some or all these factors. Figure 20.4 outlines the unemployment problem of Fred Webster of Liverpool.

Business and a changing population

1. Changes in the population cause changes in the demand for the products of the business community. A population with a high proportion of people over the age of forty-five will have a different pattern of demand for goods and services than a younger population. The "baby boom" of the 1960s saw the growth of businesses like Mothercare which targetted the baby and toddler market and the needs of the pregnant woman. As this market became less important, Mothercare expanded the range of goods it sold.

When people start to move out of an area, the businesses in that area decline. There is less custom for shops, also businesses are less willing to set up in that region because the labour force is smaller.

A rising population gives businesses an expanding market – provided people have money to spend.

2. Changes in the age structure of the population can also alter the way in which businesses are run. In the early 1990s the number of school leavers looking for jobs will be very low compared with the numbers in the 1980s. Businesses that traditionally recruited large numbers of school leavers are already looking to their recruitment policies. They will have to look at other age groups, for example, and make more effort to persuade women to return to work after maternity leaves. This means changing their advertising, their training programme and possibly the way in which the work is organised.

Figure 20.5 shows some of the ways in which changes in the structure of the population and employment can affect business.

Population change	Some results for business
Increase/decrease in the birthrate	*Change in product mix for businesses producing baby products *Look for new market e.g. export
Increase/decrease in the number of school leavers	*Changes in recruitment policy *Switch to new technology if supply of labour is falling *Offer training, re-training, creches to attract people to work
Increase in the 60+ age group	*Changes in product mix e.g. building firms produce more retirement homes *Increase in services e.g. nursing homes

Figure 20.5 *Business and population change*

JUST TESTING

1. Using Figure 20.4 as a guide, draw a diagram to show the different types of unemployment that make up Fred's problem in finding a job.

2. Give two ways in which a small house building business might be affected if people start to move away from that area.

155

Inflation

The word inflation describes a situation in which the general level of prices is rising. Buyers and sellers are not sure what the price will be in the future. As a result they lose confidence in the value of money and this changes the way in which they behave.

1. People save money for a "rainy day". Inflation means that the amount of money needed to buy goods and services rises, so savings might increase until people think they are large enough to protect them. There is thus less demand for the goods and services being produced. This is more likely to happen if inflation goes hand-in-hand with rising unemployment.

2. When the price of goods and services rises, the standard of living will go down unless incomes also rise. Businesses face demands for higher wages and the threat of industrial action. If this happens in a large number of industries then it will fuel inflation. The businesses will put up the price of their products to try to earn the same profit that they did before.

3. It is not only the price of the final product that will go up. The cost of raw materials and components will also rise. Interest rates will also go up so investment will become more expensive.

4. If the rate of inflation in the United Kingdom rises faster than the rate of inflation in other countries it will make our exports less competitive.

Inflation that goes on for a long period of time can mean a loss of confidence, less investment and a fall in the demand for goods – especially exports. When this happens the economy can start to fail. Unemployment will start to go up so there will be even less demand and less incentive for businesses to invest. This is one of the causes of cyclical unemployment.

JUST TESTING

1. The pound is worth $1.50. As a result of inflation a car that once sold at £3 000 is now sold at £4 500. What difference would this make to its price in the USA?

2. A man earned £100 a week and spent it all on goods and services. Three years later his earnings had risen to £150 per week but the goods and services would now cost him £200. He cannot borrow any money. Give two ways in which this inflation could affect a business.

Economic growth

A growing economy means a growing market for business. People are richer and can afford to buy more. Owners and managers feel more confident so they are more willing to invest – so more jobs are created – the economy grows and so on.

Growth comes from the activities of business and from factors over which they have little or no control.

1. When the level of **investment** rises in a country, the amount of goods and services produced will also rise. Businesses want to grow to increase profits but will not invest if they do not feel confident of getting a good return on their money. Governments also invest by building roads, schools and hospitals among other things and also by making money available to industry.

2. The discovery of a new **technology** can lead to growth. The development of the micro-chip has increased the efficiency of computers, made them cheaper, their use more widespread and changed the way in which goods are produced. It also resulted in a whole range of new products for both consumers and industry.

Not everybody benefits from this type of growth. The skills that industry needs change so it can cause higher unemployment. People feel threatened and try to resist the change by industrial action. Businesses that do not adapt lose their share of the market which can lead to further unemployment.

3. Businesses can increase their profits by improving their own organisation. When the economy is in a down turn and profits are falling, a business will look closely at its costs. When the economy begins to improve the leaner, fitter businesses will be in a position to take advantage of the new state of affairs – provided they have not starved themselves and lack the energy to do so.

The business can become more efficient by:

  * introducing flexible working practices. Instead of people being employed to do just one type of job they will be expected to do a variety of jobs depending on what is needed to keep production going

  * taking over or merging with other businesses to benefit from economies of scale

  * looking closely at the organisation of the business. Improved record keeping and communication, for example, can do a lot to lower costs.

156

4. An improvement in the **resources** of the economy can lead to growth:

    * a healthier, better educated labour force will produce more, using the same equipment, than the same number of people who do not understand what they are doing and lack energy

    * an increase in **raw materials** can stimulate growth. The discovery and exploitation of North Sea oil and gas gave the economy of the United Kingdom a boost in the 1980s.

5. Economies grow when the people in them can and do take advantage of the opportunities offered to them. People who have been made redundant as a result of technological change are more likely to find a new job if they are able to retrain. Owners and managers of businesses must be willing to move their resources into new types of production – and must have the imagination to see it is necessary. It is easy to say this but the process of change is very complicated. The government may have to do a great deal in the way of educating, communicating the need for change and financial support if a complex society is going to take advantage of the opportunities offered to it.

JUST TESTING

Look at Figure 20.6. How can the decisions these people are making lead to economic growth? In each case give two things that could hinder growth.

The balance of payments

The balance of payments is the money that flows into the country from the sale of goods and services to people in other countries and the money invested in this country from abroad minus the amount of money flowing out of the United Kingdom to pay for goods, services and investment from abroad. The statement of the balance of payments is divided into:

    * the **current account** which deals with payments for goods (**visible**), services and other income (**invisibles**)

    * the **capital account** which is concerned with investment.

Like the balance sheet, the balance of payments must always balance. The UK has to pay its debts. The third item, therefore is **official financing**. When we spend more abroad than we earn, the extra is paid for out of the reserves of gold and other currencies held by the government. It is like someone overdrawing on their current bank account and transferring money from their savings account to cover the overdraft. Balance of payments accounts are illustrated in Figure 20.7.

1. When there is more money flowing out of the country than coming in (i.e. a negative balance) the balance of payments is said to be in **deficit**.

2. When the reverse happens the account is in **surplus**.

Figure 20.6 *Decisions and growth*

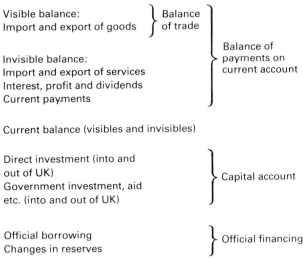

Visible balance:
Import and export of goods } Balance of trade }

Invisible balance:
Import and export of services
Interest, profit and dividends
Current payments } Balance of payments on current account

Current balance (visibles and invisibles)

Direct investment (into and out of UK)
Government investment, aid etc. (into and out of UK) } Capital account

Official borrowing
Changes in reserves } Official financing

Figure 20.7 *Balance of payments accounts*

Some people argue that we should not buy goods and services from abroad that we can produce for ourselves. But this ignores specialisation. If countries specialise in producing the things at which they are most efficient, then prices will be kept down and the consumer will benefit. The argument against this is that low prices come from low costs, at the expense of the workers in some countries who are paid very low wages and have a miserable standard of living.

In the short term, businesses are not greatly affected by whether or not the balance of payments is in surplus or deficit. However, they are affected by the measures governments take to correct any problems. A government running out of reserves and unable to borrow money from abroad will try to stop people buying goods from abroad.

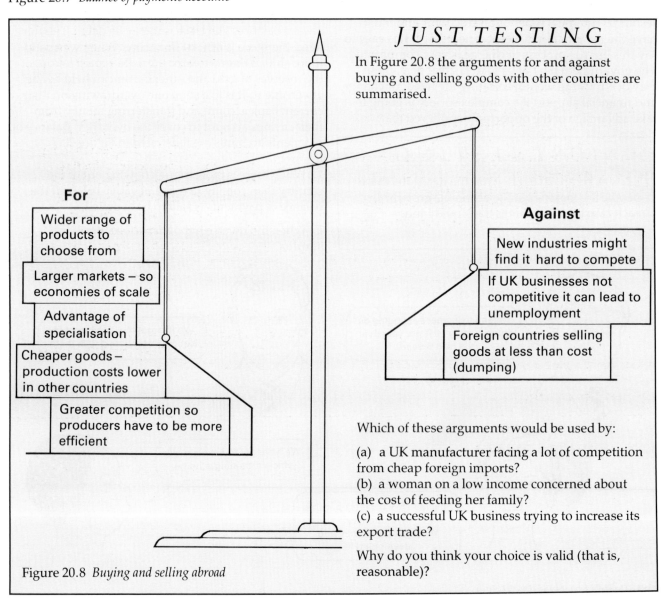

JUST TESTING

In Figure 20.8 the arguments for and against buying and selling goods with other countries are summarised.

For

Wider range of products to choose from

Larger markets – so economies of scale

Advantage of specialisation

Cheaper goods – production costs lower in other countries

Greater competition so producers have to be more efficient

Against

New industries might find it hard to compete

If UK businesses not competitive it can lead to unemployment

Foreign countries selling goods at less than cost (dumping)

Which of these arguments would be used by:

(a) a UK manufacturer facing a lot of competition from cheap foreign imports?
(b) a woman on a low income concerned about the cost of feeding her family?
(c) a successful UK business trying to increase its export trade?

Why do you think your choice is valid (that is, reasonable)?

Figure 20.8 *Buying and selling abroad*

Finding out

(N.B. For the purposes of assignment 1, a **region** is defined as any part of the country you select. It should be large enough to take in several different types of community.)

1. This assignment is an investigation into the population of a region and how it affects local businesses. There is a great deal of research in this exercise so you will probably do better working in groups and reporting your findings as a group presentation.

Task A   Collect all the information you can on the age, sex and distribution of population in a chosen region. Is the population growing or declining? Which are the most popular areas for people to live in? (A survey of house prices in the local newspapers can help with this research.)

Task B   Select three separate areas. The areas should be as different as possible. You might choose an area in which there are a large number of retired people, a large proportion of high income groups, an area in which the population is declining. Survey the local shops in the areas. How does the merchandise differ from area to area?

Task C   Interview the personnel manager of a local business. Does the business have any problems recruiting suitable employees? How do local population and unemployment conditions affect the business?

Task D   Prepare a group presentation on the theme of business and the local community.

2. By the early 1990s there will be fewer school leavers coming onto the labour market. In some areas this will mean that businesses will have to compete for labour.

The following will again work better as a group activity.

Task A   Arrange visits to several businesses that employ school leavers. What problems do they foresee as a result of the fall in the number of school leavers? What plans have they got to deal with the situation?

Task B   As a group, compare the results of your research. How far does the type and size of the businesses influence the way in which they intend to deal with this problem?

Task C   You are the personnel team of a manufacturing business that normally recruits twelve school leavers each year for technical and clerical training. You have had no problems finding recruits in the past, even though the pay you offer is not high compared with other businesses in the area. Draw up a recruitment package designed to attract applicants to your business. You should include pay, conditions of work, training and promotion opportunities in your report.

Task D   Comment on the ways in which changes in the structure of population can affect business.

Trying it out

1. Happidays is a private limited company designing and manufacturing gadgets for the house and garden. The product range includes garden tools for people with handicaps or reduced mobility. This range was initiated by the managing director whose wife, despite suffering from arthritis, is a keen gardener. In 1989 the managing director presented the figures shown in Figure 20.9 to his marketing and production managers. His only comment was "Interesting. We must do something about this."

(a) Draw a graph to show the changes in the age structure of the population over the period given in Figure 20.9.

(b) Give two reasons why the managing director thought that this data was of interest in planning the future of the range of garden tools.

Size of population (millions)		Birth rate (no. of births per 1000 population)		Death rate (no. of deaths per 1000 population)	
1961	52	1961	17	1961	12
1971	55	1971	15	1971	12
1981	57	1981	14	1981	11
1991	57*	1991	12*	1991	11*
2001	57*	2001	10*	2001	10*
2011	58*	2011	10*	2011	10*

Population by age (1900s)

	1961	1971	1981	1991*	2001*	2011*
Under 15	23%	24%	23%	22%	21%	20%
15 - 64	65%	62%	62%	61%	60%	59%
Over 65	12%	14%	15%	17%	19%	21%

* means estimated

Figure 20.9 *Population projections*

(c) Explain how the personnel department could be affected by changes in the population structure.

2. Sam Imraim is the managing director of a high technology business which designs and builds equipment for the manufacturing industry. Forty-five per cent of the firm's output is exported, its main market being the United States. The average market price of each piece of equipment is £80 000. Imraim's receives £65 000 of this after expenses have been paid.

(a) Explain how each of the following could affect the sales of the business.

(i) The value of the pound rises against the dollar.
(ii) A report that the American economy is expected to boom in the coming year.
(iii) A lowering of the rate of inflation in the UK economy.

(b) Imraim's is located in an area of high unemployment yet still finds it difficult to recruit labour with the required skills. Give two reasons for this difficulty.

UNIT 21:
GOVERNMENTS AND BUSINESS

Like business, governments have objectives. Some of the things a government wants to do will concern social issues:

* to give everybody a fair share in the wealth of the country

* to improve law and order

* to make sure the environment is clean and safe – in other words, to limit pollution

* to make sure everybody has adequate housing.

The possible list of social goals for a government is endless. Governments, like businesses, only have a certain amount of resources so they have to decide which goals shall have priority. Whatever decision the government makes will affect business. In Figure 21.1 the government has decided to increase the money given to local authorities to build council houses.

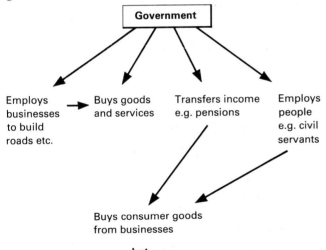

Too much government spending can lead to shortages of labour, materials and capital. Prices can start to rise so there is inflation.

Figure 21.1 *How government spending affects business*

Governments also have economic goals. The main ones are:

* to keep unemployment low

* to control inflation

* to improve the standard of living

* to sell enough exports to pay for our imports.

None of these goals is easy to reach. For example, trying to keep unemployment low and improving the standard of living can lead to inflation and more imports than exports.

British business is not only affected by the legislation of Parliament. It is also influenced by the agreements the government enters into with other governments to regulate trade. Figure 21.2 outlines the hierarchy of government.

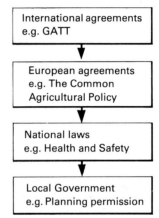

Figure 21.2 *The hierarchy of government*

JUST TESTING

The government has decided to put more money into the National Health Service (NHS). As a result the NHS is planning to build a large new hospital on a derelict site in a city. Using Figure 21.1 to help you, work out how local business would benefit – or suffer – from this decision.

The European Community (EC)

The European Community (also known as the European Economic Community or the Common Market) was founded by the Treaty of Rome in 1957. There were six founder members: France, Belgium, West Germany, Italy, the Netherlands and Luxembourg. Since 1957 the United Kingdom, Eire, Denmark, Greece, Spain and Portugal have joined.

The EC has two major objectives:

* the creation of a united Europe that would be so interdependent that there would be no future wars

* the creation of a single market for all goods and services. This would mean that European businesses would enjoy the same economies of scale as their competitors in America and Japan.

Setting up a common market was not simply a matter of removing the import duties between different countries. To make competition fair, the member countries have had to adapt the same safety standards, laws governing employment and make sure that their policies relating to competition between businesses were in line with each other. To do this the EC has developed common policies.

1. The *Common Agricultural Policy* (CAP). This supports farmers by setting **target prices** for some crops and setting **quotas** (the amount each country can produce of these crops). If the price the farmer can get on the market is less than the target price the EC makes up the difference. This payment to the farmers is called a **subsidy**. The EC also gives grants to farmers to improve their output.

2. *Regional Policy.* There is a very wide variation in wealth, not only between the countries of the EC but also between different parts of the same country. The regional policy distributes grants and aid to try to remove these inequalities.

3. The *European Social Fund* (ESF). This gives grants to bring the welfare system of each country in line with the others. For example, it offers funding to improve the vocational education of 16–19 year olds.

4. *Competition Policy.* This makes sure that competition is fair. It restricts such things as price fixing and the ability of national governments to keep businesses from other countries competing in their home markets.

The progress of the EC towards its objectives has been slow with many prolonged arguments over policy. 1992 is the year when completely free markets, not only in goods and services but also in labour, will operate.

JUST TESTING

The photographs in Figure 21.3 are of different parts of the EC.

Figure 21.3 *Standards of living in the EC*

What EC policies could help in each case? Give two ways in which local business might be affected. Explain your answer.

International agreements

The improvement in communications in the last fifty years have made it increasingly difficult for national governments to work on their own in managing their economies. This is because money can be shifted so rapidly from one country to another and in such large amounts that it can work against government policy. Countries trade together so much that a slump in the economy of one country will lead to a fall in demand in other countries and a rise in unemployment.

Governments work together through international organisations to improve world trade and to try to reduce the effects of changes in the world economy.

1. The *General Agreement on Tariffs and Trade* (GATT). This tries to increase world trade by lowering tariffs on goods and reducing the amount of subsidies that national governments give to their own businesses. For example, it is against the agreement for a business to sell goods in a foreign country for less than the cost of producing them (**dumping**). The United States protested strongly about the subsidies given to the European steel industry by the EC.

2. The *Organisation for Economic Co-operation and Development*. This has as members the developed countries of the world. Agreements cover a wide range of topics which are important to the development of a prosperous world economy.

JUST TESTING

Figure 21.4 gives information on the ways in which agriculture is protected in different countries.

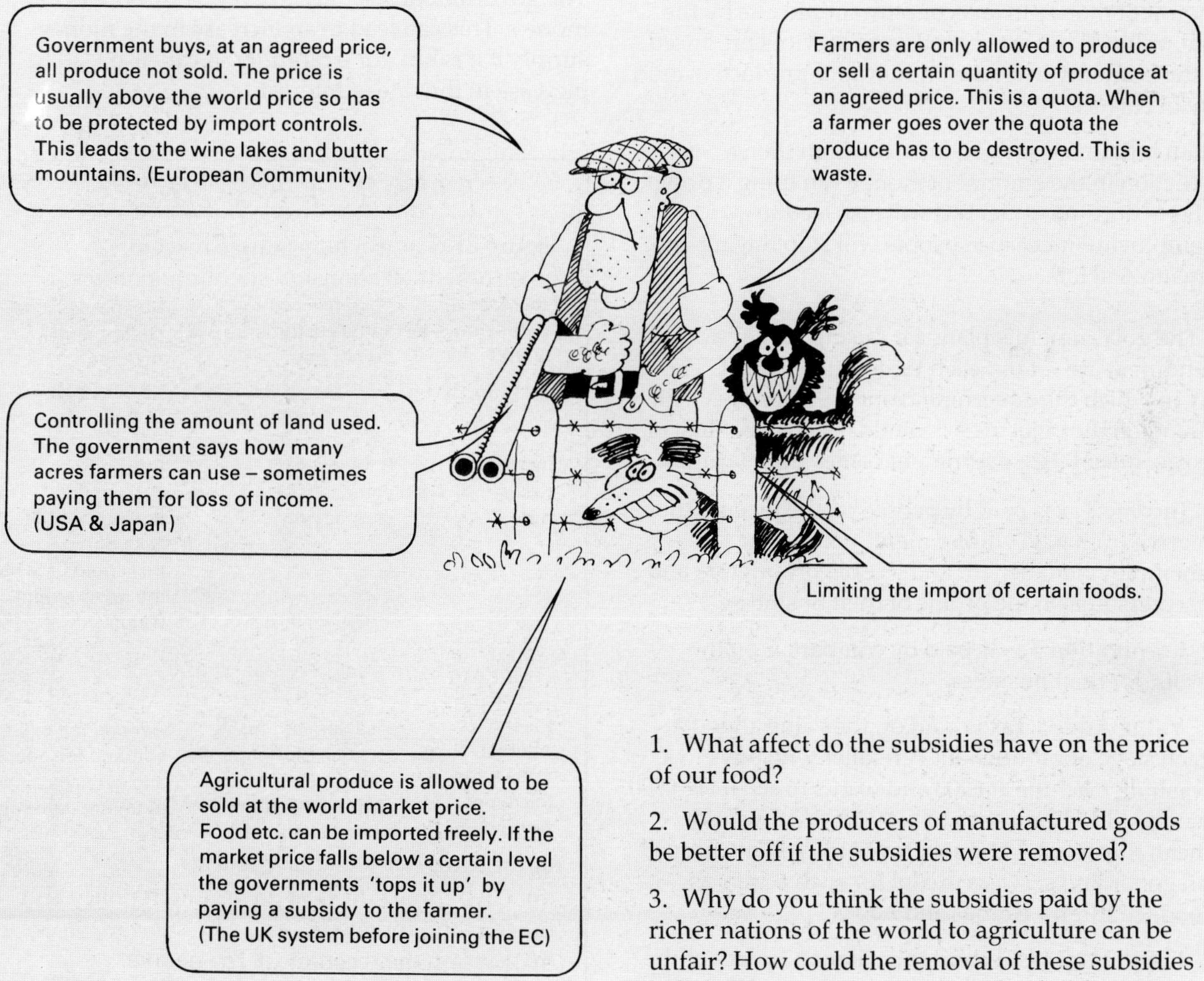

Government buys, at an agreed price, all produce not sold. The price is usually above the world price so has to be protected by import controls. This leads to the wine lakes and butter mountains. (European Community)

Farmers are only allowed to produce or sell a certain quantity of produce at an agreed price. This is a quota. When a farmer goes over the quota the produce has to be destroyed. This is waste.

Controlling the amount of land used. The government says how many acres farmers can use – sometimes paying them for loss of income. (USA & Japan)

Limiting the import of certain foods.

Agricultural produce is allowed to be sold at the world market price. Food etc. can be imported freely. If the market price falls below a certain level the governments 'tops it up' by paying a subsidy to the farmer. (The UK system before joining the EC)

1. What affect do the subsidies have on the price of our food?

2. Would the producers of manufactured goods be better off if the subsidies were removed?

3. Why do you think the subsidies paid by the richer nations of the world to agriculture can be unfair? How could the removal of these subsidies help businesses who export to the developing economies?

Figure 21.4 *Protecting agriculture*

Managing the economy

Governments manage the economy to achieve their objectives. They can do this by:

* controlling the amount of money in the economy

* changing how they raise and spend money

* controlling how people behave by law.

1. Controlling the money supply (**monetary policy**) reduces or expands the amount of money circulating in the economy. Because banks and building societies play an important part in making money available to people the government controls the amount of money they can lend and the rate of interest that is charged.

If there is too much money in an economy then this will lead to inflation. Prices will rise because there is too much money chasing too few goods. Ideally the amount of money in an economy should rise by the same value as the extra goods and services produced by the economy in a year. Money and products would stay in balance.

When inflation is judged to be too high then a restriction in the amount of money can bring it down. If this is done too quickly it will also lead to unemployment because people will stop buying and demand will fall.

2. The government's plans for raising money and spending it are set out each year in the **Budget**. The way in which the government spends its money will depend on the objectives it wants to achieve. Most of the revenue of the government comes from taxation.

* **Income Tax** is paid by people on the income they receive from paid employment, pension or unemployment benefit and by sole proprietors and partnerships on the profits of their business.

* **Corporation Tax** is paid by companies on the profits of their business.

* **Value Added Tax** is paid on the value added at each stage of production. A retailer who buys in a washing machine at £200 and wants to sell it for £300 has an added value of £100. A 15% VAT would mean that it would be sold for £315. VAT is charged on goods and services except for such things as food, children's clothes and books.

* **Capital Gains Tax** and **Inheritance Tax** cover the transfer of capital from one person to another (for example by gifts or inheritance) and the profit made by the sale of assets.

* some goods pay **Excise Duty** as well as VAT. These goods include petrol, alcohol and tobacco.

* **Customs Duties** are taxes on imported goods. They used to be more important than they are now.

* **National Insurance Contributions** are not called taxes but as every employed person has to pay them and every employer has to pay contributions for each employee then they act as a tax. By increasing the cost of employment they can reduce the willingness of employers to increase the workforce and to rely on overtime instead.

Taxes which are levied directly onto people or businesses are called **direct** taxes. Taxes which are levied on goods (e.g. VAT) are called **indirect** taxes. Direct taxes are collected by the **Department of Inland Revenue** and indirect taxes by the **Department of Customs and Excise**.

The government also raises revenue by borrowing money. This can lead to an increase in the money supply if it is not done carefully. It can also lead to an increase in the rate of interest.

JUST TESTING

Figure 21.5 shows how people react to government taxation and spending policies.

Increase or extension of VAT →	Price rises so some customers do not buy →	Businesses lose custom and revenue
Increase in excise duty →	Price rises so some customers stop buying →	Businesses lose custom and revenue – in the case of tobacco this could be what the government wants
Rise in interest rates adds to cost of borrowing →	Less demand for cars etc. Mortgage rates go up so people have less money to spend →	General fall in demand for goods and services – risk of unemployment

Figure 21.5 *People and governments*

(a) Give three effects of government policy and the demand for goods.

(b) Explain the reactions of the people.

(c) Which of the taxes mentioned are direct taxes and which are indirect?

3. Direct controls are used by the government when the problems in the economy do not respond to monetary or budget controls. In the past controls have been imposed on:

* the rent people pay for accommodation

* the percentage rate by which prices can rise

* the percentage rate by which incomes can rise

* the purposes for which people can borrow money

* the maximum length of time allowed to pay back a loan.

Local authorities

The social and economic objectives of local government are the same as those of central government, but the priorities can differ. Central government can see the reduction of inflation as its major priority while some local authorities would see a reduction in unemployment and improving the standards of housing in the area as more important. In this case the central government would want a reduction in spending while the local authority would try to increase spending.

Local authorities get their revenue from grants from central government, the community charge and money earned by the provision of services, for example, the admission to a leisure centre. The community charge is a fixed amount per person and is sometimes referred to as the poll tax. It was introduced in 1990 replacing rates, a property tax.

Many of the services the local authorities have to provide are laid down by law, for example education and refuse collection. It was realised that many local authorities would not be able to afford these and so the system of rate support grants was introduced.

Costs and benefits

The activities of business, central and local government, and other organisations bring benefits to the community but they can also lower the quality of life. Pollution is an example of this. The people living close to certain types of factory have to put up with increased traffic, noise, dirt and smells. With some industrial processes there is the danger of lethal chemical gases leaking into the atmosphere. The dangers of the nuclear industry are still the subject of heated argument.

The factories make goods that are in demand but without some sort of government control their costs of production would not cover the true costs to the country and the local community. Legal controls usually take the form of stating the maximum amount of emissions (smoke, gases, waste) a factory is allowed, with fines for businesses that exceed the limit. Local authorities also control the nuisance to householders by refusing permission to carry on businesses in areas where they might prove unpleasant.

The Department of the Environment acts as a court of appeal when major works are about to be undertaken and the local community – or a portion of it – objects. The arguments in this case centre on the costs to the local community and the benefits it will get from the development. Figure 21.6 lists some of the costs and benefits to a community of the development of a shopping mall.

Costs	Benefits
Dirt and traffic disruption during building	More income for local authority from community charge
Takes trade away from high street shops	Higher proportion of outsiders so transport improves
Increases traffic by attracting people from outside the town	More employment in pleasant conditions
Competition for labour pushes wages up so increases costs for small shops	Wider choice of goods and services
Best assistants employed in the Mall	Branches of national businesses move in

Figure 21.6 *Costs and benefits of a shopping mall*

JUST TESTING

1. Why do local authorities need government grants to help cover their spending?

2. Why is it necessary that local authorities and central government keep control of some aspects of business planning?

Finding out

1. The diagram in Figure 21.7 is taken from the Economic Progress report November – December 1986.

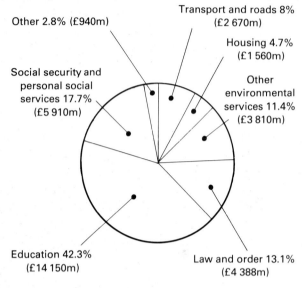

Local authority expenditure
Net, England and Wales 1986-87

Other 2.8% (£940m)

Transport and roads 8% (£2 670m)

Housing 4.7% (£1 560m)

Social security and personal social services 17.7% (£5 910m)

Other environmental services 11.4% (£3 810m)

Education 42.3% (£14 150m)

Law and order 13.1% (£4 388m)

Total spending £33.4 billion

Figure 21.7 *Local authority expenditure (England and Wales 1986–1987)*

Task A From your local authority, research the ways in which it allocated its finances from 1986 to the present date. Find out as much as you can about the reasons for the pattern of expenditure in your authority.

Task B Construct a pie chart to compare the spending of your local authority with the total for England and Wales. In terms of its size does your authority spend more or less per head than the average?

Task C Prepare a survey of local householders. From an analysis of your survey compare the priorities of the householders with the priorities of the Council. What similarities and differences are there?

Task D Explain why the spending of your local authority is:

* similar to

* different from the information given in Figure 21.7.

2. An investigation into the way in which the EC affects your local community.

Task A Find out as much as you can about EC policies and which are of use to your local community. The local authority will be able to help you here.

Task B Choose one of the policies. How useful is it to local business? What advantages is the local community getting from it?

Task C Prepare a presentation to convince local business of the value of the EC to their business. What prejudices will you have to overcome? What problems does business in your area experience as a result of the UK membership of the EC?

Task D As a result of your research do you think local business is prepared for 1992? Does it need to do more?

Trying it out

1. Figure 21.8 shows before, during, and after pictures of a town centre that has been redeveloped.

Figure 21.8 *Town centre redevelopment*

(a) Make a list of all the costs you can see in the photographs to:

   (i) traders
   (ii) customers
   (iii) the construction company.

(b) Look at the "after" photograph again. What benefits has the new development brought to the existing businesses?

(c) Give three reasons why you would be more willing to shop there.

2. Given below are some of the measures taken by the government since 1979 to improve the UK's economic performance:

* changes in the tax system. The top rate of income tax has been reduced from 83% to 40%. The standard rate of tax has been reduced from 33% to 25%

* tax relief was given on profit related pay schemes. Under these schemes part of the employees pay is based on the profits of the business

* the Enterprise Allowance Scheme which pays unemployed people £40 a week for a year while they work to start a business

* changed the system of national insurance contributions for lower paid workers. This resulted in lower contributions by both employers and employees

* instigated changes in education and training to give school pupils more chance to get to know about different jobs and to develop the necessary skills, to retrain the long term unemployed and to give skilled people a chance to update their skills

* small businesses have received relief on VAT and the small companies' rate of corporation tax has been reduced.

(a) What are:

* income tax?

* VAT?

* corporation tax?

* national insurance contributions?

(b) Which of the taxes mentioned above are direct taxes and which are indirect taxes?

(c) Explain briefly how the reduction in the level of national insurance contributions can help reduce unemployment.

(d) Reduction in income tax is said to give people the incentive to work harder. Explain how this can happen.

(e) Give two ways in which the improvements in education and training will:

(i) reduce the costs of business.
(ii) help businesses increase output.

(f) All the measures given above are likely to increase the total demand in the economy for goods and services. Give one way in which this can benefit British industry and one way in which it might cause problems for the economy.

3. Hutton Publications Ltd is a small firm of publishers specialising in books with a rural theme. Before the 1988 budget they were concerned that the Chancellor might introduce VAT on books.

(a) (i) What does VAT stand for?
(ii) Why are Hutton publications concerned about the introduction of VAT?

(b) Hutton Publications sell many of their books to shops catering for tourists. Explain why this could make it easier for them to pass on the VAT in higher prices.

(c) Hutton Publications launch a campaign in the district to persuade people to sign a petition against the introduction of VAT on books. List and give reasons for three arguments it could use to persuade people that VAT on books is not a good thing.

APPENDIX A: EXTENDED CASE STUDIES

Case study A: Glamourous Garments Limited

Joan Millwood is a director and majority shareholder of Glamourous Garments Limited. The extracts given below are the answers she gave to a group of business studies students studying the growth and organisation of her business.

"I was made redundant as a machinist in 1984. A friend in the trade suggested I start my own business and promised me work so I took the chance. There were six of us when we started, myself and five machinists. We produced 1 500 garments a week at first. I worked on the machines with the others and did the paperwork in the evening. Now, in 1989, we are producing 8 000 garments each week employing 20 machinists."

1. What is the percentage increase in output between 1984 and 1989?

2. Explain why the promise of work might have persuaded Joan to start her own business.

"It had to be a limited company. I could not take the risk of anything else. My bank provided a loan and an overdraft to see us through until the payment for the first orders started coming in. Friends lent me machines to get started. I still haven't taken any money out of the business. I don't expect to for another two years."

3. What does the word "limited" indicate in the name of the business?

4. Explain how Joan raised the starting capital for her business.

5. How has Joan financed the growth of Glamourous Garments? Give the advantages of this method of financing growth.

"These premises may not be much to look at but they are cheap and central. I don't have to worry about collecting supplies or delivering the finished goods – my customers do that – but I do have to be convenient for the people who work for me. Most of them have families to take into account and not many of them have cars."

6. Joan says her premises are cheap. List the costs she would take into account when making that decision.

7. As a machinist offered employment by Joan, give three factors you would consider when deciding whether or not the job was convenient for you.

"The customer decides on the design, materials and colour and supplies me with everything that is necessary. I provide thread and some trimmings. I work on how intricate the design is – the more complicated the design, the longer it takes to make and the higher the cost."

For each garment, Joan calculates the cost of cutting, making up, packing, thread, overheads, holidays and profit (calculated as a mark up of costs).

8. What costs will Joan include in her overheads?

9. If the total cost of making the garment is £30 and Joan wants a profit of 25%, what price would she quote her customer? Show your workings.

"Much of my business comes from recommendation. Word gets round that I do a good job and the business comes to me. I am very careful over quality control, which is why I get annoyed when given cheap material to work with. It does not matter how good your seams are, shoddy material still will not take hard wear."

10. Much of Joan's business depends on reputation. How will this affect her marketing organisation?

"All the machinists are paid by piece rate, it's normal in this business and a good machinist can make a lot of money."

11. Explain the advantages and disadvantages of paying by piece rate to:

(i) Joan   (ii) the machinists.

"I employ 20 machinists, a cutter and two pressers. I do all the administrative work, organise the production and the marketing. I check the quality control with the help of the pressers and the cutter."

12. From the information given above draw an organisation chart for Glamourous Garments Limited. Explain how the organisation chart for a larger business dealing with major clothes retailing chains would differ from this. Give reasons for your answer.

Case study B: Highway Stores

Highway Stores is a small general store, newsagent and tobacconist sited on a busy main road. Approximately 30% of its customers are local people, that is they live within five minutes walk of the shop. The rest of its trade comes from passing customers – people on their way to work or who have made the journey to the post office next door. There is a large hospital and several medium sized factories within easy walking distance. There are three supermarkets, all of which sell more cheaply than the Stores, within fifteen minutes walking distance.

1. What advantages does its site offer to Highway Stores?

2. Suggest three reasons why people might be prepared to use Highway Stores for at least some of their purchases rather than the supermarkets.

In March 1987 Highway Stores was bought by Sharon and Peter Bush who owned it in partnership. The people they bought it from provided a set of audited accounts from which Sharon and Peter extracted the following information.

Turnover		£
1986	April	4 000
	May	4 500
	June	4 000
	July	3 500
	August	3 000
	September	3 250
	October	3 750
	November	4 200
	December	5 000
1987	January	3 000
	February	3 750
	March	4 000

3. Explain what is meant by:

(i) turnover
(ii) audited accounts.

4. Suggest two reasons why the turnover of the Highway Stores varied at different times of the year.

5. What other information would Sharon and Peter need before they could calculate their net profit after tax?

The Highway Stores was in urgent need of redecoration when the Bushes took over. They invested £2 000 in painting and additional fixtures and fittings. In March 1988 annual turnover had increased to £65 000.

6. What is the percentage increase in annual turnover between the year ending March 1987 and the year ending March 1988?

Business continues to expand and Sharon and Peter decide they need to extend the shop premises. They can either incorporate part of their living accommodation into the shop or extend into some unused land at the side of the shop. They apply for planning permission to expand onto the unused land. While their planning application was going through the Bushes were informed that the Council intended to remove a zebra crossing on the road. This would mean that people living on the large housing estate on the far side of the road would find it more difficult and dangerous to cross.

7. Why is planning permission necessary?

8. Why do you think Sharon and Peter protested to the Council over the removal of the crossing?

Planning permission is given for the extension and Sharon inserts an advertisement in the local newspaper for a full time sales assistant.

9. Write a job description for the post of sales assistant.

10. Draw up an advertisement for the post of sales assistant and explain why you have included each item in it.

11. Give three other methods of recruitment Sharon could have used. Explain the advantages and disadvantages of each one.

Case study C: Transluglass PLC

In 1965 U. Brake set up in business as a **sole trader** supplying replacement windows. His starting capital was £500.

By 1974 Mr Brake had begun to see the potential of the market in double glazing. He took his son into the business as a partner and shortly after the business was registered as a **private limited company** under the name Transluglass Ltd.

During the 1970s and early 1980s the business grew steadily, although a lack of funds hindered any major expansion. In 1983 Mrs Brake suggested that they should move into the market for interior decoration. She argued that the area they lived in was expanding rapidly with two developments of private houses being built and a further four planned. Nobody buying a new house would be interested in double glazing but they would be interested in the interior of the house. There were premises in the centre of the town that were ideal for a showroom.

Mr Brake and his son were uninterested at first. The existing business brought them a good living and the risks involved in expansion seemed too high. Mrs Brake was determined. She felt that she would have a part to play in the newly expanded business. Mrs Brake conducted some market research of her own and presented the following information to her husband and son (Figure 22.1).

Sales revenue		£50 000
Cost of sales	£30 000	
Other variable costs	£5 000	
Contribution to fixed cost		£15 000
Fixed costs		£2 000
Profit		£13 000

Figure 22.1 *Budget for expansion of Transluglass Ltd*

The expansion went ahead. Figure 22.2 compares the profit and loss accounts of Transluglass before and after.

In 1988 Transluglass went public. About this time Mr Brake suggested restructuring the business. The products related to interior design were becoming more and more divorced from the double glazing division. He felt the specialist skills required were totally different.

	1983	1984	1983	1984
Sales revenue			£200 000	£260 000
Less: Cost of sales			£130 000	£140 000
Gross profit			£70 000	£128 000
Less overheads:				
Heating/lighting	£2 000	£3 500		
Rent and rates	£3 000	£10 000		
Wages/salaries	£20 000	£30 000		
Advertising	£5 000	£20 000		
Administration	£5 000	£7 000		
Net profit			£35 000	£49 500
Net profit after tax			£26 250	£37 125

Figure 22.2 *Transluglass' profit and loss accounts 1983 and 1984*

1. The following terms are mentioned in the case study. What do they mean?

   (a) sole trader
   (b) private limited company.

2. Give two reasons for the growth of Transluglass.

3. (a) When Mr Brake started his business he used £500 of his savings. If he had needed more money where could he have gone for help?
   (b) When Mr Brake's son joined him in the business they drew up a Deed of Partnership. What is a deed of partnership?
   (c) Suggest two advantages of becoming a private limited company rather than staying a partnership.

4. (a) Explain two reasons why expansion into interior design seemed a good idea to Mrs Brake.
   (b) Explain one reason why Mr Brake and his son might have been hesitant about the expansion.

5. (a) Calculate the ratio of gross profit to sales.
   (b) Calculate the ratio of net profit to sales.
   (c) What do these ratios tell you about how well the business is doing?

6. Mrs Brake did some research to find out whether or not there was a market for the interior design side of the business. Write a report outlining the stages of her research. Indicate the problems she might have met in carrying it out.

7. Explain why a showroom in the centre of the town would be useful for the new business.

8. State and explain three advantages to Transluglass of Mr Brake's proposed restructuring of the company.

Case study D: Maslin (electronics) PLC

The managing director of Maslin (electronics) PLC was not in a good mood. He had just received a report from his personnel manager that suggested the company was experiencing problems. In a meeting with the personnel manager he discussed the information given in Figure 22.3.

Staff Turnover

Department	Total number employed	Left and replaced
Research and Development	200	5
Personnel	30	1
Office	50	5
Finance	20	1
Assembly	1500	200
Maintenance	50	5
Sales	100	15

Number of days lost through absenteeism per department during the year

Research and development	100
Personnel	30
Office	200
Finance	5
Assembly	3000
Maintenance	25
Sales	100

Figure 22.3 *Personnel information for Maslin (electronics) PLC*

The meeting ended with the managing director stating his displeasure in no uncertain terms.

"These figures cover the last three years, yet this is the first time they have been brought to my notice. This is not the first time important information has been kept from me and it hardly inspires me with confidence in the ability of my management team. We need some thorough research into the problems of this company. Have an outline of the approach you intend to take on my desk by Monday."

1. (a) Calculate the ratio of the number of working days lost per employee for each of the three years.
   (b) State and explain three possible reasons for the changes you have noticed.

2. The personnel manager is particularly concerned about the figures relating to labour turnover.
   (a) Explain briefly why these are a cause for concern.
   (b) State and explain three problems the business might experience as a result of this pattern of labour turnover.

3. The personnel manager decides that recruitment, selection and training procedures will have to be examined very carefully if the business is going to alter its rate of labour turnover.

Explain briefly how each one of the above can affect labour turnover.

Over lunch the personnel manager was complaining about his boss's attitude.

"I've given him those figures every year for the past five years. The first year he read them, I doubt whether he has even glanced at them since. The trouble is he wants to make all the decisions and he does not thank anyone for taking the initiative and trying to solve problems when they arise. When things go wrong though its always our fault – never his."

4. (a) What is the managing director's style of leadership?
   (b) The managing director is not delegating to his senior management team.
   (i) What is meant by the term delegation?
   (ii) State and explain three reasons why the managing director might be reluctant to delegate.

5. The personnel manager suspects that poor communications could be a contributing cause to the problems of the business.
   (a) List four things that are necessary for good communications.
   (b) Give two examples of methods of communication used in a business.
   (c) State and explain three problems, other than the ones illustrated in Figure 22.3, that could be caused by poor communications.

6. Describe the stages the personnel manager would go through in designing a survey on the problems of Maslin (electronics) PLC.

Case study E: Carstairs PLC

Carstairs PLC is a **subsidiary** of a **multinational** company manufacturing chemical products. Its principal plant is sited near the centre of a large industrial town which suffers from a high level of unemployment.

The company has the reputation of being an excellent employer in terms of pay, working conditions and health and safety. A big attraction of working for the business is its sports and recreational facilities which are far better than those provided by the local authority.

Since 1985 the company has undertaken a major investment programme, introducing the latest technology into the plant. This has led to a slimming down of the workforce. Carstairs PLC has tried to achieve this through early retirement and **voluntary redundancy**. Aware of the impact this would have on the employment prospects of the town, Carstairs PLC has entered into a partnership with the local authority to create a **development agency**. Funds of £3 million a year are available for investment in businesses that promise rapid growth in employment prospects. Most of the businesses that benefitted from this in the first two years of its life were in the **tertiary sector**.

In the Spring of 1987 there was a leak of poisonous gas from one of the production processes. Several employees were taken to hospital. Fortunately none of the people living near the plant suffered – apart from the fright the major police, fire and ambulance operations gave them. This was the first incident involving a leaking of chemicals that Carstairs had suffered in forty years.

1. (a) What do the following terms mean?

   (i) subsidiary
   (ii) multinational
   (iii) voluntary redundancy
   (iv) development agency
   (v) tertiary sector.

   (b) Of which sector of the economy is Carstairs PLC a part?

2. (a) State and explain three reasons why the company achieved the slimming down of its labour force by voluntary redundancy.

   (b) Why are only those businesses with prospects for rapid growth of employment receiving grants from the development agency?

3. The introduction of new technology into a business can cause problems. Give two problems Carstairs PLC might experience in each of the following areas:

   (a) recruitment
   (b) training
   (c) maintenance.

As a result of the leak of poisonous gas the people living near the plant became very concerned about the health and safety standards of the company. In 1988 Carstairs PLC applied for planning permission to build an extension to the plant. A local pressure group was set up to oppose this. The town was divided between the people who were concerned about pollution and the people who were concerned about jobs.

4. (a) What is a pressure group?
   (b) List four ways in which a pressure group might attempt to achieve its aims.

5. Pollution is an **external cost** of a business. What is an external cost?

6. Carstairs PLC is a good employer. From the evidence in the passage explain two ways in which the company tried to motivate its workforce. Would these methods be successful?

APPENDIX B: SUGGESTIONS FOR COURSEWORK

Assignment A

Investigation of the production function of a business.

1. Identification of the type of product and the size of its market.

2. Reasons for locating the business in that area.

3. Description of the different types of technology used and for what purpose.

4. Plan and explanation of the production lay-out with work flow, storage areas marked.

5. Production method(s) used, reasons related to markets.

6. Sources of supply of materials, components. Problems associated with supply.

7. Quality control, importance, who does it?

8. Different labour skills employed. Job specifications, training.

9. Organisation chart of the production department.

Assignment B

Promotion of the local area as a tourist centre.

1. The resources, attractions and facilities offered in the area to tourists.

2. Organisations that exist to promote tourism, e.g. tourist boards, work of the local authority. Internal organisation and funding of at least one such organisation.

3. Problems associated with tourism as a major activity in an area, e.g. seasonal employment.

4. Education and training needs of the tourist industry. How are they being met in the area?

5. Identification of the market. Age, sex, income, interests. Draw up a consumer profile.

6. Visit to business involved in the tourist trade, e.g. hotel, theme park.

7. Social costs involved in tourism, e.g. summer overcrowding.

8. Identification of lack of provision. What needs to be done?

9. Draw up a week's activities for identified consumer.

Assignment C

Introducing information technology into a small business.

1. Identification of the needs of the business.

2. What are the available resources of the business, including finance, IT skills, etc?

3. Investigation into the hardware and software available on the market.

4. Comparison of needs and resources of the business and the available equipment.

5. Selection of most suitable equipment with reasons for selection.

6. IT and the organisation of the work space. What changes should be made and why? How will IT improve the working environment?

7. Health and Safety regulations, conditions of work.

8. Monitoring the change. What problems occurred and why.

Assignment D

Devising a promotion campaign for an organisation.

1. Analysis of the product. What are its most important features?

2. Analysis of market. Which groups of people do you need to communicate with and why?

3. Design, organise and implement a market research exercise. What have the findings told you about people's needs? What aspects of your product do you need to emphasise to each group.

4. How are you going to get your message across? What promotional and advertising methods can you use for each group? How will they differ?

5. What finance is available? How can you raise it?

6. Devise and cost a campaign using as many different promotional techniques as possible.

7. How will you account for the finance used?

8. How can you judge the success of your campaign? Increased customers? Increased awareness of the organisation? Does the success justify the money spent?

Assignment E

Present a report on the effect on business of media publicity concerning food contamination.

1. Collect information on the following:

  * medical background. What the contamination is, how does it happen and the possible effects

  * how serious is the problem? Do many people die as a result of the infection?

  * relevant legislation, e.g. Health and Safety

  * items from the media relating to the contamination.

2. Analyse the articles, news items you have collected. What approach do they take to the contamination? Is it sensational? Who do they blame and why?

3. What organisation presents the producers' case? What arguments do they use? What methods do they use to get their case across? How successful do you think they are and why?

4. Conduct a survey among consumers. Has the publicity changed their attitudes and buying patterns as far as food is concerned? What do they think of the media publicity?

5. What other groups have become involved with the issue? Central government? Consumer groups? Trading standards officers? What is the reaction of each group? Does the evidence suggest that a change in the law is needed?

6. Will the decision affect the foreign trade of the UK? For example, restrictions on imports of certain types of food may lead to retaliation against British exports by the countries affected.

7. As a result of your investigation give your opinion about the effectiveness of present legislation and control. How could it be improved? What problems could result?

Assignment F

Angela is in the sixth form of a comprehensive school following the CPVE course. She works each weekend and most of her holidays in a small hairdressing salon, and has built up a number of basic skills in hairdressing. Angela has already applied for a BTEC course in hairdressing at her local technical college. Her ambition is to start her own mobile hairdressing business.

  Assume that Angela's business will be set up in your town or city.

1. Is there likely to be a demand for a mobile hairdresser in the area? What people are likely to use the service? What proportion of the population are they?

2. What equipment will Angela need? List the equipment with the costs.

3. How much money will Angela need to provide materials and pay expenses for the first three months in the life of her business?

4. Using the totals of 2 and 3, work out the amount of money Angela will need to start her business and the possible sources of capital open to her.

5. Draw up a list of all the qualities that an employer might think desirable in an employee. Which of these do you think essential for Angela to possess to run her own business. Give reasons for your answer.

6.   Draw up a price list for the services Angela will offer. How long will it be before she breaks even?

7. What organisations could help Angela in setting up her own business? What services do they offer?

8. Arrange a visit to a bank manager to assess the work you have done so far. Include the manager's suggestions in your final report on your investigation.

Assignment G

An investigation into the effects of legislation on trade union activity.

1. Collect information on trade union legislation since 1979. What main areas of trade union activity does it affect?

2. Arrange visits to two/three trade unions. What effects has the legislation had on their organisation, finances, membership and the ability of the unions to represent the interests of their members?

3. What changes have taken place in trade union membership since 1979? How far can these changes be explained by the changes in the legislation? What other factors might have caused these changes?

4. Collect information on a number of industrial disputes in which trade unions are involved. Make a careful note of the ways in which the law has limited their power. What weapons were used against them?

5. Survey a number of members of trade unions. What is their attitude to unions and trade union legislation? In what ways has the legislation worked in their favour? What limits on trade union power would they like to see introduced? What extra freedoms would they like trade unions to possess?

6. What is the trade union history of your area, for example, has it always been a trade union stronghold? Why does your area have this attitude to the union movement?

7. As a result of your investigation write a report on the extent to which legislation has affected the trade union movement.

Assignment H

An investigation into the factors affecting the design of a product.

1. Select a product, either a good or a service. You should be able to visit the business concerned.

2. Collect all the information and promotional literature on the product that you can. What features of the product does the business think are particularly important? Why do people want this type of product?

3. How far did the business make use of new technology in the product itself and in the design process?

4. To what extent did the new product lead to re-training of the workforce? How was this carried out? What were the costs involved?

5. Did the production organisation of the business have to be altered?

6. What was the total budget for the product development and launch? How did the business decide on this sum?

7. On what information did the business decide to develop this product?

Assignment I

An investigation into the effects of Electronic Funds Transfer at Point of Sale (EFT–POS) on business and the customer.

1. What methods of payment can the customer choose from?

2. Investigation into the technology used.

3. What are the costs of the technology?

4. Organise a survey into customer attitudes to EFT–POS. What do they like about it? Do they have any worries about its introduction?

5. Organise a survey of local retailers. Which ones use EFT–POS now? Why do they use it? Could other retailers benefit from it?

6. What are the advantages/disadvantages of EFT–POS to the banks?

7. Will EFT–POS result in an increase in the amount of credit used in the economy? Give an explanation for your answer.

8. As a customer explain which method of payment you would use for each type of purchase you might make.

GLOSSARY

(Note: the words marked with an asterisk (*) are defined elsewhere in this glossary.)

A

ACAS: The Advisory, Conciliation* and Arbitration Service set up by the Employment Protection Act 1974. It works to settle industrial disputes and improve industrial relations.

Accountability: The people running a business* are responsible to owners and lenders for the way in which they have used the resources of the business.

Accounting ratio: A number obtained from the accounts of a business* and used to assess the performance and viability of the business.

Administration: Putting a decision into practice. There are forms to design, people to be delegated* to take responsibility* to do the jobs needed. This is the role* of the administrator.

Advertising: To make known loudly. Advertisers tell people how good their product is by using television, radio, newspapers, magazines, posters. Advertising is part of promotion*, the way in which businesses tell customers that their product is best.

Advice note: This is a document sent by a business to a customer to tell them their order has been dealt with. It can be sent before the goods are delivered or at the time of delivery. Usually it is used to tell (that is advise) the customer that the goods are on their way. It does not mention price or terms*.

Agent: A person who has the authority to act on behalf of another person. This means that if the agent buys or sells goods the person for whom he is buying and selling must go through with the sale.

Appropriation account: The part of the profit and loss account* that shows how the business* has divided up the profit it has made.

APR: The annual percentage rate charged. The rate of interest will depend upon the method used to calculate it, e.g. 3% per month. The APR indicates the true cost of credit and must be displayed whenever credit is offered.

Assets: Anything owned by the business*, e.g. property, machines, money.

Assisted areas: Parts of the United Kingdom which have problems of high unemployment and so receive special government grants to industry.

Auditor: A person appointed by a business* to inspect the accounts on behalf of the owners.

Authorised capital: The amount of money a business* is allowed to raise as stated in the memorandum of association.*

Authority: The power to direct work and make decisions.

B

Balance of payments: A statement of the total amount of money a country has received by selling products and from investment abroad and the amount of money it has had to pay out to other countries for products bought and investments made.

Balance of trade: The part of the balance of payments* that summarises the trade in actual goods, that is **visible**∗ imports and exports.

Balance sheet: A statement produced by an organisation that shows all the assets* and liabilities* of the organisation on a particular date.

Bankruptcy: A state in which a person, sole trade or a partnership lack the money to pay their debts. Creditors* can appeal to the law to force them to sell their assets* to pay.

Barriers to communication: Anything that stops people understanding the message that is being sent to them. Noise, distance or the fact that they don't want to hear the message can cause the blockage.

Batch production: This is where a group of products are moved from one part of the production process to another as a group.

Blue collar workers: Manual workers whose job means that they have to wear overalls.

Bonus: Money paid to employees over their basic wage, usually because they have produced more work than the amount agreed.

Book keeping: The act of recording the transactions of a business*.

Break-even chart: A diagram showing the costs and revenue of a business*.

Break-even point: The level of sales at which the revenue* received just covers the costs of production.

Breaking bulk: The term used to describe the actions of wholesalers* and retailers* when they buy a large quantity of a good and resell it in smaller quantities.

British Overseas Trade Board: An organisation to promote UK exports and give advice to business about exporting.

Budget: A detailed plan showing how a business* or part of a business hopes to reach its goals. It shows the costs involved and the hoped for revenue.

Business: An organisation that buys in goods and services which it uses to produce other goods and services which it sells for a profit*.

C

Called up capital: Companies do not always want the total amount of money, promised by their shareholders all at once. The called up capital is the money the company has asked for.

Capacity: The maximum production of which a business is capable with the resources it has.

Capital expenditure: Money spent on the fixed assets* of a business.

Cash discount: Money taken off the advertised price for a good because the buyer is paying in cash.

Cash flow: A comparison between the amount of money a business* receives in a period of time and the money it will have to pay out.

CBI: The Confederation of British Industry is an organisation of employers whose main job is to put the employers' point of view on taxation, legislation or news items relating to industry. In doing this it acts as a pressure group*.

Centralisation: A situation in which decisions are made for the business* by comparatively few people.

Chain of command: The path through which instructions move from senior management to the most inexperienced employee.

Chain of production: The progress of goods from primary industry*, through secondary* and tertiary industry* until the end product reaches the final customer.

Chamber of Commerce/Trade/Industry: An association representing the interests of the industrial and commercial businesses in a geographical area.

Channel of communication: The people through which a message is passed before it gets to the final receiver.

Channel of distribution: The organisations through which goods are passed before they get to the final customer.

Closed shop: A business which has agreed with a trade union or group of trade unions not to employ anybody unless they are a member of one of the unions.

Collective bargaining: Bargaining between representatives of the owners of a business* and the people employed with the aim of settling differences, e.g. pay, conditions of work.

Commercial services: Banking, insurance, warehousing, transport, advertising. Services that are offered by businesses to other businesses.

Communication: The flow of information, ideas and attitudes between a person or group of people and other people.

Community charge: a tax levied on the individual for community services. It replaced rates in 1990. The rates were a local government tax on property. The community charge is levied on individuals whether or not they own property.

Competitive: A situation in which the product of a business* compares well with similar products of other businesses.

Component: A finished good used as part of another product, e.g. a battery put in a car during assembly.

Conciliation: A process of negotiation that tries to reconcile the differences between two parties.

Conglomerate: A business* that produces a wide variety of different goods and services from primary*, secondary* and tertiary industries*.

Consumers' Association: A non-profit making organisation that tests and reports on goods and services that are on sale to the public. The results of the tests are published in the Association's monthly magazine *Which?*.

Contract: This is a legal agreement between two or more people. It can be either written or spoken.

Contract of employment: The contract between employer and employee in which the employee agrees to do a certain job in return for pay. The Employment Protection (Consolidation) Act 1978 states that the employee must be given a written copy of the agreement within 13 weeks of starting work.

Contribution: Revenue minus variable costs. What is left over is a "contribution" to the fixed costs of production.

Contribution pricing: Setting a price that covers the variable costs and makes a contribution to fixed costs.

Convenor: The senior shop steward* in a business* who speaks to management on behalf of all the shop stewards. In a business with members of more than one union the convenor may represent all the unions.

Co-operative: A business owned by the workforce and operated for their benefit. A "**producer**" co-operative describes businesses that make things. A "**retail**" co-operative describes businesses that buy in goods for resale.

Co-operative development agency: An organisation whose purpose is to promote and advise on the setting up of co-operatives*.

Credit: The word used to describe a sale when no cash changes hands.

Credit note: A document given by a seller to a buyer when the buyer has been charged too much money or when damaged goods have been returned. It allows the buyer to order more goods without charge.

Creditor: A person or business* to whom a business owes money.

Current assets: Assets which are constantly changing, e.g. debtors*, stock and cash.

Current liabilities: Debts that have to be paid in the near future, e.g. creditors* and overdraft*.

Curriculum vitae: An outline of experience and achievements prepared by the candidate for a job in support of his or her application.

D

Data Protection Act 1984: This compels organisations that keep personal records on computer to register with the Data Protection Registrar and to keep the information in such a way that people's privacy is respected.

Debentures: A long term loan made to a company.

Debit note: A document sent to the buyer to inform him that an extra charge will be added to his account, e.g. when he has been undercharged for goods.

Debt factor: A person or business* that collects the debts of another business for a price. The debt factor might pay a business 80% of the value of its debts and collect the full (100%) value from the people who owe the money. The difference between the two values will pay the expenses of the debt collection and provide the debt factor with profit*.

Debtors: People or businesses that owe a business* money.

Decentralisation: The delegation* of decision making in organisations to different parts of the organisation.

Deed of partnership: A contract* between two or more people who are entering into partnership* together.

Delegation: Giving authority* and responsibility* to a subordinate to make agreed decisions.

Delivery note: A form listing the goods delivered to the customer and signed by the customer when the goods are received. By signing the delivery note the customer accepts the goods, so should inspect them for damage before signing.

Demarcation: The careful marking of limits between jobs, e.g. a plumber would not do a job marked as belonging to an electrician even if no special skill was required. This acts as a protection for jobs but can slow down production and lead to higher costs.

Depreciation: The amount by which the value of fixed assets* declines in the accounts of a business*. This is to take account of the fact that as an asset gets older its value gets less.

Development areas: Those parts of assisted areas* that are judged to be most in need of help.

Direct services: Services offered to people rather than to organisations, e.g. hairdressing.

Direct taxes: Taxes that are levied on people or businesses rather than on goods or services.

Distribution: The way in which the products of a business* are made available to its customers.

Diversification: The widening of the range of goods and services produced.

Dividend: The part of a company's profits received by a shareholder*. Not all the profits* are distributed to the shareholders. Some are retained in the company for investment*. The directors decide on the proportion of profits that will go to the shareholder.

Division of labour: The specialisation* of workers in one part of a production process.

E

Economies of scale: A fall in the costs of production because of an increase in the size of a business (internal) or industry (external).

Employers' organisations: Organisations formed to promote the interests of employers, e.g. the CBI*.

Employment Acts: Legislation protecting the rights of employees, e.g. the contract of employment, redundancy and dismissal. The term also covers legislation defining the rights and responsibility of trade unions.

Enterprise zone: An area of the country with a high rate of unemployment in which businesses are given tax advantages and freedom from certain planning restrictions.

Exchange rate: The price at which one currency can be exchanged for another.

Excise duty: A tax on goods produced for consumption in the UK. The number of goods affected is limited.

Exports: Goods and services produced in one country and sold in another.

External finance: Business finance that is generated neither by the business* itself nor owners' capital*.

F

Factors of production: The resources needed in any business activity: land, labour and capital*.

Fax: Equipment that allows the reproduction of an exact copy of documents (a facsimile) using the telephone network.

Feedback: A response to a message which shows the sender of the message how it has been received.

Final consumer: The person who uses a product is not necessarily the person who buys it. Children, for example, use a wide range of goods and services that are bought for them by their parents. The parent who buys the goods and services is the customer. The child who uses the goods or services is the final consumer. The final consumer often influences the choices of the customer.

Fiscal policy: Government policy on taxation and spending.

Fixed assets: Assets that stay in the business over a period of time, e.g. land, buildings, machinery.

Fixed costs: Costs that do not change as output changes as long as capacity* does not change. These costs have to be paid even if the business produces nothing.

Flexible working: Organisation of the work in a business where people do a range of jobs to speed up the production process. (See demarcation*.)

Flotation: The setting up of and raising of capital* for a public company.

Flow production: A way of organising production so that a product moves from one stage of the production process to another as soon as that stage is completed.

Formal group: A group of people put together in a working situation by the management of a business*.

Franchise: A package of product, price, promotion and place put together by one business (the **franchisor**) and used by another business (the **franchisee**) for the payment of a fee. The franchisee has to agree to run the business in the way laid down by the franchisor.

Free economy: An economy in which goods and services go to the people and organisations that can afford them. Very few services are offered "free" by the State, paid for out of tax revenue.

Free trade: The import and export of goods and services without any interference from governments.

Fringe benefits: Benefits given to employees in addition to wages and salaries, e.g. luncheon vouchers, membership of a private health care scheme.

Function: An activity such as marketing that is needed if the business is to operate.

G

Grapevine: A pattern of communications that depends on personal relationships more than the formal channels of communication* laid down by the business.

Gross pay: Total pay before tax, national insurance contributions, etc, have been deducted.

Gross profit: Revenue from sales minus the cost of sales. Overheads and tax have not been deducted.

H

Hire purchase: A method of buying on credit* by paying for the goods in instalments. The goods do not become the property of the buyer until the last payment has been made.

Holding company: A company that controls a number of other companies by owning shares. Each of the companies (**subsidiaries**) keeps their own identity, e.g. name.

I

Imports: Goods and services produced in another country and sold in the UK.

Import duty: A tax on goods from abroad brought into the UK for sale.

Indirect taxes: Taxes levied on goods and services and not directly on people.

Induction: The activity of introducing a new employee to the business* in the first days on the job.

Industrial relations: The relationships which exist between management and the workforce.

Industrial tribunal: Panel consisting of three members, the chairperson of which is always legally qualified. It passes judgement on disputes between a business and its employees in cases which involve employment, race, or sexual equality legislation.

Inflation: A general rise in the price level in the economy.

Informal group: A group of people taking part in activities together which are not laid down by the rules of an organisation.

Innovation: The introduction of something new. It can be a product, technology or organisation.

Institutional investor: Banks, insurance companies, building societies, pension funds who buy shares in a company.

Insurance: The payment of a sum of money (the **premium**) from one person or business to another on the understanding that if stated unwanted events take place the person receiving the premium will re-imburse the insured person for the loss they have suffered.

Integration: The joining together of two or more businesses.

Interdependence: Because businesses specialise* they are dependent on other businesses for the goods and services they do not produce.

Interest rate: Money paid by a borrower as the price of using another person's money, expressed as a percentage of the amount borrowed.

Intermediate areas: The less depressed parts of assisted areas*.

Internal finance: Money used by a business* that comes from owners' capital* or retained profits*.

Investment: The use of the resources of a business* to expand or start a new business. It is also used to describe the purchase of shares in a business.

Invisible trade: The import* and export* of services and money payments, e.g. profits* (**invisibles**).

Invoice: A document issued by a seller to a buyer stating the description, quantity and cost of goods and services supplied together with VAT* charges. It will also state the terms on which the goods and services have been supplied, e.g. trade/cash discount*.

Issued capital: The part of authorised capital* the company has actually made available to shareholders*.

J

Job description: A written statement outlining the duties of a job.

Job enlargement: Increasing the number of activities of a job to make it less boring.

Job enrichment: Increasing the responsibilities* of a job to make it less boring.

Job evaluation: Attempts to put jobs in order of their importance to the business*.

Job production: A method of production in which a product is made from start to finish.

Job rotation: A way of increasing the experience of an employee by moving him/her from one job to another after a period of time.

Job satisfaction: The amount of personal satisfaction a person gets from the job.

Job specification: A detailed statement, based on the job description, of the physical, and mental qualities needed for a job and the required qualifications.

L

Leadership: The ability and need of a manager to get subordinates to co-operate in the work.

Leasing: A way of getting assets* for use in the business*. The owner of the assets (**lessor**) allows another person to use them (**lessee**) for payment.

Levels of hierarchy: The number of different levels of authority* and responsibility* in a business.

Liabilities: The claims that can be made on a business by the owners and creditors*.

Limited company: A business whose owners are protected by limited liability*.

Limited liability: The liability of the owners for the debts of a business* is limited to the amount of money they have invested in the business.

Line and staff: A way of organising a business* in which authority is passed down the chain of command* to the shop floor (**line**) and line managers are helped by the service of departments such as personnel (**staff**).

Liquidation: The selling of all the assets* of a company and turning them into cash.

Liquidity: The speed with which assets* can be turned into money. Money itself is the most liquid asset.

Liquidity ratio: A ratio that compares the current assets* of a business with its current liabilities*. There are two main liquidity ratios: the current ratio and the acid test ratio.

Loan: Money made available to a business* for the payment of interest.

Logo: A distinctive symbol that appears on all the products, advertising, etc. of a business to help increase the awareness of customers.

Long term liabilities: Liabilities that will not have to be paid for more than 12 months.

M

Manual workers: People whose job activities are mostly physical.

Mark-up: A percentage of costs added on to costs to get the price at which the good will be sold. The mark-up covers expenses not already taken into account and the profit*.

Market: The total number of buyers and sellers of a product.

Market economy: See free economy*

Market niche: A group of buyers a business* is aiming to please with its product. Usually a group of buyers other businesses have not catered for.

Market oriented: When the activities of a business are ruled by the needs of the market*.

Market research: The careful gathering of information about the buyers and sellers in a market*.

Market segment: A group within a total market* for a product that shares similar characteristics, e.g. age, income, tastes.

Marketing: The business activities that are concerned with directing goods and services from the producer to the consumer.

Marketing agent: A specialist business that undertakes the marketing functions for another business.

Marketing mix: The main functions of marketing. These are market research*, product*, price, promotion* and place.

Media: The physical means by which a message is transmitted, e.g. newspapers, radio, television.

Memorandum of association: A document that must be drawn up before a business can register as a company. It is concerned with the external organisation of the business, e.g. the title, the registered address, the type of business it will undertake (the aims), the names of the directors and the number of shares they have agreed to buy.

Merger: The joining of two or more companies to form a new company.

Message: Information, ideas and attitudes being passed from one person to another.

Mixed economy: An economy in which goods and services are provided both by publicly and privately owned businesses.

Monetary policy: That part of government policy that is concerned with the supply of money in the economy and interest rates*.

Monopoly and Mergers Commission: This is a group of people appointed by the government whose job it is to investigate any business activities that restrict the amount of competition in a market*.

Mortgage: A loan made with property as a security*. If the loan is not repaid in the agreed time the lender can take the property and sell it to recover the money.

Motivation: To provide people with the incentive to work towards the goals of the business* rather than their own goals. This is usually achieved when people can see that their own needs* are satisfied by the business.

Multinational: A business* that produces goods and services in more than one country.

N

Nationalised industry: Industries wholly owned by the government.

Needs: What people desire to survive and live an enjoyable life.

Net pay: Gross pay* minus all deductions.

Net profit: Gross profit minus overheads. Net profit after tax is net profit minus tax paid.

O

Objectives: What a person or business hopes to achieve. The main objectives of business are: the best possible profit, survival, increasing market share, a standard of service to the customer.

Official strike: One which has the backing of the trade union*.

Opportunity cost: The sacrifice that has to be made when deciding between alternatives.

Ordinary shares: These are known as risk capital because the holders of ordinary shares in a company are the last to be paid if the company goes into liquidation*. To compensate for this they have the right to vote for directors and are considered the true owners of the company.

Organisation: The process of giving people jobs so that working together they can achieve the objectives* of the business*.

Organisation chart: A chart that shows the way in which authority and responsibility* is divided up in a business*.

Overdraft: Permission from the bank manager to take more money from the current account than is credited to it. A cheap way of borrowing money for a short period of time although the annual interest rate is often higher than on other types of loan.

Owners' capital: The money put into a business* by the people who own it. The owners' capital in sole traders* and partnerships* is sometimes referred to as Proprietors' Funds*, in companies as Shareholders' Funds*. Retained profits* are a part of owners' capital.

P

Par value: The value printed on a share certificate (that is the proof of ownership of the share). The price of the share can vary from this according to the way in which the company performs. If it is doing well, or expected to do well, the price will go up.

Partnership: Two or more people who operate a business* by agreement. The business is jointly owned and the Partnership Act 1890, and subsequent Acts, state that profits and risks are equally shared. Partners who wish to vary the terms of the Act (one might have put in more money than the rest) can do so by entering into a legal agreement and drawing up a deed of partnership*.

Patent: A guarantee to an inventor that nobody can use the idea for 21 years without paying the inventor. These payments are called royalties. Patents act as an incentive to research and development.

PAYE: Pay as you earn. A method of collecting income tax where it is deducted from pay before employees get it.

Penetration price: A price set low to get as large a share of the market as quickly as possible.

Picketing: Employees on strike standing outside the place of employment (the picket line) and trying to persuade employees not on strike to support them.

Piece rate: Payment according to the amount of work done rather than the amount of time it took to do it.

Planned economy: An economy in which the State decides what will be produced, in what quantities and who will enjoy the goods and services produced.

Planning permission: The Town and Country Planning Act 1971 limited the power of owners of land to change the use of the land without getting permission from the local authority.

Point of sale: The actual place where a sale takes place, usually a shop.

Poll tax: The popular name for the community charge which replaced rates in 1990.

Preference shares: These are fixed interest securities. Some preference shares have voting rights.

Pressure group: A group of people who want to influence central and local government in legislation.

Primary data: Information collected for the first time to help in solving a business* problem.

Primary industry: All businesses involved in farming, fishing, mining, quarrying and drilling.

Private limited company: A limited company with less than £25 000 share capital whose shares cannot be sold to the general public.

Private sector: All businesses owned by private individuals without any form of State ownership.

Privatisation: The act of transferring businesses owned by the State or local authorities to private ownership, usually by turning them into limited companies. The term is also used to describe the opening up of services normally provided by the State and local authorities to private business.

Product launch: Putting a product on the market* for the first time.

Product life cycle: The length of time people are expected to continue buying a product. Fashion goods tend to have a very short life.

Product mix: The different products made by one business*.

Product oriented: An attitude in a business* that tends to think of the product and the making of it without taking the market* into account.

Productivity: How much can be produced with a given amount of resources. Increased productivity means that the same number (or less) resources are being used but the output has gone up.

Productivity agreement: An agreement between management and workforce that if productivity* increases then the pay will increase by a certain amount.

Profit: The difference between revenue* and costs.

Profit and loss account: Part of the accounts that shows how much profit/loss the business* has made over a period of time. It can also show how the profit has been used.

Profit related pay: A payment system in which a proportion of pay is related to the profits a business has made and rises and falls accordingly.

Profit sharing: The distribution of some of the profits of a business to the employees. This can be in the form of a bonus* or as shares in a company.

Promotion (1): Moving to a job on another level of the hierarchy of a business*. This means more authority and responsibility* with higher pay.

Promotion (2): That part of marketing activity which is concerned with advertising, selling and sales promotion.

Proprietors' Funds: Owners' capital as a sole proprietor or in a partnership*.

Protectionism: A government policy that protects home industries from foreign competition.

Public corporations: A legal form of business ownership, established by Act of Parliament in which the State is the sole owner.

Public limited company: A form of legal ownership in which the business* has limited liability* and can sell its shares on the open market.

Public relations: The job of making sure that the relations between a business* and the general public remain good.

Public sector: Organisations controlled by the State or other public bodies.

Purchasing: The activity of buying in the raw materials and components needed for production in the right quantity, the right quality, at the right time and at the right price.

Q

Quality control: Making sure that products meet the standards of quality set down by the business*.

Quota: A limit set on the number of goods that can be imported. This can apply to a certain type of good or all the goods from a particular country.

R

Random sample: A method of taking a sample from a population so that everybody has an equal chance of being selected.

Recession: When the economy of a country is experiencing generally low demand and high unemployment.

Recruitment: The process of deciding on the type of skills required in the job and making the vacancy known.

Redundant: A situation in which changes in technology, organisation or demand mean that some skills are no longer required by a business*.

Regional aid: Central government grants and other measures directed at parts of the UK with high levels of unemployment.

Registrar of companies: A civil service function with the responsibility to ensure that businesses applying for registration as limited liability companies have satisfied the requirements of the law.

Research and development: Business activities designed to find new products, new technology and inventions.

Reserves: The undistributed profits of a company.

Responsibility: The obligation to perform the duties specified as part of the job.

Retail price: The selling price to the final customer.

Retailer: The final link in the channel of distribution. The retailer sells in small quantities to the final customer.

Retained profit: Profits* that are not distributed to the owners of a business but are kept for future investment. They appear as reserves* on a company balance sheet*.

Return on equity: Net profit* after tax expressed as a percentage of shareholders' funds*.

Revenue: The income of a business over a period of time. Also referred to as turnover*.

Role: The part played by the authority, responsibility and skills associated with a job in achieving the objectives* of a business.

Royalty: Payment made on a regular basis for the right to use a patented* invention.

S

Seasonal demand: Demand for a good or service that varies widely according to the time of year. Easter eggs at Easter are an obvious example.

Secondary data: Market research* information that was not collected primarily for the investigation in hand.

Secondary industry: Businesses that manufacture goods.

Secondary picketing: Picketing at any other business other than the one in the dispute. This is now illegal.

Secured loan: The creditor* holds some property of the debtor* that can be sold if the loan is not repaid. A mortgage* is a special type of secured loan.

Security: Something that is offered as a pledge against a loan. It is also the term applied to the document recording a loan to a business which can be traded on the stock exchange.*

Selection: The process of choosing a suitable candidate for a job from the applicants.

Shareholders: The owners of the stocks and shares of a company. They are the owners of the company.

Shareholders' funds: Owners' capital in a company.

Shop steward: An unpaid official of a trade union* who is elected by fellow workers.

Skimming price: A price set high to get the most return out of a market* in the shortest possible time.

Social benefit: The benefits enjoyed by the general public as a result of the activities of a business*.

Social cost: Costs experienced by the general public as a result of the activities of a business*. Pollution could cause higher cleaning bills for local households but this will not appear in the costs of the business concerned.

Sole trader: Also known as the sole proprietor. A business wholly owned by one person.

Span of control: The number of people whose work a manager directly controls.

Specialisation: Concentration of a country, region, business or individual on a narrow range of economic activities. Division of labour* is a type of specialisation.

Start-up capital: Money needed to start a new business.

Status: The position a person holds in society in relation to other people.

Stock: The amount of raw materials, components*, work in progress and finished goods a business* holds. The word **inventory** is sometimes used.

Stock: Fixed interest securities*. The word is sometimes used to refer to ordinary shares*.

Stock control: Making sure the business* has enough stock* to carry on its business but not so much that it is wasting money by holding it.

Stock Exchange: An organisation whose main purpose is to ease the buying and selling of fixed interest securities and the shares of businesses whose financial position is considered sound.

Structural unemployment: Unemployment as a result of changes in demand or the introduction of a new technology that makes some skills redundant*.

Subsidiary: A business controlled by another business. It can be wholly or partly owned.

T

Take-home pay: Pay after all deductions have been made.

Takeover bid: An attempt on the part of one business to buy sufficient shares in a public company to control it.

Target market: The market the product is aimed at described in terms of age, sex, income and attitudes.

Tariff: A tax on imported goods.

Taxation: Money levied by central and local government on individuals, organisations, goods and services to pay for the services government provides for the community.

Telex: An international service by which printed material can be transmitted through wires from one printer to another.

Tender: An offer made by a business* to supply a good or service, the offer will include details of what will be supplied for what price. Central and local government put contracts* out to tender, e.g. when building a road.

Terms: The agreement between a buyer and a seller about the way in which they will conduct the deal. For example, did the seller agree to credit* or discount*.

Tertiary industry: All businesses supplying services.

Time rate: A method of payment where employees are paid by the time they spend at work rather than the amount of work done.

Trade: Buying and selling for a profit*.

Trade discount: A percentage deducted from the recommended retail price by a supplier for a customer who will resell the product or use it in production of another good or service.

Trade union: An organisation representing the interests of employees who are its members.

Trades Union Congress: A federation of most of the trade unions in the UK founded in 1864. The member unions have complete independence but must obey the rules laid down by Congress.

Trading account: That part of the profit and loss account* that includes turnover* and cost of sales but does not include overheads and tax payments.

Training: Business activities designed to give employees the knowledge, skills and attitudes they need to do a particular job.

Turnover: The revenue* a business receives from sales in a certain time period.

U

Unofficial strike: A strike which does not have the backing of a trade union*.

V

VAT: Value Added Tax. A tax levied on the additional value added to goods and services as they pass through the chain of production*.

Variable costs: Costs that vary as output varies, e.g. materials.

Visible trade: Import and export of goods.

Voluntary codes: Codes of practice drawn up by trading organisations to regulate the way in which their members behave towards their customers and the general public, e.g. the Advertising Standards Authority.

W

White collar workers: People working in "clean" jobs which do not require the protection of an overall.

Wholesaler: A business that buys goods in bulk from the manufacturer for resale to a retailer.

Work study: Systematic study of the requirement of a job and the way in which it is done with the object of improving efficiency.

Work to rule: A weapon in an industrial dispute when employees obey the rules of the business, health and safety, etc. in minute detail. This slows down the work rate.

Worker participation: The involvement of employees in the policy making process of the business.

Working capital: Current assets* minus current liabilities*.

Working population: The proportion of the total population who are available for work.

YT: Youth Training. A two year training scheme for the 16+ age group that combines on the job training with further education. Previously, this was known as the Youth Training Scheme.

INDEX